Contributions to Finance and Accounting

The book series 'Contributions to Finance and Accounting' features the latest research from research areas like financial management, investment, capital markets, financial institutions, FinTech and financial innovation, accounting methods and standards, reporting, and corporate governance, among others. Books published in this series are primarily monographs and edited volumes that present new research results, both theoretical and empirical, on a clearly defined topic. All books are published in print and digital formats and disseminated globally. This book series is indexed in Scopus.

Sinem Derindere Köseoğlu
Editor

A Practical Guide for Startup Valuation

An Analytic Approach

Springer

Editor
Sinem Derindere Köseoğlu
Istanbul University
Istanbul, Turkey

ISSN 2730-6038 ISSN 2730-6046 (electronic)
Contributions to Finance and Accounting
ISBN 978-3-031-35290-4 ISBN 978-3-031-35291-1 (eBook)
https://doi.org/10.1007/978-3-031-35291-1

This Springer imprint is published by the registered company Springer Nature Switzerland AG
The registered company address is: Gewerbestrasse 11, 6330 Cham, Switzerland

"Price is what you pay. Value is what you get"—Warren Buffet

Preface

Welcome to "*A Practical Guide for Startup Valuation—An Analytic Approach*" a comprehensive guide to navigating the complexities of valuing startups in today's dynamic and ever-changing business environment. Whether you're an entrepreneur, investor, or business professional, this book is designed to equip you with the knowledge and tools you need to confidently assess the value of startups and make informed decisions.

Valuing startups is a critical element in the entrepreneurial journey. It enables entrepreneurs to accurately assess the worth of their business, attract investors, and strategically plan for the future. Investors, on the other hand, must precisely evaluate the potential value of a startup to manage risk and anticipate the potential return on investment. This book is structured to provide a practical and analytical, step-by-step approach to startup valuation. We begin by outlining the fundamentals of startup valuation, including the key drivers of value, different valuation methods, and common valuation challenges. From there, we delve into the practical application of these concepts, including financial modeling, sensitivity analysis, and valuation methods.

Then, beyond addressing concepts and traditional startup valuation methods, this book also covers several modern valuation methods, such as the venture capital method and the scorecard method. These modern approaches to startup valuation are essential for entrepreneurs and investors alike to navigate the ever-changing startup landscape. Throughout the book, we provide real-world examples and case studies to illustrate key concepts and provide practical guidance. These examples help you apply your newfound knowledge and put your insights into action.

We put our hearts and souls into creating a book that is not only informative but also engaging, accessible, and easy to understand. We hope this book will be a valuable resource for you as you wander the world of startup valuation. We invite you to join us on this exciting journey, and we look forward to sharing our insights and expertise with you.

Sincerely,

Istanbul University, Istanbul, Turkey Sinem Derindere Köseoğlu

Contents

A Practical Guide for Startup Valuation: An Analytic Approach

Sinem Derindere Köseoğlu

1 Introduction

The world is changing, and startups are leading the charge. From SpaceX to Bytedance, startups are transforming industries and creating new markets at an unprecedented pace. These companies are often founded by visionary entrepreneurs who are not afraid to take risks and challenge the status quo. But the road to success is never easy, and the challenges facing startups are numerous. One of the most critical challenges is determining the value of a startup. Unlike established companies, startups have little to no financial history, and their future potential can be difficult to predict. As a result, the valuation of a startup can vary widely, with different investors and analysts arriving at vastly different valuations. Despite these challenges, startup valuation is a crucial aspect of the investment and entrepreneurial ecosystem. Understanding how to value a startup is essential for entrepreneurs seeking funding, investors looking for promising opportunities, and business professionals seeking to acquire or merge with startups.

"*A Practical Guide for Startup Valuation – An Analytic Approach*" book is a comprehensive guide to understanding startup valuation. As an entrepreneur, investor, or business professional, understanding how to value a startup is critical to making informed decisions about investment, acquisition, or growth.

In this book, we explore the various methods used to value startups, from traditional methods like discounted cash flow analysis to more modern approaches like the venture capital method and scorecard method. We also examine the unique challenges and opportunities that come with valuing startups, such as the lack of financial history and the potential for rapid growth. Through real-world case studies and practical advice, we'll show you how to navigate the complex and dynamic

---

S. D. Köseoğlu (✉)
Istanbul University, Istanbul, Turkey

S. Derindere Köseoğlu (ed.), *A Practical Guide for Startup Valuation*, Contributions to Finance and Accounting, https://doi.org/10.1007/978-3-031-35291-1_1

world of startup valuation. We cover topics such as how to assess market potential, how to account for risk and uncertainty, and how to negotiate fair valuations.

Whether you're an entrepreneur looking to raise capital, an investor looking to make informed investment decisions, or a business professional looking to understand the valuation process, this book has something for you. Our goal is to demystify the world of startup valuation and provide you with the knowledge and tools you need to succeed.

This book is divided into 13 chapters, each of which explores a different aspect of startup valuation.

In Chap. 2, titled "*Introduction to Startup Valuation: From Idea to IPO*", we provide an overview of startups and startup valuation, discussing the different players in the startup ecosystem, explaining the fundamentals of valuation, financing methods, funding stages, and highlighting the importance of understanding startup valuation for entrepreneurs, investors, and accelerators. We also discuss the different methods used in startup valuation based on traditional and modern approaches such as discounted cash flow (DCF), relative valuation, Venture Capital, Scorecard, Berkus Method, and so on. This chapter also includes why it is important for entrepreneurs to understand startup valuation, how it affects their fundraising efforts, and how it can impact their ability to grow their business. Additionally, the chapter also addresses some of the common challenges that arise in startup valuation, such as dealing with uncertainty and limited historical financial data. Overall, the chapter is planned to serve for the more detailed discussions that will follow in the rest of the book.

In the third chapter, titled "*From Planning to Valuation: Mastering Business Planning and Sensitivity Analysis for Your Startup*", the author starts by defining the key components of a business plan, including the market analysis, marketing strategy, customer acquisition, investment strategies, financial projections, and implementation plan. The chapter also provides some details on how to write each section effectively, and how to tailor the plan to the needs of the startup and its target audience. Creating a solid business plan, building a financial model, and performing sensitivity analysis are critical for startups to succeed, but it can be challenging to apply these concepts to real-life scenarios. In this chapter, the author takes a deep dive into a real case study of a startup, and demonstrates how financial modeling and sensitivity analysis were used to develop a successful business plan and secure funding. The chapter also indicates how the financial model was used to create a proforma balance sheet and proforma income statement, which provide a snapshot of the company's financial performance and position over time. By the end of this chapter, readers will have a practical understanding of how financial modeling and sensitivity analysis can be used to develop a successful business plan and drive value creation.

"*Valuation Versus Pricing: A Conceptual and Practical Guide to Estimating an Economic Value for Early-stage Companies via DCF*" is the fourth chapter of the book. Since there is greater uncertainty involved in early-stage companies and their future performance, this chapter aims to bridge the gap in this dialectic discussion by first providing the theoretic framework to conceptualize differences in value and pricing, perhaps a key driver of the debate which summarizes key challenges in startup valuation. The article then goes on to develop a straightforward practical approach for early-stage valuation, based on the traditional discounted cash flow method for business valuation, augmented with statistical analysis and market triangulation, and finally validated with the more conventional venture capital pricing method often employed in the industry. The objective of the article is to bring enhanced robustness, at a practical level to startup valuation, via a simplified step-by-step approach, and serve as an additional conversation starter in this increasingly important theme in modern corporate finance.

Chapter 5, titled *"Hierarchical and Segmented Approaches to Startup Valuation: What They Are. Why They Work"*, attracts the attention of the reader by starting expressive with the question Why is it that startups in California attract higher valuations than those in New York? How do startups based in London attract higher valuations than those in Paris, Berlin, or Milan, even when based in similarly sized economies, share the same industries and many of the same investors? According to the chapter, while classical economic theory describes that valuations are based on revenues, growth rates, and risk-adjusted discount rates, the valuation of startups often proves the exception to the rule. Whereas startup valuations are influenced by revenues, stage of development business risks, and macroeconomic conditions, the specific valuation impacts are traditionally a black box. Given that valuations are often undisclosed, roles played by other factors (economic geography, sector, and intellectual property) can often only be guessed at. This chapter is a deep-dive and how-to guide outlining methods and approaches for the application of segmented hierarchical startup valuation and can be applied using existing data and valuation models.

Chapter 6, titled "An Analysis of Startup Valuation Methods: Understanding the Investor's Perspective" draws attention to the subjectivity of startup valuation which can lead to varying valuations from different investors, creating difficulties in determining the accurate value of the startup. This unpredictability can lead to over or undervaluation of the company, which can have a significant impact on its future financing and success. Thus, this chapter discusses some of the most popular methods of valuation with illustration along with their advantages and disadvantages generally with basic examples.

In today's fast-paced business environment, it is critical to have a thorough understanding of alternative modern valuation approaches in detail to make informed investment decisions. In the following chapters of the book, different alternative modern valuation methods are discussed in more detail on their own for readers seeking to understand the latest valuation methods and techniques. Chapter 7, Venture Capital Method; Chap. 8, The First Chicago Valuation Method; Chap. 9, Scorecard Method of Valuation; Chap. 10, Dave Berkus Method; and Chap. 11, Risk Factor Summation Method are covered in depth.

The author of the *"Venture Capital Valuation Method"* in Chap. 7 claims that the venture capital method (VC Method) is one of the most used valuation methods in the venture capital industry. This chapter starts with identifying the reasons why the venture capital method is so widely adopted and discussed the venture capital method, along with a case. Some of the critical elements in the venture capital method are deciding the quantity of investment, estimating the exit value, calculating the target multiple of the money, valuing the portion held by the VC in the startup, incorporating fund management and carried interest into the valuation, valuing the interested of general partner vs limited partners, and deciding on the investment. This chapter touches are the above points and more.

Chapter 8, titled *"The First Chicago Valuation Method"*, mention that The First Chicago valuation method can be seen as a variation of the Discounted Cash Flow (DCF) methodology. It provides a differentiated approach to analyzing companies at different stages in their lifecycle, further helping you to grasp the uncertainty involved. A further benefit of this approach is that it generates a variety of payoff scenarios for the company. Traditionally, three scenarios are constructed – the best, the base, and the worst case – and each scenario is assigned a probability. The valuation result is derived from a probability-weighted average of all three scenarios, so it includes both possible gains as well as potential losses in order to provide a precise valuation. This method is generally utilized by venture capitalists and private equity investors to appraise private companies because it incorporates both upside potential and possible downsides.

Chapter 9, titled *"Scorecard Method of Valuation: The Subjective Analysis of Valuation"*, argues that a good valuation is always not just about the numbers it is a combination of the story and the numbers, which is very well explained in the book by Aswath Damodaran, Narratives and Numbers, The value of Stories in Business. When investing in an early stage companies investors look for valuation which cannot always be based on the numbers due to the absence of a historic track record of the new company, this situation has resulted in professional valuers inventing newer qualitative valuation methods, one such method being Scorecard Method of Valuation which focuses on the various factors such as Founding team strength, Competition, Product, Customer Acquisition, etc. Some refer to this as the Benchmark Method. The chapter on the Scorecard Method of Valuation is a result of the study of the scorecard method of valuation created by the US Angel Investors and also the modified scorecard method is a result of the author's practical experience and focuses on entrepreneurship from a strategic lens.

Chapter 10 explains *"Dave Berkus Method"*. The method provides an alternative valuation framework for early-stage startups. It aims to help investors and entrepreneurs efficiently assess the potential of an early-stage startup that may not yet have significant revenue or assets on which to base a traditional valuation. The method provides a set of guidelines and criteria that can be used to evaluate the chances of success of a startup, including factors such as Sound Idea, Viability of product tested through a prototype, assessment of management capabilities, strategic relationships that the startup has built and effective product roll out and achievement of sales.

Chapter 11 explains *"Risk Factor Summation Method"*. The method considers a broader set of factors in determining the pre-money valuation. This method is particularly useful for early-stage investors as it forces them to consider important exogenous factors. It assesses various types of risks that a venture must manage to achieve a lucrative exit. These risks include management, stage of the business, legislation/political risk, manufacturing risk, sales, and marketing risk, funding/capital raising risk, competition risk, technology risk, litigation risk, international risk, reputation risk, and potentially lucrative exit.

In the final two chapters of this book, we explore two advanced methods for startup valuation: real options and data envelopment analysis. Both traditional and modern approaches to startup valuation have proven useful. Although they are not easy to estimate, advanced methods for startup valuation are also becoming increasingly popular among investors and entrepreneurs.

Chapter 12, titled *"Fintech: Startup Valuation based on the Real Options Approach"*, proposes a general startup business valuation framework based on the Real Options (RO) approach. Decisions taken by managers based on traditional approaches were inflexible based on straightforward criteria "sticky options". Even in good market conditions, the traditional criteria do not allow to extract an investment "opportunity value" referred to as Time Value, which may unmask a better than previously expected investment performance. As startups lack financial historical information and cost structures, the traditional business valuation approach based on DCF could be doubtful. Therefore, the RO is proposed not as a substitute of DCF valuation approach, but as a complementary tool for the decision-making process. Four scenarios based on the "Options Cycle for Startups" are performed related to the option to invest, to continue, to abandon, and to switch. Results revealed that when NPV rejects a startup investment, the RO suggests that there is a chance to exercise the initial investment at the expiration of the stage. Even though market conditions may go worst, the RO approach shows that there is always a Time value in any business decision-making. The scenarios emphasized Fintech startups because of their current importance in financial inclusion and financial services digitization. The RO approach should be taken with care since investment projects and startups are not marketable securities, as the Black-Scholes model assumes.

In Chap. 13, titled *"Startup Valuation with Data Envelopment Analysis"*, the author emphasizes once again the difficulties of Startup valuation such as short history, limited estimation possibilities for the future, first-year negative cash flows, and lack of comparable companies. Thus, the chapter argues that these difficulties can be partially overcome by developing various assumptions. In this chapter, first of all, DEA and the methodology of valuation with DEA are explained, then the value range of a hypothetical startup firm, as well as its maximum value, are estimated by analyzing it with real comparable firm data. As with other valuation methods, the realistic assumptions used in startup valuation with DEA will increase the success of the valuation. In this framework, it is an important requirement to select the most appropriate input-output mix in the startup valuation with DEA and to realistically estimate the selected input-output mix for the startup to be valued.

In conclusion, the world of startup valuation is a complex and ever-changing landscape that can seem daunting to even the most seasoned investor. However, by understanding the key principles and methodologies behind startup valuation, entrepreneurs and investors alike can make informed decisions that have the potential to drive innovation, fuel growth, and generate significant returns. In this book, we will delve into the intricacies of startup valuation, exploring the various approaches and techniques used to assess the worth of a startup. Whether you're an entrepreneur looking to secure funding or an investor searching for the next big opportunity, or a business professional seeking to acquire or merge with startups this book will provide you with the knowledge and tools you need to navigate the world of startup valuation with confidence. Get ready to embark on an exciting journey into the world of startup valuation.

Introduction to Startup Valuation: From Idea to IPO

Sinem Derindere Köseoğlu and Adam Patterson

Every scenario has a component of both risk and return. Valuation is the only KPI that puts them together.—Daniel Faloppa, Equidam Founder.
A (startup) firm can have value only if it ultimately delivers earnings.—Aswath Damodaran.
Startup valuation is not just a spreadsheet. It is a summarized map of future strategy, narrative and value creation.—Adam Patterson.
Good financial modeling in a startup valuation should include the full story of the company. This is the art part of the work.—Sinem Derindere Köseoğlu.

1 Startups Terminology and Processes

1.1 Startup Processes

The startup ecosystem possesses its own nomenclature and phraseology, so much so that it can seem quite overwhelming at first, especially for newcomers to the space. Therefore, in this introductory chapter, we clarify basic terms related to the ecosystem in order to elucidate grounding and provide context before progressing through the book.

The startup ecosystem is a complex network of various entities, processes, and interactions that work together to support and promote the creation and growth of new businesses. It's a complex and dynamic environment that requires a deep understanding of business, technology, and entrepreneurship to navigate successfully.

S. D. Köseoğlu (✉) · A. Patterson
Istanbul University, Istanbul, Turkey

Redirection Corporate Advisory, Curitiba, Brazil
e-mail: adam@redirection.com.br

S. Derindere Köseoğlu (ed.), *A Practical Guide for Startup Valuation*, Contributions to Finance and Accounting, https://doi.org/10.1007/978-3-031-35291-1_2

A startup is a new business enterprise that is in the process of developing and testing a unique product or service. The focus of a startup is often on innovation and disruption, aiming to create a new market or disrupt an existing one (Faster Capital, 2023).

The initial stage of a startup is *idea* generation. Once an idea has been generated, it is important to *validate* it to ensure that there is a market for the product or service. This may involve conducting market research or testing the product with potential customers. There is also an *incubation* process in which incubators provide support and resources to early-stage startups. This may include office space, mentorship, funding, and other services that help startups to grow and develop. Accelerators are similar to incubators, but they focus on providing startups with intensive, short-term programs that help them to scale up quickly. This may involve providing access to funding, mentorship, and other resources. S.M.A.R.T goals should be specific in terms of what is to be accomplished, measurable in terms of how progress will be tracked, actionable in terms of what steps will be taken to achieve the goal, realistic in terms of what is achievable given available resources, and time-bound in terms of when the goal will be accomplished. *S.M.A.R.T* is an acronym for *Specific, Measurable, Actionable, Realistic, and Time-bound*. It is a framework used to help set goals and objectives that are clear, well-defined, and achievable.

The *funding process* is also significantly important for the start-up ecosystem because entrepreneurs with new ideas often do not have enough access to funds for growth. Startup funding can come from a variety of sources, including angel investors, venture capitalists, and crowdfunding platforms. This is often a crucial stage in the startup process, as it provides the necessary resources to help the business grow and expand. *The burn rate* of startups is important for the need for funds immediately. Burn rate is a measure of how quickly a startup is spending its available funds. It is typically expressed as a monthly figure, and takes into account all of the company's expenses, including salaries, rent, marketing, and other operating costs. A high burn rate means that a company is spending its money quickly and may need to raise additional funds soon, while a low burn rate means that a company is operating more efficiently and may be able to sustain its operations for a longer period of time.

Due diligence typically comes into play during the funding stage of the startups. It is the process of conducting a thorough investigation of a company, typically by potential investors, to assess its financial, legal, and operational status before making an investment. The goal of due diligence is to help investors make an informed investment decision and minimize the risk of investing in a startup that may not be viable or may have significant legal or financial liabilities. For startups, going through due diligence can also help to identify areas where they may need to improve their business operations or address potential legal or financial issues before seeking funding.

In the startup journey, there is *a scaling phase*. Scaling refers to the process of growing a startup into a sustainable, profitable business. This may involve expanding the customer base, developing new products or services, or entering new markets. Sometimes, startups need to the process of changing the direction or focus of a startup in response to feedback or changing market conditions, which process is called *Pivot*. Pivoting may involve changes to the company's product or service offering, target market, business model, or other key elements of the business. Pivoting can be a difficult decision, as it may involve abandoning previous plans or investments, but it can also be a necessary step to ensure the long-term success of a startup.

Finally, many startups aim to eventually *exit* the market through acquisition, merger, or an initial public offering (IPO). This can provide a significant return on investment for investors and founders, while also allowing the business to continue to grow and evolve under new ownership.

After a brief description around the startup ecosystem and processes, we provide more details and discussion on some of the key points.

1.2 Startups' Different Stages

A new enterprise has different stages. There are main stages that a new company typically goes through as it grows and matures. The specific terminology and number of stages may vary depending on the source, but a common framework is:

1. *Idea stage* (pre-seed stage): This is the initial stage of a startup, where the entrepreneur has an idea and is exploring its potential. Idea stage is the very earliest stage of a startup, where the entrepreneur or team has an idea for a new product, service, or business model, but has not yet developed a fully functioning prototype or business plan. At this stage, the focus is on researching the market, identifying a target audience, and assessing the feasibility of the idea. The goal is to determine whether the idea has the potential to be turned into a viable business. Seed funding may be required to help the entrepreneur or team develop a more concrete plan and start building the business.
2. *Seed stage:* This is the earliest stage of a startup, where the company is just getting started and may still be developing its product or service. Seed-stage companies often rely on funding from friends, family, or angel investors. During the seed stage, the focus is on refining the startup's idea, developing a minimum viable product (MVP), and identifying a target market. The goal is to create a product or service that solves a real problem for customers and can be brought to market quickly and cost-effectively. Seed-stage companies often have a high degree of uncertainty and risk, but they also have the potential for significant growth and success if they can develop a strong product and attract early customers.
3. *Lean stage*: This is a stage of rapid experimentation and iteration, where the startup focuses on building a minimum viable product (MVP) and testing it with customers. This stage advocates the creation of rapid prototypes designed to test market assumptions, and uses customer feedback to evolve them much faster than via more traditional product development practices.

4. *Early stage:* This is the stage where a startup has a functioning product or service and is beginning to generate revenue. Early-stage companies may also receive funding from venture capitalists (VCs) or other institutional investors.
5. *Growth stage:* In this stage, the startup has a proven business model and is experiencing rapid growth. The focus is on scaling the business and expanding into new markets. Growth-stage companies often receive significant funding from VCs or private equity firms.
6. *Expansion stage:* This is the stage where the company has established itself as a successful business and is expanding into new regions or markets. The focus is on continuing to scale the business while maintaining profitability.
7. *Mature stage/late stage:* In this stage, the company is a well-established player in its industry and has a stable market position. The focus is on maintaining market share and profitability, and the company may consider going public or being acquired.
8. *Exit stage:* At this stage, the founders or investors of the company may consider selling the company or going public. This is the final stage in the company's growth journey.

It's important to note that not all startups will progress through all of these stages, and some may exit the startup phase earlier or later than others. In other words, the startup lifecycle is not always linear. Additionally, there may be other stages or variations of this framework depending on the industry or specific business.

1.3 Startups' Classification Based on Their Value

There is another classification that startups take according to the value they reach, in which startup titles can be Unicorn, Decacorn, and Hectacorn (Alpha, 2023):

1. *Unicorn:* A startup that has reached a value of $1 billion or more.
2. *Decacorn:* A startup that has reached a value of $10 billion or more.
3. *Hectacorn:* A startup that has reached a value of $100 billion or more.

2 Startup Ecosystem in the World

The startup ecosystem is a global phenomenon that has grown rapidly in recent years. The startup ecosystem is not limited to any specific region or country, and startups are being founded and funded all over the world. While the United States is often considered the epicentre of the startup ecosystem, other regions such as Europe, Asia, and Latin America are also home to thriving startup communities (Startup Blink, 2022).

According to the Startup Blink Global Startup Ecosystem Index 2022, the top 10 countries for startups are (Table 1):

Table 1 Top 10 countries for startups

1. United States
2. United Kingdom
3. Israel
4. Canada
5. Sweden
6. Germany
7. Singapore
8. Australia
9. France
10. China

Data Source: Startup Blink Global Startup Ecosystem Index 2022

These rankings are based on factors such as the number of startups, quality of startups, level of funding, support infrastructure, and entrepreneurial culture. However, rankings like these can change rapidly over time as the startup environment evolves and new players emerge.

When we look at the industry-based distribution of startups, we see that the fintech, life sciences, and AI industries have a high share (Fig. 1).

The Crunchbase Unicorn Board is a compiled list of the most valuable private companies in the world depending on Crunchbase's extensive market data. According to the Crunchbase Unicorn Board list the top ten valued companies, operations, origins, and post-money value are shown in Table 2.

There are many factors that contribute to the success of the most valued startups in the world. When we analyse the most valued startups we can conclude that the most successful startups are those that are able to combine the factors of innovation and disruptive technology, strong leadership and vision, market opportunity and scalability, access to capital and talent, and customer focus and user experience. Above all, the best startup companies can be seen to seamlessly solve a problem or provide a new product or service at the right time.

3 The Importance of Startup Valuation

Startup valuation and due diligence are of fundamental importance in the ecosystem. We can summarize some of the reasons why startup valuation is important as follows:

1. *It is focused on determining the investor's share in the company:* When a startup raises capital from investors, they usually do so in exchange for equity, which represents ownership in the company. The percentage of equity that an investor receives is determined by the startup's valuation. It determines the investor's share in the company, which can impact their return on investment, as well as the company's ability to attract future investment and partnerships.

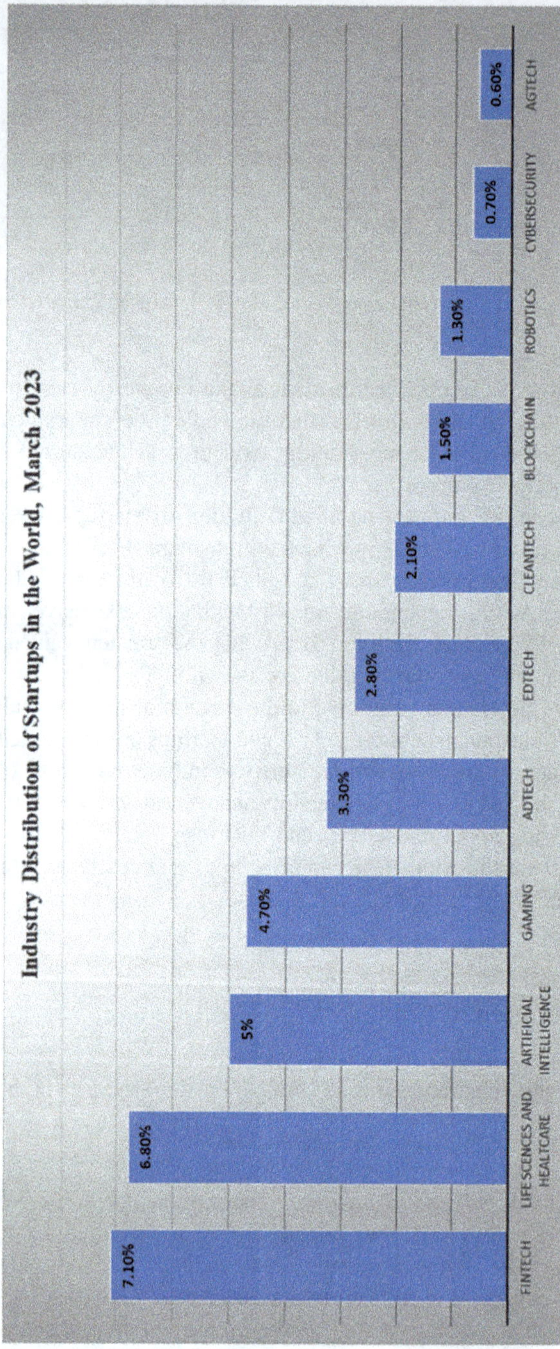

Fig. 1 Industry distribution of startups in the world. Data Source: statista.com

Table 2 The Crunchbase Unicorn Board list of the top 10 global startups by valuation (2023)

	Company	Operations	Origin country	Post money value
1	ByteDance	ByteDance is the parent company of popular social media app TikTok, as well as other apps such as Douyin and Toutiao.	China	$220 Billion
2	Ant Group	Ant Group is a financial technology company that offers services such as mobile payments, wealth management, and credit scoring.	China	$150 Billion
3	SpaceX	SpaceX is a space exploration company founded by Elon Musk. The company's primary focus is on developing reusable rockets and spacecraft for commercial spaceflight and space exploration.	United States	$125 Billion
4	Shein	Shein is an e-commerce company that sells fast fashion and accessories primarily to women. The company is headquartered in Nanjing, China, and operates in various markets around the world. Shein has faced criticism for its labour practices and environmental impact.	China	$100 Billion
5	Stripe	Stripe is a financial technology company that provides payment processing and other services for businesses. Stripe has been rapidly expanding its product offerings and has recently entered the realm of cryptocurrency.	United States	$50 Billion
6	Canva	Canva is a graphic design platform that allows users to create graphics, presentations, and other visual content. The company is headquartered in Sydney, Australia, and has users in various markets around the world. Canva has been rapidly expanding its product offerings and recently launched a video editing platform.	Australia	$40 Billion
7	Checkout.com	Checkout.com is a financial technology company that provides payment processing and other services for businesses. Checkout.com has been rapidly expanding its product offerings and recently acquired a payment processing company in the United States.	United Kingdom	$40 Billion
8	Instacart	Instacart is a grocery delivery and pick-up service that allows users to order from various retailers and have their groceries delivered or picked up at a designated location.	United States	$39 Billion
9	JUUL	JUUL Labs is a company that produces e-cigarettes and vaping products. JUUL has faced regulatory challenges and public scrutiny due to concerns about its marketing practices and appeals to young people.	United States	$38 Billion
10	Databricks	Databricks is a software company that provides a unified data analytics platform, designed to help businesses manage and analyse their data effectively. The platform is built on top of Apache Spark, an open-source data processing engine, and allows users to work with large datasets in a scalable and collaborative manner.	United States	$38 Billion

2. *Attracting investment:* A startup's valuation is a key factor in attracting investment from venture capitalists, angel investors, and other sources of funding. Investors use a startup's valuation to determine how much equity they will receive in exchange for their investment, as well as to evaluate the potential return on investment.
3. *Negotiating deals:* A startup's valuation can be used as a bargaining chip in negotiations with potential partners, customers, or vendors. For example, a startup with a high valuation may be able to negotiate better terms with suppliers or secure more favourable deals with customers.
4. *Exit strategy:* A startup's valuation is also important in determining the potential exit strategy for investors and founders. Large and growing valuations and fundraising can be used for IPO or acquisitions.
5. *Employee compensation:* A startup's valuation can also impact how much equity employees receive as part of their compensation package. Employees can receive stock options or other forms of equity in lieu of high salaries, so a high valuation can be a strong motivator for employees to join and stay with the company.
6. *Competitive advantage:* A startup's valuation can also provide a competitive advantage in the market by signalling to customers, partners, and competitors that the company is financially stable and has the potential for long-term growth. A high valuation can also increase a startup's credibility and brand recognition, which can help attract new customers, talent, and business opportunities.
7. *Risk management:* A startup's valuation can also play a role in risk management, as it can help identify potential areas of weakness or vulnerability in the company's operations or financial structure. By monitoring changes in valuation over time, startups can better understand the risks and challenges they face and make informed decisions about how to mitigate them.
8. *Partnership opportunities:* A startup's valuation can also open up partnership opportunities with other companies in the ecosystem, such as strategic investors, corporate venture funds, or accelerator programs. Moreover, high valuations can unlock commercial opportunities with broader market players. These partnerships can provide valuable resources and expertise to help the startup grow and scale.
9. *Strategic financial management based on business value:* Companies that regularly monitor business value are aware of value drivers. They are thus better placed to develop strategies based on valuation performance indicators by taking into account the factors that positively and negatively affect the value of the company.

Overall, startup valuation is a crucial factor in the success and growth of a startup. As such, it's important for startups to carefully consider their valuation and work to maximize their value proposition in the market.

4 Startups Valuation Methods

Startup valuation is the process of determining the value of a startup company, which is important for various reasons such as attracting investment, selling the company, or establishing a partnership. It is also an important part of investment due-diligence. Startup valuation methods are basically divided into two principal approaches as traditional and modern valuation methods. There are different methods under these two distinctions. The methods will be discussed in more detail in the following chapters in the book and only general definitions of these methods are therefore mentioned in this introductory chapter (Fig. 2).

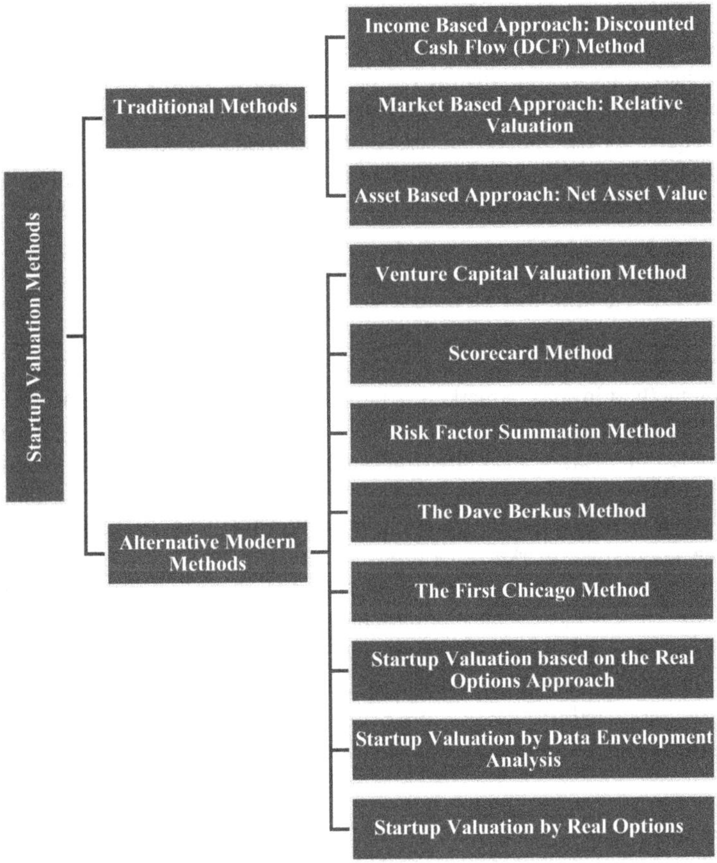

Fig. 2 Startup valuation methods

4.1 Traditional Valuation Approaches and Methods

Traditionally, startup valuation has relied on classical data-driven approaches.

4.1.1 The Discounted Cashflow (DCF) Valuation Method

The most well-known income-based method is the DCF method. These include the discounted cash flow (DCF) valuation approach, which takes several forms, which discount different measures of firm-income, revenue, or cashflow, using the appropriate risk-adjusted discount-rate. The DCF model requires forecasting the future cash flows of the startup, determining a discount rate to reflect the perceived risk of the investment, and adding the discounted cash flows to determine firm value. Approaches include the free-cashflow-to-firm (FCFF) method, which discounts sales revenues, discounting them with the weighted-average cost of capital, as well as the free-cashflow-to-equity (FCFE) method, which discounts net income by the cost of equity as per the capital asset pricing model (CAPM), and the Gordon Growth Model, which mitigates discount rates in accordance with revenue growth rates (Goker & Köseoğlu, 2020).

4.1.2 Relative Valuation Method

Relative Valuation Method is a market-based approach. A prominent alternate valuation method in startup markets is the relative valuation method. Mechanically, this method relies on estimating valuation as a multiple of the firm's balance sheet and income statement or cash flow components. In other words, this method values the startup based on many multiples of comparable companies. Valuation multiples, in turn, are driven by averages drawn from comparable firms, which typically share the same contextual market conditions, such as industry, business model, and economic geography. This method is useful when there is a sufficient number of comparable companies with similar business models. Empirically speaking, regressions-based approaches supplement these models by controlling for contextual market conditions (Berre & Le Pendeven, 2022). These range from macroeconomic conditions to industry-level market-dynamics, to relevant entrepreneur characteristics.

4.1.3 Net Asset Value

Net asset value is an asset-based valuation method. This method values the startup based on its tangible and intangible assets. This method considers the value of the company's assets, including cash, equipment, inventory, and intellectual property, and subtracts its liabilities to determine the net asset value.

4.2 Alternative Modern Methods

4.2.1 Venture Capital Method

The venture capital (VC) method, which was created in 1987 by Bill Sahlman, is a modern method for startup valuation that is commonly used by investors, such as venture capitalists, angel investors, or other investors who invest in early-stage companies. This method involves estimating the potential return on investment (ROI) for the investor by using the expected future valuation of the startup (Payne, 2011a).

The VC method involves estimating the expected future value of the startup, typically within a period of 2–5 years, and then calculating the expected return on investment for the investor. This is done by determining the investor's required rate of return, which is the minimum rate of return that the investor expects to earn on their investment, taking into account the level of risk involved in the investment and their opportunity cost. Once the expected future value of the startup is estimated, the post-money valuation of the company is calculated by adding the amount of investment to the expected future value. The pre-money valuation is then calculated by subtracting the amount of investment from the post-money valuation. Finally, the percentage of ownership in the startup is calculated by dividing the amount of investment by the calculated valuation (Dealstation, 2022) (see chapter "Venture Capital Method" for the details of this method).

4.2.2 The First Chicago Method

The First Chicago valuation method is a tool for determining the value of a company based on the analysis of its expected future cash flows in multiple scenarios, therefore, it can be seen as a variation of the DCF method. As an extension of the standard DCF, the First Chicago method runs three or more separate DCFs under varying assumptions and then weights the values based on the probability of each outcome occurring (Reinfeld, 2018) (see chapter "The First Chicago Valuation Method" for the details of this method).

4.2.3 Scorecard Method

The Scorecard Method involves assessing the startup's value on various factors such as the management team, market size, product, etc., and assigning scores based on these factors to arrive at a valuation. The scorecard method can provide a more qualitative and forward-looking assessment of a startup's value. The overall score from the scorecard can then be used to estimate the value of the startup by comparing it to similar companies or by using multiples such as price-to-sales or price-to-earnings ratios (Payne, 2021) (see chapter "Scorecard Method of Valuation: The Subjective Analysis of Valuation" for the details of this method).

4.2.4 The Dave Berkus Method

This approach provides a set of guidelines and criteria that can be used to evaluate the chances of success of a startup, including factors such as sound idea, viability of product tested through a prototype, assessment of management capabilities, strategic relationships that the startup has built and effective product roll out and achievement of sales. In this method, the corresponding amount is given by evaluating five basic criteria, and the total value of these criteria gives the company value. The amount given to each criterion cannot exceed 500 thousand dollars, and the total amount given cannot exceed 2.5 million dollars. However, since each country and each sector has its own dynamics, amounts should be adjusted in different countries and sectors (Myvaluation, 2022) (see chapter "Dave Berkus Method" for the details of this method).

4.2.5 Risk Factor Summation Method

The Risk Factor Summation Method assigns a score to 12 different criteria and is given an amount based on the assigned scores. It is a more comprehensive valuation method which is a combination of the Scorecard method and the Berkus method. All aspects of management, enterprise, political system, production, sales/marketing, fund/capital, competition, technology, legal status, international position, reputation, and exit from investment criteria are evaluated and evaluated individually, and a value is reached depending on the relative risks of the criteria (Payne, 2011b) (see chapter "Risk Factor Summation Method" for the details of this method).

4.2.6 Startup Valuation by Real Options Approach

Lastly, more niche-case approaches such as the real options valuation approach, depend on the accurate and detailed estimation of risk and volatility (see chapter "Fintech: Startup Valuation Based on the Real Options Approach" for the details of this method).

4.2.7 Startup Valuation by Data Envelopment Analysis (DEA)

DEA is a non-parametric tool. The method finds a frontier and analyses the efficiency of each unit in the comparison set relative to its distance from this frontier. This method can provide the integrity that traditional methods cannot provide for the evaluation of multiple inputs and multiple outputs with the logic of total factor productivity. In the DEA technique, the weights of inputs and outputs are used for Decision Making Units (DMUs) to maximize their efficiency ratios. Weights are allocated for the inputs and outputs of each decision-making unit separately (Kutlar

& Babacan, 2008). Firm valuation via DEA, where valuation tests have been performed for mature firms in the literature and it has been seen that quite satisfactory results are obtained, can also be used in the valuation of startup firms if the input and output data to be used in the analysis can be estimated with various assumptions (see chapter "Startup Valuation with Data Envelopment Analysis" for the details of this method).

5 Startup Financing Methods

Startups begin with ideas. An idea to improve or innovate an existing product or service disrupts or solves a problem in the market. Success however does not depend solely on an idea. Timing, effort, technological and management capacity, luck—one recalls Napoleon's "I'd rather have lucky generals than good one's" quote—and of course adequate financial resources also play key roles. Moreover, because they lack financial history and collateral, unlike mature companies, startups cannot easily get financing from traditional organizations like banks (Hellwig, 1991). According to Ostgaard and Birley (1994), the inherent uncertainty in startups' future trajectory makes it challenging for them to secure external, third-party, capital. A startup financing ecosystem with angel, seed, and venture capital investors has therefore grown to fill the gap.

Startup funding enables entrepreneurs to execute their ideas by developing new products, hiring staff, investing in R&D endeavours and competing with other firms. Essentially then, funding is essential to the success of startup companies as it helps accelerate a good business idea. Famously, even Steve Jobs had to sell his car to help fund the creation of Apple.

It is estimated that more than 60% of all startups need investment from external sources (TecnoIdentity, 2022) and moreover that 47% of startup failures in 2022 were due to a lack of financing, nearly double the percentage that failed for the same reason in 2021, whilst running out of cash was behind 44% of failures (CNBC, 2023). Despite the boom in venture capital funding over the last few years, statistics reveal that for each startup that VC investors allocate capital, they look at a further 400 and that "only 0.91% startups get funded by the angel investors, while a mere 0.05 percent are funded by the VCs. In comparison, 57% startups get funds through credit and personal loan, while 38% get startup funding from friends and family" (Marquee Equity, 2021). OECD research (2014) contends that almost 55% of entrepreneurs report "obtaining finance" as a major startup difficulty.

Startups use, or following industry terminology, "burn", capital to help get the company off the ground, get a good team in place, invest in software, give the company external credibility and support marketing, commercial and technological development activities. A startup is a business proposal (Sandler, 2015) and financing therefore helps transform the proposal into business reality. Moreover, VC investment can be classed as "smart" for the incremental value it brings to the table beyond financial resources, such as business know-how, networking, and help to develop new commercial opportunities. Baum and Silverman (2004) maintain that external investment helps identify potential, provides validation and the coaching a startup needs to succeed. Historically, the main sources of startup funding have been traditional, or somewhat subsidized, credit lines and bank loans—in summary: debt instruments—and early-stage financing which encompass angel and VC investment. These funds are usually in exchange for equity, or ownership stakes in companies that exhibit high growth potential.

Georges Doriot, a professor at Harvard Business School, is often regarded as the "Father of Venture Capital". In order to invest in businesses that commercialized technologies created during the second world war, he founded the American Research and Development Company (ARDC) in 1946 and raised a $3.5 million investment fund. Prior to this, venture finance, similar to the broader private equity universe, was primarily the purview of high-net-worth individuals (HNWI) and large banking groups. Since then, we have seen a significant uptick in VC funds. Today there are roughly 1000 active venture capital firms in the United States and over 800 in Europe (Zippia, 2022). Over the last few years there has been an increase in the available sources and volumes of startup funding, which will be described in more detail below:

- *Bootstrapping:* In the startup universe, bootstrapping refers to the process of starting and expanding a firm without exogenous funding or succour. At the macro level therefore, instead of relying on investors or loans, the approach entails building up a business using personal funds, savings, or existing resources in a self-sustaining process. The term was first described by Bhidé (1992) in the Harvard Business Review. As Carter and Auken (2005) argue, bootstrap finance is probably one of the most widely used forms of financing by companies, especially for emerging firms. The etymology of the term can trace its origins to the nineteenth century expression of "Pulling oneself up by one's bootstraps" which refers to carrying out an action independently, without the aid of external actors, usually in a more challenging fashion in order to acheive success. For Grichnik et al. (2014) bootstrapping is "an alternative resource management approach directed at avoiding market-based resource transactions". Of course, companies can be "bootstrapped" until maturity, as was the case of software development firm company, GitHub, which developed through bootstrapped resources for its first 4 years before raising large VC financing rounds with major funds and ultimately being bought by Microsoft for $7.5 billion in 2018, a decade after being founded. At the practical level however, bootstrapping is often a financing mechanism for only the embryonic months or years of a startup's life cycle before external financing rounds or options are sought.
- *The Famous 3Fs*: Burke et al. (2014) state that the term "3Fs" (designating "family, friends, and fools") refers to those who invest or loan resources informally to entrepreneurs usually through personal relationships at the start of a startup's life cycle. Such "investors" frequently allocate capital informally, with far less assurances and due diligence of the venture's viability—hence the "fool" element of the abbreviation—usually because they have faith in the

entrepreneur's skill or in the concept or essentially due to familial or friendship connections. Thus, a startup founder without a history of business success may find it simpler to get funding from these "investors" than from other sources of funding. According to an OECD study (2014): "The 3Fs of founder, family and friends are the main source of startup finance" across different socio-demographic groups. As there is typically not much financing required at the ideational stage, the majority of 3Fs will invest or loan nominal capital amounts, which makes sense from their perspective by limiting potential losses. For the entrepreneur, market validation is the 3Fs phase's goal by providing empirical factual proof that they can develop the concept into a scalable business model.

- *Startup Accelerators:* A startup accelerator is a fixed-term mentor-based program that adds value through guidance, networking, practical support, and initial seed funding streams, often in exchange for a small equity component. For Karimi et al. (2022) they are the "crucial foundations that influence development of the entrepreneurial ecosystem and new venture creations". Y-Combinator, then based out of Massachusetts, is widely considered the world's first accelerator program, founded in 2005 (Drover et al., 2017). Since then and in line with the growth of the broader startup nexus, it is estimated that there are approximately 8000 business accelerators worldwide with more than half of them set-up between 2014 and 2022 (Aljalahma & Slof, 2022), including initiatives led by Governments and large corporates. In general, the acceleration methodology is centred around an, usually competitive, open application process, team-focused cohort-learning and graduation-style conclusions, often with a "demo or pitch day" (Gilani & Dettori, 2011). The business model is based on generating venture-style returns, via equity, rather than charging for teaching, rental, or service fees. There have been multiple cases of accelerator program successes. AirBnB, Y-Combinator class of 2008, for instance, went public in 2020 with an IPO that was quickly valued at $100 billion dollars.
- *Government Incentives and Grants:* According to Sheriff and Muffatto (2015), institutions and the government are crucial in the development of entrepreneurial networks. Afterall, as Auerswald (2015) argued, governments and non-governmental organizations are increasingly turning to startups in order to expand their economies and productivity growth. Startup grants are essentially a type of financing, most commonly from the government and third-sector organizations, intended to support business expansion and innovation. Occasionally, business guidance and mentoring are included with financing. Governments can boost entrepreneurship by enacting macro-level public policies that encourage improved access to funding, education, and training, as well as by cutting bureaucratic red tape. Government organizations can specifically assist in providing money for startups by offering grants, loans, and financial incentives for businesses, such as tax breaks for R&D operations. Many subsidies and incentives are available in both developed and emerging countries for new startups. For instance, the Canadian government has a mentoring program that pairs aspiring entrepreneurs with seasoned business mentors. Small businesses can get free business advice from the US Small Business Administration's SCORE program,

and the US government's Small Business Innovation Research (SBIR) program offers funds to help them create cutting-edge goods and services for the US government. According to the British Business Bank, 2022, there are over 200 government grants for small businesses available in the UK. These grants include capital grants for the acquisition of machinery or IT equipment as well as subsidized business loans, lower rent, and local government rates. Most incentives for small businesses are given to new or fledgling companies, and though there are many grants available, obtaining a government grant for a small business can be a challenge. Government financial assistance via grants for new companies can be advantageous for three conceptually separate reasons, according to Söderblom et al. (2015). Government financial contributions can legitimize the new venture, signal that the startup is certified by a reliable source and increase its appeal to potential investors. Government financial contributions are particularly relevant to new ventures, as they are able to reduce information asymmetries and market failures.

- *Angel Investors:* An angel investor is an individual or organization that provides capital for a business, including startups, typically in exchange for convertible debt or ownership equity, at an early stage when failure risk is high and when most investors are not prepared to support them. Angel investors are also referred to as business angels, informal investors, or angel funders. The term "angel" in the financing context first appeared in the theatre and cultural sector, where it was used to refer to wealthy people who contributed funds to plays that would otherwise have had to be cancelled. Historically, angel investors have been high net-worth individuals who have privately invested in new startup firms during their initial life cycle. In addition to providing funding, angel investors add value by giving the entrepreneur access to their network, coaching and offering business advice. According to University of New Hampshire (2021) data, the overall amount of US angel investments in 2020 was $25.3 billion, up 6% from 2019. [Moreover], "angel investments went to 64,480 business initiatives in total, up 1.2% from 2019 investments. Moreover, a 3.5% increase in active investors brought the total to 334,680 from 323,365 in 2019. In addition, angel investments at the seed and startup stage were 39% {of total investment] in 2020, with an average deal size of $392,025". As such, angel investment is a fundamental part of the early-stage startup financing equation.
- *Venture Capital:* Venture capital (VC) is an asset class that offers financing and operational know-how to founders and startup businesses, generally in disruptive and technology-based industries. Data from Dealroom, based on the UK market, shows that the sectors that received the most VC investment in 2022 were fintech, health, energy, transportation, and marketing. Firms look for venture capital investment for a myriad of reasons, including expanding their operations, improving product development and building out their teams. VCs can provide both early-stage funding and growth capital in an individual or multiple-sector approach at varying investment levels. Many of the most well-known technology blue-chip companies today received venture capital funding in their early stages of development, including Google and Facebook. VCs often invest together with

other VCs and investors in minority ownership in companies. Early-stage businesses raise capital through "rounds" (Series A, B, C, etc.), where additional funds are invested by the same investors or new ones to support the business as it expands. VC plays an essential role in the promotion, creation, and establishment of new business ventures (Subhash, 2006).

- *Private Equity:* A private equity (PE) firm is an investment management company that offers financial support for direct investments in, mostly privately held, businesses using a variety of investment theses. Leveraged buyouts and venture capital are only two examples of the many capital allocation and raising strategies that fall under the umbrella of private equity. Investors will pay a private equity firm a recurring management fee and a portion of the profits (or "carried interest"). A minority or a majority equity stake might be used to fund investments (Avdeitchikova, 2008). Private equity businesses also often issue debt to boost the return on their equity investment, but their capital, or "dry powder", primarily comes from institutional investors such as pension funds, endowments, large corporates, and Family offices (Dawson, 2011). Private equity firms' main goal is to maximize their financial returns by selling their equity stakes at the highest possible capital gain after a medium-term investment period, which is typically between 4 and 7 years. The global private equity market was valued at $4.74 trillion in 2021, according to Prequin (2021) data. Research from Bain estimates that private equity investors closed $284 billion in tech deals in 2021, accounting for 31% of all sector deals and 25% of the total buyout value (Bain, 2022). Of the top 10 firms in the 2021 *HEC-DowJones Private Equity Performance ranking*, more than half are focused on technology investments. PE has become a more important part of financing larger funding streams as international technology companies have remained private for extended periods of time.
- *Crowdfunding:* Crowdfunding is a method of collectively obtaining funds to finance projects and companies. The strategy makes it possible for fundraisers to use online platforms to collect smaller sums of money from a big number of donors. Websites that facilitate communication between fundraisers and the public are known as crowdfunding platforms. The crowdfunding platform can be used to solicit and collect financial pledges. Equity crowdfunding, peer-to-peer lending, and funding in exchange for future earnings or profit sharing are the main types of crowdfunding finance. Data from Statista (2021) shows that the global crowdfunding industry was valued $13.64 billion in 2021 and was expected to double in size by 2028. Crowdfunding uses social media and specific websites to connect investors and entrepreneurs. By enlarging the pool of investors outside the typical circle of owners, family, and venture capitalists, crowdfunding has the potential to boost entrepreneurship and startups. After first starting as a way to jointly finance music and artists, crowdfunding has since become a source of funding for a variety of enterprises. Indeed, for new ventures, crowdfunding is viewed as a solution to close the early-stage funding gap (Hemer et al., 2011). If the fundraising campaign is successful, crowdfunding platforms typically charge fundraisers a fee on raised capital and potentially even future rounds. In return,

crowdfunding platforms are expected to provide a secure, quick, and easy-to-use service.

- *ICOs:* Initial Coin Offerings, or ICOs, are a cutting-edge new form of fundraising that are also known as token sales (Fisch, 2019). They combine aspects of crowdsourcing and digital currencies to finance company growth whilst utilizing blockchain technology. In his 2013 "The Second Bitcoin White Paper", software developer J.R. Willet introduced the idea. ICOs were especially popular from 2017 as an innovative way for projects to raise funds, and they took off quickly, bringing in more than $5 billion that year. While conducting an ICO, a blockchain-based firm creates a specific number of its own native digital tokens and commercializes them to early investors. ICOs are thus a form of digital crowdfunding and provide entrepreneurs the ability to not only raise money without ceding equity but also to build a community of users who are financially motivated to see the project grow so that their presale tokens appreciate in value. The blockchain technology transfers some of its implications and qualities, including immutability, decentralization, and openness, to attributes of the ICO, according to Kher et al. (2020), making ICOs distinct from traditional crowdfunding. Startups can generate money through ICOs by offering investors digital tokens, or "coins", in return for financial resources. The business owner agrees to only take the coins issued as payment for the goods and services on their platform and agrees to stop issuing coins after the predetermined number has been reached. If the platform is successful, buyers may additionally profit from increased token value and access to the service that the token grants. Tokens can be either utility tokens or security tokens.
- *Convertible Debt and Bridge Financing:* A startup may raise a "bridge financing round" if it requires extra funding in between two rounds of funding. Bridge financing is thus a temporary unpriced finance round. The company typically offers preferred equity or convertible notes. As they can set a valuation cap or discount price for shares sold in the following pricing round, investors favour convertible notes, especially as they are interest-bearing instruments. Convertible debt notes are a viable alternative to traditional bank loans and allow startups to raise cash more rapidly and cheaply than equity without having to define a new valuation (Craigmile & Hermann-Friede, 2021). The investor-provided discount rate on the future round valuation and the valuation cap to reduce potential dilution are the two fundamental features that set a convertible debt note apart from a regular loan. Bridge funding, an unpriced round of financing, is frequently led by one of the company's current investors. According to Lewis et al. (1999), businesses with corporate governance challenges are more likely to employ convertible sources of financing to lower the adverse selection costs associated with using straight debt and regular equity. Hence, bridge rounds frequently suggest unfavourable connotations with the business's financial situation. However, these rounds may also offer a temporary infusion of finance to capitalize on strong growth, seize unanticipated business possibilities, or prepare for an IPO. Also, they permit a company to raise money without affecting its valuation in a down round, which dilutes current shareholders and can slow the pace of

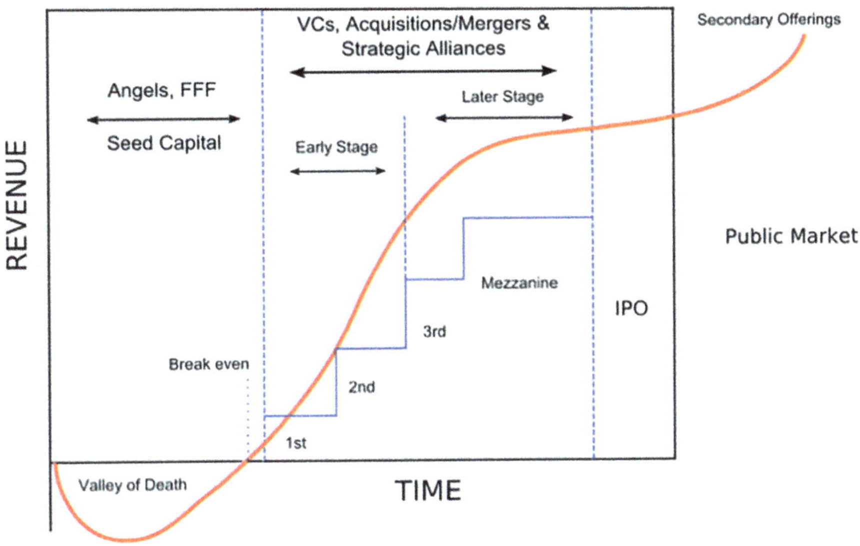

Fig. 3 Startup financing cycle. Source: https://startupxplore.com/en/blog/types-startup-investing/

expansion. When insiders and outsiders differ on a company's risk or worth, firms can reduce information asymmetry issues by choosing convertible finance (Brennan & Schwartz, 1988). A startup may also make use of a finance instrument called a Simple Agreement for Future Equity (or "SAFE") to raise money during its seed fundraising rounds. Some see SAFEs as a more founder-friendly option than convertible notes. This type of financing gives investors the option to convert their capital into equity at a later-priced funding round or liquidation event. This idea was first presented by Y Combinator partner Carolynn Levy in 2013 (Graham, 2013). On AngelList, a large platform for startups, investors, and fund managers, SAFEs are considered the most widely used investment model (Fig. 3).

6 Startup Funding Stages

As per Simon (1993), we can conceive of the advance of companies in evolutionary terms. This is especially the case for startups who by definition are "designed to grow fast" as the legendary startup investor and Co-founder of Y Combinator Paul Graham famously contended. Growth is a crucial phenomenon for small businesses. Expansion reduces the likelihood of small firms failing or closing down (Rauch & Rijskik, 2013). After all, a huge percentage of startups fail in the very beginning and only about one-third of them succeed in becoming mature businesses (Vesper, 1990). Research on startup lifecycles has been a key area of academic focus over the last few years (see, for example, Salamzadeh & Kawamorita Kesim, 2015).

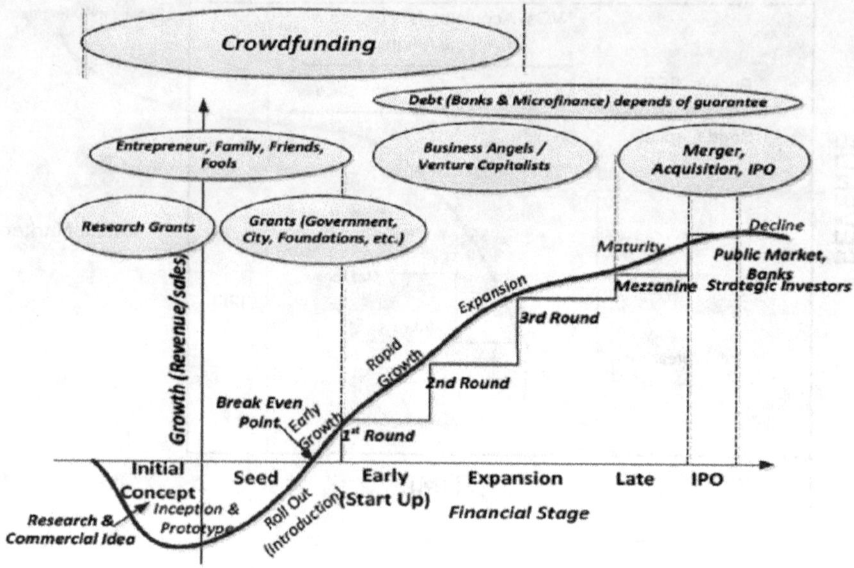

Fig. 4 New venture financing lifecycle. Source: Rossi (2014)

Nonetheless, we do note a certain vagueness and lack of consensus in defining lifecycle stages. We shall thus aim to contextualize and summarize the key concepts and literature review around this topic. In general, these terms are only referring to points within a broad and challenging continuum of gaining traction and growing. Essentially, an early-stage startup begins with a potentially scalable ideation for a product or service targeting a market that is poised to generate value and solve a market problem which in turn attracts funding. The authors contend that at a meta-level, there are therefore three principal startup stages: early-stage, venture-funded (growth) stage, and maturity phase with each stage requiring bespoke types of financing. At the product level, we can expand these three stages to encompass: (1) Problem/Solution Fit, (2) Minimum Viable Product (MVP), (3) Product/Market Fit, and finally (4) Scale. Depending on a startup's current phase, the lifecycle can be separated into seed funding, stage A, stage B, stage C, and stage D (Tripathi et al., 2019). The below model developed by Rossi (2014) illustrates the relationship between stage and funding source, from concept to IPO (Fig. 4).

At the practical level there is overlap between stages and funding profiles. A lot depends on the specific sector, geography, and timing. On average each funding should provide between 6 months and 2 years in cash-flow "runway". To elucidate this concept Marcus et al. (2013) segment the lifecycle into four macro stages, from Bootstrapping to IPO, each of whose characteristics are correlated in terms of potential investments (Table 3).

Here, we briefly discuss the key funding stages to amplify comprehension and link these phases to operational moment, capital amounts, and valuations. Broadly

Table 3 Types of possible investment in different stages of the startup lifecycle

	Seed	Young	Growing	Mature
FaF, bootstrapping, own capital	X			
Government	X			
Crowdfunding	X	X		
Angel Investors	X	X		
Corporate venturing	X	X	X	
Banks	X	X	X	X
Venture capital		X	X	
Private equity			X	X
Profit retention		X	X	X
Institutional investors				X
Stock market—IPO				X

Source: Marcus et al. (2013)

speaking, startup strategic planning, and specifically funding, is based on operational and financial milestones and performance (Block & MacMillan, 1985). Moreover, to simplify the discourse in defining and explaining funding levels, we borrow the argument put forth by Dibner (2018) who asserts that effectively there are only three main startup funding stages: (1) Early-Stage, (2) Series A, and (3) Growth, or as the author contended:

> When you meet startups and VCs these days, there's usually a lot of verbiage spent on defining stage (pre-seed, seed, post-seed, pre-A, Early A, A, Late A, B, C. . .). Some of this struggle comes from startups trying to define their stage in a way that will support their fundraising efforts. Some of this struggle comes from VC firms trying to define a rational or differentiated investment strategy. In summary nomenclature changes with time, there are "phases" of a startup's life, not "rounds" and that Series A is an absolutely critical milestone. While it's always possible to add additional distinctions and classifications, I think in reality these are really only three stages that matter. So that's it: three stages, three types of investors and three sets of challenges.

We expand upon this definition, by adding some brief insight around funding via mergers and acquisitions and public markets paths.

Early-Stage

- *Pre-Seed:* This is the earliest stage of a startup external funding. Capital is usually raised via bootstrapping resources, 3Fs, or angel investors. Startups at this stage are still ideating the concept, starting to build out and test the product, determining the product-market fit and beginning to incorporate the nascent business which is generally pre-revenue. In essence, the pre-seed stage is the idea funding stage with founders usually working alone or with a small team towards developing the MVP. According to data from Salesflare (2019), in the United States, pre-seed investments range from $50,000 to $200,000, typically for a 5%–10% equity stake.
- *Seed stage:* This is considered the first "official" capital raising round (some startups skip pre-seed altogether) and from the investor perspective one of the

riskiest. Nevertheless, cheque sizes are modest. Seed startups are often still working on their MVP and identifying their ideal customer base and putting into place a strong core team, early traction and customer experiences showcasing the opportunity for future growth. Iteration happens very quickly as the firm looks for product-market fit and revenue streams, the product offering evolves and company strategy pivots. Using the US market as a benchmark, seed startups have typically raised between $1-5 million. One study by Finmark (2021) found that the median seed investment amount for 2020 was "$4 million [which was] 4x the median from 10 years prior". Seed rounds have historically been the optimal terrain for the angel investor but in recent years VC firms and new crowdfunding platforms have increasingly migrated to the space as round sizes have grown and the search for future "homerun" investments intensifies.

Series A

Series A is the first formal financing round, usually with institutional, that is professional, investor groups such as venture capital firms and is thus an important milestone in the startup lifecycle. It is estimated that "less than 10% of companies that raise a seed round are successful in then raising Series A capital" (Fundz, 2023). Series A financing occurs when "a Series A investor is convinced that a company could scale. . .Building and de-risking that capability [to scale] is the main activity during this phase" (Dibner, 2018). Equity investment in the round is usually based on preferred stock rather than the common stock issued during the seed round. In this stage startups generally have more solid operational and financial foundations, such as a working product, reasonably defined product-market fit, a growing customer base and initial revenue. Funding ranges for Series A vary on industry and scale-up requirements. Based on CB Insights data (2023b) for the American market, in 2022 median Series A funding was $10.4 million with median valuations at $63.4 M, increases of 48,6% and 67,7% over 2020 figures, respectively. Overall, series A financing provides up to 24 months runway for the startup to further develop or expand its products, increase hiring and begin to execute on its go-to-market (sales, marketing, and operations) strategy.

Growth Funding (Series B+)

As the startup grows and establishes itself in the market, post-Series A rounds can be expected to fuel further expansion, revenue and, eventually, profitability. These funding rounds are frequently used to expand into new sectors, market geographies and ramp up R&D endeavours. According to Y-Combinator (2022): "Growth stage startups have identified product market fit. They know who their customers are, and they're on their way to capturing as many of them as possible. There's typically an emphasis on user growth and scalability, including rapidly expanding the team and any physical assets needed to serve the startup's growing customer base". As Dibner (2018) goes on to argue, "the key is, that if the Series A stage has been successful, the company has already built the machinery of growth and can prove that is it working". Furthermore, in contrast to prior rounds, these stages also attract a variety of new categories of investors, including investment banks, later-stage VCs, private

Table 4 Average round raises and valuations in the growth funding phase

Funding phase	Year 2020	2021	2022
Series B			
Median deal size	$15.0 M	$25.0 M	$24.4 M
Median valuation	$109.3 M	$192.8 M	$200.0 M
Series C			
Median deal size	$30.3 M	$50.0 M	$44.0 M
Median valuation	$283.0 M	$567.1 M	$517.6 M
Series D+			
Median deal size	$61.1 M	$110.0 M	$80.0 M
Median valuation	$1.0B	$1.6B	$1.4B

Source: CB Insights, Tech Valuations Report, 2022 recap (2023a)

equity firms, and other institutional funds. Current investors may participate in future rounds as they helped set terms and objectives for later rounds of investment during the series A investment. As the funding rounds advance, investors usually pay a higher share price for investing in the company than earlier investors. As such then, B, C, and D investment rounds essentially rank investor payments to guarantee that earlier investors receive preferential treatment as a reward for taking earlier investment risks in previous rounds. However, return on investment and performance is clearer and more solid, helping to support competition for funds and putting upwards pressure on valuations. According to CB Insights data we can visualize average and median investment and valuations per stage (Table 4):

Unit economics, that is the startups' revenues and costs in relation to an individual customer, are increasingly important, as firms have to "prove profitable and scalable product-market fit" (Qapita, 2021). A company will often conclude its external equity funding with Series C as the startup increasingly targets exits—so-called liquidity events—either through IPOs or M&A activity. Based on research from Rowley and Techcrunch (2017) on funding data from around 15,600 U.S.-based technology companies founded between 2003 and 2013, it is estimated that only around 25% of startups who raise early-stage funding advance to a Series B round and ultimately only around 1% of firms have raised a Series F round. There is a positive correlation between startup funding stages and survival, indeed, financing strategy can predict firm success (Keogh & Johnson, 2021). The below graphic illustrates this trend (Fig. 5).

Mergers and Acquisitions (M&A) in the Startup Context

Whereas investors have different preferences and aspirations for the firms they invest in, it is evident from the literature that investors consider their ability to convert their investment into cash with a good return through M&A as a positive result (Ahluwalia & Kassicieh, 2021). A M&A exit is also deemed a successful outcome for a startup (Bernstein et al., 2016). At a practical level this involves larger corporates or investment funds purchasing startups at an earlier stage, enhancing the probability of a liquidity event for existing investors as an alternative to a

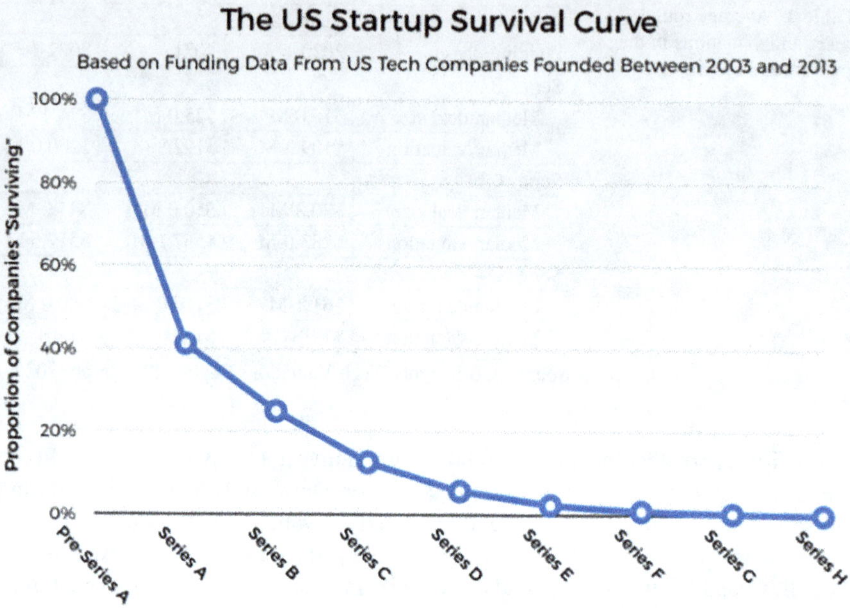

Fig. 5 The startup survival curve. Startups that raised capital in previous rounds raise in the next one. Source: Rowley and Techcrunch (2017)

potential, more challenging and less probable, IPO. Ultimately, startups can take many years to exit, if at all. The acquisition of smaller startups by larger companies has significantly affected the funding of startups (Chaudhary, 2023). Indeed, in recent years the level of M&A activity for startups has increased substantially, with more than 1070 VC-backed startups in the United States getting acquired in 2022 according to Metinko (2023). Moreover, "over the course of 2011 to 2018, 7 per cent of startups so far have made exits, 0.8 per cent via a public offering". Technically, of course, exits are not financing rounds. In some respects, they can be seen as an effective conclusion to a startup's journey, at least considered from the existing investor base. In others, acquired startups which maintain the original founders, although by definition diluted, can continue to raise future, presumably larger, rounds and carry on the fundraising cycle, even onwards to an IPO, indirectly with the new shareholder or directly through a spin-off IPO. Another element in the startup M&A universe is startups conducting their own M&A activity to in-organically grow their business. As Chudzinski (2014) contends, M&A activity can therefore be beneficial to startups, even at the early stages, and furthers this argument by listing the following motives behind these strategies:

(a) Entrepreneurs buy a small company/underdeveloped product to further develop it. This helps them jump over the phase of gaining initial traction and product market fit, speeding up time to market.

(b) A startup buys another startup in a different country to speed up/enable international expansion.
(c) Market consolidation. Competitors go together to create a company with a stronger market position.
(d) Product range expansion.
Source: Chudzinski (2014).

And as such, startups who have built up their capacity, teams, technology, and service offerings via M&A transactions thus become a more robust prospect for further funding raises. Afterall, it can be "easier to buy than build".

IPOs and Capital Market Operations
Historically, going public on a significant stock exchange used to be the main objective of most startup businesses. Initial public offerings (IPOs) are a way for private companies to raise money by selling shares to the general public and broader institutional investors. The IPO is a key time to realize gains as shares can sell at a premium to previous valuations. As Singh (2021) argued: "Ever since Apple and Google went on to become public with their stocks being traded as a ticker symbol in the market, raising an IPO has become something of an endgame for emerging tech companies". Moreover, Pagano et al. (1998) found that larger companies and companies with higher growth rates such as technology firms are more likely to go public. Nonetheless, the fact is that initial public offers are complex, and the overriding majority of firms remain privately held.

Ultimately however, public companies go public to optimize access to public investment, making it simpler to raise long-term capital and expand the business. Moreover, increased share liquidity, some outside monitoring, improved company image and publicity, motivating management and employees, and cashing in have all been highlighted in prior studies (Pagano et al., 1998). Indeed, the post 2009 market is often described as the second-best time for tech firms to list, after the dot com era of the early 2000s. To aid in these capital market strategies, many leading stock exchanges have established secondary, unregulated markets to enable small, high-tech businesses to go public without being burdened by onerous restrictions (Vismara et al., 2012). And yet, increasingly, companies are staying private for longer, or even not targeting IPOs. According to one study, the average age of a new publicly listed firm in the technology space increased from 4.5 years in 1999 to more than 12 years in 2020.

The fact is that public companies are subject to many additional regulations and reporting requirements, which can be expensive and burdensome to manage especially for "lean" tech companies. There are also the added financial costs of structuring the operation to consider. Founders can also maintain greater shareholder control in private companies. Furthermore, the subpar performance of many recent, high-profile IPOs has led to a more challenging market, further dissuading founders to take the public listing route. Indeed, according to Refinitiv data, 2022 saw the lowest volume of new listings since 2009. Smaller private companies are increasingly being acquired by large, listed corporates before they themselves go public. In effect "36% of IPO firms delist within the first 5 years after the IPO, with 12% being due to poor performance and 24% because they are acquired".

Nevertheless, IPOs are not the only capital market options for tech firms, another two key strategies are Direct Listings and Special Purchase Acquisition Companies ("SPACs"). Rather than going public through an IPO, Direct Listings, a process whereby a company can go public by selling existing shares instead of offering new ones, and thus without either a primary or secondary underwritten offering, are therefore "an innovative structure that provides companies with an alternative to a traditional IPO". In summary, equity prices are driven by the market rather than banks and brokers. Spotify's 2018 direct listing, at a $29,5B valuation, helped pioneer this type of operation for technology firms. By May 2022, more than 13 tech companies had followed Spotify's lead (Ritter, 2022).

SPACs, commonly labelled "blank cheque companies", are also an alternative way to take a company public. They can offer a more streamlined and economical public-path than traditional IPOs (Deloitte, 2021). SPACs have been around in different modalities for many years, but came to prominence in the United States in the 2019–2021 period (Bazerman & Patel, 2021). Moon (2021) provides more detail: "Rather than going through the traditional IPO process to access public markets, the SPAC is a shell [company] that raises money through an IPO. After raising IPO proceeds the SPAC typically have a 2-year period to find a private company to take public via merger". Based on research from Mackintosh (2022) in 2021, "there were 613 SPAC listings, raising a total of $145 billion – an increase of 91% from the amount raised in 2020". Despite this, data from PwC (2022) suggests that "SPAC transactions accounted for just 2% of total tech deal activity in 2022". And yet, they remain a potential funding option for private companies who may not meet "the eligibility requirements for a traditional IPO or corporate acquisition" (Deloitte, 2021).

7 The Inherent Challenges in Startup Valuations

Early-stage valuation is certainly replete with technical and practical challenges. Understanding new market dynamics and trends, dealing with a lack of historical financial data, defining realistic forecast assumptions and having access to market benchmarks add extra levels of complexity above and beyond traditional company valuation assignments. In this book, we explore in Chapters "Valuation Versus Pricing: A Conceptual and Practical Guide to Estimate Economic Value for Early-Stage Companies Via DCF" and "An Analysis of Startup Valuation Methods: Understanding the Investor's Perspective" in more detail some of these challenges. Nevertheless, let us briefly illustrate some of the many difficulties practitioners face when confronted with the task in valuing startups.

We start on the return side of the valuation ledger. Most startups lack the detailed financial background necessary to predict future cash flows and value. They may even be pre-revenue without an established business model that can be monetized.

Making logical assumptions about key value drivers such as growth, efficiency, cost structure, and investment needs pose problems for business value. This is particularly true if the firms are currently loss-making. Moreover, the business model and market are fundamentally uncertain. Research by Gompers and Lerner (2001) highlights the inherent risks and uncertainties associated with starting a new business, which can result in approximately equal opportunities for success or failure in the market. Startups, similar to the broader private company universe, are also somewhat illiquid. In these situations, the appraiser must modify valuation inputs by adding liquidity discounts, which in effect act as an additional return, or safety margin, to the investor for investing in such firms. What is more, startups famously rely on investor capital as they seek scale and profitability rather than on internal cash flow generation. If the proverbial taps are tuned off how is value affected? On the risk side of the coin, startups are typically riskier than both listed companies or mature enterprises. How is this incremental risk calculated in both discount rates and survival factors? In summary then, as Damodaran (2009) contends: "Many of the standard techniques we use to estimate cash flows, growth rates and discount rates either do not work or yield unrealistic numbers". And yet, startups are an interesting asset class that can provide large returns and portfolio diversification. They are also an increasingly important part of the modern economy. And thus, developing robust valuation approaches and solutions to these multiple challenges has never been more vital.

8 Final Considerations for Startup Valuation

For entrepreneurs, valuation plays an essential role in the fundraising process as well as being a key tool in strategic planning and value-based management. As we have seen, different types of financing and funding rounds are intrinsically linked to valuation. And yet they also raise additional questions. From a valuation perspective these questions need not just to be asked but throughout this book, should be answered as well. In this section, we aim to start closing out our introduction by flagging several related common themes in fundraising endeavours that can impact on startup valuation. They are thus important questions for founders to keep on their strategic radar. Afterall, to paraphrase Sir Francis Bacon, the process of asking sensible questions is one-half of attaining wisdom.

- *Dilution:* Valuation and dilution are two intricately linked fundamental concepts. It is a given that when founders raise equity their ownership percentages decrease. Thus, there is often a diametric discussion in play: founders seek to maximize valuation while minimizing dilution whilst incoming investors prefer the axiom in reverse. The golden rule is for the startup's value to increase to the point when you own a smaller percentage of a much larger company. But what is the interplay between percentage and economic dilution? How do down rounds impact on valuation and equity dilution? Do both primary and secondary stock issuance equally affect valuation and dilution levels? How can we model dilution over multiple rounds? What is the role of anti-dilution mechanisms? Should startups raise less to restrict the dilution effect or at the very least better crystalize their investment plans? Afterall, how much capital does the company require for a 12–18-month cash flow runway whilst hitting target metrics? How do employee stock option plans (ESOP) and their implicit dilution impact on valuation? Alternatively, can a heavily diluted founder team still attract leading VCs or quality talent? Can founders apply strategies to mitigate the impact of dilution on the ownership targets for them and their investors which in turn clearly impact valuation? Moreover, can equity dilution be delayed until the next financing round with the use of convertible debt and SAFEs?

- *Preferred Stock*: In the startup fundraising universe, paraphrasing George Orwell, some shares are more equal than others. Investors usually negotiate for preferred stock, whilst founders and employees receive ordinary shares. Preferred shares are a type of hybrid security that firms offer that combines certain characteristics of fixed income and equity investments. The value of the preferred stock will rise in line with the price of the underlying common stock but will not fall below par value. Investors who own preferred shares receive benefits such as liquidation privileges and protective provisions, which assist in risk reduction. They also have stronger claims on assets. This dynamic also raises key questions. How do liquidation preferences, pro-rata rights and anti-dilution provisions impact on valuation and the invest attractiveness of your startup? How about "double-dip" provisions which combine preference and liquidity? Overall then, how does preferred stock impact on startup valuation? According to DLA Piper (2017), "VC's "post-money valuation" is not intended to represent the current value that a third party would pay to acquire the company or that a valuation firm would likely place on the current value of the business. Instead, it is driven by the investor's belief in likely exit scenarios for the company and the investor's investment criteria. The empirical data from these valuations shows that the common stock per share value typically falls in a range of about 20 per cent to 0 per cent of the preferred stock value". As such, while estimating the possible value of their common stock, founders and employees must be aware of the preferred stock's liquidation preferences.
- *Contractual Terms:* A term sheet is a framework of the proposed key terms of startup investment. The terms outline the investment and contractual conditions between the company and investors. A large body of literature points to contracts being especially favourable to VC investors, potentially to the detriment of the founder (as argued by Moskowitz & Vissing-Jørgensen, 2002). However, the current market scenario—"bull" or "bear" territory—at the time of fundraising is also a key driver, as is the quality of the investor. Ewens et al. (2022) contend that contracts materially affect startup values, with both value-increasing and decreasing components: "Despite the reduction in firm value that results from a suboptimal equity share (and other contract terms), the VC benefits from a higher expected payoff". How do, for example, full ratchet anti-dilution provisions and cumulative or payment-in-kind dividends impact valuations? Research by

Kramer et al. (2015), based on analysis of unicorn valuations—essentially private companies with a valuation above a billion dollars—in that year found that 100% of unicorn fundraisings that year possessed liquidation preferences whereby "valuations of these companies could fall on average by 90% before the unicorn investors would suffer a loss of their investment", meaning that investors received terms that deliver significant of downside protection. The other side of the coin, or in other words enhanced founder-friendly provisions can also occur. Kramer (2017) asserts that "a significant percentage of the highest valuation unicorns had dual class common stock which provided founders/management and in some cases other shareholders with super voting rights". Ultimately, the return on investment that investors expect from a startup also effects its valuation. And this ROI is heavily impacted by the contractual terms that define future returns.

- *Startup Survival Risk:* It is an aphorism that startups are inherently risky assets. The market and business models are uncertain. Survival risk is high. The data supports this. For example, according to data compiled by insurance company Embroker (2020), "about 90% of startups fail. 10% of startups fail within the first year. Across all industries, startup failure rates seem to be close to the same. Failure is most common for startups during years two through five, with 70% falling into this category". A broader study by Knaup and Piazza (2007) argued that only 31% of companies still exist after 7 years of operating. Risk is therefore a major component of startup value and not a side-effect. From a fundamental perspective, ceteris paribus, the higher the forecasted cash flows and the lower the perceived risk in a firm, the higher its valuation is likely to be. Wiegelmann (2012) defined risk as a possibility of negative or unfavourable impacts from a present process or future event to an asset. Risk can be measured, including by lifecycle stage and sector. Damodaran (2009) determines processes for estimating discount rates for private companies and for adjusting the present value for the possibility of failure. And as such, for startup valuations there are multiple questions that need to be addressed to contemplate real or perceived risks. How does the perceived survival risk impact startup valuations? Moreover, how does risk in startup projections transform into estimating economic value? How do venture capitalists utilize discount rates to quantify valuation? Does survival risk change over time? What statistical approaches can help better quantify risk and therefore valuation?
- *Startup Culture:* Culture is multifaceted but generally encompasses the processes, approaches, values, and human capital environment throughout business operations. In summary, organizational culture can be defined as "the patterns of thinking and behaving that are recognized and espoused" (Laker, 2021). These concepts can come across as "fuzzy" but corporate culture is an important driver of business value (Graham et al., 2022). Essentially then, business managers use organizational culture to set their company apart from rival organizations (Weber & Tarba, 2012). According to O'Connor and Byrne (2015), organizational culture benefits corporate governance and management. At a practical level an optimal business culture can thus help improve financial controls, technology development, productivity and commercial strategy. All these factors add not

only indirect qualitative value but can directly impact on startups' bottom line. Moreover, if corporate culture is unable to quickly make sound decisions at all levels and across functions and put them into action, value growth can be affected. A large volume of academic and corporate literature has looked at this space and the data infers positive affirmation of the link between culture and value, for instance:

> Does culture influence corporate valuation and actions? Starting with the former, we document that executives strongly believe that an effective corporate culture enhances firm value: 91% of executives consider corporate culture to be "important" or "very important" at their firm. While it may not be surprising that executives say culture matters, it might be surprising that it matters so much that 54% of executives would walk away from an M&A target that is culturally misaligned, while another one-third would discount a misaligned target by between 10%–30% of the purchase price. In fact, when executives rank 'the things that contribute to long-term firm value', culture ranks highest (Graham et al., 2022).

What's more, the average annual returns for businesses that make Fortune's annual list of the 100 Best Companies to Work For are also greater, with cumulative returns as high as 495% rather than 170% (Russell 3000) and 156% (S&P 500) for the broader market based on analysis by Grant Thornton (2018). A PwC (2019) survey of PE firms found that over half agree that cultural issues hamper value creation. Company culture is even more important for startups who generally scale quickly. A team can grow from two founders to 30 employees relatively rapidly. A founder needs to be aware of some crucial questions: how can an early-stage firm quickly implement a sustainable corporate culture? How to evaluate and assess this culture? How can culture positively impact corporate governance, controls, transparency, and compliance? And how can founders effectively communicate the culture narrative to potential investors?

- *Professional Valuations and Accounting Standards:* A 409A valuation is an estimate of the fair market value (FMV) of the common stock of a private corporation undertaken by an impartial third party and named after section 409A of the IRS Internal Tax Code (IRC). Startups frequently contract these reports before funding rounds to determine the price at which employees can acquire or be granted shares or options of the company's common stock. A 409A incorporates all the different advantages and rights that don't exist with common shares into a robust valuation framework.

> In broad strokes, a 409A valuation is a three-step process: The first step determines how much a company is worth (i.e., "enterprise value" — more on that below). The enterprise value is then allocated across the various equity classes to arrive at the fair market value (FMV) for the common stock. Finally, the last step is to apply a discount to the FMV to take into account that the stock is not publicly traded (Moon, 2020).

Accounting standard IFRS 2, defined by the International Accounting Standards Board (IASB), seeks to standardize valuations on share-based payments and primarily affects stock options granted to employees (or even contractors). As we have seen ESOPs are a key component of startup strategic planning and impact on valuations. As startups grow, attention to international reporting standards is increasingly important, in both developed and emerging markets. In addition, as part of IFRS 2, the firm is required to calculate the fair value of the share options employees receive.

9 Closing Thoughts

As we have seen throughout this chapter, startup growth is a journey and valuation is an important strategic companion that assists in decision-making around funding rounds, capital sources and advancing through growth stages. There are multiple startup valuation techniques. For robust valuation estimates it is fundamental that startup financial projections and the business plan are linked to the real world and economic drivers as well as be based on strong, feasible and dynamic assumptions. Unit economics help track performance and create the building blocks for valuation. Both qualitative and quantitative factors impact on economic value. As do contractual terms. In this book, we provide a comprehensive and detailed discussion not only on the technical and practical approaches to conduct robust startup valuations but also connect these topics to the broader early-stage universe, developing an end-to-end holistic paradigm for understanding startups, their ecosystem, funding methods, and the use of valuation tools. As such, we feel that this book adds value to the academic and practical discussion playbook.

References

Ahluwalia, S., & Kassicieh, S. (2021). Effect of financial clusters on startup mergers and acquisitions. *International Journal of Financial Studies, 10*(1), 1–13.

Aljalahma, J., & Slof, J. (2022). An updated systematic review of business accelerators: Functions, operation, and gaps in the existing literature. *Journal of Open Innovation: Technology, Market, and Complexity, 8*(4), 214. https://doi.org/10.3390/joitmc8040214

Alpha, J. W. C. (2023, January 4). Ventures, differences between unicorn, decacorn and hectocorn. https://www.alphajwc.com/en/the-differences-between-unicorn-decacorn-and-hectocorn/

Auerswald, P. E. (2015, October 1). Enabling entrepreneurial ecosystems: Insights from ecology to inform effective entrepreneurship policy. *Kauffman Foundation Research Series on City, Metro, and Regional Entrepreneurship*. Available at SSRN: https://ssrn.com/abstract=2673843 or https://doi.org/10.2139/ssrn.2673843

Avdeitchikova, S., Landstrom, H., & Månsson, N. (2008). What do we mean when we talk about business angels? Some reflections on definitions and sampling. *Venture Capital: An International Journal of Entrepreneurial Finance., 10*, 371–394. https://doi.org/10.1080/13691060802351214

Bain. (2022). *How private equity keeps winning in software* (By D. Lipman, C. Perry, J. Zecha, & J. Holliday). Available at: https://www.bain.com/insights/software-global-private-equity-report-2022/

Baum, J., & Silverman, B. (2004). Picking winners or building them? Alliance, intellectual, and human capital as selection criteria in venture financing and performance of biotechnology startups. *Journal of Business Venturing, 19*, 411–436. https://doi.org/10.1016/S0883-9026(03)00038-7

Bazerman, M. H., & Patel, P. (2021). SPACs: What you need to know: A guide for the curious and the perplexed. *Harvard Business Review, 99*(4), 102–111. Available at: https://hbr.org/2021/07/spacs-what-you-need-to-know

Bernstein, S., Giroud, X., & Townsend, R. R. (2016). The impact of venture capital monitoring. *The Journal of Finance, 71*, 1591–1622.

Berre, M., & Le Pendeven, B. (2022). What do we know about start-up valuation drivers? A systematic literature review. *Venture Capital*, 1–45. https://doi.org/10.1080/13691066.2022.2086502

Bhidé, A. (1992). Bootstrap finance: The art of start-ups. *Harvard Business Review, 70*(6), 109–117. Available at: https://hbr.org/1992/11/bootstrap-finance-the-art-of-start-ups

Block, Z., & MacMillan, I. C. (1985). Milestones for successful venture planning. *Harvard Business Review, 63*(5), 184. Available at: https://hbr.org/1985/09/milestones-for-successful-venture-planning

Brennan, M. J., & Schwartz, E. S. (1988). An equilibrium model of bond pricing and a test of market efficiency. *Journal of Financial and Quantitative Analysis, 17*, 301–329.

British Business Bank. (2022). How to get government grants for your start up business. Available at: https://www.startuploans.co.uk/business-advice/get-small-business-government-grant/.

Burke, A., van Stel, A., Hartog, C., & Ichou, A. (2014). What determines the level of informal venture finance investment? Market clearing forces. *Small Business Economics, 42*(3), 467–484. http://www.jstor.org/stable/43552940

Carter, R., & Auken, H. (2005). Bootstrap financing and owners' perceptions of their business constraints and opportunities. *Entrepreneurship and Regional Development, 17*, 129–144. https://doi.org/10.1080/08985620500067548

CB Insights. (2023a). Tech valuations 2022 report, recap. Available at: www.cbinsights.com/reports/

CB Insights. (2023b). Tech valuations 2022 report. Available at: https://www.cbinsights.com/research/report/tech-company-valuations-2022/#:~:text=Download%20the%20tech%20valuations%202022%20report,-First%20name&text=Global%20late%2D%20and%20mid%2Dstage,21's%20levels%20in%20Q4'22.

Chaudhary, H. (2023). Rise in M&A deals as startup funding slow down. Available at: https://blog.ipleaders.in/rise-in-ma-deals-as-startup-funding-slow-down/

Chudzinski, P. (2014). M&A for startups. Available at: https://medium.com/point-nine-news/m-a-for-startups-d929ef96556e

CNBC. (2023). The 3 biggest reasons startups failed in 2022, according to a poll of almost 500 founders, based on Skynova/CB Insights. Available at: https://www.cnbc.com/2023/01/20/top-reasons-why-startups-failed-in-2022-study.html#:~:text=Lack%20of%20financing%20or%20investors,was%20behind%2044%25%20of%20failures

Craigmile, C, & Hermann-Friede, J. (2021). Convertible notes. Available at: https://sswm.info/financing-water-impact/financing-instruments/qe%3A-convertible-notes

Damodaran, A. (2009). *Valuing young, start-up and growth companies: Estimation issues and valuation challenges*. Stern School of Business, New York University.

Dawson, A. (2011). Private equity investment decisions in family firms: The role of human resources and agency costs. *Journal of Business Venturing, 26*, 189–199. https://doi.org/10.1016/j.jbusvent.2009.05.004

Dealstation. (2022). White paper the venture capital method: An introduction. dealstation.io, https://uploads-ssl.webflow.com/6295e2b444d4bb66bd950b69/630f72e94edc6bd55c350f6f_DealStation_Whitepaper_VC_Method_20220830.pdf

Deloitte research. (2021). SPACs dominate headlines, but it's traditional technology M&A that's booming: What the rise of SPACs means for technology executives. Available at: https://www.

deloitte.com/global/en/our-thinking/insights/industry/technology/rise-of-spacs-and-technology-m-and-a.html

Dibner, G. (2018). There are only three startup stages. Angular Ventures, Medium. Available at: https://medium.com/angularventures/there-are-only-three-stages-for-startups-b8783d6b0f1

DLA Piper research paper. (2017). The two faces of startup valuation. Available at: https://www.dlapiperaccelerate.com/knowledge/2017/the-two-faces-of-startup-valuation.html

Drover, W., Busenitz, L., Matusik, S., Townsend, D., Anglin, A., & Dushnitsky, G. (2017). A review and road map of entrepreneurial equity financing research. *Journal of Management, 43*(6), 1820–1853.

Embroker analysis. (2020). Startup statistics and trends. Available at: https://www.embroker.com/blog/startup-statistics/

Ewens, M., Gorbenko, A., & Korteweg, A. (2022). Venture capital contracts. *Journal of Financial Economics, 143*(1), 131–158.

Faster Capital. (2023, October 7). What is the difference between a startup and an established company. https://fastercapital.com/content/What-is-the-difference-between-a-startup-and-an-established-company.html#What-is-a-Startup

Finmark. (2021). Startup funding explained: Pre-seed, seed, & series A-D. Available at: https://finmark.com/seed-series-a-b-c-d-funding/

Fisch, C. (2019). Initial coin offerings (ICOs) to finance new ventures. *Journal of Business Venturing, 34*(1, 1), –22. Available at SSRN: https://ssrn.com/abstract=3147521 or https://doi.org/10.2139/ssrn.3147521

Fundz. (2023). Series A, B, C funding: Averages, investors, valuations. Available at: https://www.fundz.net/what-is-series-a-funding-series-b-funding-and-more#:~:text=In%20fact%2C%20less%20than%2010,issued%20during%20the%20seed%20round

Gilani, A., & Dettori, G. (2011). *Incubators in US and Europe – Speed and scale in capital formation* (p. 21). Kauffman Fellow Program.

Goker, O., & Köseoğlu, S. D. (2020). Chapter 4: Challenges in valuation by using discounted free cash flow method. In *Valuation challenges and solutions in contemporary businesses*. IGI Global.

Gompers, P., & Lerner, J. (2001). The venture capital revolution. *Journal of Economic Perspectives, 15*(2, Spring), 145–168. Available at: https://www.aeaweb.org/articles?id=10.1257/jep.15.2.145

Graham, P. (2013). *Announcing the safe, a replacement for convertible notes*. Y Combinator. Available at: https://www.ycombinator.com/blog/announcing-the-safe-a-replacement-for-convertible-notes/

Graham, J., Grennan, J., Harvey, C., & Rajgopal, S. (2022). Corporate culture: Evidence from the field. *Journal of Financial Economics, 146*(2), 552.

Grant Thorton analysis. (2018). Beyond measure: Making culture count. Available at: https://www.grantthornton.com/insights/articles/advisory/2018/beyond-measure-making-culture-count.

Grichnik, D., Brinckmann, J., Singh, L., & Manigart, S. (2014). Beyond environmental scarcity: Human and social capital as driving forces of bootstrapping activities. *Journal of Business Venturing, 29*(2), 310–326.

Hellwig, M. (1991). Banking, financial intermediation and corporate finance. In *European financial integration* (pp. 35–63). Cambridge University Press.

Hemer, J., Schneider, U., Dornbusch, F., & Frey, S. (2011). *Crowdfunding und andere Formen informeller Mikrofinanzierung in der Projekt-und Innovationsfinanzierung*. Fraunhofer Verlag.

Karimi, A., Mohammadi, N., & Sakhteh, S. (2022). "Opportunities and threats facing early-stage digital startups during the COVID-19 pandemic," Contributions to economics. In N. Faghih & A. Forouharfar (Eds.), *Socioeconomic dynamics of the COVID-19 crisis, chapter 0* (pp. 83–99). Springer.

Keogh, D., & Johnson, D. K. N. (2021). Survival of the funded: Econometric analysis of startup longevity and success. *Journal of Entrepreneurship, Management and Innovation, Fundacja Upowszechniająca Wiedzę i Naukę "Cognitione", 17*(4), 29–49.

Kher, R., Terjesen, S., & Liu, C. (2020). Blockchain, bitcoin, and ICOs: A review and research agenda. *Small Business Economics, 56*, 1699–1720.

Knaup, A. E., & Piazza, M. (2007). Business employment dynamics data: Survival and longevity, II. *Monthly Labor Review, 130*, 3–10.

Kramer, B. (2017). *The terms behind the unicorn valuations*. Fenwick West LLP. Available at: https://www.jdsupra.com/post/contentViewerEmbed.aspx?fid=fcbdbd33-b629-4500-9e72-2f457b533a1a

Kramer, B., Patrick, M., & Harper, N. (2015). *The terms behind the unicorn valuations*. Fenwick West LLP. Available at: https://assets.fenwick.com/legacy/FenwickDocuments/The-Terms-Behind-the-Unicorn-Valuations.pdf

Kutlar, A., & Babacan, A. (2008). CCR efficiency-scale efficiency analysis in public universities in Turkey: Application of DEA technique. *Kocaeli University Journal of Social Sciences, 15*(1), 148–172.

Laker, B. (2021). Culture is a company's single most powerful advantage. Here's why', article in Forbes (published on 23/04/2021). Available at: https://www.forbes.com/sites/benjaminlaker/2021/04/23/culture-is-a-companys-single-most-powerful-advantage-heres-why/?sh=52f1ae6679e8

Lewis, C. M., Rogalski, R. J., & Seward, J. K. (1999). Is convertible debt a substitute for straight debt or for common equity? *Financial Management, 28*(3), 5–27.

Mackintosh, P. (2022). A record pace for SPACs in 2021. Nasdaq. Available at: https://www.nasdaq.com/articles/a-record-pace-for-spacs-in-2021

Marcus, A., Malen, J., & Ellis, S. (2013). The promise and pitfalls of venture capital as an asset class for clean energy investment. *Organization & Environment, 26*(1), 31–60. https://doi.org/10.1177/1086026612474956

Marquee Equity. (2021). The ultimate guide to startup funding. Available at: https://marquee-equity.com/blog/startup-funding-guide/

Metinko, C., & Crunchbase. (2023). Forecast: Startup M&A could pick up in 2023 as fundraising tightens further. Available at: https://news.crunchbase.com/ma/startup-forecast-2023-fundraising-venture-valuations/

Moon, C. (2020). *16 things to know about the 409A valuation*. Andreessen Horowitz. Available at: https://a16z.com/2020/02/13/16-things-about-the-409a-valuation/

Moon, L. (2021, December 2). An overview of SPACs and the 2020–2021 SPAC surge. Available at SSRN: https://ssrn.com/abstract=3979359 or https://doi.org/10.2139/ssrn.3979359

Moskowitz, T. J., & Vissing-Jørgensen, A. (2002). The returns to entrepreneurial investment: A private equity premium puzzle? *American Economic Review, 92*(4), 745. Available at: https://www.aeaweb.org/articles?id=10.1257/00028280260344452

Myvaluation. (2022). The Berkus method. https://myvaluation.in/wp-content/uploads/2022/01/THE-BERKUS-METHOD.pdf

O'Connor, T., & Byrne, J. (2015). Governance and the corporate life-cycle. *International Journal of Managerial Finance, 11*, 1–23.

OECD. (2014). Policy brief on access to business start-up finance for inclusive entrepreneurship. Available at: https://www.oecd.org/cfe/leed/Finacing%20inclusive%20entrepreneurship%20policy%20brief%20EN.pdf

Ostgaard, T. A., & Birley, S. (1994). Personal networks and firm competitive strategy—A strategic or coincidental match? *Journal of Business Venturing, 9*(4), 281–305.

Pagano, M., Panetta, F., & Zingales, L. (1998). Why do companies go public? An empirical analysis. *The Journal of Finance, 53*(1), 27–64. http://journals.sagepub.com/doi/abs/10.1177/014920

Bill Payne, 2011a, Valuations 101: The venture capital method., https://gust.com/blog/startup-valuations-101-the-venture-capital-method/.

Bill Payne, Valuations 101: The-risk-factor-summation-method, 2011b., https://gust.com/blog/valuations-101-the-risk-factor-summation-method/.

Payne, B. (2021). *Scorecard valuation methodology establishing the valuation of pre-revenue.* Start-up Companies. https://seedspot.org/wp-content/uploads/2021/02/Scorecard-Valuation-Methodology.pdf

Prequin. (2021). Preqin global private equity & venture capital report. Available at: https://www.preqin.com/insights/global-reports/2021-preqin-global-private-equity-and-venture-capital-report

PwC paper. (2019). Creating value beyond the deal: private equity: Pulling the right levers to lock in real value creation. Available at: https://www.pwc.es/es/publicaciones/transacciones/assets/creating-value-beyond-deal-private-equity.pdf

PwC Research. (2022). *Technology: US deals 2023 outlook*. PwC. Available at: https://www.pwc.com/us/en/industries/tmt/library/technology-deals-outlook.html

Qapita. (2021). Types of funding rounds: Seed, series A, B, C…'. Available at: https://www.qapita.com/blogs/types-of-funding-rounds

Rauch, A., & Rijskik, S. A. (2013). The effects of general and specific human capital on long term growth and failure of newly founded businesses. *Entrepreneurship Theory and Practice, 3*, 923–941. https://doi.org/10.1111/j.1540-6520.2011.00487.x

Reinfeld, P. (2018). *Startup valuation: Solving the valuation puzzle of new business ventures*. Paris University, Finance Institute.

Ritter, J. (2022). *Initial public offerings: Direct listings through May 19, 2022*. Eugene F. Brigham Department of Finance, Insurance, and Real Estate, Warrington College of Business, University of Florida. Available at: https://site.warrington.ufl.edu/ritter/files/Direct-Listings.pdf

Rossi, M. (2014). The new ways to raise capital: An exploratory study of crowdfunding. *International Journal of Financial Research, 5*, 28.

Rowley, J., & Techcrunch. (2017). Here's how likely your startup is to get acquired at any stage. Available at: https://techcrunch.com/2017/05/17/heres-how-likely-your-startup-is-to-get-acquired-at-any-stage/

Salamzadeh, A., & Kawamorita Kesim, H. (2015). Startup companies: Life cycle and challenges. In *4th international conference on employment, education and entrepreneurship (EEE), Belgrade, Serbia*. Available at SSRN: https://ssrn.com/abstract=2628861 or https://doi.org/10.2139/ssrn.2628861

Salesflare. (2019). Startup funding rounds: The ultimate guide from pre-seed to IPO startup funding masterclass: Part four. Available at: https://blog.salesflare.com/startup-funding-rounds

Sandler, S. (2015). Substitute for Silicon Valley: The case of the round house startup factory. *Journal of Organization Design, 4*, 31–36.

Sheriff, M., & Muffatto, M. (2015). The present state of entrepreneurship ecosystems in selected countries. *African Journal of Economic and Management Studies, 6*, 17–54. https://doi.org/10.1108/AJEMS-10-2012-0064

Simon, H. A. (1993). Strategy and organizational evolution. *Strategic Management Journal, 14*(S2), 131–142.

Singh, S. (2021). *A tech entrepreneur guide to initial public offering (IPO) process*. Appinventiv. Available at: https://appinventiv.com/blog/entrepreneur-guide-to-ipo/

Söderblom, A., Samuelsson, M., Wiklund, J., & Sandberg, R. (2015). Inside the black box of outcome additionality: Effects of early-stage government subsidies on resource accumulation and new venture performance. *Research Policy, 44*(8), 1501–1512.

StartupBlink. (2022), Global startup ecosystem index. https://www.startupblink.com/startupecosystemreport

Statista Research Department. (2021). Market size of crowdfunding worldwide in 2021 with a forecast for 2028. Available at: https://www.statista.com/statistics/1078273/global-crowdfunding-market-size/

Subhash, K. (2006). How to teach "The Big Baby" to walk: Case of the Indian venture capital industry. *The Journal of Private Equity: JPE; strategies and techniques for venture investing, Institutional Investor, 9*(4), 76–91.

TecnoIdentity. (2022). Startup funding 101. Available at: https://www.technoidentity.com/insights/startup-funding101/#:~:text=Most%20entrepreneurs%20do%20not%20have,help%20find%20the%20best%20fit

Tripathi, N., Seppänen, P., Boominathan, G., Oivo, M., & Liukkunen, K. (2019). Insights into startup ecosystems through exploration of multi-vocal literature. *Information and Software Technology, 105*, 56–77.

Vesper, K. H., & New Venture Strategies. (1990). University of Illinois at Urbana-Champaign's Academy for Entrepreneurial Leadership Historical Research Reference in Entrepreneurship. Available at SSRN: https://ssrn.com/abstract=1496217

Vismara, S., Paleari, S., & Ritter, J. R. (2012, January 4). Europe's second markets for small companies. Available at SSRN: https://ssrn.com/abstract=1957140 or https://doi.org/10.2139/ssrn.1957140

Weber, Y., & Tarba, S. (2012). Mergers and acquisitions process: The use of corporate culture analysis. *Cross Cultural Management: An International Journal, 19*, 288–303. https://doi.org/10.1108/13527601211247053

Wiegelmann, T. (2012). *Risk Management in the Real Estate Development Industry: Investigations into the application of risk management concepts in leading European real estate development organisations*. Institute of Sustainable Development & Architecture Bond University.

Y-Combinator. (2022). Stages of startups. Available at https://www.ycombinator.com/library/Ek-stages-of-startups

Zippia. (2022). The Eight Largest VC Firms in the United States. Available at: https://www.zippia.com/advice/largest-venture-capital-firms/

From Planning to Valuation: Mastering Business Planning and Sensitivity Analysis for Your Startup

Sinem Derindere Köseoğlu

1 Introduction

A business plan can be thought of as a roadmap for a business. It outlines the goals, strategies, operations, and tactics that a business will use to achieve its objectives over a specific period, usually 3–5 years. It should include market analysis, competitive analysis, marketing and sales strategies, operational plans, and financial projections, besides the description of the business (Haag, 2013). Based on the results of Welter (2021), the study found that business planning activity was found to be correlated with performance according to the analysis of a sample of 120 entrepreneurs across the United States. This suggests that a well-crafted business plan is an essential tool for entrepreneurs in achieving long-term success. According to Haag (2013), developing a business plan is essential for the survival and success of startups. A business plan helps entrepreneurs identify potential challenges and opportunities, allocate resources effectively, and make informed decisions. By outlining key areas of concern and developing a roadmap for success, a business plan can increase the likelihood of survival for startups in their early stages.

A comprehensive business plan can include the components below:

Executive Summary
Table of Contents

1. Idea Uniqueness
2. What Problem the Business Is Trying to Solve?
3. Business Structure and Product/Service Description
4. Market Analysis

S. D. Köseoğlu (✉)
Istanbul University, Istanbul, Turkey

S. Derindere Köseoğlu (ed.), *A Practical Guide for Startup Valuation*, Contributions to Finance and Accounting, https://doi.org/10.1007/978-3-031-35291-1_3

(a) Economic Analysis
(b) Which Industry?
(c) Total Industry Market Size
(d) Ascertainable Market Size for the Specific Market
(e) Target Market
(f) Market Share of the Company Wants to Capture
(g) Phased Wise Market Penetration Strategy
(h) Market and Competitor Analysis—Tools Used

5. Technology

    (a) History of the Respective Technology/Evolution in that Specific Space
    (b) Technology—Backend, Frontend, Cloud space, Tools used, AI, ML, Block Chain, Design, Data Analytics
    (c) Technology Roadmap
    (d) Cost

6. Customer Acquisition

    (a) Acquisition Strategy
    (b) Cost of Acquisition
    (c) Switching Cost
    (d) Customer Retention Strategy
    (e) Customer Satisfaction Criteria Assessment and Close Loop Strategy

7. Business Model

    (a) Cost
    (b) Competitive Advantage
    (c) Mix

8. Revenue Model—Streams
9. Diversified or Focused
10. Investment Strategy

    (a) Capital Structure—VC, Bootstrapping, etc.
    (b) Milestones and Exit Plan
    (c) Cost

11. Feasibility Study and Financial Modelling/Forecasting/Sensitivity analysis (changes with respect to cost/expense/asset/liability/valuation/investment other factors)

    (a) Revenue
    (b) Cost

        (i) Employee
        (ii) Marketing
        (iii) Technology
        (iv) Capex

(v) Working Capital—Inventory, Cash, Bank, Bill Receivable, Bills Payable
(vi) Long-term Debt
(vii) Short-term Debt
(viii) Ratio Analysis (Standards in Various Industries)

12. Benchmark of Cost/Expenses Versus Revenue/Employee—Metrics
13. Impact of Human Capital Management, Corporate Governance, Innovation, Structural Framework, Use of Technological Tools, Cultural Aspects, Leadership Principles, Moral Values, Teamwork
14. How Can We Take into Account of These Qualitative Aspects into Financial Value?
15. Company Specific Risk Premium, Unsystematic Risk

Appendix

2 Key Components of a Business Plan

2.1 Idea Uniqueness

It is very crucial to start by introducing your business idea and what makes it unique compared to other businesses in the same industry in a business plan. The idea should be different from existing solutions. It can also include information on any patents, trademarks, or other intellectual property that you have or plan to obtain to protect your idea.

2.2 Problem the Business Is Trying to Solve

It is important to explain how the idea aims to solve a specific problem or pain point. It can add value to discuss any research or data you have gathered to support the existence of this problem and its impact on your potential customers.

2.3 Market Analysis

(a) *Economic Analysis:* Provide an overview of the current economic conditions and trends that may impact the industry and market you are targeting. Analyze the buying habits and behaviors of consumers and businesses in the current economic climate.

(b) *Which Industry?:* Identify the industry or industries that your business operates in. Provide an overview of the industry and its characteristics, such as market size, growth rate, and major players.
(c) *Total Industry Market Size:* Define the total market size for the industry you are targeting. Identify the key trends, drivers, and challenges that are affecting the industry and its overall market size. Use research and data to support your market size estimates and projections.
(d) *Ascertainable Market Size for the Specific Market:* Define the specific market segment or niche that your business targets and determine the market size of this segment, taking into account factors such as geography, demographics, and psychographics.
(e) *Target Market:* Analyze the target market in detail, define the characteristics of this market, including demographics, psychographics, and behavior and provide insights into how this market makes buying decisions and what factors influence their purchasing behavior.
(f) *Market Share of the Company Wants to Capture:* Define the specific market share that your business aims to capture and explain how your business plans to capture this market share and what strategies you will use to differentiate yourself from competitors.
(g) *Phased Wise Market Penetration Strategy:* Define the phased approach that your business will use to penetrate the market and define the timelines, resources, and milestones for each phase of your market penetration strategy.
(h) *Market and Competitor Analysis:* Tools Used: Identify the tools and techniques that you used to conduct your market and competitor analysis such as SWOT Analysis, PEST Analysis, market surveys, customer interviews, and focus group analysis.

2.4 Technology

In today's business landscape, technology is often at the core of many startups. Whether it's a new software application, a hardware device, or an online service, technology plays a crucial role in creating and delivering value to customers. Because of this, it's important to include a detailed discussion of technological milieu in your business plan. This can help you demonstrate your technical expertise, showcase your unique selling proposition, and moreover how such technology is an upgrade on current options and helps with the market pain points highlighted in Sect. 2.2.

2.5 *Investment Strategy*

A business plan should discuss on the business' overall investment strategy, including how it plans to raise capital and the sources of funding it plans to pursue. This includes considering a dialog around venture capital, angel investing, crowdfunding, or bootstrapping strategies, as well as any potential benefits or drawbacks of each approach. This also includes Milestones and Exit Plans such as acquisition or IPO, to show potential investors or partners it's the long-term vision for the business.

3 Financial Modelling and Sensitivity Analysis

Lasher (1994) emphasizes in his book the importance of financial projections in a business plan. Financial projections are a key element of any business plan as they demonstrate the potential financial performance of the business over time. These projections typically include forecasts of revenue, expenses, profits, and cash flows for a specific period of time. For financial backers, such as investors or lenders, the financial projections are a crucial element of the business plan as they want to see the potential return on investment and the likelihood of the business's success.

When starting a new company, it's important to have a solid financial projections, a business plan, and understand the funding requirements. A financial projection outlines the financial objectives of the business and how it intends to achieve them. It typically includes a budget, cash flow projection, and financial forecast. The budget outlines the expected income and expenses for the business, while the cash flow projection shows the expected free cash inflows and outflows. The financial forecast is a prediction of the financial performance of the business over time. By developing a robust financial plan, it becomes easy to understand the funding requirements and so decide where the capital will come from. This may include personal savings, loans from banks or investors, or crowdfunding. A clear understanding of the funding requirements will help ensure that the business has enough capital to get started and can continue to grow and succeed.

As seen in Fig. 1, these basic parameters determine the company's future performance. There are also many other parameters, which are not seen in Fig. 1. These parameters are also related to each other. Depending on these parameters, the company attains profitability. This constitutes the company's own Equity. Equity is also a resource of a company like financial debt. Financial debt requires interest payments. This in turn affects net profit, thus affecting equity. Companies need to model it very accurately financially. They influence each other in the form of a network.

I provide a detailed financial modeling case study in this chapter. Depending on the financial modeling I provide sensitivity analysis of some key factors and proforma financial statements are created to provide a clear and comprehensive financial analysis of the startup.

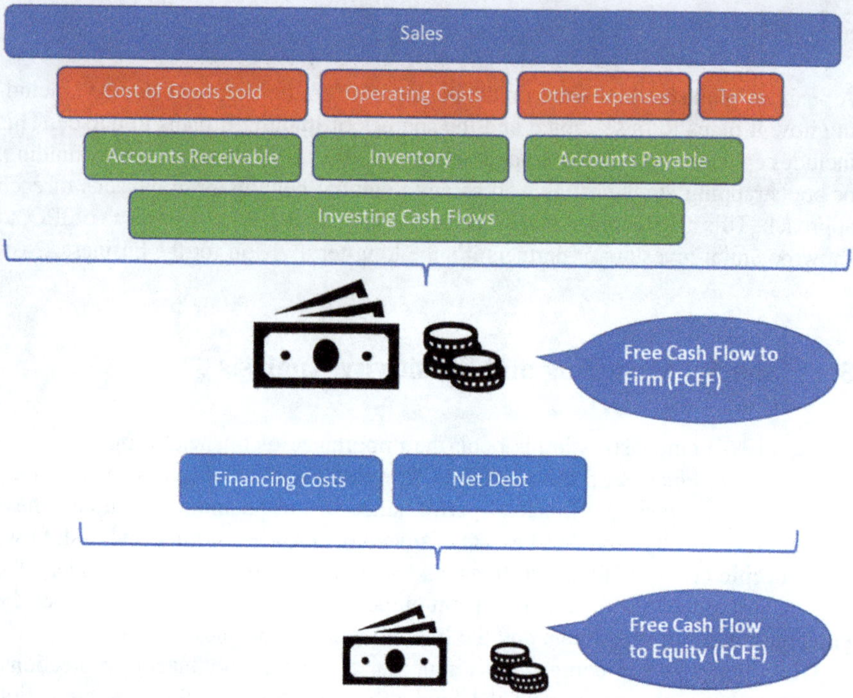

Fig. 1 Free cash flow parameters. Authors own creation

- *Financial Modelling* to demonstrate financial feasibility: Financial modeling is a crucial component of any business plan, as it helps to demonstrate the financial viability of the startup. By including a financial modeling example, it is possible to show potential investors or lenders that the business has a realistic plan for generating revenue and profits.
- *Sensitivity Analysis* to identify potential risks and opportunities: A sensitivity analysis helps the business to identify potential risks and opportunities within their business. By testing various scenarios and assumptions, it can determine how changes in the market or other external factors may impact the financial performance of the startup.
- *Proforma Financial Statements* to provide a basis for financial proposals: Proforma statements provide a detailed forecast of the startup's financial performance over a specific period of time. These statements are crucial for providing the basis for financial proposals, such as a request for funding or investment.

3.1 Case Study

Mrs. Derindere plans to set up a domestic company based on her international personal networking and connections. The company's main field of activity is to purchase domestically produced dry fruits like dry fig and dry apricot and sell them abroad. In this context, it will establish an international transportation network by engaging its solution partners abroad.

Mrs. Derindere can put up to $125,000 in capital. The Company will meet the financial requirement while carrying out its main activities by debt.

- The company plans to generate $2.5 million in sales for the first year. In this context, agreements have been made with the relevant suppliers.
- The company's cost of sales for the first year is estimated at 90% of the sales. This rate will continue to be 85% in the second year, 80% in the third year, and 75% in the following years. It is estimated that these ratios will decrease as the turnover of the company increases.
- The company plans to grow aggressively in the first few years, and after making sales of $2.5 million in the first year in dollar terms, the sales growth rate will be 30%, 25%, 20%, 15%, 10%, 5%, respectively, and 1.5%, equivalent to annual dollar inflation, over the following years.
- The company plans to focus on e-commerce and sell its products through its own website. Therefore, the website must comply with all security rules and be able to store a large amount of data. In this framework, the company's technology investments will be $250,000, $200,000, $175,000, and $150,000, respectively, over the forecast period.
- The company will purchase a $300,000 building in the first year.
- After the investments are made, maintenance and repair expenses of these investments will also occur every year. The maintenance and repair costs of technology investments will be 10% for the building and 5% for the technology investment each year.
- The company's trade receivables turnover period, the inventory turnover period, and accounts payable payment turnover are estimated to be 30, 20, and 15 days respectively.
- The corporate tax rate is 15% in the domestic country.
- Operating expenses on the basis of percentages of the cost of goods sold will be as follows (Table 1) and the discount rate inputs are in Table 2.

Industry beta shows the average regression beta across companies in the industry group (Table 3). Relative risk of sector

In this context, I create a 10-year FINANCIAL PLAN and MODEL for the company. To do so, the chapter will

1. Create the projection of the Company's Sales, Cost of Sales, Operating Expenses, etc.
2. Determine how much financial borrowing will be incurred in the coming years if the company starts its activities with a capital of 125,000 dollars.

Table 1 Operating expenses as a percentage of cost of goods sold

Marketing, advertising, and promotion expenses	1.25%
Transport/logistics	1.50%
Packaging	1.31%
Customs	2.00%
Storage	2.00%
Insurance	1.00%
Salaries	5.00%
Other general and administrative expenses	1.00%
Outsourcing expenses	3.00%
Other expenses	3.00%

Table 2 Inputs for cost of equity, cost of debt, and WACC

Long term treasury bond rate =	3.88%
Risk premium to use for equity =	5.94%
Expected inflation rate in US $ =	1.50%
Industry beta=	0.67
Std dev in stock=	28.26%

Source: Aswath Damadoran, WACC calculations

Table 3 Cost of debt lookup table (based on std. dev in stock prices)

Standard deviation	Standard deviation	Basis spread
0	0.25000	0.85%
0.250001	0.50000	1.62%
0.500001	0.65000	2.00%
0.650001	0.80000	3.13%
0.800001	0.90000	5.26%
0.900001	1.00000	7.37%
1.000001	10.00000	11.57%

Source: Aswath Damadoran, WACC calculations

3. Revenues, expenses, taxes, interest payments, etc. Determine the net profit of the company for each year after offsetting.
4. Determine the company's equity amounts for each year, together with the determination of the net profit.
5. Determine the company's resource need and resource generation power for each year.
6. Determine when the company will pay off all its financial debts.
7. Find out how many years the company will not make any profits for the first year and after which year it will make a profit to the partners.
8. Determine the value of the investment.
9. Prepare the proforma balance sheet and income statement of the investment and the company for the coming years (Tables 4, 5 and 6).

Net working capital requirement (NWCR) is a concept that represents the amount of working capital that a company needs to operate its business. NWCR is calculated as:

Table 4 Cost of goods sold of the Startup

	0	1	2	3	4	5	6	7	8	9	10
Sales		**6,250,000**	**8,125,000**	**10,156,250**	**12,187,500**	**14,015,625**	**15,417,188**	**16,188,047**	**16,430,868**	**16,677,331**	**16,927,491**
Sales growth rate			*30.00%*	*25.00%*	*20.00%*	*15.00%*	*10.00%*	*5.00%*	*1.50%*	*1.50%*	*1.50%*
Cost of goods sold		**5,625,000**	**6,906,250**	**8,125,000**	**9,140,625**	**10,511,719**	**11,562,891**	**12,141,035**	**12,323,151**	**12,507,998**	**12,695,618**
Cost of goods sold/ sales		***90.00%***	***85.00%***	***80.00%***	***75.00%***	***75.00%***	***75.00%***	***75.00%***	***75.00%***	***75.00%***	***75.00%***

Table 5 Operating expenses of the startup (on the basis of percentages of the cost of goods sold)

	0	1	2	3	4	5	6	7	8	9	10
Total operating expenses		**1,203,516**	**1,609,191**	**1,942,266**	**2,237,150**	**2,588,148**	**2,838,563**	**2,866,616**	**2,873,295**	**2,882,077**	**2,893,471**
Packaging		*73,828*	*90,645*	*106,641*	*119,971*	*137,966*	*151,763*	*159,351*	*161,741*	*164,167*	*166,630*
Storage		*112,500*	*138,125*	*162,500*	*182,813*	*210,234*	*231,258*	*242,821*	*246,463*	*250,160*	*253,912*
Customs		*112,500*	*138,125*	*162,500*	*182,813*	*210,234*	*231,258*	*242,821*	*246,463*	*250,160*	*253,912*
Transport/logistics		*84,375*	*103,594*	*121,875*	*137,109*	*157,676*	*173,443*	*182,116*	*184,847*	*187,620*	*190,434*
Insurance		*56,250*	*69,063*	*81,250*	*91,406*	*105,117*	*115,629*	*121,410*	*123,232*	*125,080*	*126,956*
Salaries		*281,250*	*345,313*	*406,250*	*457,031*	*525,586*	*578,145*	*607,052*	*616,158*	*625,400*	*634,781*
Marketing, advertising, and promotion expenses		*70,313*	*86,328*	*101,563*	*114,258*	*131,396*	*144,536*	*151,763*	*154,039*	*156,350*	*158,695*
Other general and administrative expenses		*56,250*	*69,063*	*81,250*	*91,406*	*105,117*	*115,629*	*121,410*	*123,232*	*125,080*	*126,956*
Outsourcing expenses		*168,750*	*207,188*	*243,750*	*274,219*	*315,352*	*346,887*	*364,231*	*369,695*	*375,240*	*380,869*
Other expenses (3% of sales)		*187,500*	*243,750*	*304,688*	*365,625*	*420,469*	*462,516*	*485,641*	*492,926*	*500,320*	*507,825*
Depreciation expenses		*0*	*118,000*	*170,000*	*220,500*	*269,000*	*287,500*	*188,000*	*154,500*	*122,500*	*92,500*
Operating expenses/ sales		***19.26%***	***19.81%***	***19.12%***	***18.36%***	***18.47%***	***18.41%***	***17.71%***	***17.49%***	***17.28%***	***17.09%***

[a] Percentages are used in this table to calculate operating expenses as a percentage of the cost of sales; however, other expenses are calculated as a percentage of sales. Annual Depreciation expense is calculated by dividing the cost of assets by the useful life of 5 years. The annual depreciation expense is calculated using the linear depreciation method

Table 6 Net working capital change of startup

	0	1	2	3	4	5	6	7	8	9	10
Operating periods (days)		**35.0**	**35.0**	**35.0**	**35.0**	**35.0**	**35.0**	**35.0**	**35.0**	**35.0**	**35.0**
Trade receivable collection period		*30.0*	*30.0*	*30.0*	*30.0*	*30.0*	*30.0*	*30.0*	*30.0*	*30.0*	*30.0*
Inventory turnover period		*20.0*	*20.0*	*20.0*	*20.0*	*20.0*	*20.0*	*20.0*	*20.0*	*20.0*	*20.0*
Accounts payable payment period		*15.0*	*15.0*	*15.0*	*15.0*	*15.0*	*15.0*	*15.0*	*15.0*	*15.0*	*15.0*
Net working capital requirement	**0**	**541,294**	**696,283**	**866,243**	**1,034,989**	**1,189,603**	**1,308,909**	**1,379,034**	**1,401,212**	**1,423,640**	**1,446,303**
Trade receivables		*513,699*	*667,808*	*834,760*	*1,001,712*	*1,151,969*	*1,267,166*	*1,330,524*	*1,350,482*	*1,370,740*	*1,391,301*
Inventories		*308,219*	*378,425*	*445,205*	*500,856*	*575,985*	*633,583*	*665,262*	*675,241*	*685,370*	*695,650*
Accounts payable		*280,624*	*349,950*	*413,723*	*467,580*	*538,351*	*591,841*	*616,753*	*624,511*	*632,469*	*640,647*
Net working capital change		**541,294**	**154,989**	**169,959**	**168,746**	**154,614**	**119,306**	**70,125**	**22,178**	**22,428**	**22,663**

NWCR = Operating Cycle Time* Daily Operating Expenses

The operating cycle time is the amount of time it takes for a company to convert its inventory into cash. It includes the time it takes to purchase raw materials, manufacture products, sell them to customers, and collect payment. The NWCR is an important metric for companies to track because it helps them to determine how much working capital they need to keep on hand to operate their business. A company with a high NWCR may need to maintain a larger cash reserve or have access to a line of credit to meet its ongoing cash flow needs. Conversely, a company with a low NWCR may have excess working capital that could be invested in growth opportunities or returned to shareholders.

Trade Receivable Collection Period: This is the average amount of time that a company takes to collect payment from its customers after a sale has been made. It is calculated by dividing the average accounts receivable balance by the average daily sales and multiplying the result by the number of days in the period.

Inventory Turnover Period: This is the average amount of time that a company takes to sell its inventory. It is calculated by dividing the average inventory balance by the cost of goods sold per day.

Accounts Payable Payment Period: This is the average amount of time that a company takes to pay its suppliers for goods or services that it has purchased. It is calculated by dividing the average accounts payable balance by the average daily purchases and multiplying the result by the number of days in the period.

To calculate future trade receivables, inventories, and accounts payable using operating periods (days), the following formulas are used:

Trade Receivables = Sales* Trade Receivable Collection Period/365

Inventories = (Cost of Sales* Inventory Turnover Period/365)

Accounts Payable = (Cost of Sales + Operating Expenses)*

(Accounts Payable Payment Period/365)

In the case study company's trade receivables turnover period, the inventory turnover period, and accounts payable payment turnover are estimated to be 30, 20, and 15 days respectively. Trade Receivables, Inventories, and Accounts Payable have been calculated for these turnover periods.

Net working capital change, on the other hand, refers to the difference in net working capital from one period to another. It can be calculated as follows:

Net Working Capital (**NWC**) **Change** = Net Working Capital (End of Period) – Net Working Capital (Beginning of Period)

A positive NWC change indicates that a company's working capital has increased from one period to another, while a negative net working capital change indicates that the working capital has decreased. Managing net working capital is important for businesses as it helps to ensure that the company has enough liquidity to cover its short-term expenses and operations. By monitoring the changes in net working capital, businesses can make better decisions about managing their cash flow, inventory levels, and accounts receivable and payable.

A positive NWC change means that the company's current assets have increased more than its current liabilities during the period. This result from an increase in accounts receivable, an increase in inventory, or a decrease in accounts payable, which result in a cash outflow (Table 7).

Capital expenditures (CapEx) are funds that a company invests in long-term assets, such as property, plant, and equipment (PP&E), that are expected to generate benefits over a period of time greater than 1 year. Capital expenditures are typically made to maintain or expand a company's production capabilities or improve its efficiency and are considered to be essential for the growth and success of a business (Table 8).

- The company will purchase a $300,000 building in the first year.
- The company's technology investments will be $250,000, $200,000, $175,000, and $150,000, respectively, over the forecast period.
- After the investments are made, maintenance and repair expenses of these investments will also occur every year. The maintenance and repair costs of technology investments will be 10% for the building and 5% for the technology investment each year (e.g., 1. year 40.000 = 300.000*0,05 + 250.000*0,10; 2. year 60.000 = (300.000*0,05) + (250.000 + 200.000)*0,10 and so on.

Estimating Cost of Debt

$$\textbf{Cost of debt} = \text{Long Term Treasury Bond Rate} + \text{Basis Spread based on the std dev in industry stock prices}$$

$$\textbf{Cost of debt} = 3.88\% + 1.62\%$$

$$\textbf{Cost of debt} = 5.50\%$$

Estimating Cost of Equity

$$\textbf{Cost of Equity} = \text{Long Term Treasury Bond Rate} + (\text{Beta}^{*}\text{Equity Risk Premium})$$

$$\textbf{Cost of Equity} = 3.88\% + (0.67^{*}5.94\%)$$

$$\textbf{Cost of Equity} = 7.86\%$$

Free cash flow (FCF) is a measure of a company's cash flow available for distribution to investors, debt repayment, or reinvestment in the business. It represents the amount of cash generated by a company's operations that is available after capital expenditures and working capital requirements have been met. While Free Cash

Table 7 Capital expenditure of startup

	0	1	2	3	4	5	6	7	8	9	10
Capital expenditures	0	**590,000**	**260,000**	**252,500**	**242,500**	**92,500**	**92,500**	**92,500**	**92,500**	**92,500**	**92,500**
Property	*0*	*300,000*	*0*	*0*	*0*	*0*	*0*	*0*	*0*	*0*	*0*
Internal use software, website development, and other technological expenditures	*0*	*250,000*	*200,000*	*175,000*	*150,000*	*0*	*0*	*0*	*0*	*0*	*0*
Maintenance/repair/renovation investments	*0*	*40,000*	*60,000*	*77,500*	*92,500*	*92,500*	*92,500*	*92,500*	*92,500*	*92,500*	*92,500*

Table 8 FCFE calculation from both net profit and operating income

From net profit	From operating income
Net profit +Depreciation +Net working capital change –Capex –Principal payments +Paid in capital *=FCFE (free cash flow to equity)*	*Operating income* +Depreciation –Tax provision +Net working capital change –Capex –Interest expenses –Principal payments +Paid in capital *=FCFE (free cash flow to equity)*

Flow to Equity (FCFE) the amount of cash flow available to a company's equity investors after accounting for capital expenditures, debt repayments, and working capital requirements. It represents the cash flow available for distribution to a company's equity holders, such as dividends or share buybacks.

$$\textbf{FCF} = \text{Operating Income} + \text{Depreciation–Tax} \pm \text{Change in NWC–CapEx} + \text{Capital Raised}$$

$$\textbf{FCFE} = \text{Operating Income} + \text{Depreciation} - \text{Tax} \pm \text{Change in NWC} - \text{CapEx} - \text{net interest expenses} - \text{Debt Repayments} + \text{Net New Debt Issuances} + \text{Capital Raised}$$

If Free Cash Flow to Equity (FCFE) is negative, it means that a company's cash outflows, such as capital expenditures, debt repayments, and working capital requirements, are greater than its cash inflows from operating activities and net new debt issuances. In other words, the company is spending more cash than it is generating from its operations, and it may need to raise additional capital to finance its activities through debt or equity issuances. Therefore, in our financial model, when the FCFE is negative, I calculate the additional capital need from debt financing (Goker & Derindere Köseoğlu, 2020).

Considering that the company has only invested \$125,000 in capital at the beginning of the project and will not add to it later, the company will choose a debt financing strategy. Thus, the FCFE will not be negative because outside finance will enter the company. We should solve this problem as to make FCFE zero. Goal Seek what-if analysis in excel[1] can be used to find the debt level need that makes the FCFE level zero. We repeat this during periods of negative FCFE. When FCFE turns positive, I stop this process.

1. In the **Set cell** box, enter the reference for the cell that contains the formula that you want to resolve. In the example, FCFE cell.

[1]On the **Data** tab, in the **Data Tools** group, click **What-If Analysis**, and then click **Goal Seek**.

2. In the **To value** box, type the formula result that you want. In the example, **this is 0 (zero).**
3. In the **By changing cell** box, enter the reference for the cell that contains the value that you want to adjust. In the example, this reference is **total financing debt principal cell** (Table 9).

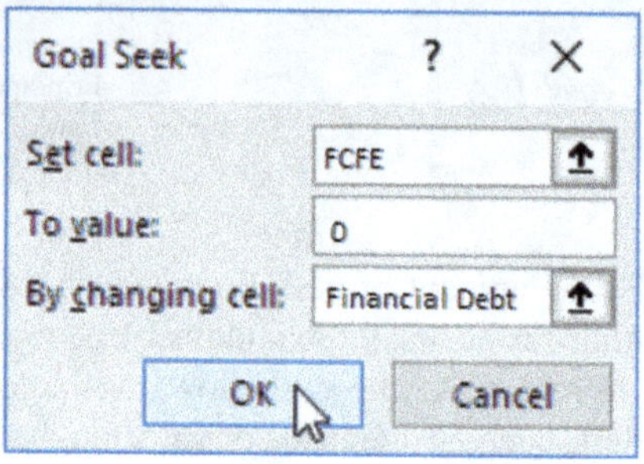

- Corporate tax rate and rules can change from country to country. In this example, I take 15% as the corporate tax rate.
- Interest expenses are calculated from the average total financial debt principal (e.g., 48.349 = [((0 + 1.758.159)/2)*5,5%] and so on (Tables 10 and 11).

Sensitivity Analysis

Sensitivity Analysis is an important tool used in financial modeling to assess the potential impact of changes in key variables or assumptions on the financial performance of a business or investment. It involves varying one or more input variables of a financial model while keeping all other variables constant, and then examining how changes in these variables affect the output or results of the model (Saltelli et al., 2004).

1. One-way sensitivity analysis: This involves varying one input variable at a time while keeping all other variables constant. This helps to identify the most important drivers of the financial model and assess their impact on the output.

   One-way sensitivity analysis is conducted for **"change in sales growth"** (Fig. 2) and **"change in cost of goods sale percentage"** (Fig. 3) for the financial model above.

2. Two-way sensitivity analysis: This involves varying two input variables simultaneously while keeping all other variables constant. This can help to identify the interdependencies between different variables and assess how changes in one variable affect the sensitivity of another variable.

   Two-way sensitivity analysis is conducted for **"Trade Receivable Collection Period"** and **"Accounts Payable Payment Period"** changes for the financial model above.

The sensitivity of the Startup value to the growth rate changes in sales was analyzed. If the growth rate in Sales is 1% lower each year during the projection

Table 9 Financial model and valuation of the startup

Business Plan (USD)	0	1	2	3	4	5	6	7	8	9	10	Terminal Value
Sales		**6,250,000**	**8,125,000**	**10,156,250**	**12,187,500**	**14,015,625**	**15,417,188**	**16,188,047**	**16,430,868**	**16,677,331**	**16,927,491**	
Sales growth rate			*30.00%*	*25.00%*	*20.00%*	*15.00%*	*10.00%*	*5.00%*	*1.50%*	*1.50%*	*1.50%*	
Cost of goods sold		**5,625,000**	**6,906,250**	**8,125,000**	**9,140,625**	**10,511,719**	**11,562,891**	**12,141,035**	**12,323,151**	**12,507,998**	**12,695,618**	
Cost of goods sold		*5,625,000*	*6,906,250*	*8,125,000*	*9,140,625*	*10,511,719*	*11,562,891*	*12,141,035*	*12,323,151*	*12,507,998*	*12,695,618*	
Gross profit		**625,000**	**1,218,750**	**2,031,250**	**3,046,875**	**3,503,906**	**3,854,297**	**4,047,012**	**4,107,717**	**4,169,333**	**4,231,873**	
Gross profit margin		***10.00%***	***15.00%***	***20.00%***	***25.00%***	***25.00%***	***25.00%***	***25.00%***	***25.00%***	***25.00%***	***25.00%***	
Total operating expenses		**1,203,516**	**1,609,191**	**1,942,266**	**2,237,150**	**2,588,148**	**2,838,563**	**2,866,616**	**2,873,295**	**2,882,077**	**2,893,471**	
Operating income		**−578,516**	**−390,441**	**88,984**	**809,725**	**915,758**	**1,015,734**	**1,180,396**	**1,234,422**	**1,287,256**	**1,338,402**	
Operating income margin		−9.26%	−4.81%	0.88%	6.64%	6.53%	6.59%	7.29%	7.51%	7.72%	7.91%	
Depreciation cost (+)		**0**	**118,000**	**170,000**	**220,500**	**269,000**	**287,500**	**188,000**	**154,500**	**122,500**	**92,500**	
Tax provision (15%)		**0**	**0**	**0**	**99,252**	**119,575**	**141,067**	**173,218**	**185,163**	**193,088**	**200,760**	
Income before taxes		**−626,865**	**−509,313**	**−60,672**	**661,678**	**797,169**	**940,445**	**1,154,783**	**1,234,422**	**1,287,256**	**1,338,402**	
Net working capital requirement	**0**	**541,294**	**696,283**	**866,243**	**1,034,989**	**1,189,603**	**1,308,909**	**1,379,034**	**1,401,212**	**1,423,640**	**1,446,303**	
Net working capital change		**541,294**	**154,989**	**169,959**	**168,746**	**154,614**	**119,306**	**70,125**	**22,178**	**22,428**	**22,663**	
Capital expenditures	**0**	**590,000**	**260,000**	**252,500**	**242,500**	**92,500**	**92,500**	**92,500**	**92,500**	**92,500**	**92,500**	
Equity	**125,000**	**−501,865**	**−1,011,178**	**−1,071,851**	**−509,424**	**168,169**	**967,547**	**1,949,113**	**2,998,372**	**4,092,539**	**5,230,181**	

(continued)

Table 9 (continued)

Business Plan (USD)	0	1	2	3	4	5	6	7	8	9	10	Terminal Value
Paid in capital	*125,000*	*0*	*0*	*0*	*0*	*0*	*0*	*0*	*0*	*0*	*0*	
Net profit		*— 626,865*	*— 509,313*	*−60,672*	*562,426*	*677,593*	*799,378*	*981,566*	*1,049,259*	*1,094,167*	*1,137,642*	
New financial debt principal		**1,758,159**	**806,303**	**313,131**	**0**	**0**	**0**	**0**	**0**	**0**	**0**	
Total financial debt principal	**0**	**1,758,159**	**2,564,462**	**2,877,593**	**2,505,913**	**1,806,434**	**931,361**	**0**	**0**	**0**	**0**	
Financial debt interest expenses		**48,349**	**118,872**	**149,657**	**148,046**	**118,590**	**75,289**	**25,612**	**0**	**0**	**0**	
Total financial debt principal payments		**0**	**0**	**0**	**371,680**	**699,479**	**875,073**	**931,361**	**0**	**0**	**0**	
Total financing requirement		**1,179,643**	**2,086,334**	**2,340,250**	**2,405,891**	**2,051,578**	**1,525,290**	**652,612**	**— 1,319,497**	**— 2,383,310**	**— 3,490,617**	
Cash and cash equivalents	**125,000**	**125,000**	**125,000**	**125,000**	**125,000**	**125,000**	**125,000**	**200,579**	**1,289,660**	**2,391,399**	**3,506,377**	
Free cash flow to equity		**0**	**0**	**0**	**0**	**0**	**0**	**75,579**	**1,089,080**	**1,101,739**	**1,114,979**	**29,102,965**
Cost of equity		*7.86%*	*7.86%*	*7.86%*	*7.86%*	*7.86%*	*7.86%*	*7.86%*	*7.86%*	*7.86%*	*7.86%*	
Discount factor	**1.00**	**0.9271**	**0.8596**	**0.7969**	**0.7389**	**0.6850**	**0.6351**	**0.5888**	**0.5459**	**0.5061**	**0.4692**	**0.4692**
Discounted free cash flow to equity		**0**	**0**	**0**	**0**	**0**	**0**	**44,503**	**594,543**	**557,625**	**523,203**	**13,656,554**
Market value	**15,376,428**											

Table 10 Proforma balance sheet for 10 years of the startup

Year/term	0	1	2	3	4	5	6	7	8	9	10
Balance sheet											
Assets	**125,000**	**1,536,918**	**1,903,233**	**2,219,466**	**2,464,068**	**2,512,954**	**2,490,749**	**2,565,866**	**3,622,883**	**4,725,008**	**5,870,828**
Cash and cash equivalent	**125,000**	**125,000**	**125,000**	**125,000**	**125,000**	**125,000**	**125,000**	**200,579**	**1,289,660**	**2,391,399**	**3,506,377**
Accounts receivable	**0**	**513,699**	**667,808**	**834,760**	**1,001,712**	**1,151,969**	**1,267,166**	**1,330,524**	**1,350,482**	**1,370,740**	**1,391,301**
Inventories	**0**	**308,219**	**378,425**	**445,205**	**500,856**	**575,985**	**633,583**	**665,262**	**675,241**	**685,370**	**695,650**
Net tangible fixed assets	**0**	**590,000**	**732,000**	**814,500**	**836,500**	**660,000**	**465,000**	**369,500**	**307,500**	**277,500**	**277,500**
Tangible fixed assets	0	590,000	850,000	1,102,500	1,345,000	1,437,500	1,530,000	1,622,500	1,715,000	1,807,500	1,900,000
Accumulated depreciation	0	0	–118,000	–288,000	–508,500	–777,500	–1,065,000	–1,253,000	–1,407,500	–1,530,000	–1,622,500
Total liabilities	**125,000**	**1,536,918**	**1,903,233**	**2,219,466**	**2,464,068**	**2,512,954**	**2,490,749**	**2,565,866**	**3,622,883**	**4,725,008**	**5,870,828**
Financial debts	**0**	**1,758,159**	**2,564,462**	**2,877,593**	**2,505,913**	**1,806,434**	**931,361**	**0**	**0**	**0**	**0**
Accounts payables	**0**	**280,624**	**349,950**	**413,723**	**467,580**	**538,351**	**591,841**	**616,753**	**624,511**	**632,469**	**640,647**
Equity	**125,000**	**–501,865**	**–1,011,178**	**–1,071,851**	**–509,424**	**168,169**	**967,547**	**1,949,113**	**2,998,372**	**4,092,539**	**5,230,181**
Paid in capital	125,000	125,000	125,000	125,000	125,000	125,000	125,000	125,000	125,000	125,000	125,000
Retained earnings	0	0	–626,865	–1,136,178	–1,196,851	–634,424	43,169	842,547	1,824,113	2,873,372	3,967,539
Period net profit/loss	0	–626,865	–509,313	–60,672	562,426	677,593	799,378	981,566	1,049,259	1,094,167	1,137,642

Table 11 Proforma income statement for 10 years of the startup

Year/term	0	1	2	3	4	5	6	7	8	9	10
Income statement											
Net sales	0.00	6,250,000	8,125,000	10,156,250	12,187,500	14,015,625	15,417,188	16,188,047	16,430,868	16,677,331	16,927,491
Cost of goods sold	0.00	5,625,000	6,906,250	8,125,000	9,140,625	10,511,719	11,562,891	12,141,035	12,323,151	12,507,998	12,695,618
Gross profit	0.00	625,000	1,218,750	2,031,250	3,046,875	3,503,906	3,854,297	4,047,012	4,107,717	4,169,333	4,231,873
Operating expenses	0.00	1,203,516	1,609,191	1,942,266	2,237,150	2,588,148	2,838,563	2,866,616	2,873,295	2,882,077	2,893,471
Net operating profit	0.00	–578,516	–390,441	88,984	809,725	915,758	1,015,734	1,180,396	1,234,422	1,287,256	1,338,402
Interest expenses	0.00	48,349	118,872	149,657	148,046	118,590	75,289	25,612	0	0	0
Income before tax	0.00	–626,865	–509,313	−60,672	661,678	797,169	940,445	1,154,783	1,234,422	1,287,256	1,338,402
Income tax expense	0.00	0	0	0	99,252	119,575	141,067	173,218	185,163	193,088	200,760
Net profit/loss for the period	0.00	–626,865	–509,313	−60,672	562,426	677,593	799,378	981,566	1,049,259	1,094,167	1,137,642

15,372,374	
-5%	10,290,265
-4%	11,190,850
-3%	12,146,431
-2%	13,159,869
-1%	14,234,147
0%	**15,372,374**
1%	16,577,787
2%	17,853,757
3%	19,203,790
4%	20,631,536
5%	22,140,790

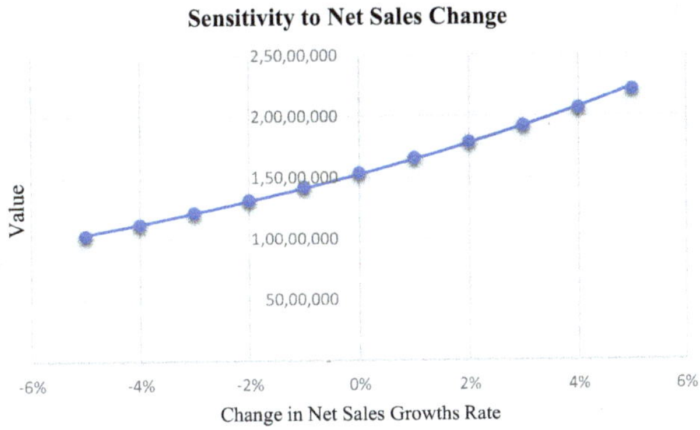

Fig. 2 One-way sensitivity analysis for **"change in sales growth"** (The sensitivity analysis is conducted in Excel using the "What-If Analysis-Data Table" feature, which is located under the "Data" tab on the Excel ribbon)

15,372,374	
-5%	29,708,802
-4%	26,842,967
-3%	23,977,132
-2%	21,111,297
-1%	18,245,462
0%	**15,372,374**
1%	12,492,205
2%	9,612,036
3%	6,731,868
4%	3,851,699
5%	962,026

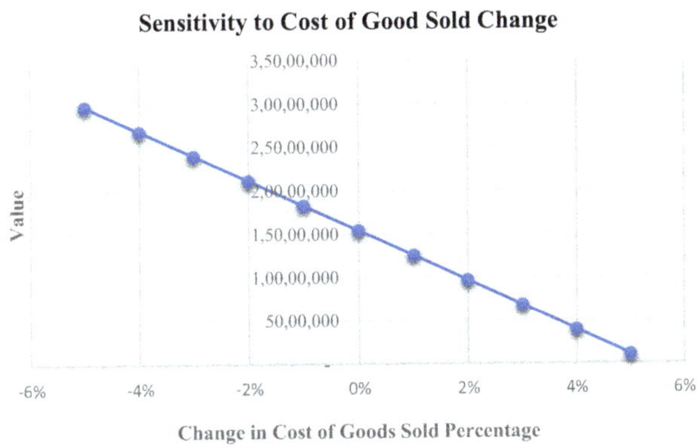

Fig. 3 One-way sensitivity analysis for **"change in cost of goods sale percentage"**

period, the value of the startup is 14,234,147 and if it is 1% higher each year, the value is 16,577,787. On the other hand, the effect of the cost of goods sales value on the Startup value was also analyzed. If the Cost of Goods Sales ratio is 1% lower each year during the projection period, the value of the startup is 18.245.462 and if it is 1% higher each year, the value is 12.492.205. Thus, the changes in the costs of the company affect the value of the company more than the changes in its sales. Strategies to reduce costs should therefore be developed and prioritized (Tables 12 and 13).

A company's Trade Receivable Collection Period and Accounts Payable Payment Period can impact its valuation. A company that has a shorter Trade Receivable Collection Period and a longer Accounts Payable Payment Period may be seen as a more attractive investment opportunity due to its stronger cash flow position. Conversely, a company that has a longer Trade Receivable Collection Period and

Table 12 Value of the startup depending on the changes of net sales and costs of goods sold

Change	Value (USD)	effect
1% increase in net sales	16,582,600	108%
Base scenario	15,376,428	100%
1% decrease in Costs of Goods Sales	18,250,035	119%

a shorter Accounts Payable Payment Period may be seen as a riskier investment due to its weaker cash flow position. Therefore, a shorter Trade Receivable Collection Period and a longer Accounts Payable Payment Period at the same time, impact a company's valuation in a positive way in two ways.

4 Conclusion

In conclusion, mastering the art of business planning, financial modeling, and sensitivity analysis is crucial for any startup looking to succeed in the long run. By creating a solid business plan, startups can identify their strengths, weaknesses, opportunities, and threats, as well as the resources they'll need to achieve their goals. Remember, planning is an ongoing process that requires continuous monitoring, evaluation, and revision. As startups grow and evolve, so should business plans and sensitivity analysis. By staying agile and adaptable, startups can navigate through the challenges and opportunities of the ever-changing business landscape and increase their chances of success.

As illustrated in a real case study, creating a solid business plan that incorporates financial modeling, valuation, and proforma financial statements can help startups identify key performance indicators, monitor their financial performance, and make informed decisions. Additionally, performing sensitivity analysis can help startups understand the impact of different variables on their business's financial performance, enabling them to make more informed decisions and adjust their plans accordingly.

Finally, seeking feedback and advice from others, including mentors, advisors, and investors, can provide valuable insights and perspectives that can help startups refine their business plan, financial modeling, valuation, and sensitivity analysis, identify blind spots, and uncover new opportunities. By incorporating a real case study that includes financial modeling, valuation, sensitivity analysis, and proforma financial statements in this chapter, I try to provide practical examples that illustrate the concepts I discussed and help readers apply them to their own startups.

Table 13 Two-way sensitivity analysis for "**Trade Receivable Collection Period**" and "**Accounts Payable Payment Period**" changes

		Trade receivable collection period change										
Accounts payable change	15,372,374	−10	−8	−6	−3	−1	0	1	3	6	8	10
	−10	15,416,967	15,326,222	15,235,478	15,099,361	15,008,617	14,963,244	14,917,872	14,827,128	14,691,011	14,600,266	**14,509,522**
	−8	15,499,604	15,408,859	15,318,115	15,181,998	15,091,253	15,045,881	15,000,509	14,909,764	14,773,648	14,682,903	14,592,159
	−6	15,582,240	15,491,496	15,400,751	15,264,635	15,173,890	15,128,518	15,083,146	14,992,401	14,856,284	14,765,540	14,674,795
	−3	15,706,195	15,615,451	15,524,706	15,388,590	15,297,845	15,252,473	15,207,101	15,116,356	14,980,239	14,889,495	14,798,750
	−1	15,788,832	15,698,088	15,607,343	15,471,226	15,380,482	15,335,110	15,289,737	15,198,993	15,062,876	14,972,132	14,881,387
	0	15,830,150	15,739,406	15,648,661	15,512,545	15,421,800	**15,376,428**	15,331,056	15,240,311	15,104,194	15,013,450	14,922,705
	1	15,871,469	15,780,724	15,689,980	15,553,863	15,463,119	15,417,746	15,372,374	15,281,630	15,145,513	15,054,768	14,964,024
	3	15,954,105	15,863,361	15,772,616	15,636,500	15,545,755	15,500,383	15,455,011	15,364,266	15,228,149	15,137,405	15,046,660
	6	16,078,060	15,987,316	15,896,571	15,760,455	15,669,710	15,624,338	15,578,966	15,488,221	15,352,105	15,261,360	15,170,616
	8	16,160,697	16,069,953	15,979,208	15,843,091	15,752,347	15,706,975	15,661,602	15,570,858	15,434,741	15,343,997	15,253,252
	10	**16,243,334**	16,152,589	16,061,845	15,925,728	15,834,984	15,789,611	15,744,239	15,653,495	15,517,378	15,426,633	15,335,889

References

Goker, O., & Derindere Köseoğlu, S. (2020). Challenges in valuation by using discounted free cash flow method. In S. D. Köseoğlu (Ed.), *Valuation challenges and solutions in contemporary businesses* (p. 67). IGI Global.

Haag, A. B. (2013). Writing a successful business plan: An overview. *Workplace Health and Safety, 61*(1), 19–21.

Lasher, W. (1994). *The perfect business plan made simple*. Doubleday Dell.

Saltelli, A., Tarantola, S., Campolongo, F., & Ratto, M. (2004). *Sensitivity analysis in practice: A guide to assessing scientific models*. Wiley Pub.

Welter, C. (2021). The road to entrepreneurial success: Business plans, lean startup, or both? *New England Journal of Entrepreneurship, 24*(1), 21–42.

Valuation Versus Pricing: A Conceptual and Practical Guide to Estimate Economic Value for Early-Stage Companies Via DCF

Adam Patterson

> *(A cynic) is a man who knows the price of everything but the value of nothing—Oscar Wilde (1892), in Lady Windermere's Fan*
> *Price is what you pay. Value is what you get—Warren Buffet (1966)*
> *It might feel positively retro to apply discounted-cash-flow valuation to hot start-ups and the like. But it's still the most reliable method—Mckinsey & Company*

1 Chapter Context

The past decade has seen a huge increase in technology-based innovation, disruption in multiple industries, the advent of "unicorns"—billion-dollar private companies—and early-stage technology investment. Indeed, Global Venture Capital (GVC) investment has grown significantly over the last few years, increasing at a 13.5% compound annual growth rate (CAGR) between 2015 and 2020 (Nolting et al., 2021). Global venture capital investments nearly doubled in 2021, setting a record of $671 billion invested over 38,644 deals (Moore, 2021). US VC fundraising has grown by 18.7% in the 10 years to 2021 (Stepstone, 2022).

Large investors, including family offices, mutual funds, endowments, corporates, pension funds and sovereign wealth funds have been enhancing their exposure to the private equity (PE) and venture capital assets because of its capacity to deliver alpha-returns and provide portfolio diversification benefits due to low or even negative correlations with other asset classes (Invesco, 2020). VC has performed "extremely well over the last 5, 10, and 15 years, beating the S&P 500 by more than 700 basis points on average" (Cambridge Associates, 2022).

Nonetheless, the cyclical nature of venture capital and the broadly illiquid nature of the investment universe often lead to questions around asset class valuation during

A. Patterson (✉)
Redirection Corporate Advisory, Curitiba, Brazil
e-mail: adam@redirection.com.br

S. Derindere Köseoğlu (ed.), *A Practical Guide for Startup Valuation*, Contributions to Finance and Accounting, https://doi.org/10.1007/978-3-031-35291-1_4

periods of both upside and downside pressure in financial markets. Market discourse therefore oscillates between bubbles to downturns and can highlight differing approaches to the issue of valuation for start-ups, early-stage companies and even the technology universe more broadly. This chapter contends then that there is a potential disconnect between "price" and "value" which is partly responsible for such valuation uncertainty. Nonetheless, due to the size of global investment allocation in the space, the issue of start-up valuation is of practical importance for corporate finance professionals, investors, and startup founders.

The author often hears it said, especially from early-stage investors that it is impractical and unnecessary to value young and pre-revenue companies with traditional techniques (in particular discounted cash flow or 'DCF'). It seems that it is not the industry norm to use fundamental valuation for early-stage or 'idea' companies, and thus finance professionals should therefore expand their traditional toolboxes and employ shortcuts and other solutions that seem to offer a simpler or more 'practical' way to value these types of companies. In other words: the future is way too uncertain; business models are still dynamic, prone to 'pivoting' and the asset class suffers from significant survival risk. It has been estimated that 90% of startups fail within 3 years (Patel, 2015). Experienced venture capitalists maintain that the multiple assumptions that are required for DCF analysis can lead to a lack of confidence in financial projections and subsequently, economic value estimates.

Nonetheless, the central argument of this chapter is that discounted cash flow analytics, when used together with a broader market triangulation approach and statistical methods, is a robust startup valuation tool and helps provide not only insight around intrinsic value but also a holistic understanding of the business model, external economic environment and key value drivers that other approaches simply cannot. Afterall, it is also used for some intellectual heavy lifting in other financial fields, such as valuation adjustments for derivative contracts (E&Y, 2014); Expected-Loss-Based Accounting and provisions under IFRS 9 (BIS, 2015) and Credit Portfolio Management in the banking industry (Tschirhart et al., 2007).

This begs the question, if it can be used to price derivatives and credit provisions—arguably much more complex and technical fields why is it not the early-stage valuation tool of choice? According to a Harvard Business Review survey (Gompers et al., 2015), "the vast majority of PE investors rely on gross IRR and MOIC [techniques] and over 70% also incorporate comparable company multiples. In contrast, relatively few [VC investors] use DCF methods, fewer than 20% use APV or WACC-based DCF methods to evaluate investments". Furthermore, a Grant Thornton professional survey (2015) supported this insight: the most popular valuation method typically utilized—by more than 80% of survey respondents—was the Public Multiple method. We can safely assume then that the proportion for venture capitalists using DCF, especially at early-stage, is lower still. Consequently, does that mean corporate finance professionals can't use the method for startups? Some of the world's leading corporate finance firms and professionals argue that we can and, in light of the alternatives, should. What's more, the global authority on valuation, Professor Damodaran (2012) argues that alternative approaches could even be labelled 'the dark side of valuation'. This is not just an academic and conceptual discussion but has significant practical implications for asset valuation. Valuation is an important part of entrepreneurial economics, which prompts the question of how it should be employed in such an important market segment. A lack of visibility and robustness in economic viability analytics can generate valuation and investment risk (broadly, the risks of losses arising from the difference between the accounting value of an asset and the fair market value). As per Deshpande (2020):

> Investors need to know the fair value of their investment; fund managers need to demonstrate their internal rate of returns (IRRs) and calculate accrued carried interest for financial reporting. Simply put [valuation risk] is risk of incorrectly valuing an asset. Fair value under U.S. GAAP represents an exit price that would be exchanged between market participants (willing knowledgeable buyers and sellers). It is possible for market participants to have diverse opinions of fair value. However, such opinions tend to be within a stated range based on access to information. Practical challenges in valuation arise from: (i) lack of available information for a particular investment; (ii) using significant inputs or assumptions that are not supportable; or (iii) uncertainty relating to either the portfolio company or the macro-economic conditions in general.

The fact is that valuing startups is certainly challenging. There are extensive uncertainties involved but an 'ostrich'—head in the sand—approach to utilizing DCF, does not make such uncertainties go away. As Wharton finance professor Luke Taylor argues: "It's difficult to value companies that are very young, that don't have positive cash flows or even revenues [but that] discounted cash flow model is simply correct finance" (Siegel & Amit, 2013).

By applying some common sense and well-worn investment principles, we can build in consistency checks and forward visibility into our startup forecasts and business plans. High growth and innovative businesses do not exist in a parallel universe where finance theory does not hold. The *raison d'être* of this chapter is therefore to map out a comprehensive framework, based on best practices in corporate finance literature and statistical analysis, to value even the most disruptive new startup.

2 Introduction

The goal of this chapter is restricted to a theoretical analysis of existing valuation frameworks before proposing a simplified adjusted approach to DCF which contemplates supplementary statistical and benchmark analytics and result validation via relative valuation methods. In other words, the aim is to build upon current valuation methods.

First though, we must define what is a startup. In the literature, there is not a unanimous consensus. We utilize as a starting point the definition of Kolvereid (2006) of a "new businesses which are started from scratch" before calibrating to take account of the technological angle of many of these New Economy Firms (NEF). Steve Blank, a well-known American entrepreneur, described a startup as a transient firm looking for a scalable, repeatable, and successful business model (Blank, 2020). The global startup economy is indeed massive, creating nearly $3 trillion in value, a figure on par with the GDP of a G7 economy (Fisk, 2019). On average across OECD countries, young firms account for only a fifth of total employment but are responsible for almost half of aggregate job creation (OECD, 2021). Given the prevalence and significance of startups to the economy, it is therefore crucial to comprehend the proper techniques for estimating their worth (Sander & Kõomägi, 2007). Startups are notoriously difficult to value due to their opacity, brief histories, and a wide variety of intangible assets (Damodaran, 2009). This has led to the emergence of a variety of valuation methodologies (Montani et al., 2020).

Let us reflect on some of the myriad challenges in applying standard valuation techniques to young and pre-revenue companies, before touching on the philosophy of price versus value and then mapping out a fundamental value-based framework for startups. Afterall, it is frequently said that a major problem is often not understanding the problem.

3 The Startup Valuation Challenge

1. Startups often have no, or little, operational history and key performance indicators. Unlike valuing mature companies where it is possible to identify trends, growth and margins, startups, by definition, don't have extensive financial statements or management controls. We generally use these current and historic profit and loss and balance sheet records to estimate future cash flows. However, startups are focused on building and growing their operations. Either financial data simply doesn't exist yet or it's at an embryonic and dynamic stage. We also miss out on additional cyclical or macro insight of how the firm's business model copes with economic downturns, operational and execution issues or stochastic shocks.
2. This dynamism and the associated volatility mean that growth metrics and unit economics are in a constant state of flux and identifying fixed patterns is harder. Numbers and margins can change significantly from 1 month to the next. Also, as companies start from a low base, growth of a 1000% in users, revenues and costs could be part and parcel of the process. A startup passes through several phases of growth—how can we model that?
3. High burn rates. Burn rate is a metric that illustrates how much money a startup is spending and how quickly it 'burns' through its initial investment. Thus, it's the amount of money a business needs to have on hand over a specific window of time to pay for overhead expenses, investment needs and liabilities. Even if we have a few months or a year of revenue data, startups burn through capital to grow, consequently profit and cash flow are likely to be negative. However, Finance 101 tells us that companies that do not (eventually) generate earnings do not generate economic value. How can we then model high burn rates?

4. A startup needs growth assets to expand and then maintain its operations. How can we project future investment requirements in fixed assets, working capital and return on capital?
5. Lack of owner diversification. The first source of external capital for new companies is often the "3Fs" of 'friends, family and fools'. This is the startup equivalent of going 'all in' in poker. From a technical point of view, this impacts on our calculations of opportunity cost. The major risk and return models at our disposal—such as Capital Asset Pricing Model—assume that the marginal investor has a diversified asset portfolio and as such that the only risk worth worrying about is non-diversifiable risk. For most startups, at least at the beginning of their operational life that is not necessarily the case. All risk is on the table. Are traditional risk models valid in such a context? This diversification risk, like most operational metrics should also evolve throughout the startup life-cycle and as such, so should opportunity costs for the marginal investor. Standard deviation evaluates total risk, which is both systematic and unsystematic. Beta, a key concept in valuation, measures only systematic risk (or market risk). Most successful startups go through distinct funding phases, after the 3Fs or 'bootstrapping', which refers to endogenous funding without requiring external capital, before evolving to Angel/Seed and then Venture Capital before institutional or capital market investment. Each investor profile brings differentials to costs of capital. How to model this dynamic?
6. Along the same lines how can we account for illiquidity in startup investments? In financial markets, asset liquidity is a key and active consideration. Liquidity refers to the ease in which an asset can be converted into cash, with cash being fully liquid and other securities liquid to varying degrees. Investors value liquidity and would pay more for an asset that is fully liquid than for an otherwise identical asset that is not fully liquid. The illiquidity discount is then the discount applied to the valuation of an asset as compensation for the reduced saleability. In other words, liquidity describes the degree to which an asset can be quickly bought or sold in the market at a price reflecting its intrinsic value. Public companies and other popular assets can be bought and sold pretty much immediately. It can be much harder for small, private companies, where a potential sale could take months. This lack of liquidity and marketability—where marketability is linked to transaction velocity and not the certainty of its selling or conversion price—needs to be factored into startup valuation. How do we compute this?
7. Risk. Here we are talking about the full spectrum of operational, regulatory, financial, and human risks. Risk being the generation of hazard or the probability of an outcome different to the expected result. What are some of the key startup risks? What happens if the founder leaves? What about if planned investment doesn't materialise? What if revenue next year is only 50% of the forecast value? And if your patent doesn't come through or if the technology doesn't actually work? These factors and multiple others can translate into an acute risk of failure and bankruptcy. Paraphrasing Helmuth von Moltke: no business plan survives first contact with the market. Again, most startups fail or don't achieve

their initial targets. As valuation is innately based on future projections, a robust financial analysis must contemplate such risks.

8. Founder optimism. This is a key ingredient for startup success. However, "the tendency to expect positive outcomes even when such expectations are not rationally justified" (Sander & Kõomägi, 2007), can also be a key occupation hazard. Afterall, the origin for the word "passion" in Latin, is to "suffer". From a valuation standpoint, where owner feedback is important to understand the business model, financial potential, and future narrative, over confidence, amongst other things, can lead to non-plausible projections and planning. Inaccurate forecasts often come from misinterpreting data or simply from the lack of accurate information altogether. Demand forecasting is often inaccurate because of the inherent complexity of the problem. Valuation professionals are also not immune to the sometimes-contagious confidence of founders or a "new investment paradigm". Furthermore, as Damodaran (2016a) has argued, all valuations are biased. How can we deal with this?
9. Uncharted territory. Niels Bohr, the Nobel laureate in Physics and father of the atomic model, is quoted as saying, 'Prediction is very difficult, especially if it's about the future!'. That rationale is especially true for startups. New company trajectories often do not follow linear curves but rather exhibit exponential, logistic or multiple order polynomial properties (and many more statistical trajectories). Top line metrics such as future active users and revenue per client, which directly impact on the valuation bottom line, can be extremely difficult even for experienced econometricians to project and accurately extrapolate.

That is certainly a long and complex, and yet non-exhaustive, list of technical financial issues that need to be quantified in a solid valuation. There are numerous ways to examine the proposed questions above both through theoretical and empirical lenses. Nonetheless, it is a function of these many assessment challenges that lead some investors and analysts to focus on "pricing" shortcuts that may not be consistent with fundamental valuation principals and can in fact lead to estimation errors—both over and under—in forecasting economic value.

4 The Venture Capital Method: Startup Pricing

> Intrinsic value can be calculated based on a set of rules, whereas pricing is inferred by other references. The definition of pricing is best answered by the economist's refrain: An asset is worth whatever the market will bear (Lapidus, 2017).

Before clarifying the impact of this definition through the prism of startup valuation, we will briefly examine one of the most popular approaches employed to quantify early-stage startup potential: the Venture Capital Method, to highlight the 'pricing' concept, which essentially aims to estimate what the market, via a potential liquidity event, would 'bear'.

The approach was first described by Professor William Sahlman from Harvard Business School in a now famous essay in the 1980s (Sahlman & Scherlis, 1987). Sahlman's core formula involves multiplying the company's projected revenue with its projected margin and industry price-to-earnings to decide on its future value. In its most basic form, the idea is to project revenue or earnings over a short-term period until a potential "exit" event, normally between 3 and 5 years. This terminal value is then an estimate of how much an investor can sell their stake for in the future. The next step is multiplying this figure by a comparable sector equity (usually earnings/net income) or enterprise (usually GMV, sales, gross profit, EBITDA) multiple from the public markets or recent private transactions to estimate at a future "harvest" value. We then discount this value at a, generally high, target rate or expected absolute return on investment (ROI) to arrive at the pre and post "valuations" (adjusting for invested capital). Below we illustrate the technique with a high-level example of a single financing round, assuming no adjustment for future dilution:

$$\text{Post Money Valuation} = \text{Financial Metric}^{\text{Year N}} \times \text{Market Multiple} = \text{Future Value}$$

$$\text{Post Money Valuation} = \frac{\text{Future Value}^{\text{Year N}}}{\text{ROI}^{\text{Year N}}}$$

$$\text{Pre Money Valuation} = \text{Post Money} - \text{Investment}$$

*where investment is the capital allocated in the funding round.

What are some of the "valuation" issues in this approach looking from a fundamental viewpoint?

- By basing the valuation on a short-term horizon when the company is in early-stage mode, we are artificially halting earnings growth before the company reaches maturity. Even after an increase in unicorn numbers and growth rates, data shows that the median age of a billion-dollar technology company was 8 years (Priceonomics, 2018). That being so, can a 3- or 5-year forecast period account for long-term value generation?
- The method can also confuse the potential intrinsic value added in the firm's operations (valuation) with a possible investor exit. Moreover, the method often ignores the possible losses, or gains, that happen between investment and exit which would be factored into a standard valuation. In some versions, the model also includes adjustments for future potential equity dilution. The question being, does future equity investment and changes to cap-tables impact economic value? In the VC universe, it does, as before an investor can compute their future returns, they must first determine ownership stakes in the company post-investment. Moreover, a broader question to discuss: should the only difference between pre and post-money scenarios be an integral function of investment?

- Venture capitalists use two main metrics to measure returns: cash-on-cash return and internal rates of return (or IRR). Both measures can be directly compatible. IRR shows the annualized per cent return an investor's portfolio company or fund has earned (or expects to earn) over the life of an investment. For example, an expected return of 38% over a 5-year period would be equivalent to a cash-on-cash return of five times invested capital (expected multiples are usually not adjusted for the element of time). High "target" discount rates—of up to 50–70% or higher—are common in the venture capital industry and are generally based on arbitrary IRR "targets" that often do not reflect the specific risk characteristics of the company, sector or country in which the investment is made. Basically, the cost of capital is then potentially not based on theoretically accepted risk and return models such as CAPM, APV and Multi-Beta models (which we discuss below). Computed target rates are often much higher than these traditional metrics and even average VC industry returns. Most early-stage investors anticipate an annual net IRR of between 20% and 30%, depending on the investment stage of their portfolio vintage — a level that many venture capitalists have generally easily met over the last few years. For late-stage financial backers, the normal IRR target reference is nearer to 20% (Lewis, 2022). These higher effective demanded discount rates, compared to mature company WACCS, reflect the fact that the bulk of returns are centred around a small proportion of portfolio investments which translates into a greater risk profile. Venture returns are often skewed: 65% of investment rounds fail to return 1× capital and only 4% return greater than 10× capital (Levine, 2007), the veritable 'homerun'. Furthermore, they also consider returns exclusively from equity investor viewpoints (rather than a weighted cost approach).
- Data quality. The golden rule of financial modelling is 'rubbish in, rubbish out'. Or in other words, robust and meaningful assumptions help create robust and meaningful projections. That is why solid and comparative data around growth, margins and risk are so important to assertive value estimates. If estimates of startup multiples or margins are based around private transactions, sample sizes could be small and therefore noisy. Such private market data, unlike their public counterpart, is also not updated regularly so it's hard to keep track of temporal performance and return metrics. If public multiples are used, how do we account for illiquidity, country risk or different fundamentals? Can practitioners be sure multiples are like-for-like?

As a paper by global consultancy Mckinsey has stated: "these shorthand methods [used in the VC Method] can't account for the unique characteristics of each company in a fast-changing environment, and they provide little insight into what drives valuation" (Goedhart et al. 2015). This normative declaration gets to the crux of the argument of this chapter. The VC Method, and indeed other approaches such as Balanced Scorecards and qualitative checklists do not seek a priori to quantify value, but rather focus on pricing dynamics, and what the market is willing to absorb. In summary, price and value are not necessarily identical or even mutually exclusive concepts. They may even be fundamentally different.

5 Defining Economic Value

Economic theory tells us that the price of a good is the point where the curve of supply meets the curve of demand. Ceteris paribus, greater demand should mean higher prices. Demand meaning not only willing, but capable buyers. However, demand alone cannot impart price to a commodity. Value, on the other hand, "confers the explicit advantage on account of ownership of a given good whereas price depicts the sacrifice or outlay required (or expected) to acquire that object" (Aristotle ~350 BC). Value is then our opinion on the importance or utility of the good. Or as Warren Buffet said in one of this chapter's introductory quotes: "price is what you pay, value is what you get". But isn't value determined by the market and the market perceptions of that good? This is certainly a valid point and indeed IFRS and US GAAP accountancy standards all require market value to be the basis of fair value or in other words what an asset could sell for in an orderly transaction at the valuation date. That of course assumes that the market is "efficient", and that any given time it reflects all available information about the businesses that comprise it. The overarching idea is that stocks are optimally priced according to their inherent investment properties.

> Theoretically, the market value methodology should bring you to the same valuation as fundamental value. But, in practice, market value tends to be higher than fundamental value when markets are rising—and lower when they are falling. Emotion and momentum are among the factors leading markets to tend to overshoot on both the upside and the downside in the short term (PwC, 2022).

However, if value is based purely on market perceptions, when price diverges from value, and the basic expectation is that someone else will buy the asset for more than you paid, that is a trading version of the 'pass-the-parcel' game that could eventually lead to market bubble economics. By definition, a bubble denotes trade in an asset at a price that strongly deviates from the corresponding asset's intrinsic value.

Economic history, as always, can act as our guide to illustrate this concept. Was a tulip really "worth" over 10 times the average annual craftsman's salary during the spring of 1637? Or Cisco worth more than 150 times earnings at the height of the dot. com bubble? In an efficient market, price can stray only a certain amount from value before 'valuation gravity' kicks in and the market corrects. Over the last decade, we have seen a secular trend in technology stock value appreciation. Between 2011 and 2021 the Nasdaq Composite Index, heavily weighted toward the technology sector, increased by around 500% in value. And yet 2022 saw significant downside pressure on technology stocks. As is to be expected, the correction in public-markets is causing a rethink in private markets around the accuracy of sector valuations. Employing another Warren Buffet quote: 'it's only when the tide goes out that you learn who has been swimming naked'.

Volatility in startup valuations has been a key market theme over the last few years. Multiple leading institutional investors have written down their valuations in technology companies and down rounds have been increasing. The United States market watchdog, the Securities and Exchange Commission, has been investigating into mutual funds procedures for valuing startups since at least 2015, focusing on the procedures and tools companies are using to make sure the values are appropriate (Grind, 2015). As a side note, many of the headline "valuations" of startups are often based on complex and opaque structures of downside protections built into investment terms, such as ratchets and features, convertible notes and multiple share classes rather than fundamental estimates of enterprise value. In other words, many startups pay for their high valuations with lopsided terms that favour the latest investors. Public-company valuations are instantly dynamic whilst the valuations of private companies shift only during fundraising. As venture capitalist Keith Rabois of Khosla Ventures once stated, "private-market valuations are more of an art than a science. They are a negotiation, with the venture capitalist asking, 'At what price will somebody who doesn't need my money take my money?'"

Given that context, let us consider what finance professionals mean by 'value'. For millennia, scholars and theorists have tried to deduce how assets attained their 'value'. For Fogarty "the historical evolution of the value debate became locked into a centuries old dialectical conflict between the objective and subjective approaches". That is, our discussion is novel only in that this debate is now being applied to what constitutes startup value.

Plato argued that a man "should not attempt to raise the price, but simply ask the value" (Plato (~375 BC), implying that value is an absolute quality inherent in the asset. Intrinsic value then refers to the value of a company, stock, currency or product determined through fundamental analysis without reference to its market value. Value is a function of the capacity of an asset to deliver positive cash flows, after adjusting for risk (see below). In practice, value can only ever be a guide for the determination of price. The actual can be higher or lower, based on a range of both quantitative and qualitative factors.

In accounting terms, value is the monetary worth of an asset, business entity, goods sold, services rendered, or liability or obligation acquired. In economic terms, value is the sum of all the benefits and rights arising from ownership. According to traditional corporate financial theory, the value of a firm is the present value of expected future cash flows discounted back at a cost of capital that reflects both the sources and costs of financing (Damodaran, 1999). The idea of discounting future cash flows is one of the main principles of corporate finance. An asset's value is based on cash flow generation and risk. The Discounted Cash Flow (or DCF) analysis is the key framework that captures this idea.

As accounting criteria like net income do not accurately reflect economic value, cash flow is used instead. Even though a company's net income may be positive, its cash flow may be negative, which would be detrimental to the business's economics. At the end of the day, investors prefer cash rather than accounting profit (hence the expression: 'cash is king'). Simply put, cash flow, or more specifically Free Cash Flow (FCF) is the amount of money generated by a firm that can be given to investors or reinvested in the company after paying for costs, expenses, taxes and reinvestment needs. In other words, free cash flow is the cash left over after a company pays for its operating expenses (OpEx) and capital expenditures (CapEx).

Indeed, we use valuation models to assess if an asset is under or overvalued based on the assumption that markets are inefficient, and "mistakes" could have been made in ascertaining value. As Damodaran (1999) has argued, valuing an asset based on perceptions makes sense if the asset is a Picasso or Matisse but isn't an optimal guide for financial assets where value is based on cash flows.

Value—and robust assumptions—should therefore always be the anchor for price. Of course, these assumptions can and should change in response to internal and external events which will impact value estimates. One is reminded of the quote ascribed to Keynes in relation to facts and opinions ('When the facts change, I change my mind. What do you do, sir?'). Nevertheless, ceteris paribus a startup's price should be less volatile if based around fundamentals rather than merely "story telling" and market perceptions. Damodaran (2016b) has argued that venture capital is broadly speaking a "price" game rather than a "value" game. This distinction may surprise entrepreneurs and first-time founders. It is also not a normative judgement—after all venture capital routinely delivers higher returns than other asset classes. That being said, the distinction is also not just semantics. The essential point is where the numbers originate and how value is calculated or understood.

Valuation and pricing require different mindsets, data points and possess different objectives. It is then important to align which method is being used to evaluate startup potential. In general, when people talk about early-stage "valuation" they are often talking about pricing. We can value a company based on its intrinsic characteristics of returns, growth and risk or we can price it based on either similar asset transactions or via the VC method mapped out above. Pricing is essentially a play on the direction the asset's price will move going forward, relative to what the market can 'bear'. Apart from demand and supply dynamics, mood, momentum and company-specific analysis are all key factors. Damodaran (2016a, 2016b) brings some excellent insight around this point to help elucidate the mechanics (Fig. 1):

In summary, pricing and valuation are two different questions that can give you different answers. Pricing will tell you if an asset is cheap or expensive based on

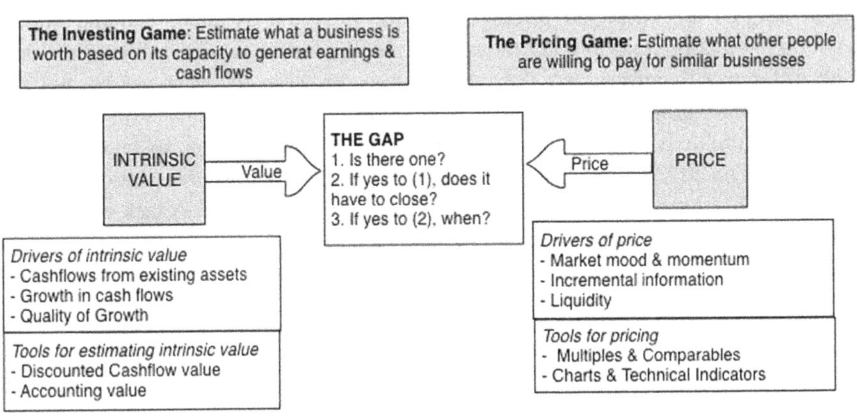

Fig. 1 Investing X Pricing. Source: Damodaran (2016a, 2016b)

what others are paying whilst valuation will tell you how much an asset is "worth". Or as Damodaran (ibid.) goes on to say:

> In public investing, I have argued that this plays out in whether you choose to play the value game (invest in assets where the price < value and hope that the market corrects) or the pricing game (where you trade assets, buying at a lower price and hoping to sell at a higher).

In venture capital, where "what good looks like" is a successful exit to another fund, larger company or even an IPO it makes sense to focus on pricing dynamics. That is after all how the industry works and is remunerated, at least over the early stage: estimating a "harvest value" and then work backwards to quantify funding levels and equity shares (whilst estimating expected dilution and future financing rounds). Ultimately, VCs are measured on their IRRs. If a company over the short-term does not generate positive cash flows, then that is less important for startup investing when the projected exit is generally only 3 to 5 years away and price is often based on top-line metrics. Invested capital is also expected to cover near-term burn rates. Valuation analysts focused on fundamental value concerns may be forgiven for seeing this, as mentioned, as a 'pass-the-parcel' analogy masquerading as valuation. In a sense it is. We have already described the skewed nature of venture capital returns which do not follow normal distributions, overall, they adhere more to power law curves (Mallaby, 2022) whereby a small percentage of firms capture a large percentage of industry returns. Essentially, that equates to investing in a diversified portfolio requiring high returns (and thus higher discount rates) to enhance the probability of success and one or two "bets" scaling successfully for unicorn success or merger & acquisitions (M&A) and IPO liquidity events.

Of course, from a purely intrinsic value perspective, it doesn't make sense to invest in an asset where there is little potential for value added in the form of risk-adjusted cash flows over a reasonable time frame. However, if an exit event is the priority, then trading, and thus asset pricing, may well do. Along the same lines, if the startup can survive on investor capital injections, then (potentially negative) annual cash flow until that liquidity event may indeed be a secondary consideration.

Even so, we need to be clear that most of the time, the numbers used to justify future returns are based on pricing (and not valuation as such) and the inbuilt assumption that prices will continue to move higher for those successful companies. The difference therefore isn't the methodology to estimate value per se, but the broad-based assumption that value is a function of how much investors can profit from a future exit. That approach can be construed more as speculating than investing. The 2022 correction in technology stocks shows, as have past corrections and no doubt future ones will do, that not always this is the case. A lack of focus on financial fundamentals can create fragility in valuation estimates and leave founders and investors even more dependent on market conditions.

6 Startup Valuation Solutions

The objective of this chapter is to suggest that fundamental valuation, despite the inherent uncertainties, can be straightforwardly employed for early-stage investment. Let us briefly illustrate how, by responding at a macro level to the earlier challenges to DCF valuation that were flagged up.

1. No operational history and financial data? Instead of looking at the past, we can look at the future and what the company could look like in steady state based on similar companies and conduct financial reverse engineering. What are average user growth rates and revenue paths? Average operational margins and reinvestment needs? This "triangulation" approach based around sector averages—usually publicly traded firms—also provide inbuilt constraints and "reality" checks. The use of statistical distributions around point-estimates can also help reduce forecast errors given the context where the past may not be able to act as a guide for future financial planning.
2. How to model growth phases? The above approach will help us project a "path to profitability" whereby the startup experiences acute growth before reaching maturity as per similar companies in either the same sector or those with similar characteristics. A three-stage DCF model helps us account for changes in growth, risk and market dynamics over time. Trend interpolations can then help us fit curves to model these phases.
3. High burn rates and negative cash flows? Again, we can rely on modelling the company reaching maturity which means that revenue growth and high investment should eventually lead to self-generating positive earnings, in line with market averages.
4. How can we forecast investment? Investment needs are one of the more difficult line items to forecast, especially separating investment from operational costs. How much capex as a percentage of revenue will be needed? How about inventory and working capital? One approach is to use sales/capital ratios or average capex and net working capital numbers and check for reasonableness against sector average returns on capital.
5. Lack of owner diversification? This is a complex—and controversial—discussion in the valuation profession (Patterson, 2016). The Capital Asset Pricing Model (CAPM)—the most widely used model to price expected returns—is based on the concept of the marginal investor having a diversified market portfolio (see for example Fama & French, 2004) and as such, only market risk will be rewarded and priced. In the broader private equity universe, this rarely occurs. We can therefore adjust for this lack of diversification via the Beta and adapt the traditional CAPM to ensure we capture the risk of the startup as a stand-alone asset or in other words encompass both systematic and non-systematic risk. We call this approach the Total Cost of Equity by utilizing the Total Beta, a concept introduced by Professor Damodaran and formalized by other practitioners (Butler, 2010) which seeks to capture total company risk. There are valid counter arguments to the use of Total Beta of course (e.g. Kadper, 2013) in the broad sense

that even startup founders can obtain market diversification. The author however would suggest that for most valuation practitioners, total beta better captures the risk associated with a privately held investment, as per Butler (2013) and thus for quantifying unsystematic risk for small and privately held companies, arguably more so than the standard practice of estimating and adding small-cap premiums to the WACC.

6. Lack of liquidity? All non-publicly traded assets are—to a greater or lesser degree—less liquid and marketable than public securities. Quantifying this "liquidity" discount is a major valuation challenge. Industry rules of thumb often range from 20 to 30%. However, we can look at restricted securities or value premiums pre and post IPO events to ascertain potential discounts. Damodaran (2008) has argued that: "In private company valuation, illiquidity is a constant theme. The illiquidity discount tends to be smaller for firms with higher revenues, decreases as the block offering decreases and is lower when earnings are positive". The central point then is that any discount is dynamic over time, sector, company performance and the composition of the cap-table, or the makeup of marginal investors in the startup. As the company scales, reaches profitability and raises capital from institutional investors, the estimated discount rate should, ceteris paribus, reduce over the forecast period or a smaller final discount be used to contemplate earlier, less liquid periods. It also seems reasonable to argue that due to greater venture capital transactions than private equity equivalents, startup illiquidity could actually be less than the average private company. Nonetheless, this can be assessed on a case-by-case basis.
7. Quantifying additional risk factors? Risk can be modelled. For standard failure risk, we can look at how many companies in the sector survive each year and adjust our cash flows or final equity values accordingly. These failure rates can also be adjusted upwards or downwards, using a qualitative scorecard approach, based on the startup's relative position *vis-à-vis* their competitors.
8. Founder optimism? As discussed, all valuations are biased, it just depends on how much and in what direction. But we should always seek to ground our growth, risk and reinvestment estimates in sector averages and similar company trajectories. Above all, we need to ensure that our numbers are "possible, plausible and probable" (Damodaran, 2014). The startup narrative therefore needs to be connected to the endogenous and exogenous value drivers. Qualitative factors can help with 'story-telling', a key component in private equity, M&A and public company growth and fundraising. A useful model, potentially first described by Cameron (2010) and adjusted by other authors, such as Deeb (2016), is called the "4-Ms", four important topics all starting with the letter M: market, model, management and momentum which assist in relative assessments.
9. Increased uncertainty in startups? We need to accept this uncertainty as a fact of life for startup modelling. We can though, use statistical tools to help us better understand this uncertainty by migrating from single and static point-estimates and use sensitivity analysis, weighted scenarios, regressions and Monte Carlo simulations to get a better handle on probability distributions, value drivers and

risks. Afterall, one is reminded of the mathematical axiom that the probability of a single event is zero on a continuous interval.

Now, of course, these steps will not necessarily lead to a more "accurate" estimate of economic value than other pricing approaches. They are likely to be "wrong" just as often, that's because there's no "right" answer, equity valuations are always imprecise. Uncertainty is a fact of life. Your author contends that there is no such thing as a "perfect" valuation. That being so, this chapter argues that they provide a more robust framework to quantify and keep track of startup potential across their life-cycle and help weave together numbers and narrative. That's not to say, pricing models do not have a key role to play. As always for all complex issues there is rarely a single answer. They can help validate value estimates and sometimes may indeed even provide a more realistic estimate of current value. And vice versa, we can use valuation to verify and understand current pricing scenarios. The "First Chicago method", for example, although outside the scope of this chapter, can also be a valuable tool here, as it can combine both multiples and DCF views and scenario analysis and in essence estimates the value of a company by taking the probability-weighted sum of three different valuation models (Achleitner & Lutz, 2008). Real Options and Monte Carlo analysis are also effective statistical tools to help model uncertainty, probabilities and result distributions. Real Options methods, help show "how a firm's value is affected by stochastic 'higher moments' behaviour", incorporating analysis of asymmetry and kurtosis (Milanesi & Pesce, 2013) as well but often work better when there is a level of exclusivity in the product offer. In summary, fundamental valuation techniques, such as DCF but also broader value approaches such as Adjusted Present Value (APV) and Economic Value Added (EVA), can be employed on any cash flow generating asset, even in cases where forward visibility is limited such as with early-stage growth companies. The same economic principles apply. A startup is, again, not a work of art to be admired but a financial asset.

These detailed approaches also provide an added dimension by allowing entrepreneurs to evaluate the potential of new business lines, quantify cost-cutting endeavours and assess the viability of new projects which "pricing" shortcuts cannot. A detailed view of the financials—the principal building block of valuation—can also facilitate future conversations around M&A synergies. Moreover, by linking financial planning to key value drivers—or in other words Value Based Management (VBM)—we can get a big picture view of the business, and to paraphrase Oscar Wilde, understand the value of everything. Even startups.

7 A Step-by-Step Practical Approach to Startup Valuation

Given this theoretical introduction, let us now map out at a practical level how we can apply these approaches and solutions to model and value early-stage companies. We note that this guide is not supposed to be an exhaustive manual, rather a simple

Table 1 Summarized P&L (LTM)

Metric	Value	Vertical analysis (value as a % of net revenue)
Gross revenue	3,750,000	
Revenue Churn[a]	150,000	4.0%
Net revenue	3,600,000	100.0%
(−) COGS	720,000	20.0%
(=) gross profit	2,880,000	80.0%
(−) OpEx	1,500,000	41.7%
(−) Staff expenses	2,000,000	55.6%
(=) Operating profit	−620,000	−17.2%
(−) Taxes	–	–

Source: Author's own creation

[a] Where revenue churn is the percentage of customer subscriptions that the business loses or retains existing contracts over a period of time

step-by-step approach to illustrate some key ideas and provide the key building blocks of a DCF valuation. Multiple complex technical points are overtly simplified. Ideally valuations should not be conducted in a vacuum but anchored to market numbers, company estimates, common sense and financial best practices. Researching the market and competitor performance though can require a great deal of time. Note as well, that this guide intends to be none-geography specific to enhance its adaptability for startups in different countries.

Let us begin. We are evaluating a small software-as-a-service (SaaS) startup that has been in business for just over 2 years but has previously been working on technological development and product beta tests. We have operating and accounting data for the last 12 months (LTM). The company provides a customer relationship management and BI software tool for SME's. The software adds new functionalities, user experience and helps solve customers' corporate pain points. The company is owned by a single founder, it's CEO, and has not previously conducted an external financing round. It is therefore debt free. Its startup capital was provided from the founder's savings, which in the LTM totalled two million in a none-specific currency unit (¤). The company has grown significantly over the past year and has already hit 3.75 million in gross revenue. It currently trades at an operating loss of 620 thousand (and thus a negative margin of 17.2%), financed by its initial investment (Table 1).

We also analyse the breakdown of revenue over the same period to better understand the company's unit economics. Here we focus on customer numbers, average ticket price and revenue churn. Note that for SaaS companies, it would also be important to dig deeper into broader KPI metrics including gross profit and cost per customer, CAC, LTV, net client churn, average customer lifetime and cost per feature et al. to provide greater robustness. Our startup currently has 250 customers, a monthly ticket price of 1250 and monthly recurring revenue (MRR) of 315.5 thousand, which with a revenue churn of 4.0% equates to a net annual recurring revenue (ARR) of 3.6 million (Table 2).

Table 2 Revenue model overview

Metric	LTM
Number of customers (x)	250
Average ticket (y)	1250
Monthly recurring revenue (x*y)	312,500
Annual recurring revenue (x*y*12)	3,750,000
Gross revenue churn (z)	4.0%
Net revenue (ARR*(1−z))	3,600,000

Source: Author's own creation

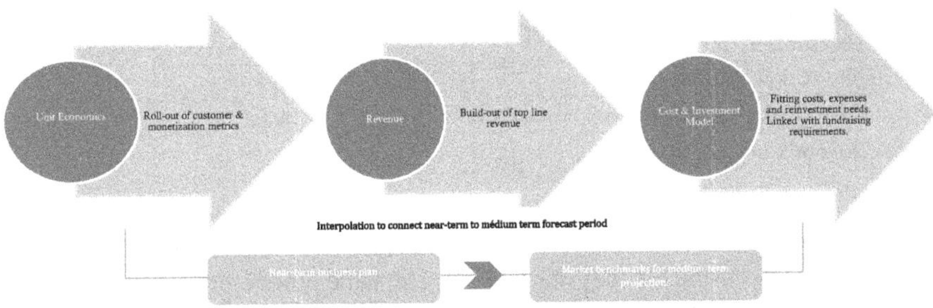

Fig. 2 Approach to startup financial projections. Source: Author's own creation

We now look to project future performance. We adopt a three-stage approach where we first estimate the customer/unit economics roll-out, build out revenue on top of these metrics before finally constructing the cost and investment structure necessary to hit these targets. At a practical level it would be commonplace to utilize as a foundation the startup's near-term (1 to 2 years) business plan and ensure that these targets make sense and are feasible before triangulating revenues, costs, expenses, and investments in a future steady state before interpolating backwards to our near-term financial plan and current performance. We summarize this approach as follows (Fig. 2):

Revenue is arguably the single most important financial metric for a startup to measure, especially at early-stage, and for valuation purposes serves as the 'top line' to drill down to profit and cash flow. It is after all a key foundation of your startups' narrative. A revenue-first mindset also helps set up the business to scale and puts it on the path to profitability. The first step in projecting startup performance is to benchmark the company against its competitors or sector—where data is available—including analysing their KPIs, growth trajectories and profitability.

We decide on a 5-year forecast period as our analysis suggests similar SaaS companies reach maturity over this timeframe. We break this down into an accelerated growth phase over the first 3 years and scale growth by year four and five. After the fifth year, we calculate terminal value.

We start with estimating customer numbers for future years. Our company's CEO is targeting 4000 customers by the end of year 5 when he expects the company to reach operational maturity. It is natural that founders opt for optimistic values, the valuation professionals' job is to validate and understand the feasibility of such

Table 3 Competitor benchmarking

Competitor	Number of customers—year 5
Company 1	5200
Company 2	4000
Company 3	3450
Company 4	4500
Company 5	3600
Average	4150
Standard deviation	714
Probability of hitting market average	70%
Downside estimate	3500
Probability of downside scenario	30%
Weighted average customer projection in year 5	3955

Source: Author's own creation

numbers. We first select our benchmark group of similar companies in the sector and check how many customers they reached over the same timeframe, which in our case was an average of 4150 (Table 3).

Based on our understanding of the relative strengths of the company, market dynamics and alignment with the company CEO, we utilize this average number as our 5-year target but to aim for the financial principle of conservativism we adopt probability theory whereby the expected forecast value is a generalization of the weighted average. This being so, we estimate a 70% probability of the startup reaching the market average, and a 30% probability of reaching a downside projection of 3500, which equates to a weighted average target of 3955 customers over 60 months (calculated as: 4150*70% + 3500*30%).

With this target we map out growth rates between current customer numbers and this future target. There are many ways this can be done. In this valuation, we opt to utilize a statistical sigmoid, or s-curve, to fit the trajectory between our points A (250 customers) and B (3955 customers). This logistic curve can help explain the evolution of a successful startup or product launch and many other phenomena in finance and even nature (Kucharavy & De Guio, 2007), progressively over time. The formula can be computed as follows:

$$\text{New Users in Period} = ((\text{users} * \text{contagion rate}) * ((\text{population} - \text{users})/\text{population}), 0)$$

Upon analysis, we define our contagion rate, or the growth rate new users are added expressed as a ratio of the current customer base, at 0.1 and a financial spreadsheet program helps facilitate the analysis and forward extrapolation over our forecast period (60 months) (Fig. 3 and Table 4).

In our simplified illustrative approach, we use the above model to calculate average customer numbers per year, which we round to the nearest integer. Nonetheless, the correct approach would be to calculate effective monthly customers to

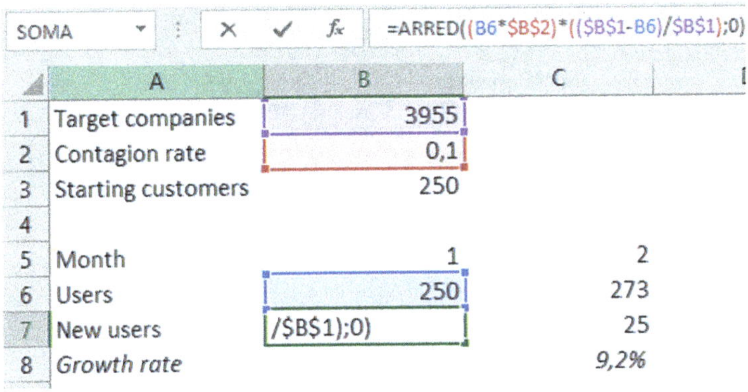

Fig. 3 Calculating model contagion rate

Table 4 Estimating customer numbers

Period	Average clients	Rounding	Growth rate (%)	Sector average
Current	250.0	–		
Next twelve months (NTM)	421.7	421	68.7%	75.0%
24 months	1081.8	1081	156.5%	150.0%
36 months	2163.1	2163	100.0%	105.0%
48 months	3180.0	3180	47.0%	50.0%
60 months	3754.9	3754	18.1%	20.0%
Total end of period	3955.5	3955		
Average annual growth rate %			78.1%	80.0%

Source: Author's own creation

quantify unit economics month by month. The table below shows our average customer forecast each year over the forecast period. We validate projected annual growth trajectory with the wider sector at the equivalent timeframe. With this insight we can see that our customer projections are therefore in line with the market: client growth is projected to grow at an average growth rate of 78.1% over 5 years whilst the market average over the same period is 80.0%. Having these growth targets can help a startup develop its commercial and marketing plan, based on accompanying key metrics such as efficiency of lead generation, Click-Through-Rates, conversion and Return-On-Ad Spend to deliver this expected performance.

We then estimate the second key component of revenue, the average ticket price. The CEO plans to maintain the basic SaaS package at the current price point of 1250 (in ¤) for the next 2 years but we will adjust by the monthly upsell percentage which over the forecast period is expected to reach the market average of 15% by year five from the current rate of 10% (in SaaS land, upselling means amplifying revenue streams and increasing the customer lifetime value through subscription upgrades and add-ons for existing customers). Note again that we are not projecting new product/service offerings (Table 5).

Table 5 Estimating average ticket

Period	Current monthly ticket	Management estimate (AT)	Upsell	Total average monthly ticket (AT * (1 + Upsell %))	Rounding
Current	1.250				
NTM		1.250	10%	1.375	$ 1.375
24 months		1.250	11%	1.391	$ 1.390
36 months		1.500	13%	1.688	$ 1.687
48 months		1.500	14%	1.706	$ 1.706
60 months		1.500	15%	1.725	$ 1.725

Source: Author's own creation

Table 6 Projecting unit economics

Year	Customer estimates (x)	Estimated ticket (y)	Gross ARR (xy*12)	Growth %
LTM			3,600,000	
NTM	421	1.375	6,946,500	93.0%
24 months	1081	1.390	18,031,080	159.6%
36 months	2163	1.687	43,787,772	142.8%
48 months	3180	1.706	65,100,960	48.7%
60 months	3754	1.725	77,707,800	19.4%
Average				92.7%
Average sector growth in the period				95.0%

Source: Author's own creation

Table 7 Estimating annual gross revenue churn

Period	Rate
Current	4.0%
NTM	5.0%
24 months	6.0%
36 months	7.0%
48 months	7.0%
60 months	7.0%

Source: Author's own creation

With our customer number forecasts and average ticket we can now forecast recurring revenue for the next 5 years. The company is expected to grow from 3.75 million to 77.7 million. The average growth rate over the period of 92.7% is again in line with our competitor group average over the same period of 95% during the equivalent growth phase (Table 6).

Based on our forecasts of customer numbers and average ticket we can now forecast recurring revenue for the next 5 years. To arrive at net revenue, we extrapolate our current annual revenue churn of 4.0% to the market average of 7.0% by year 5. The extrapolation formula is given as follows (Table 7):

Table 8 Reasonableness check market share

Year	Market share (%)
Company 1	10.0%
Company 2	4.5%
Company 3	12.5%
Company 4	7.5%
Company 5	14.0%
Total top 5	48.5%
Average	9.7%
Estimated market size in 5 years	800,000,000
Estimated company market share %	9.7%

Source: Author's own creation

$$\text{Period to forecast} = \text{Starting point} + \frac{\text{end point} - \text{starting point}}{\#\text{periods}}$$

We can exogenously check for the reasonableness of these revenue forecasts and how they convert into market share. Market data points to a future size of the specific SaaS segment at 800 million by year five. Based on our year 5 revenue forecast of 77.7 million we are implicitly assuming a future market share of 9.7%. We again look at our competitor group to analyse comparative market shares and see that our company's projected market share is in line with the market average. This compares to our relative qualitative analysis of the company's product offering and management team experience, who have had success with previous startups and exits. We also note that with the top five players being responsible for less than half of the market size, and thus fragmented, there is adequate space for the company to grow over the coming years, as per our estimates (Table 8).

With our top line revenue forecasts, we now look at broader financial performance. Here we again show the simplified profit-and-loss view of LTM results, together with a vertical analysis. However, we should always seek—where possible—to analyse each accounting line, at a micro level, to get a better handle on company financials, cost structure in addition to examine the company's Balance Sheet. With a gross profit margin of 80%, and total OpEx of 3.5 million the company currently has an operating loss of 620 thousand. With capital to cover these losses and healthy growth potential, the company is in a reasonably comfortable position. It is after all common for startups to have negative profitability over early periods as has been previously discussed (Table 9).

We now turn our attention to benchmarking expected performance against market metrics in the future. For cost of goods sold, we calculate that the market average of both our segment competitors and broader SaaS sector is a cost margin of 15.0% over revenue which we use as our target for year 5 and extrapolate from the 20.0% current margin in LTM. This cost reduction makes sense as startups in particular can maximize economies of scale as they grow. We then project out sales and marketing (S&M) expenses which consist of costs related to growth activities. We again turn to our benchmark group to understand the proportion of these expenses against

Table 9 Summarized P&L (LTM)

Metric	Value	Vertical analysis (%NR)
Gross revenue	3,750,000	
Revenue churn	150,000	4.0%
Net revenue	3,600,000	100.0%
(−) COGS	720,000	20.0%
(=) Gross profit	2,880,000	80.0%
(−) Total OpEx	3,500,000	97.2%
(−) Sales & marketing	500,000	13.9%
(−) Staff expenses	2,000,000	55.6%
(−) General & Administrative	1,000,000	27.8%
(=) Operating profit	−620,000	−17.2%
(−) Taxes	–	–
(=) NOPAT	$−620,000	−17.2%

Source: Author's own creation

Table 10 Average COGS margin %

Competitor	%
Company 1	12.5%
Company 2	15.5%
Company 3	18.5%
Company 4	12.5%
Company 5	16.0%
Average	15.0%
Broader SaaS segment	15.0%

Source: Author's own creation

revenues. To forecast outwards, we utilize a simple regression analysis, which is a statistical method used for the estimation of relationships between a dependent variable and one or more independent variables, in our case revenue and S&M expenses. The formula for simple linear regression is given as:

$$Y = mX + b$$

where Y is the dependent variable, X is the predictor, or independent variable, whilst m and b are the estimated coefficient and intercept respectively.

We can use the results of the regression to assess fit and statistical significance of our variables, and thus projection model. There is a good statistical fit. To illustrate how we use this regression, the S&M estimated value for 36 months, 9.2 M, is computed as the intercept plus the revenue estimate for the same period multiplied by the regression coefficient, or −471,492 + 43.8 M*0.22. Over the forecast period S&M estimates are in line with the market average of around 20.0% as a per cent of revenue, but with our calculation, are more assertively scaled with revenue growth (Tables 10 and 11).

Table 11 Competitor sales & marketing expenses

Competitor	ARR	S&M	S&M/Revenue (%)
Company 1	35,496,425	7,099,285	20.0%
Company 2	15,973,391	3,034,944	19.0%
Company 3	44,370,531	8,208,548	18.5%
Company 4	26,622,319	5,856,910	22.0%
Company 5	49,694,995	11,429,849	23.0%
Average	34,431,532	7,058,464	20.5%
Regression analysis results			
R-squared	93.7%		
F statistic	0.0015		
Interception	−471,492		
Coefficient	0.22		

Source: Author's own creation

With our sector churn, cost averages and regression analytics around S&M expenses, we plot out our key assumptions to year 5, as per the below tables. For staff and general expenses, we consider the 2-year estimation horizon based on the company's business plan but to contemplate potential uncertainty around the deterministic estimates we utilize the Program Evaluation Review Technique (PERT) weighted average, a beta distribution, which can be described by the following formula:

$$\text{PERT estimate} = (\text{Upside estimate} + (\text{Basecase estimate} \times 4) + \text{downside estimate})/6$$

For these expense lines through years 3–5 we project how they should grow over the forecast period based on company estimates, our understanding of our infrastructure capacity and market benchmarking. In a more detailed analysis, these growth estimates could also be weighted based on probability distributions. As a general principal, the level of detail should reduce as we become more uncertain about a firm's future prospects. Afterall, we do not have crystal balls and less can certainly be more, especially if we utilize scenarios, statistical tools and targets based on valid market aggregates and ranges.

We project staff expenses to grow between 50.0% and 15.0% between years 3 and 5 and general expenses to grow between 70.0% and 10.0%, scaling down as the company reaches its mature phase. We note that it is important to validate our staff expense against sector Revenue/Headcount or FTE metrics (full-time employment). To compute taxes, we use a marginal tax rate of 20% to cover all required taxes as per local fiscal regulations. For internal consistency we note three additional points. To simply our analyses in this example, we will not consider potential gains from net operating losses that could be carried forward to be used on future positive earnings, nor will we consider deprecation expenses (and thus in our example we implicitly assume a net-capex position). Lastly, we will not contemplate potential

Table 12 Forecast assumptions (%)

Metric	LTM	NTM	24 months	36 months	48 months	60 months
Revenue churn %	4.0%	5.0%	6.0%	7.0%	7.0%	7.0%
COGS %	20.0%	25.0%	20.0%	18.3%	16.7%	15.0%
(−) Sales & marketing	Via *regression equation*					
(−) Staff expenses				50%	35%	15%
(−) General & administrative				70.0%	25.0%	10.0%
Taxes			20.0%	20.0%	20.0%	20.0%

Source: Author's own creation

Table 13 Forecast assumptions ($)

Accounting Line	NTM	24 months
(−) Staff expenses (PERT)	3,500,000	5,750,000
Upside estimate	4,000,000	6,500,000
Company estimate	3,562,500	5,675,000
Downside estimate	2,750,000	5,300,000
(−) General & Administrative (PERT)	2,500,000	4,000,000
Upside estimate	2,750,000	4,400,000
Company estimate	2,487,500	3,975,000
Downside estimate	2,300,000	3,700,000

Source: Author's own creation

lags in costs and expenses whereby they would be anticipated to deliver future revenue. In other words, spending on marketing and staff costs could be required in one period to deliver revenue over future periods (Tables 12 and 13).

With these assumptions we can compute a 5-year P&L forecast. Gross revenue is expected to reach 77.7 million by year 5, gross profit at 61.4 million and operating profit at 22 million. Net Operating Profit after tax is estimated at 17 million. Looking at our path to profitability, we note that both costs and OpEx fall as a proportion of revenue over the forecast period and that subsequently operating margin increases. To validate our projections for reasonableness, we analyse key metrics against market averages in steady state by year 5. We find that S&M and G&A expenses over time converge with the comparable market, as does the operating profit margin. Again, in order to simplify our model, we note that none of these OpEx lines contemplates fixed asset development. Software capitalization is when a company recognizes software development costs internally as an asset (in other words, investment is capitalized on a company's balance sheet instead of being expensed). To capitalize is to record the cost of developing a bespoke software as an expenditure spread over its lifetime. It is also important that our financial models are based on local and international accounting standards (Tables 14 and 15).

We now estimate free cash flow. In our example we will utilize Free Cash Flow to Firm (or "FCFF") which represents the cash generated by the core operations of a company that belongs to all providers of capital, and thus, debt and equity. Although

Table 14 Forecast P&L

Metric	LTM	NTM	24 months	36 months	48 months	60 months
Gross revenue	$ 3,750,000	$ 6,946,500	$ 18,031,080	$ 43,787,772	$ 65,100,960	$77,707,800
Revenue churn	$150,000	$347,325	$ 1,081,865	$3,065,144	$4,557,067	$5,439,546
Net revenue	$ 3,600,000	$ 6,599,175	$ 16,949,215	$ 40,722,628	$ 60,543,893	$72,268,254
(−) COGS	$720,000	$ 1,649,794	$ 3,389,843	$7,465,815	$ 10,090,649	$10,840,238
COGS margin %	*20.0%*	*25.0%*	*20.0%*	*18.3%*	*16.7%*	*15.0%*
(=) Gross profit	$ 2,880,000	$ 4,949,381	$ 13,559,372	$ 33,256,813	$ 50,453,244	$61,428,016
Gross margin %	*80.0%*	*75.0%*	*80.0%*	*81.7%*	*83.3%*	*85.0%*
(−) Total OpEx	$ 3,500,000	$ 7,075,000	$ 13,139,843	$ 24,601,089	$ 34,015,686	$39,389,862
OpEx %	*97.2%*	*107.2%*	*77.5%*	*60.4%*	*56.2%*	*54.5%*
(−) Sales & marketing	500,000	$ 1,075,000	$ 3,389,843	$9,176,089	$ 13,871,936	$16,649,549
(−) Staff expenses	$ 2,000,000	$ 3,500,000	$ 5,750,000	$8,625,000	$ 11,643,750	$13,390,313
(−) General & Administrative	$ 1,000,000	$ 2,500,000	$ 4,000,000	$6,800,000	$8,500,000	$9,350,000
(=) Operating profit	$−620,000	−2,125,619	419,529	8,655,724	16,437,558	22,038,154
Operating margin %	*−17.2%*	*−32.2%*	*2.5%*	*21.3%*	*27.1%*	*30.5%*
(−) Taxes	–	–	83,906	1,731,145	3,287,512	4,407,631
(=) NOPAT	$−620,000	−2,125,619	335,623	6,924,579	13,150,046	17,630,523

Source: Author's own creation

Table 15 Reasonable check P&L assumptions (fifth year)

Metric	Company result	Market average
Sales & marketing % ARR	21.4%	20.5%
General & administrative % ARR	12.0%	14.0%
Operating margin %	30.5%	30.0%

Source: Author's own creation

the key focus for startups is usually on the equity component, here we align the common enterprise approach widely used in investment banking.

To get to cash flow from the P&L we need to project reinvestment needs which are a function of net working capital and capex. Startups have different investment profiles than traditional companies. There is greater focus on R&D, data centres/servers, marketing, team equipment and even bringing forward operating expenses such as hiring. Growth is not free and as such reinvestment is an essential step in calculating valuation. Investment impacts cash flow negatively and may create the need for capital injections from investors to keep the company afloat (the latter point could affect the startups cap-table through dilution).

To calculate reinvestment, we have three main options: (a) use company estimates or again look at the market via (b) average NWC and capex investments as a percentage of sales, profit or operational cycle or (c) compute based on sales/capital ratios. We decide to utilize the latter approach. The sales to capital ratio tells us how efficiently a company can transform capital into revenue dollars. To estimate how much our company needs to reinvest to reach its future revenue targets we use the sector average sales/capital ratio of 5.25 over the first 5-year cycle of competitor companies. Depending on the data available we could also use dynamic, or annual, targets that evolve over the initial life-cycle, as firms may need to invest more over the first few years. The calculation for NTM is given as the delta between incremental revenue from LTM to NTM divided by this ratio (or ~ 3.2 M/5.25 = ~609 K). For the NTM period we add an explicit additional capex forecast based on short-term CEO estimates to ensure conservatism. We again note that in this example we are not lagging our reinvestment. Reinvestment as a percentage of sales should be higher during a high growth phase and scale down as the company matures (in our model reinvestment as a proportion of revenue declines from 16.0% to 3.1% over the projection period). With our NOPAT and reinvestment estimates we can now compute free cash flow. We also note that, generally, profit becomes positive before cash flows do; the latter are impacted by the needs to invest for future growth. This may not always be the case for SaaS companies who can often 'front-load' annual subscriptions. In our model, we simplify by assuming a basic monthly subscription model with zero setup or cancellation costs (which would impact revenue). Free Cash Flow is projected to become positive from the third year and in year 5 is estimated at 15.2 million. Negative cash flows mean that additional capital will be needed, either by existing equity holders or new investors.

Table 16 Estimating free cash flow

Metric	LTM	NTM	24 months	36 months	48 months	60 months
Gross revenue	3,750,000	6,946,500	18,031,080	43,787,772	65,100,960	77,707,800
Delta		3,196,500	11,084,580	25,756,692	21,313,188	12,606,840
Sales/capital ratio		5.25	5.25	5.25	5.25	5.25
Reinvestment		608,857	2,111,349	4,906,037	4,059,655	2,401,303
NOPAT		–2,125,619	335,623	6,924,579	13,150,046	17,630,523
Reinvestment (via sales/capital)		608,857	2,111,349	4,906,037	4,059,655	2,401,303
Additional capex		500,000				
Total reinvestment		1,108,857	2,111,349	4,906,037	4,059,655	2,401,303
Reinvestment %GR		*16.0%*	*11.7%*	*11.2%*	*6.2%*	*3.1%*
FCFF		–3,234,476	–1,775,725	2,018,543	9,090,391	15,229,220
FCFF %GR		*–46.6%*	*–9.8%*	*4.6%*	*14.0%*	*19.6%*

Source: Author's own creation

We summarize the formula to arrive at Free Cash Flow to the Firm (FCFF), noting again that in our simplified example we are not contemplating depreciation expenses (Table 16):

$$\text{FCFF} = \text{EBIT} * (1 - \text{tax}) - \text{Variation in NWC} - \text{Capex} + \text{Depreciation/Amortization}$$

We then conduct additional consistency checks. We first look at the much commented "SaaS rule of 40" which states that to be sustainable software companies combined revenue growth rate and profit/cash flow margin should equal or exceed 40%. On a 2-year rolling average, we see that this is indeed the case for our company. We also seek to validate our investment estimates to verify if the company is investing enough. We calculate the capital invested each year, starting with the initial capital investment of two million made by the founder/CEO, adding to this amount the reinvestment each year to arrive at the cumulated capital invested at the end of each forecast period. We compare this to the sector average by year 5 of 35.0% and see that our return on capital estimate is in line over a similar time frame. Returns on capital should decline in perpetuity (or even be equal to costs of capital). We note that in this step, it is important to analyse the issue of software capitalization previously discussed, and other accounting principles, to ensure a like-for-like approach for how much firms are reinvesting when we look at return on capital metrics (Tables 17 and 18).

Table 17 SaaS rule of 40

Metric	LTM	NTM	24 months	36 months	48 months	60 months
Gross revenue	$ 3,750,000	$ 6,946,500	$ 18,031,080	$ 43,787,772	$ 65,100,960	$ 77,707,800
Growth % (x)		85.2%	159.6%	142.8%	48.7%	19.4%
FCFF %GR (y)		*−46.6%*	*−9.8%*	*4.6%*	*14.0%*	*19.6%*
Total (x + y)		*38.7%*	*149.7%*	*147.5%*	*62.6%*	*39.0%*
2 year rolling average			94.2%	148.6%	105.0%	50.8%

Source: Author's own creation

Table 18 Reasonable check cost of capital (fifth year)

Metric	LTM	NTM	24 months	36 months	48 months	60 months
NOPAT	− 620,000	− 2,125,619	335,623	6,924,579	13,150,046	17,630,523
Total reinvestment	2,000,000	1,108,857	2,111,349	4,906,037	4,059,655	2,401,303
Capital invested at beginning of year		2,000,000	3,108,857	5,220,206	10,126,242	14,185,897
Capital invested at year end		3,108,857	5,220,206	10,126,242	14,185,897	16,587,200
Average invested capital		2,554,429	4,164,531	7,673,224	12,156,070	15,386,549
Return on capital (NOPAT/ average invested capital)	−31.0%	−83.2%	8.1%	90.2%	108.2%	114.6%
Accumulated average		−57.1%	−35.4%	−4.0%	18.5%	34.5%
Market average—after first 5 years						35.0%

Source: Author's own creation

We now calculate the cost of equity (COE) to be able to discount our future cash flow. We use the CAPM model, whose basic formula is given as follows:

$$\text{COE} = \text{Risk Free Rate} + \text{Beta} * \text{Equity Risk Premium}$$

We calculate three phases of COE to align up with our cash flows. The inputs should evolve over time based on market perspectives. We utilize the zero-coupon 5-year treasury bond for the first two periods and a 30-year bond yield in perpetuity.

Table 19 Long term cash flow estimation

Metric	Perpetuity
Long-term growth rate	3.0%
NOPAT in perpetuity	18,159,439
Cost of equity in perpetuity	11.50%
Fundamental reinvestment rate (=long term growth rate / COE)	26.09%
FCFF in perpetuity (NOPAT—reinvestment)	13,422,194

Source: Author's own creation

We calculate the Equity Risk Premium—the expected returns of the stock market over the risk-free rate—via implied premiums. We utilize and maintain stable the average unlevered beta over the forecast periods but adjust for the estimated lack of diversification of the marginal investor via the total beta approach. This diversification factor, measured at first by correlation, is projected to reduce over time as the company grows, raises qualified investment and aims to eventually IPO. In other words, in perpetuity, we expect the company's cost of capital to approximate publicly traded firms in the sector. The cost of capital over the first 3 years, at 32.0% is similar to the lower range VC IR's (equivalent to a COCR of 4× over 5 years) and declines to 11.5% in perpetuity. The company's founder is confident that debt will not be required over the forecast period, and we also note that the average debt/equity (D/E) ratio for our competitor group is nevertheless minimal, at 0.02. Note that without computing debt capital, including in perpetuity, our COE based on CAPM is equal to WACC. We simplify in our example but in reality, depending on sector debt/equity ratios and company capital requirements, it could make sense to include debt acquisition in future growth phases, perhaps scaling to market D/E averages.

Note as well, that although we adopt a geography neutral approach, for emerging market valuations, additional inputs around country risk premiums (both credit and equity factors) and inflation differentials to estimate local currency rates may be required. Moreover, we argue that the total beta approach, and posterior liquidity and broader risk adjustments, can better contemplate the specific factors targeted in the often used small-cap-premium. Adding an implied liquidity premium to WACC could also be an optimal route to quantify additional risk, but the author is mindful that the cost of capital should not serve as a panacea for all risk factors which could be better calculated via adjustments directly to cash flow.

We then utilize the fundamental reinvestment equation to calculate reinvestment needs in perpetuity where we essentially incorporate the endogenous relationship between growth and value. Based on long-term growth rate of 3.0% and COE of 11.5% in perpetuity we calculate that the company will need to reinvest 26.09% (3.0%/11.5%) of its post-tax operating income. We calculate this as =NOPAT* (1–26.09%) or ~4.7 M. Thus, NOPAT less reinvestment is equal to our FCFF estimate for the perpetuity phase (Table 19).

We can now compute our valuation estimate based on our 5-year and perpetual free cash flow projections. We utilize the mid-year convention for cash flow discounting and assume super-economic growth in perpetuity—where the company delivers returns over the cost of capital threshold—based on our analysis of the sector. Put simply, we assume that over the long-term ROC is above COC (as mentioned previously, this may not universally be the case).

We utilize the standard formulas to discount cash flow over the two periods:

$$EV = \sum_{i=1}^{n} FCFFi/(1 + WACC)^{i} + TV/(1 + WACC)n$$

$$TV = FCFFn + 1/(WACC - g) = FCFFn * (1 + g)/(WACC - g)$$

where:

EV = Enterprise Value
FCFF = Free Cash Flow to Firm
COE = Cost of Equity
TV = Terminal Value (or perpetuity value)
WACC = Weighted Average Cost of Capital (note again that in our example WACC = COE and thus the two terms are used interchangeably).

Enterprise Value is computed at 73.2 million (7.9 M plus 65.3 M), which without debt is equal to Equity Value. Note that much of the economic value is based on value generation in perpetuity. We make two further adjustments directly to EV. Based on market averages of failure rates in the SaaS sector we calculate the probability of survival over the first 3 years before the company scales and raises qualified investment, strengthening its financial and operational viability. We quantify this at 27.5%. This execution or operational risk could also be calculated year-by-year on revenue or cash flows, discounting these metrics over the period. Alternatively, this risk could also be calculated in distinct scenarios, or in other words one DCF model contemplating zero operational risk in delivering our forecasts and another contemplating such risk and potential cash flows from reduced performance scenarios or even asset liquidation. In this example, we adopt a fixed discount to our EV estimates to simplify.

We then estimate a liquidity discount which, as discussed, can be calculated via fixed discounts, bid-stock regressions, pre-IPO transactions, directly in the COE or deltas between similar public and private transactions. In our example, we use a fixed discount of 15%. According to Damodaran (2017), "In both cases, the discount is estimated to be the difference between the market price of the liquid asset and the observed transaction price of the illiquid asset". We apply these adjustments of 27.5% and 15% respectively to arrive at a total adjusted EV value of 45 million (computed as =73.2 million*(1–27.5%)*(1–15%)) (Table 20).

To validate our DCF valuation we compute relative valuation based on current revenue and also via the Venture Capital approach. Note that we utilize the same financial projections. The first step is estimating the market multiple. We can select from public equity valuations or M&A transactions. In our case we use the average revenue multiple from the sector and for consistency also discount for liquidity

Table 20 Estimating economic value

Metric	NTM	24 months	36 months	48 months	60 months	FCFF in perpetuity
FCFF	–3,234,476	–1,775,725	2,018,543	9,090,391	15,229,220	13,422,194
Discount period (mid-cap convention)	0.5	1.5	2.5	3.5	4.5	4.5
Cost of equity	32.00%	32.00%	32.00%	21.69%	21.69%	11.50%
DCF (=CF/(1 + COE)^period)	–2,815,250	–1,170,887	1,008,331	4,573,216	6,296,088	
Perpetuity (=CF/(COE-long term growth)						157,908,164
Value 1–5 years (forecast period, x)	7,891,498					
Present value of perpetuity (y)	65,282,642					
Enterprise value (x + y)	73,174,141					
Failure risk (1–3 years)	27.5%					
Total liquidity discount	15.0%					
Adjusted valuation	45,093,564					
Net debt	–					
Equity value	45,093,564					

Source: Author's own creation

(as the multiple here is based on publicly traded firms). We could also calculate as well other multiples such as GMV (gross merchandise value) or profit as previously discussed. In our example the adjusted revenue multiple of 6.6× (or 7.75× * (1–15%)), calculated then as the gross multiple less the impact of liquidity, which we will adopt for both the Relative and VC approaches. In some cases, a premium could be calculated over the public market multiple if there is enhanced demand for M&A activity in the sector by larger strategic or financial players. In general, we must be attentive to potential adjustments to the multiple—and potential discounts—based on market timing and the firms' characteristics at the time of valuation (for instance adopting a higher multiple for early-stage higher growth). For simplicity we use the projected market revenue multiple of similar publicly traded firms which we

Table 21 Relative valuation

Metric	Values
Revenue—NTM	6,946,500
Revenue multiple	6.6
Enterprise value (=revenue*multiple)	45,760,069
Net debt	–
Equity value	45,760,069

Source: Author's own creation

Table 22 Venture capital method

Metric	Values
Revenue—year 5	77,707,800
Adjusted revenue multiple	6.6
Future EV (=revenue*multiple)	511,900,133
Venture capital IRR (=COCR of 10× in 5 years)	58.0%
Period (same as DCF model)	4.5
Enterprise value (VF/(1 + 58%^4.5))	65,347,406
Failure risk (1–3 years)	27.5%
Adjusted valuation (EV*(1–27.5%))	47,376,869
Total reinvestment—2 years (same as DCF model)	3,220,206
Pre-money valuation (post money—investment)	44,156,663

Source: Author's own creation

find is also in line with the 3-year average. We need to define if we are using total revenue or recurring revenue multiples. We opt to use publicly market multiples in the broader SaaS market, as the firm intends on conducting an IPO or be acquired by a large public company—hence our lower COE in perpetuity—over the long-term allied to the fact that public valuations are much more liquid, updated and less impacted by noise than private transactions, which are often harder to research. To enhance comparability with public firms, we could also conduct regression analysis on the key value drivers, such as size, growth, profitability and risk which impact publicly trade multiples to better understand if we can generate assertive multiple estimates. Note that for current relative valuation we do not compute survival risk as we are analysing current or near-term performance. Also note that for the Venture Capital Method we adopt a more aggressive target IRR as our discount rate to better align with VC pricing, as previously discussed. After this analysis we see that the results are in broadly line with our DCF valuation, with current relative valuation estimated at 45.8 million and VC pricing at 44.2 million. Relative valuations, especially those based on revenue metrics, are often higher than DCF results, because they do not contemplate negative cash flows during early years. And yet as mentioned the key focus on early-stage companies has traditionally been revenue generation. The average valuation is computed as 44.0 million. In summary then, the relative and VC method estimates go a certain way to validate our principal valuation via DCF (Tables 21, 22 and 23).

Table 23 Startup valuation results summary (EV)

Approach	Value
Discounted cash flow	45,093,564
Relative valuation—NTM revenue	45,760,069
Venture capital method (pre-money)	44,156,663
Valuation average	45,003,432
Valuation median	45,093,564
Standard deviation	805,494

Source: Author's own creation

Table 24 DCF value scenarios

Approach	Values	Estimated probability
PERT method		
Discounted cash flow—basecase	45,093,564	
Discounted cash flow—upside	52,759,470	
Discounted cash flow—downside	33,820,173	
PERT DCF (=(52.8 + (45.1*4) + 33.8)/6	44,492,317	
Weighted probability method		
Discounted cash flow—basecase	45,093,564	55%
Discounted cash flow—upside	52,759,470	25%
Discounted cash flow—downside	33,820,173	20%
Probability weighted average DCF (=px1 + px2 + px3)	44,755,363	100%

Source: Author's own creation

We could also have calculated distinct DCF valuation scenarios and then compute weighted average of the results via PERT or probability estimates to get a better handle on potential results scenarios or even conducted Monte Carlo analysis around our projection and volatility intervals. We illustrate the weighted scenario approach via both PERT and probability analysis in the below table without specifically calculating such scenarios in this chapter. It may also be necessary to compute additional discounts and adjustments for key person discounts—what happens if the funder leaves?—and for equity claims and control differences, however for simplicity we will close out our valuation here (Table 24).

8 Conclusion

As we have described throughout this chapter, early-stage valuation is certainly a technical and practical challenge. Understanding new market dynamics and trends, dealing with a lack of historic performance or even zero accounting numbers, aligning up reasonable and consistent financial projections with founders and researching adequate market benchmarks. From a valuation perspective however, it is an increasingly important segment and can be rewarding. The biggest challenge is often between quantifying price and value. However, in this chapter paper, we have discussed conceptual challenges and subsequent solutions and through simple examples have developed some laid-out principles and approaches that can be used to compute more robust valuation estimates for start-ups via the traditional DCF method. The author contends that a DCF valuation is not just a spreadsheet but a quantitative answer to the question of 'what drives value'. These approaches help us to quantify uncertainty, risk at both the qualitative and quantitative levels and ultimately value start-ups, helping to ensure alignment between value and price, to paraphrase our Oscar Wile quote at the beginning of this chapter.

References

Achleitner, A.-K., & Lutz, E. (2008). First Chicago method: Alternative approach to valuing innovative start-ups in the context of venture capital financing rounds. *Betriebswirtschaftliche Forschung und Praxis (BFuP), 57*(4), 333–347. Available at: https://ssrn.com/abstract=1133004

Aristotle. (~350BC). Metaphysics, Book 7, Chapter 7 in McKeon, "The basic works of Aristotle", Modern Library Classics.

Bank for International Settlements. (2015). Basel Committee on Banking Supervision. Guidance on credit risk and accounting for expected credit losses. Available at: https://www.bis.org/bcbs/publ/d350.pdf

Blank, S. (2020). *The startup owner's manual: The step-by-step guide for building a great company*. John Wiley & Sons.

Buffet, W. (1966). Letter to partners, 20 January 1966, in Warren Buffett Speaks (2007). Available at:https://www.oxfordreference.com/view/10.1093/acref/9780191866692.001.0001/q-oro-ed6-00012078

Butler, P. (2010). Beta or total beta? The answer depends on the "company" it keeps. *The Valuation Journal, The National Association of Authorized Romanian Valuers, 5*(1), 4–21.

Butler, P. J. (2013). The total beta debate: A real-world analysis. *Business Valuation Review, 32*(4), 227.

Cambridge Associates. (2022). US venture capital report, index and selected benchmark statistics Q222. Available at:https://www.cambridgeassociates.com/private-investment-benchmarks/

Cameron, C. (2010). *The 4 M's of attracting investors to your startup*. Readwrite. Available at: https://readwrite.com/the-4-ms-of-attracting-investors-to-your-startup/

Damodaran, A. (1999). Financing innovations and capital structure choices. *Journal of Applied Corporate Finance, 12*, 28–39.

Damodaran, A. (2008). *The cost of illiquidity*. Stern Business School, New York University. https://pages.stern.nyu.edu/~adamodar/pdfiles/country/illiquidity.pdf

Damodaran, A. (2009). *Valuing financial service firms*. Stern Business School, New York University. http://people.stern.nyu.edu/adamodar/pdfiles/papers/finfirm09.pdf

Damodaran, A. (2012). The dark side of valuation: A Jedi guide to valuing difficult-to-value companies. Cited in https://pages.stern.nyu.edu/~adamodar/pdfiles/country/darkside2012full.pdf

Damodaran, A. (2014). *Possible, plausible and probable: Big markets and networking effects*. Stern Business School, New York University. Available at: https://aswathdamodaran.blogspot.com/2014/07/possible-plausible-and-probable-big.html

Damodaran, A. (2016a). *Valuation: Art, science, craft, magic?* Stern Business School, New York University. Available at: https://pages.stern.nyu.edu/~adamodar/pdfiles/country/valalldayEurope2016.pdf

Damodaran, A. (2016b). Venture Capital: It is a pricing, not a value, game! Available at: https://aswathdamodaran.blogspot.com/2016/10/venture-capital-it-is-pricing-not-value.html

Damodaran, A. (2017). *Consider the effect of illiquidity* (p. 143). Stern Business School, New York University. Available at: https://pages.stern.nyu.edu/~adamodar/podcasts/valUGspr17/session22.pdf

Deeb, G. (2016). *Before investing in a startup, study their 4 M's*. Forbes. Available at:https://www.forbes.com/sites/georgedeeb/2016/03/16/before-investing-in-a-startup-study-their-4-ms/?sh=2c4d057d6b7f

Deshpande, G. (2020). Q4 2020 - Addressing venture capital valuation challenges. *Eisner Amper*. Available at:https://www.eisneramper.com/venture-capital-valuation-ea-1220/

Ernst & Young. (2014). EY Global CRS. Credit valuation adjustments for derivative contracts (IFRS 13). Available at: https://www.ey.com/en_gl/ifrs-technical-resources/credit-valuation-adjustments-for-derivative-contract-ifrs-13

Fama, E. F., & French, K. R. (2004). The capital asset pricing model: Theory and evidence. *The Journal of Economic Perspectives, 18*(3), 25–46.

Fisk, P. (2019). The $3 trillion global start-up economy . . . where and how start-up ecosystems are driving new growth. Available at:https://www.peterfisk.com/2019/10/the-3billion-global-start-up-economy-where-and-how-start-up-ecosystems-are-driving-new-growth/

Goedhart, M., Koller, T., & Wessels, D. (2015). *Valuation: Measuring and managing the value of companies* (6th ed.). John Wiley & Sons. Available at: "Valuing high-tech companies": https://www.mckinsey.com/capabilities/strategy-and-corporate-finance/our-insights/valuing-high-tech-companies

Gompers, P., Kaplan, S. N., & Mukharlyamov, V. (2015). *What do private equity firms say they do?* Harvard Business School, Working Paper 15-081. Available at: https://www.hbs.edu/ris/Publication%20Files/15-081_9baffe73-8ec2-404f-9d62-ee0d825ca5b5.pdf

Grant Thornton. (2015). Private equity valuations: Best practices and pitfalls. *A Grant Thornton LLP 2015 survey*, p. 7. Available at:https://www.grantthornton.pr/globalassets/1.-member-firms/puerto-rico/advisory-articles/private-equity-valuations%2D%2D-best-practice-and-pitfalls.pdf

Grind, K. (2015). Regulators probe mutual funds' startup valuations. Market Watch. Available at: https://www.marketwatch.com/story/regulators-probe-mutual-funds-startup-valuations-2015-11-18

Invesco. (2020). The case for venture capital. *The Invesco White Paper Series*. Available at: https://apinstitutional.invesco.com/dam/jcr:1f35880c-bdf9-42ea-8afe-ab69b85bc7a4/The%20Case%20for%20Venture%20Capital.pdf

Kadper, L. J. (2013). Total beta—A capital market analysis with empirical evidence. *Business Valuation Review, 32*(4), 212–226.

Kolvereid, L. (2006, November). New business start-up and subsequent entry into self-employment. *Journal of Business Venturing, 21*(6), 866–885.

Kucharavy, D., & De Guio, R. (2007). Application of S-shaped curves. In *TRIZ Future Conference 2007*. LGECO - Design Engineering Laboratory, INSA Strasbourg - Graduate School of Science and Technology.

Lapidus, B. (2017). *What's the difference between valuation and pricing of assets? FP&A should know*. Association for Financial Professionals. Available at: https://www.afponline.org/ideas-inspiration/topics/articles/Details/what's-the-difference-between-valuation-and-pricing-of-assets-fp-a-should-know#:~:text=Thus%2C%20intrinsic%20value%20can%20be,whatever%20the%20market%20will%20bear

Levine, S. (2007). Venture capital returns are more skewed than people realize. *Times of Entrepreneurship*. Available at: https://timesofe.com/vc-fund-returns-are-more-skewed-than-you-think/

Lewis, A. (2022). *Early 2022 data shows a drop in median IRR across funds*. Carta Blog. Available at: https://carta.com/blog/irr-q2-2022/

Mallaby, S. (2022). *The power law: Venture capital and the making of the new future*. Penguin Press.

Milanesi, G., & Pesce, G. (2013). Technology-based startup valuation using real options with edgeworth expansion. *Journal of International Financial & Accounting, 1, 54*, –61.

Montani, D., Gervasio, D., & Pulcini, A. (2020). Startup company valuation: The state of art and future trends. *International Business Research Archives, 13*(9), 31.

Moore, C. (2021). *Venture pulse Q421*. KPMG Private Enterprise.

Nolting, C., Višić, I., & Singh, S. (2021). Deutsch Bank Wealth Management. Growth and the COVID-19 pandemic. Available at: https://deutschewealth.com/en/insights/investing-insights/asset-class-insights/venture-capital-investing-closer-look/venture-capital-trends.html

OECD. (2021). Measuring job creation by start-ups and young firms. Available at: https://www.oecd.org/industry/dynemp.htm

Patel, N. (2015). 90% of startups fail: Here's what you need to know about the 10%. Available at: https://www.forbes.com/sites/neilpatel/2015/01/16/90-of-startups-will-fail-heres-what-you-need-to-know-about-the-10/?sh=543ad7066792

Patterson, A. (2016). Diversification, valuation & total beta. Available at: https://www.linkedin.com/pulse/diversification-valuation-total-beta-adam-paul-patterson/

Plato, Book XI, (~375BC). Persons of the dialogue: An Athenian speaker. Available at: http://www.classicallibrary.org/plato/dialogues/laws/book11.htm.

Priceonomics. (2018). How old are the $1B+ Tech Unicorn Companies?. Available at: https://priceonomics.com/how-old-are-the-s1b-tech-unicorn-companies/

PWC. (2022). PWC: Private equity's fair value judgement. Available at: https://viewpoint.pwc.com/dt/us/en/pwc/accounting_guides/fair_value_measureme/fair_value_measureme__9_US/chapter_4_concepts_u_US/42_definition_of_fai_US.html

Sahlman, W. A., & Scherlis, D. R. (1987). A method for valuing high risk, long term investments: The 'Venture Capital Method'. Available at: https://www.hbs.edu/faculty/Pages/item.aspx?num=6515

Sander, P., & Kõomägi, M. (2007). Valuation of private companies by Estonian private equity and venture capitalists. *Baltic Journal of Management, 2*(1), 6–19. https://doi.org/10.1108/17465260710720219

Siegel, J., & Amit, R. (2013). How VCs are driving a tech-valuation 'feeding frenzy'. *Knowledge at Wharton Staff*. Available at: https://knowledge.wharton.upenn.edu/article/how-vcs-are-driving-a-tech-valuation-feeding-frenzy/#:~:text=%E2%80%9CIt's%20difficult%20to%20value%20companies,finance%20professor%20at%20Wharton%2C%20concurs

StepStone. (2022). VC's unique ability to navigate volatile markets. Available at: https://www.stepstonegroup.com/news-insights/vcs-unique-ability-to-navigate-volatile-markets/

Tschirhart, J., O'Brien, J., Moise, M., & Yang, E. (2007). *Federal Reserve Board, Finance and economics discussion series, divisions of Research & Statistics and monetary affairs*. Bank Commercial Loan Fair Value Practices. Available at: https://www.federalreserve.gov/pubs/feds/2007/200729/200729pap.pdf

Wilde, O. (1892). Lady Windermere's fan. *Bloomsbury, Act, III*, 340.

Hierarchical and Segmented Approaches to Startup Valuation: What They Are. Why They Work

Max Berre

1 Introduction

Why do startups in some cities attract higher valuations than those elsewhere in the country, can be observed in California vis-à-vis New York or Boston? In Europe, similar things are true both within and among European markets. Not only do valuation differentials exist between Paris and Lyon, for example, but also between Paris and London. This is the case even when the startups in question are based in similarly-sized economies, share the same industries and many of the same investors?

Although classical economic theory describes that valuations are based on revenues, growth-rates, and risk-adjusted discount rates, the valuation of startups often proves the exception to the rule. Fundamentally, due to their short histories, difficult-to estimate intangible assets, and opaque details, startups are notoriously difficult to value, a phenomenon described in detail by Damodaran (2009). Over the past 30 years, scholars have been attempting to formalize both valuation and valuation-drivers within startup markets.

Whereas overall published knowledge is both sparse and dispersed across several academic fields, Bellavitis et al. (2017) and Budhwar et al. (2022) agree on the importance of focusing on startup valuations as a key avenue of research, with potential to tie together, financial, entrepreneurial, and macroeconomic microeconomic theoretical perspectives, thereby forging dynamic and innovative insights.

Traditionally, startup valuation has relied on classical data-driven approaches. These include the discounted cashflow (DCF) valuation approach, which takes

This article has been sponsored by the Partners of the "Finance for innovation" Chair at Audencia Business School. Special thanks is accorded to Benjamin Le Pendeven.

M. Berre (✉)
Université de Lyon, Lyon, France
e-mail: maxens.berre@univ-lyon3.fr; mberre@audencia.com

S. Derindere Köseoğlu (ed.), *A Practical Guide for Startup Valuation*, Contributions to Finance and Accounting, https://doi.org/10.1007/978-3-031-35291-1_5

several forms, which discount different measures of firm income, revenue, or cashflow, using the appropriate risk-adjusted discount-rate. Approaches include the free-cashflow-to-firm (FCFF) approach, which discounts sales revenues, discounting them with the weighted average cost of capital, as well as the free-cashflow-to-equity (FCFE) approach, which discounts net income by the cost of equity as per the capital asset pricing model (CAPM), and the Gordon Growth Model, which mitigates discount-rates in accordance with revenue growth-rates. A prominent alternate valuation approach in startup markets is the relative-valuation approach, which is described in detail by Damodaran (2010). Mechanically, this approach relies on estimating valuation as a multiple of the firm's balance sheet components, income statement components, or cashflow statement components. Valuation multiples, in turn, are driven by averages drawn from comparable firms, which typically share the same contextual market conditions, such as industry, business model, and economic geography. Empirically speaking, regression-based approaches supplement these models by controlling for contextual market-conditions (Berre & Le Pendeven, 2022). These range from macroeconomic conditions to industry-level market-dynamics, to relevant entrepreneur characteristics. Lastly, more niche-case approaches such as the real options valuation approach depend on the accurate and detailed estimation of risk and volatility.

In contrast to the classical valuation approaches which dominate peer-review empirical finance literature, industry practitioners often use summation-based segmented models to estimate valuation in a piecemeal fashion (Ernst & Young., 2020). While this approach is widespread due to its straightforward architectural simplicity, its use is often confined to specific industry-sectors or economic geography, rather than being applied in a more general fashion. Mechanically, this approach relies on attaching estimate values to a wide range of valuation factors, which are ultimately aggregated to produce the final valuation estimate. Overall, economic theory holds that these diverse approaches to valuation are equivalent to one another (Fama, 1970; 1991; Damodaran, 2002).

Fundamentally, this is intended to constitute a detailed, in-depth how-to guide describing methods and approaches for the application of segmented hierarchical startup-valuation, as well as how they can be applied using existing data and regression-models. The rest of the study proceeds as follows: The subsequent section describes segmented startup-valuation models, describing their emergence and use in both practitioner-focused grey-literature, as well as in peer-review literature. Following this, section three describes how segmented models can be made hierarchical, as well as explaining how this modelling-approach can be used for microtargeting-based valuation approaches. Lastly, a discussion and conclusion section describes why segmented, hierarchical, and microtargeting valuation approaches are used by industry practitioners, by describing their added-value vis-à-vis more traditional valuation-approaches.

2 Segmented Models: How Contextual Factors Play a Role

A useful theoretical approach used by a minority of scholars is that of the scorecard-based approach. A critical advantage of scorecard valuation-approaches is the ability to incorporate qualitative, geographic, sectoral or other types of categorical valuation-factors in several ways ranging from the non-financial and deal-characteristics prevalent in a given municipal or industry-specific sectoral ecosystem, to the role of national-level or macroeconomic and macrofinancial market-conditions. This approach is capable of shedding light into valuation even as detailed related economic and financial information is missing, scare, or unevenly available.

Segmented valuation-methods are modular and relatively straightforward valuation-approaches based on summation of key valuation-determinants, firm-characteristics, market-conditions, and deal-conditions developed mainly by industry practitioners. One principle advantage of this type of approach is that valuation can be modelled, captured, and contextualized via the inclusion of specific categorical information, which could be general, highly-specific, and/or be organized as joint, combined, or hierarchical segmentation.

2.1 *Practitioners: Segmented Models in Markets*

In industry, scorecard approaches are typically employed by business angels. Industry-emergent techniques for scorecard valuation include Berkus (2016) and Payne (2011). Perhaps the most well-established segmented startup valuation model is the Scorecard Model, outlined by Payne (2011). Outlined in Table 1, the scorecard model segments the impact of valuation factors into management team, target market, competitive environment, and need for further funding. Valuation is established via summation of the model's component factors:

Alternatively, another well-known alternative to Payne's Scorecard model can be found in the Berkus Model (EY, 2020). Outlined in Fig. 1, the Berkus model segments valuation into component risks. Valuation is established via summation.

2.2 *Segmented Models in Peer Review*

While the segmented valuation-model approach has made considerable traction among industry practitioners, within published economic literature, this same concept appears in the form of summation-based valuation models, such as the models outlined in Hand (2005) and Sievers et al. (2013). Concretely, Eq. (1) for example, outlines the Hand (2005) startup-valuation model, describing the model's component deterministic valuation-factors as being segmented into financial-statement data

Table 1 Abbreviated Payne Scorecard Model

Weighting		**Impact on Startup Valuation**
0–30%	*Impact*	*Merits of the entrepreneur and management team*
	+	Several years of overall business experience
	++	Experience in the industry in question
	+++	Experience as a CEO
	++	Experience as a COO, CFO, CTO
	+	Experience as a product manager
	−	Experience in technology or sales
	−−	No business notable experience
		Size of the opportunity
0–25%	*Impact*	*Scale of target market (measurable in total sales)*
	−−	<$50 million
	+	$100 million
	++	>$100 million impact
		5-year potential for revenues of target company
	−−	<$20 million
	++	$20 to $50 million – >$100 million (will require substantial additional funds)
0–15%	**Impact**	**Strength of the product and intellectual property**
	−−−	Not well defined, still seeking or developing a prototype
	0	Well defined, prototype looks interesting
	++	Good feedback from potential customers
	+++	Orders or early sales from customers
0–10%	**Impact**	**Competitive environment**
		Strength of competitors in this marketplace
	−−	Dominated by a single large player
	−	Dominated by several players
	++	Fractured, many small players
	Impact	**Strength of competing products landscape**
	−−	Competing products are excellent
	++	Competing products are weak
0–10%	**Impact**	**Marketing/sales/partners**
		Impact sales channels, sales and marketing partners
	−−−	Haven't even discussed sales channels
	++	Key beta testers have been identified and contacted
	+++	Channels secure, customers placed trial orders
	−−	Firm has not identified partners
	++	Key partners in place
0–5%		**Need for additional rounds of funding**
	+++	None
	0	Another angel round needed.
	−−	Need venture capital

Source: Ernst and Young (2020)

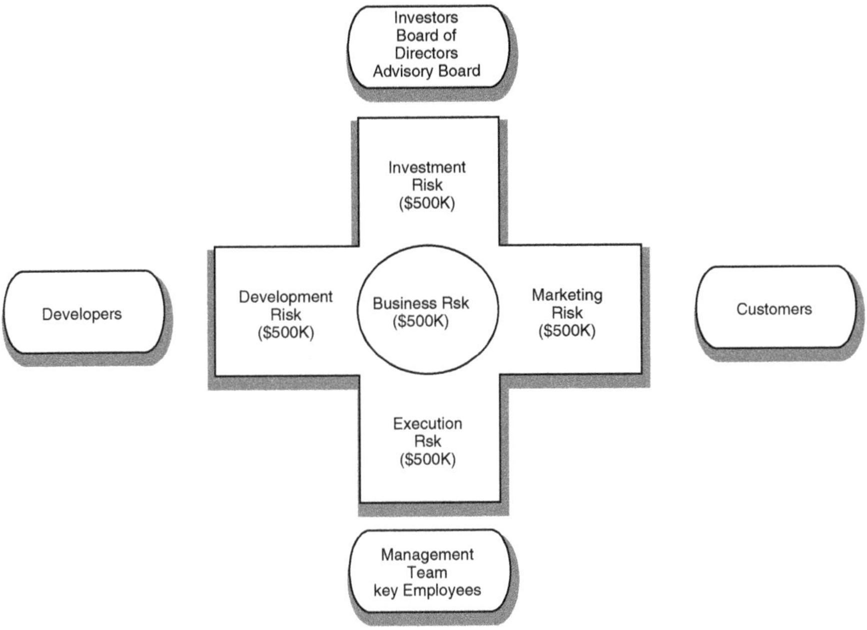

Fig. 1 Berkus model for startup valuation. Source: Berkus (2016)

such as Net Income, Cashflows, and Assets on one hand, and operational and industry-related data on the other.

Equation 1: Hand (2005) Summation-based Segmented Valuation Model

$$\begin{aligned} &\text{HAND (2005)}\ Ln(\text{Pre} - \text{Money Valuation}) \\ &= \sum \Theta_b Ln(\text{Financial Statement Data}_{bik}) \\ &+ \sum \Upsilon_c Ln(\text{NonFinancial Statement information}_{cik}) + \varepsilon_{ik} \end{aligned} \tag{1}$$

Meanwhile, Eq. (2), outlines another prominent segmented startup-valuation model developed by Sievers et al. (2013) as a summation-based valuation model, assigning valuation based on summation of financial, and non-financial firm-attributes, as well as deal-characteristics along with their relevant valuation-coefficients. Essentially, whereas Hand (2005) segments valuation-factors into accounting and non-accounting data, with each segment contributing to valuation with its own coefficient, Sievers et al. (2013)'s model uses similar model-architecture to segment valuation-factors into financial factors such as risks and revenues drawn from a firm's income statement and balance sheet, and assets and capital-invested drawn from balance-sheet data, as well as, non-financial factors such as industry-level data and firm-level operational data, and deal characteristics such as investor-syndication, and shareholder-agreement clauses such as tag-along, redemption, and ratchet clauses in the venture capital investment deal.

Equation 2: Sievers et al. (2013) Summation-based Segmented Valuation Model

$$\log(\text{Valuation}_{it}) = \sum \Phi\text{Non} - \text{financial}_{it} + \sum \Delta\text{Financial}_{it} + \sum \Psi\text{Deal Characteristics}_{it} \quad (2)$$

As with the Payne and Berkus valuation models, the startup's valuation is established via summation of the established segments. What these model-models have a tendency to overlook, however, are interactions and hierarchies among the identified valuation-determinants. Architecturally speaking, a closely-related alternate functional form for segmented valuation-models can be elaborated as multistage valuation approaches, such as the Startup-Valuation Meta-Model described by Berre and Le Pendeven (2022) outlined in Eq. (3). This would account for phases, hierarchies and interactions among valuation-determinants. Formally this can be expressed as:

Equation 3: Berre and Le Pendeven (2022) Startup Valuation Meta-Model[1]

$$\text{Pre} - \text{Money Valuation} = f\left(\left(\left(\sum \text{Start} - \text{Up Value}\right)\sum \text{Deal Value}\right)\sum \text{Deal Valuation}\right) \quad (3)$$

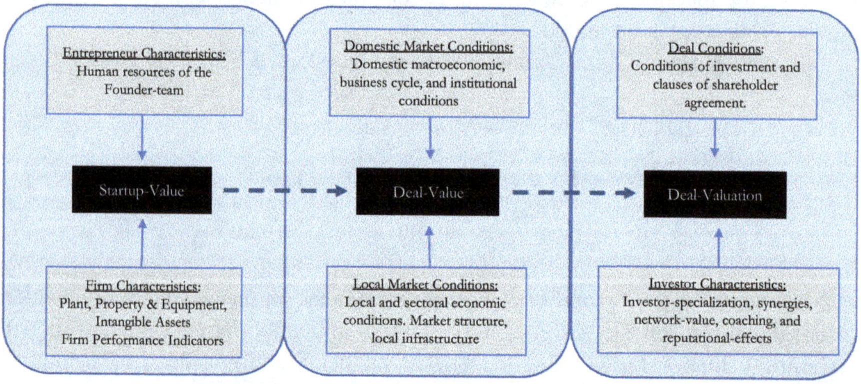

[1] Source: Berre and Le Pendeven (2022).

3 From Segmentation to Microtargeting: The Hierarchical Modelling Approach

The recent emergence of ever-developing machine learning techniques has led to increasing methodological sophistication of scorecard approaches, as predictive techniques incorporating to categorical, geo-spatial, and qualitative data become widespread.

Mechanically, microtargeting by means of data mining is described by Murray and Scime (2010), as the process of inductively analyzing data to find patterns, fault-lines and relationships among the data, on the basis of trends related to both descriptive and numerical characteristics, such as average age, number of family members, and geographic area, via construction of decision trees. Essentially, this is an analytical technique which is both explanatory and predictive, and is useful for both variable predictions, as well as to provide key insight regarding structure, segmentation, and interrelationships among data.

This approach provides insight into how specifically the outcome variable's value is dependent on the model's deterministic factors, with each identifiable fault-line constituting a segment of individual observations. Data-mining-driven microtargeting, for instance, allows scorecard-based valuation-approaches to incorporate categorical and qualitative data to a potentially-extreme degree of detail, given the added explanatory power of variable-hierarchy for accurately modelling relationships among explanatory variables.

Functionally speaking, a hierarchically-structured valuation-model that would result from a microtargeting approach can be expressed via a staged valuation approach, such as the Startup-Valuation Meta-Model described in Eq. (2). Figure 2

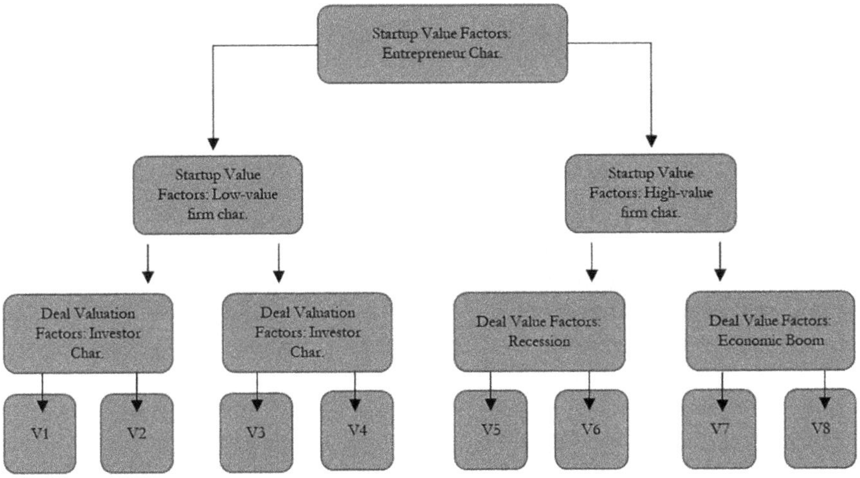

Fig. 2 Decision tree based on the Berre-Le Pendeven Meta-Model. Source: Author's own creation

displays the form that the Berre-Le Pendeven Meta-Model would adopt as a hierarchical decision tree.

3.1 Why Hierarchical Approaches Work: Regression Trees and Random Forests

In principle, CART-based microtargeting using regression-trees and random forests, which aggregate multiple regression-trees can reorganize valuation-determinant data such that several key insights emerge, which regression-model approaches might otherwise overlook, as well as by more rudimentary valuation-models. First, data consisting of qualitative and categorical valuation-factors such as sectoral geographic, and business-model details, which carry the potential information-density are taken into account. Second, CART trees demonstrate areas and subsections of the data where given valuation-determinants might be more or less-influential, granting very precise insight into how valuation emerges. Third, fundamental fault-lines are displayed as values along which branches diverge.

For the purposes of startup valuation, the informational content of descriptive and categorical characteristics such as geographic location, industry-sector, and business model are often overlooked, despite the general possibility that these characteristics might possess explanatory power equivalent to multiple associated numerical variables. Meanwhile, incorporation of descriptive categorical-characteristics into econometric models via use of fixed-effects suffers losses in explanatory-power as the number of descriptive-characteristics increases, whereas decision-tree-based microtargeting approaches see improved accuracy as the number of categorical and qualitative characteristics increases. Consequently, a principal advantage of this approach is that it is viable to microtarget valuation by including ever small-scale and highly-specific categorical information.

3.2 Functional Form of Segmented Valuation Models

Krzywinski and Altman (2017) explain that CART approaches do not develop a prediction equation per se. Instead, data are partitioned along the predictor axes into subsets with homogeneous values of the dependent variable. This process is represented by a decision tree that can be used to make predictions from new observations. Accordingly, several functional-form options exist mathematically, which can be used both in markets and in research settings. Furthermore, the combination and/or selective use of these can be a useful way to investigate valuation in detail, as this may serve to maximize nuances.

3.2.1 Log Transformation

Given that log transformation makes multiplication and summation interchangeable, the log transformation of regression-variables can architecturally simplify regression models and mathematical relationships for purposes of empirical specification (Neter, 1990; Wooldridge, 2010; Benoit, 2011), while also lending themselves to model-flexibility. Since log transformation brings the product property of logarithms to bear, it is possible to represent any model in its entirety in the form of a summation-model for intermediate-stage purposes, given the interchangeability of logarithm summation and multiplication (Miller et al., 2010). Strictly-speaking, this means that intermediate-stage functional forms can be functionally reoriented both in terms of variable-order and in terms of interaction-effects.

Furthermore, log transformation serves to "flatten" relationships, by restraining outlier impact on dataset means and medians. Given that regression trees and partitioning methods outputs in general can be sensitive to the influence of dependent-variable outliers (Khan et al., 2013), outlier-flattening has potential to add substantial explanatory power to regression-tree models, as log-transformation reduces estimation-issues associated with percentage changes from baseline (Keene, 1995), while maximizing data-scale flattening (Ribeiro-Oliveira et al., 2018). Additionally, variables showing skewed distribution can be made symmetric using log transformation (Keene, 1995).

On the other hand, given that log transformation also impacts multiplicative models and functional-forms (Benoit, 2011), the specific architectural shape of the valuation-function becomes unclear, as multiplication, summation, ratios, and other functional form elements inherent in the valuation-function might also become unclear.

In order to reach a viable comprehensive valuation-outlook, it is necessary to examine the model's log-transformed expression alongside its original version, whose functional-form would capture both variable-order and possible interaction terms in detail. In order to establish a decision-tree model however, both variable-order and relative variable-importance need to be established. Fundamentally, regression variable-interaction terms can convey how specifically a model's explanatory variables interact with one another. This serves to indicate variable-position within the model's decision tree, granting more complete and wholistic insights on the details of relationship's causality structure.

3.2.2 Regression-Model Equations

Functionally speaking, regression-model equations consist of a summation of key-variables, modified by factor-coefficients, alongside constant and error-terms. Structurally, this model-architecture lends itself to near-direct transposition of segmented valuation approaches, as well as the approximation of most classically-established firm-valuation models, ranging from the discounted cashflow valuation (DCF) approach, to a multiples-valuation approach.

Since regression-model equations are structured as summation functions, with each term consisting of a variable and a coefficient, valuations can ultimately be expressed as a summation of variables, coefficients, constants, the error-term. For instance, a discounted-revenue-based valuation model approach, incorporating similar information to a discounted cashflow valuation (DCF), can approximate an FCFE approach by regressing startup-valuation on historic and current Net Income figures, thereby capturing both the free cashflow and its growth rate, as well as risk factors which would drive the discount rate, which can be expressed as a combination of the risk-free-rate and the applicable equity risk-premium described in the CAPM model. This is captured in Eq. (4).

Equation 4: Regression model simulating free cashflow to equity

$$\begin{aligned}\text{Valuation}_{it} = {} & \alpha_i + \beta_1(\text{Net Income}_{it}) + \beta_2\,(\text{Net Income}_{it-n}) \\ & + \beta_3(\text{Risk} - \text{Free rate}_t) + \beta_4(\text{Risk} - \text{Premium}_{it}) + u_{it}\end{aligned} \quad (4)$$

On the other hand, multiples-valuation approaches, whose widespread popularity flows, in part, from its simplicity and ease with which these models communicate valuation, as well as its ability to convey the market's current mood (Damodaran, 2002), might seek to estimate valuation from as few as one valuation-determinant factor drawn from a firm's income-statement, balance-sheet, or cashflow-statement. This however, comes at the cost of sample-selection, as choosing the sample of relative firms and assets against which to compare, can lead to standardization (or assumption of standardization) of variables outside the valuation-model. According to Damodaran (2002), the most widespread multiples-valuation model is the price/sales ratio, describing valuation as a function of a firm's sales revenues, as demonstrated in Eq. (5):

Equation 5: Price-to-Sales Ratio

$$\text{Price} - \text{to} - \text{Sales} = \frac{\text{Firm's Total Market Share} - \text{Price}}{\text{Sales Revnue}} \quad (5)$$

Equation (6) expresses the valuation-impact of the Price-to-Sales ratio as an Ordinary-Least-Squares (OLS) regression-model, given by the parameter Sales Revenue, while β estimates the Price-to-Sales ratio. Outside factors ranging from quantitative valuation-factors such as total assets, borrowing costs, or CAPEX, to qualitative valuation factors such as factors driven by sector, industry-specialization, or economic geography can be sample-selected to be constant, or assumed to be constant across the sample.

Equation 6: Price-to-Sales Ratio as an OLS regression model

$$\text{Valuation}_i = \alpha_c + \beta_c(\text{Sales Revnue}_i) + u_i \quad (6)$$

Beyond the use of regression-model functional-form to convey or approximate classical firm-valuation models such as DCF or relative-valuation, the OLS regression-model's functional form can also be used for summation-based segmented valuation-models, such as those outlined in Eqs. (1) and (2). Moreover, this is even the case for models using hierarchical approaches, such as Mahmoud et al. (2022) express random forest regressions using OLS-style regression-model equations, simulating the summation-based segmented functional form used by OLS models.

3.2.3 Decision Tree Functional-Forms

Architecturally speaking, there is flexibility regarding the function forms that decision tree model could adopt considering the possible contexts in which they can be deployed, the factors enumerated, and both their relative and hierarchical explanatory power. While Krzywinski and Altman (2017) describe that the CART approach does not express a prediction equation (i.e., that this approach is backwards-looking), CART regression tree results can be used to extend and modify segmented models. Fundamentally, the regression tree model's outputs make possible two architecturally-viable segmentation approaches.

For example, Mahmoud et al. (2022) express random forest regression models using OLS-style regression-model equations, simulating the summation-based functional-form of an OLS model. This modelling-approach has the advantage of capturing the overall directionality of the causal relationship to be tested empirically, without specifically precluding existence of complex model functional-forms.

Comparative Model Explanatory Power and Goodness-of-Fit

In general, the accuracy of regression tree models can be compared to those of equivalently-constructed regression models on the basis of their goodness-of-fit indicators. Whereas explanatory power of OLS and panel-data regression models are evaluated on the basis of R^2, Sandeep (2014) and Firmin (2021) outline that regression trees are to be evaluated on the basis of $1 - R^2$ root-mean-squared-error.

Weighted Summation Segmentation

First, a rudimentary "back-of-the-envelope" segmentation-approach can essentially be considered a modification of Payne's Scorecard Model, which includes model-weighting to its segmentation approach. In order to obtain regression-tree model-weights from the CART approach, it would suffice to examine variable-importance. While CART variable-importance outputs can aggregate to a maximum of 100%, as demonstrated by Table 2, aggregate variable importance model-outputs might also add to less than 100%. While for CART models whose aggregate variable

Table 2 OLS Model Using DCF Valuation-Factors and Business Model

OLS Coefficients:	Estimate	Std. Error	T-Value	P-Value
(intercept)	5.10E+08	6.12E+07	8.326	5.02E-16***
Revenue	4.27E-01	6.20E-02	6.892	1.31E-11***
Country-risk-premium	−4.19E+09	3.18E+09	−1.317	0.188
Sectoral-Beta	−4.61E+08	6.02E+07	−7.664	6.67E-14***
B2B & C	3.06E+08	6.13E+07	4.995	7.59E-07***
B2B	9.80E+07	6.25E+07	1.569	0.117
B2C	6.37E+08	6.28E+07	10.138	<2.00E-16***
*** p < 0.01, ** p < 0.05, *p < 0.1				
Residual standard error:	546,900,000 on 644 degrees of freedom			
Multiple R-squared: 0.279		Adjusted R-squared: 0.273		
F-statistic: 41.6 on 6 and 644 DF, p-value: <2.20E-16				

Source: Berre (2022)

importance adds to 100%, it suffices to assign the model's variable-importance figures as valuation-model factor-coefficients, for instances in which variable-importance outputs aggregate to less than 100%, factor-importance proportionalities would need to be calculated as an initial step, as outlined in Eq. (7):

Equation 7: CART Variable-Importance Proportionality

$$\text{Factor} - \text{Coefficient}_i = \sigma_i(X)_i = \frac{\text{Variable Importance}_i}{\sum_n^i \text{Variable Importance}_i} \tag{7}$$

Fundamentally, this approach is highly useful as a generally applicable model-approach, giving rise to a Payne-style scorecard valuation model, which can be applied in a general fashion to startup markets as a whole. For example, a Payne-style scorecard valuation-model, involving valuation-weights, which could be constructed on the basis of firm characteristics and market characteristics, can take the form outlined in Eq. (8), combining the FCFE valuation-factors with Payne valuation-factors outlined in Table 1:

Equation 8: Weighted Summation Segmentation Regression-Tree Valuation Model Simulating FCFE Valuation Model

$$\begin{aligned}\text{Valuation}_i = \; & \sigma_1\beta_1(\text{Net Income}_i) + \sigma_2\beta_2(\text{Risk} - \text{Free rate}_i) \\ & + \sigma_3\beta_3(\text{Risk} - \text{Prem.}_i) + \sigma_4\beta_4(\text{Size of Opportunity}_i) \\ & + \sigma_5\beta_5(\text{Competitive Environ.}_i) + \sigma_6\beta_6(IP_i)\end{aligned} \tag{8}$$

Where:

$\sum_{i=1}^{n} \sigma_i = 1$ but where $\sum_{i=1}^{n} \widehat{\sigma}_i \leq 1$.

Here, σ expresses the weighting-coefficient n of startup i (e.g., the scale of Net Income's impact on startup i's valuation), driven by the factor's variable-importance drawn from the CART output, while β expresses the impact-coefficient n of startup i (e.g., country-level sovereign risk-premium is a valuation-determinant known to be a constituent of DCF-model discount-rates (Damodaran, 2009), and as such, can be expected to have negative valuation-impact and therefore a negative β-coefficient).

Mechanically, this functional-form approach can work for either continuous valuation-determinants drawn from firm-level financial statements (i.e., Net Income, Fixed Assets, etc.) and from market indicators (i.e., business-cycle and macroeconomic indicators), or for binary factors such as intellectual-property or entrepreneur-characteristics. Moreover, because CART regressions segregate data into dichotomous subsets along the predictor axes, categorical variables (i.e., classifications such as sectoral-industry classifications and business-model classifications, as well as variables linked to economic geography such as cities, counties, inclusions in regional-clusters) which are treated as binary-variables.

Hierarchical Ordinal Segmentation

A second approach could be called the hierarchical ordinal segmentation approach. Given that the data are partitioned along predictor axes into subsets with homogeneous dependent-variable values, a more complex hierarchical modelling-approach is also possible. The basis of this model-approach begins with adoption of terminal-node average-values as ω-coefficients. These can be multiplied by the regression-tree's branch-thresholds and branch-conditions, as follows:

$$\omega_i(X)_j \left(\begin{cases} = 1 & \text{if } X \text{ is true} \\ = 0 & \text{if } X \text{ is false} \end{cases}\right.$$

Or

$$\omega(X)_j \left(\begin{cases} = 1 & \text{if } X \text{ is above threshold} \\ = 0 & \text{if } X \text{ is below threshold} \end{cases}\right.$$

Thereafter regression-tree models can be elaborated for specific given startups, following any given startup's position within the regression tree. Eq. (9) describes this model functional-form.

Equation 9: Valuation Regression-Tree Model Using Hierarchical Ordinal Segmentation

$$\text{Valuation}_i = \omega_i \left(\prod_{i1}^{in} \text{Branch Threshold}_{ii} \right) + \ldots$$
$$+ \omega_n \left(\prod_{n1}^{nn} \text{Branch Threshold}_{nn} \right) \tag{9}$$

As a specific example building on Eq. (9), establishing a specific startup valuation-model, Eq. (10) applies the hierarchical ordinal segmentation approach to Eq. (8)'s combined FCFE-market-conditions valuation-model, while ranking the nodes in hierarchical-order following their order in Eq. (8). Note that this causes the factor-order described in the equation to change somewhat to reflect the conditionality-relationship.

Equation 10: Valuation Regression-Tree Using Hierarchical Ordinal Segmentation Model Approach

$$\text{Valuation}_i = \omega_i \left(\prod_{i}^{I} \text{Net Income}_{ii} \right) + \omega_j \left(\prod_{j}^{J} Risk - \text{Free rate}_{jj} \right)$$
$$+ \omega_k \left(\prod_{k}^{K} \text{Risk} - \text{Premium}_{kk} \right) + \omega_l \left(\prod_{l}^{L} \text{Size of Opportunity}_{ll} \right)$$
$$+ \omega_m \left(\prod_{m}^{M} \text{Competitive Env.}_{mm} \right) + \omega_n \left(\prod_{n}^{N} IP_{nn} \right) \tag{10}$$

A fundamental difference between the hierarchical ordinal approach and a weighted-summation approach is that the hierarchical ordinal model-approach is specific to the individual startup's position within the decision tree. Essentially, this means that the segmentation's functional-form differs from that of weighted-summation approach, since a startup's regression-tree branch-placement may indicate functional form featuring either an omission or a repetition of some of the regression model's valuation-determinants, a feature which may be functionally-indicative of either conditional valuation-impacts or variable interaction-effects.

Another core difference between the two model approaches, is that while the weighted-summation approach can grant a holistic view of σ-weights across the dataset as a whole, the ordinal-model approach can directly provide a valuation-estimate by placing the firm along regression-tree's terminal-nodes (i.e., the regression-tree's leaf-nodes).

3.2.4 Two-Tiered Approach

Given that the inclusion of categorical variables is able to grant key insights on valuable information, of both qualitative and quantitative nature, and holds the explanatory-power potential to be as information-dense as the joint-inclusion of multiple numerical variables, their use for research purposes remains a very valuable tool. This is in particular the case with fixed-effects regressions, given that they can meaningfully incorporate categorical indicators such as geographical or industry-level designations. In the face of multiple information-dense categorical variables however, this approach is subject to a hard-limit, taking into consideration that the explanatory power of joint-fixed-effects can be limited as the number of categorical variables grows.

What this means therefore is that either OLS or fixed-effects regressions can be deployed in order to capture the general causal-overview among the valuation-drivers and in order to detect information-density and explanatory-power of relevant categorical labels. In order to elaborate on any OLS or fixed-effects findings, CART (or possibly-other cluster-driven approach) can be utilized.

With this in mind, combined empirical approaches are possible, with the potential to outperform single-method analysis in terms of detailed insights in two important ways. First, this approach can outperform an OLS-based summation model in terms of model-accuracy, model sophistication, and explanatory power, because it can grant insights on the roles, relative-position, and hierarchy of near-significant explanatory-factors. Second, the two-tiered approach can provide detailed insight vis-à-vis scale and sign of factor-impacts (i.e., β-coefficients), thereby improving upon pure CART-based weighted-summations.

4 Example of CART-Based Microtargeting with One Categorical Variable

Tables 2 and 3 demonstrate both OLS and CART approaches to examine valuation-regression-models, which include revenues, and discount-factor components consisting of country-risk-premium (conveying country-level risk-free-rate), and sector-level CAPM-beta (conveying sector-level risk-premium) as discounted-cashflow valuation-factors alongside business model.

In principle, one can expect firm revenues to have positive β-coefficients, given their positive valuation-impact, while the DCF-discount-factor components (country-risk-premium and sector-level CAPM-beta) can both be expected to have negative coefficients. Meanwhile, business model is a categorical variable, which may take the value "business-to-business" (B2B), "business-to-customer" (B2C), business-to-business-and-customers" (B2B & C), or business-to-government" (B2G).

First, Table 2 uses an OLS model to examine the relationship between DCF-factors, business model, and startup-valuations, splitting business-model into dummy-variables, finding that the valuation-impact of revenue is DCF-consistent, while the discount-factor appears to be driven by sector-level CAPM-beta, and the valuation-impact of B2B is outweighed by both B2C and B2B & C.

Table 3 DCF Valuation-Factors and Business Model CART

Observations:	1048			
End nodes:	15			
Complexity parameter	No. of Split	RMSE	Cross-validation error	Cross-validation St. dev.
0.1280	0	1.0000	1.0024	0.1634
0.0623	2	0.7441	0.8255	0.1484
0.0574	3	0.6817	0.8100	0.1479
0.0376	4	0.6243	0.7245	0.1398
0.0285	5	0.5867	0.7133	0.1397
0.0241	7	0.5296	0.7016	0.1385
0.0148	8	0.5055	0.6458	0.1366
0.0132	9	0.4906	0.6200	0.1317
0.0132	11	0.4643	0.6219	0.1318
0.0102	12	0.4512	0.6242	0.1318
0.0100	13	0.4409	0.6154	0.1318
Variable importance				
Revenue	Business model	Beta	Country-risk premium	
35	24	23	18	

Source: Berre (2022)

Meanwhile, Table 3 outlines a decision-tree-based CART valuation which includes revenue, country-risk-premium (capturing country-level risk-free-rate), and sector-level CAPM-beta (capturing sector-level risk-premium) as discounted-cashflow valuation-factors alongside business model, and describes premoney startup-valuations ranging from €27 Million to €3.1 Billion, and are partitioned hierarchically.

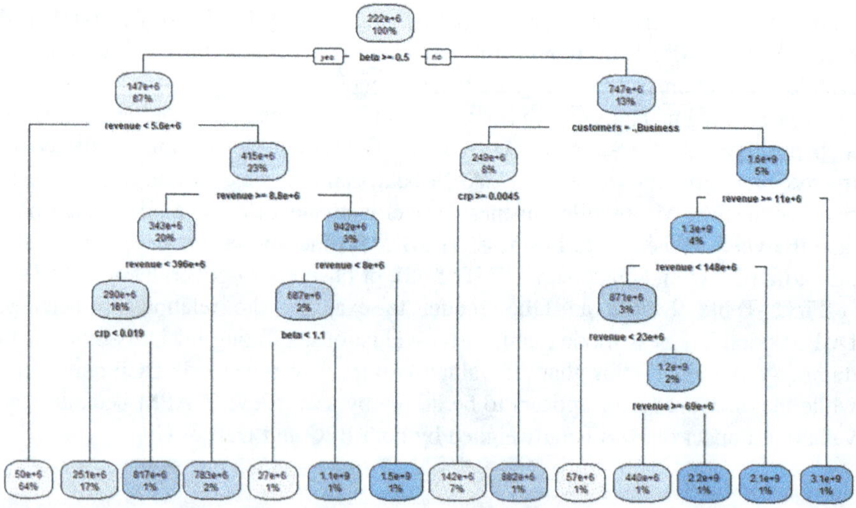

Given the architectural shape of Table 3's regression-tree, the weighted-summation approach and the hierarchical-ordinal approach would lead to somewhat-different functional-forms. Eq. (11) demonstrates a weighted-summation functional-form expression of the valuation-model resulting from the regression-tree outlined in Table 3, taking the resulting variable-importance indicators as σ-coefficients.

Equation 11: Valuation Regression Tree Model Using Weighted-Summation Segmentation

$$\begin{aligned}\text{Valuation}_i = {} & 0.35\beta_1(\text{Revenue}_i) + 0.24\beta_2(\text{Business Model}_i) \\ & + 0.23\beta_3(\text{Sectoral} - \text{Risk Beta}_i) + 0.18\beta_4(\text{Country} - \text{Risk Premium}_i)\end{aligned} \quad (11)$$

As per this approach, the highest-valuation tranche would first and foremost be startups with substantial revenue figures. This is followed by firms which have business models focusing on B2C, B2B & C, or B2G commerce, and whose revenues are discounted by low sector-level CAPM-betas, as well as by low country-risk premiums. Essentially, this means that the highest-valuation EU startups are firms combining substantial revenue figures with a B2C, a B2G, or a B2B & C, business model, and which are located in a low-volatility industry, and based in a AAA-rated home-market such as Denmark, Germany, or Switzerland (Damodaran, 2021), whereas lowest-valuation EU startups are more likely to be based in higher-risk EU markets (for example in the CEE or Euro-Med region), and are characterized by low-revenues, high-risk industry-sectors, and a B2B business model. Table 3 presents the regression-tree results outlined in Table 2, as a Payne-Style valuation-scorecard.

By also drawing on the OLS findings outlined in Table 2 as a source of β-coefficients, a two-tiered approach is possible. Here, Eq. (12) and Table 5 capture the revisions possible by inclusion of β-coefficients drawn from Table 2. Because Business Model has been re-transcribed as its constituent (statistically-significant) dummy variables, B2C and B2B & C, the valuation-model's functional-form includes terms and coefficients for both of these business-models, but excluding B2B and B2G.

Equation 12: Valuation Regression Tree Model Using Weighted-Summation Segmentation

$$\begin{aligned}\text{Valuation}_i = {} & (0.35 * 0.4273)(\text{Revenue}_i) + (0.24 * 637{,}000{,}000_{B2C}) \\ & \times (\text{Business Model}_i) + (0.24 * 305{,}900{,}000_{B2B\&C})(\text{Business Model}_i) \\ & + 0.23\beta_3(-460{,}900{,}00_i) + 0.18\beta_4(\cdot_i)\end{aligned} \quad (12)$$

Building on this revision, Table 5 represents a revision of the Payne-style summation scorecard outlined in Table 4, featuring the incorporation of β-coefficients drawn from use of a two-tiered valuation-approach.

Alternatively, hierarchical ordinal segmentation, a second segmentation modelling-approach, gives rise to a significantly more extensive valuation-model

Table 4 CART-based Valuation as Weighted-Summation Segmentation Results Presented in Payne-Style Scorecard

Weighting	Sign of β Coef.	Impact on startup valuation
35%	**Impact**	*Revenue*
	+	Valuation is positively impacted by revenues
		Business model
24%	**Impact**	*Client focus of the business*
	–	Business-to-business (B2B)
	+	Business-to-customer (B2C)
	+	Business-to-business and customer (B2B & C)
	+	Business-to-government (B2G)
		Discount factor
23%	**Impact**	*Sector-level CAPM-beta*
	–	Valuation negatively impacted by sectoral risk
18%	**Impact**	*Country-risk premium*
	–	Valuation is negatively by country-risk-premium
Total		
100%		

Source: Author's own creation

functional-form, as each of the regression-tree's branch and terminal-nodes can be represented in the model. Equation (13) demonstrates an example of this second valuation-segmentation approach, outlined in Eq. (8). Because the CART results include 14 terminal-nodes, as well as numerous branch-nodes, the complexity and size of the entire long-form valuation equation is substantial.

Equation 13: Valuation Regression Tree Hierarchical Ordinal Segmentation Model Approach

$$\text{Valuation}_i =$$

$$50{,}000{,}000(Sectoral - Beta \geq 0.5) * (Revenue_i < 5{,}600{,}000)$$

$$+251{,}000{,}000(Sectoral - Beta \geq 0.5) * (Revenue_i \geq 5{,}600{,}000) * (Revenue_i \geq 8{,}800{,}000) * (Revenue_i < 369{,}000{,}000) * (Country - Risk - Premium_i < .019)$$

$$+817{,}000{,}000(Sectoral - Beta \geq 0.5) * (Revenue_i \geq 5{,}600{,}000) * (Revenue_i \geq 8{,}800{,}000) * (Revenue_i < 369{,}000{,}000) * (Country - Risk - Premium_i \leq .019)$$

$$+783{,}000{,}000(Sectoral - Beta \geq 0.5) * (Revenue_i \geq 5{,}600{,}000) * (Revenue_i \geq 8{,}800{,}000) * (Revenue_i \geq 369{,}000{,}000)$$

Table 5 Two-Tiered Revised-Valuation as Weighted-Summation Results Expressed as a Payne-Style Scorecard

Weighting	Sign of β Coef.	Impact on Startup Valuation
35%	**Impact**	*Revenue*
	0.427	Valuation is positively impacted by revenue. Per EUR of revenue.
		Business model
24%	**Impact**	*Client focus of the business*
	.	Business-to-business (B2B) —— (not significant)
	637,000,000	Business-to-customer (B2C)
	305,900,000	Business-to-business and customer (B2B & C)
	.	Business-to-government (B2G) —— (not significant)
		Discount factor
23%	**Impact**	*Sector-level CAPM-beta*
	– 460,900,000	Valuation is negatively impacted by sectoral risk. Per 1.00 of CAPM-Beta
18%	**Impact**	*Country-risk premium*
	–	Valuation is negatively impacted by country-risk-premium. But not statistically significant using a European EU/EEA dataset. Near-significance of coefficient indicates that CRP is likely to be significant in more diverse datasets.
Total		
100%		

$$+27{,}000{,}000(Sectoral - Beta \geq 0.5) * (Revenue_i \geq 5{,}600{,}000) * (Revenue_i < 8{,}800{,}000) * (Revenue_i < 8{,}000{,}000) * (Sectoral - Beta < 1.1)$$

$$+1{,}100{,}000{,}000(Sectoral - Beta \geq 0.5) * (Revenue_i \geq 5{,}600{,}000) * (Revenue_i < 8{,}800{,}000) * (Revenue_i < 8{,}000{,}000) * (Sectoral - Beta \geq 1.1)$$

$$+1{,}500{,}000{,}000(Sectoral - Beta \geq 0.5) * (Revenue_i \geq 5{,}600{,}000) * (Revenue_i < 8{,}800{,}000) * (Revenue_i \geq 8{,}000{,}000)$$

$$+142{,}000{,}000(Sectoral - Beta < 0.5) * (Business\ Model_i = B2B) * (Country - Risk - Premium_i \geq .0045)$$

$$+882{,}000{,}000(Sectoral - Beta < 0.5) * (Business\ Model_i = B2B) * (Country - Risk - Premium_i < .0045)$$

$$+57{,}000{,}000(Sectoral - Beta < 0.5) * (Business\ Model_i = B2C\ or\ B2B\&C\ or\ B2G) * (Revenue_i \geq 11{,}000{,}000) * (Revenue_i < 148{,}000{,}000) * (Revenue_i < 23{,}000{,}000)$$

$$+440{,}000{,}000(Sectoral - Beta < 0.5) * (Business\ Model_i = B2C\ or\ B2B\&C\ or\ B2G) * (Revenue_i \geq 11{,}000{,}000) * (Revenue_i < 148{,}000{,}000) * (Revenue_i \geq 23{,}000{,}000) * (Revenue_i \geq 69{,}000{,}000)$$

$$+2{,}200{,}000{,}000(Sectoral - Beta < 0.5) * (Business\ Model_i = B2C\ or\ B2B\&C\ or\ B2G) * (Revenue_i \geq 11{,}000{,}000) * (Revenue_i < 148{,}000{,}000) * (Revenue_i \geq 23{,}000{,}000) * (Revenue_i < 69{,}000{,}000)$$

$$+2{,}100{,}000{,}000(Sectoral - Beta < 0.5) * (Business\ Model_i = B2C\ or\ B2B\&C\ or\ B2G) * (Revenue_i \geq 11{,}000{,}000) * (Revenue_i \geq 148{,}000{,}000)$$

$$+3{,}100{,}000{,}000(Sectoral - Beta < 0.5) * (Business\ Model_i = B2C\ or\ B2B\&C\ or\ B2G) * (Revenue_i < 11{,}000{,}000) \quad (13)$$

An interesting detail about the regression-tree described in Table 3 is that several of the nodes indicate unicorn valuation. Stated otherwise, this decision tree appears to describe the recipe for the establishment of unicorn-valuations. Furthermore, we see that revenue drives the majority of the lower and intermediate branches, corroborating revenue's dominant-position in terms of variable-importance.

Nevertheless, while the entire regression-tree valuation-function outlined in Eq. (13) is sizable and cumbersome, it is not necessary to estimate the function as a whole. Rather, because segments of the function where the criteria are not met are zero, it suffices to estimate the branches and terminal-node where the firm actually finds itself. For example, for a startup located in the rightmost terminal-node, whose sectoral beta would be larger than 0.5, and whose revenue is less than €50,000,000, Eq. (14) reduces to:

Equation 14: Valuation Regression Tree Model Reduced-form Ordinal Segmentation Model Approach

$$\text{Valuation}_i = 50{,}000{,}000(\text{Sectoral} - \text{Beta} \geq 0.5) * (\text{Revenue}_i < 5{,}600{,}000) \quad (14)$$

While this reduced-form is both compact and immediately-useful for practitioner purposes, substantial detail is lost in terms of other-path branches and terminal nodes, as well as their distributions and threshold-values.

5 Discussion, Conclusion, and Further Research

Overall, segmented valuation-models are historically underappreciated within empirical finance literature, with segmented models surfacing in but a small, obscure fraction of startup-valuation literature (Berre & Le Pendeven, 2022). Nevertheless, appearance of these models in practitioner and industry-sourced grey literature (e.g., Ewing Marion Kauffman Foundation (2007), Goldman (2008), Payne (2011), Berkus (2016), and Ernst and Young. (2020)), can be taken as indication that segmentation valuation approaches have established traction among industry practitioners ranging from venture capital investors and business angels to consultancy and auditing practitioners.

5.1 *Why Do Segmented Models Work?*

While these segmented valuation-models may be presently under-represented within the literature, the ongoing emergence and proliferation of machine learning techniques can be expected to increase the viability, diversity and popularity of segmented models within the literature, given that there are several empirical approaches drawn from both econometrics and machine-learning empirical approaches, to which segmented models can be adapted. In principle, the industry-popularity and usefulness in markets of segmented valuation-models can be attributed to several noteworthy positive qualities which characterize them.

First, segmented models are mechanically and mathematically straightforward, making them easy to intuit and understand, as well as easy to communicate to investors, clients, and stakeholders. This characteristic quality may partially explain widespread popularity of the Berkus and Payne methods among industry practitioners and among industry-sources. Indeed, Damodaran (2002) ascribes this quality to models using this approach.

Second, segmented models can be estimated quickly. Because of their mechanical simplicity, rough valuation-estimations can be executed quickly, in the field, and perhaps even with only partial information available. This detail contrasts more complex valuation approaches, which might require substantial access or estimation to key figures.

Third, segmented models are directly transposable to empirical modelling, making the investigation of their validity and accuracy relatively straightforward. Fundamentally, this is the case because both CART and OLS models can be expressed in segmented functional-form.

Fourth, segmented models have substantial flexibility. Because the segmented valuation-models' functional-form are readily-transposable for the purposes of empirical modelling, they are also highly-adaptable. This means that they can be altered by adding or modifying the impacts of valuation-determinant factors as the need arises, for example by adding segments to capture interaction terms or niche functional-form segments. Furthermore, they can be constructed by modifying other styles of valuation-models. For example, relative-valuation models can be combined into two-factor or three-factor segmented valuation-models.

The rise and proliferation of hierarchical empirical approaches, including not only CART-based regression-trees, but also related tree-based empirical approaches, such as the bottom-up Hierarchical Ascending Classification decision-trees, and Random Forest has yielded the proliferation of increasingly-accurate and flexible prediction-models, which can not only be used for valuation purposes, but also for speedy decision-making, as well as the construction of increasingly-flexible segmented valuation models. This indicates that the use of such approaches across business, market, and investment landscapes can only be expected to proliferate in the future.

5.2 *Contributions and Further Research*

Because this study focuses on the implementation of methodological approaches imported and drawn from industry practitioners, as well as from marketing and political science journals, within entrepreneurial finance literature, this study adds to the existing body of research in several ways by both addressing existing theory gaps, and by elaborating on currently-existing published empirical findings.

First, this study links practitioner-approaches with trends in peer-review literature. While practitioner-derived or industry-oriented sources such as Ewing Marion Kauffman Foundation (2007) or Ernst and Young (2020) point to segmented valuation-models such as valuation-approaches described by Payne (2011) and Berkus (2016), this approach, seen in studies such as Hand (2005) or Sievers et al. (2013) for valuation models and Siskos and Zopounidis (1987) for selection-models, has heretofore received relatively-little attention within peer-review literature. Principally, this is owed to overall need for model-sophistication in order to incorporate interaction-effects and variable-hierarchies within valuation models. This study provides an overview and synthesis of these approaches, which can be generally deployed by practitioners and valuation-experts across a wide variety of markets, while also providing context, as well as developmental-direction for the ongoing debate within peer-review literature concerning valuation-approaches for startup markets.

Second, by elaborating on already existing entrepreneurial finance research, this study gives rise to justification for a second-look at existing empirical findings, a research avenue which may indeed prove fertile. Existing studies which use segmented approaches devote little space to exploring model functional-form. Here again, the overall need for model-sophistication in order to meaningfully incorporate variable interaction-effects and variable-hierarchies within valuation-models is not only apparent, but also likely more relevant for startup markets than for more established (i.e., information-rich) markets.

Third, this study describes the use of newly-emergent empirical techniques and describes how to systematically make use of them in a consistent way. While hierarchical decision-tree-based microtargeting can take multiple forms in terms of machine learning algorithms (i.e., recursive-partitioning, agglomerative hierarchical clustering, random forest), the modelling functional-form that can be applied for startup valuation, startup-selection, or startup-survival intended to accompany such modelling-approaches has heretofore not yet appeared in the literature. This may be due to the overall novelty of such approaches within published entrepreneurial-financial literature up until now.

Given that machine learning approaches generally confront questions of model-selection and algorithm-selection relatively early-on, further research using the principles outlined in this paper should consider both model-complexity and shape of functional-form as a fundamental part of model-selection and algorithm-selection, as a combined model-outlook. Furthermore, this combined-outlook can and should be taken into consideration for all applications of machine learning approaches within economics, finance, or firm-strategy, or entrepreneurship research, as well and practice thereof in the professional marketplace.

Implications of this research are far-reaching. For markets and industry practitioners, elaboration on why and how segmented valuation models work, as well as how specifically they relate to emerging machine learning approaches can lead to the development of new and bespoke valuation-models going forward, as industry practitioners may increasingly adopt this style of valuation-approach. Meanwhile, the emergence of investors linked to the big data and machine learning industries (ranging from CVCs to specialized consultants and experts) may someday try to automate tree-based segmented-valuation approaches, in contexts where it may be appropriate to do so (for instance, implementation of trading-algorithms in a crowdfunding-platform or P2P-lending-platform setting). For investors, as well as for third-parties, implications are also far-reaching because these models can hypothetically deliver accurate valuation-estimations via microtargeting, which in its least numerical forms is able to bypass difficult-to-obtain or confidential firm-level accounting data, making accurate valuations considerably more widespread within startup markets.

For policy-maker circles meanwhile, the implications segmented model proliferation as machine learning approaches develop and evolve, are the rise of a more niche and targeting understanding of startup markets, a body of knowledge which may be very useful for the purposes of SME policy, as well as in targeting key sectors, asset-classes, regions, or municipalities going forward.

Fundamentally, future research will be able to build on this study by deploying modelling principles described here for empirical studies featuring hierarchical machine learning approaches for the development of segmented startup-valuation models. Since this approach is still in relatively-early phases of emergence, it may be feasible to "push the envelope" on what is empirically feasible. Doing so can be helped, for instance by development of taxonomy studies of entrepreneurial-finance-relevant configurations, clusters, and categorical variables, so that future microtargeting research can grow beyond reliance on industry-sector, business-model, and economic-geography variables (e.g., regions, cities, municipalities, or postal-codes).

Additionally, future research may build on this study by expanding the use of hierarchical empirical approaches to construct segmented models in other areas of entrepreneurial finance. Two topics adjacent to startup-valuation, which are also core to the entrepreneurial finance field are startup-selection (Berre & Le Pendeven, 2022), and startup-survivability. In principle, hierarchical empirical-approaches can be used to create segmented models to describe and predict these as areas as well. In particular, the approach can be useful for scholars interested in predicting startup-selection, as well, since qualitative factors play a more prominent role here than in startup-valuation (Berre & Le Pendeven, 2022), which may require a more sophisticated approach than OLS, capable of using both qualitative and quantitative data in order to estimate predictions. Startup-survivability on the other hand, would be most useful in an industry practitioner setting, where a way to accurately model any given startup's likelihood of survival or bankruptcy has the potential to substantially impact a VC's commercial outcomes.

Lastly, this research can be used as a roadmap for forthcoming studies intending to make use of hierarchical machine learning techniques within entrepreneurial finance, for industry practitioners interested in deploying machine learning techniques to establish bespoke segmented valuation models, or machine learning professionals interested in deploying their expertise for entrepreneurial finance (for example in a fintech setting).

References

Bellavitis, C., Filatotchev, I., Kamuriwo, D. S., & Vanacker, T. (2017). Entrepreneurial finance: New frontiers of research and practice: Editorial for the special issue embracing entrepreneurial funding innovations. *Venture Capital: An International Journal of Entrepreneurial Finance, 19*(1–2), 1–16.

Benoit, K. (2011). *Linear regression models with logarithmic transformations*. Methodology Institute London School of Economics. Working Paper.

Berkus, D. (2016). *The Berkus method - Valuing the early-stage investment*. Berkonomics.

Berre, M. (2022). Which factors matter most? Can startup valuation be micro-targeted? In *International conference on small business (ICSB) world conference, Washington DC. Working paper.*

Berre, M., & Le Pendeven, B. (2022). What do we know about start-up valuation drivers? A systematic literature review. *Venture Capital*, 1–45. https://doi.org/10.1080/13691066.2022.2086502

Budhwar, P., Cumming, D., & Wood, G. (2022). Entrepreneurial finance and the legacy of Mike Wright. *British Journal of Management, 33*, 3–8.

Damodaran, A. (2002). *Investment valuation: Tools and techniques for determining the value of any asset* (Wiley Finance Series). John Wiley & Sons.

Damodaran, A. (2009). Valuing young, start-up and growth companies: Estimation issues and valuation challenges. SSRN Scholarly Paper ID 1418687. : Social Science Research Network

Damodaran, A. (2010). *It is all relative... multiples, comparables and value!* NYU Stern. Retrieved December 2022, from http://pages.stern.nyu.edu/~adamodar/pdfiles/country/relvalAIMR.pdf

Damodaran, A. (2021). Equity Risk Premiums (ERP): Determinants, estimation, and implications – The 2021 edition. Available at SSRN: https://ssrn.com/abstract=3825823 or https://doi.org/10.2139/ssrn.3825823

Ernst & Young. (2020). Startup funding full eGuide - The Factory. EY - The Factory. Retrieved June 30, 2022, from https://thefactory.works/wp-content/uploads/2020/10/Eguide_Funding_A4.pdf?mc_cid=df85bfb95a&mc_eid=f80b29de26

Ewing Marion Kauffman Foundation. (2007). *Valuing pre-revenue companies*. Angel Capital Association. https://www.angelcapitalassociation.org/data/Documents/Resources/AngelCapitalEducation/ACEF_-_Valuing_Pre-revenue_Companies.pdf

Fama, E. (1970). Efficient capital markets: A review of theory and empirical work. *The Journal of Finance, 25*, 383–417.

Fama, E. (1991). Efficient capital markets: II. *The Journal of Finance, 46*(5), 1575–1617.

Firmin, S. (2021). Understanding the outputs of the decision tree tool. *Alteryx Designer Knowledge Base*. Retrieved September 1, 2022, from https://community.alteryx.com/t5/Alteryx-Designer-Knowledge-Base/Understanding-the-Outputs-of-the-Decision-Tree-Tool/ta-p/144773

Goldman, M. (2008). Valuation of startup and early-stage companies. *The Value Examiner*. http://www.michaelgoldman.com/Publications/Goldman%20Valuation%20of%20Start-ups.pdf

Hand, J. R. M. (2005). The value relevance of financial statements in the venture capital market. *The Accounting Review, 80*(2), 613–648.

Keene, O. N. (1995). The log transformation is special. *Statistics in Medicine, 14*(8), 811–819.

Khan, I., Capozzoli, A., Corgnati, S. P., & Cerquitelli, T. (2013). Fault detection analysis of building energy consumption using data mining techniques. *Energy Procedia, 42*(2013), 557–566.

Krzywinski, M., & Altman, N. (2017). Classification and regression trees. *Nature Methods, 14*, 757–758. https://doi.org/10.1038/nmeth.4370

Mahmoud, F., Zahoor, A., Hussain, N., & Younes, B. Z. (2022). Working capital financing and firm performance: A machine learning approach. In *Financial economics meeting (FEM-2022). Paris*.

Miller, J., O'Neill, M., & Hyde, N. (2010). *Intermediate Algebra* (2nd ed.). McGraw-Hill Higher Education.

Murray, G. R., & Scime, A. (2010). Microtargeting and electorate segmentation: Data mining the American National election studies. *Journal of Political Marketing, 9*(3), 143–166. https://doi.org/10.1080/15377857.2010.497732

Neter, J., Wasserman, W., & Kutner, M. H. (1990). *Applied linear statistical models: Regression, analysis of variance, and experimental design* (3rd ed.). McGraw-Hill, Inc.

Payne, B. (2011) Scorecard valuation methodology: Establishing the valuation of pre-revenue, start-up companies. https://www.angelcapitalassociation.org/blog/scorecard-valuationmethodology-rev-2019-establishing-the-valuation-of-pre-revenue-start-up-companies/

Ribeiro-Oliveira, J. P., Garcia de Santana, D., Pereira, V. J., & Machado dos Santos, C. (2018). Data transformation: An underestimated tool by inappropriate use. *Acta Scientiarum Agronomy., 40*(1), e35300. https://doi.org/10.4025/actasciagron.v40i1.35300

Sandeep. (2014). (https://stats.stackexchange.com/users/45985/sandeep), Difference between rel error and xerror in rpart regression trees. URL (version: 2014-07-02): Retrieved September 1, 2022, from https://stats.stackexchange.com/q/105536

Sievers, S., Mokwa, C. F., & Keienburg, G. (2013). The relevance of financial versus non-financial information for the valuation of venture capital-backed firms. *European Accounting Review, 22*(3), 467–511.

Siskos, J., & Zopounidis, C. (1987). The evaluation criteria of the venture capital investment activity: An interactive assessment. *European Journal of Operational Research, 31*(3), 304–313.

Wooldridge, J. M. (2010). *Econometric analysis of cross section and panel data* (2nd ed.). The MIT Press Cambridge.

Analysis of Startup Valuation Methods: Understanding the Investor's Perspective

Faisal Usmani, Mohd Sarim, and Atif Ghayas

1 Introduction

One of the available options for the potential entrepreneurs to finance their dream business is to approach venture capitalists. A key question to such a financing option is the determination of the fair cash flow trajectories and enterprise valuation of the startup. The cash flows projected by the budding entrepreneurs most often seem like dream cash flows to the venture capitalist. As a result, the venture capitalist determines its own expected returns considering the chance of success under given circumstances. This makes the valuation of a startup challenging and represents a trade-off situation between the entrepreneur and the venture capitalist. Therefore, the part of the book aims at examining the relationship of entrepreneur and the venture capitalist from principal-agent theory perspective to determine the factors for trade-offs. Also, the part of the book attempts to determine the factors considered by venture capitalists for determining the hurdle rate and its effect on the exit valuation.

A startup firm still has a lot of obstacles to overcome even though it may have the potential to grow profitably. Startups need a variety of funding sources to enable them to create a successful company from the ground up. Understanding startup valuation is crucial for this reason (Damodaran, 2009). It is challenging to value businesses early in their life cycles, in part because there is no operating experience and in part because the majority of startup businesses fail during these crucial early years.

Startup valuation is the process of calculating a startup company's overall value in order to determine the present value of all the expected cash flows for the startup in the market. This is typically done in order to attract investors in exchange for a

F. Usmani (✉)
Vellore Institute of Technology (VIT) University, Vellore, Tamil Nadu, India

M. Sarim · A. Ghayas
GITAM School of Business, GITAM (Deemed to be University), Bengaluru, Karnataka, India

S. Derindere Köseoğlu (ed.), *A Practical Guide for Startup Valuation*, Contributions to Finance and Accounting, https://doi.org/10.1007/978-3-031-35291-1_6

share of the company's profits. Startup values show how well a company will be able to use the additional funding to expand, satisfy shareholders and customers, and attain the next standard. Block et al. (2014) stated that when evaluating startups as investment targets, venture capitalists (VCs) encounter difficulties. These issues are brought on by the significant information gaps between venture capitalists and startups.

According to fundamental theory, positive news about an industry's prospects should lead to a rise in search volume and firm valuations due to the expectations of higher future profits. When investors perceive an industry as having positive future prospects, they are more likely to search for information about the industry and the companies operating within it (Ramelli & Wagner, 2018). This increase in search volume can signal an increase in investor interest and confidence, leading to a rise in firm valuations. Additionally, positive news about an industry's prospects may lead investors to adjust their expectations of future earnings upward, resulting in a rise in firm valuations (Que & Zhang, 2021). Overall, fundamental theory suggests that positive news about an industry's prospects can have a significant impact on investor behavior and firm valuations.

Valuing a new venture is a crucial step in the process of entrepreneurial financing, and it is important to understand the factors that influence VCs' valuations. This chapter develops an integrated theoretical framework to examine whether venture capitalists' valuation of a new venture can be explained by factors identified in the strategy theories as important to firm performance. To address this issue, several theoretical frameworks were developed by Jensen and Meckling (1976), Barney (1991), and Li and Zahra (2012) to examine whether VCs' valuations of a new venture can be explained by factors identified in strategy theories as important to firm performance. The framework proposed by Li and Zahra (2012) integrates the resource-based view (RBV), agency theory, and social network theory. The RBV suggests that resources and capabilities are critical to firm performance, and that firms with valuable, rare, inimitable, and non-substitutable resources have a competitive advantage (Barney, 1991). Agency theory highlights the importance of aligning the interests of principals (i.e., VCs) and agents (i.e., the startup's founders) to reduce conflicts of interest and maximize firm value (Jensen & Meckling, 1976). Social network theory emphasizes the role of social relationships and networks in creating value for firms (Burt, 1992).

Using a sample of 57 VC-funded startups, Li and Zahra (2012) found that VCs' valuations of new ventures were positively associated with the startup's human capital, technological innovation, and network centrality. Specifically, VCs placed a higher value on startups with founding teams that had prior entrepreneurial experience, technical expertise, and industry knowledge. In addition, VCs valued startups with more innovative technologies and those that were more central in their industry networks.

This study provides insights into the factors that VCs consider when valuing new ventures, and highlights the importance of human capital, innovation, and network centrality in determining the success of startups. By understanding these factors, entrepreneurs can better position their ventures to attract VC funding and maximize their chances of success.

Startups typically have negative but going to grow cash flows (Moro-Visconti & Moro-Visconti, 2021), limited or no historical financial data and forecasts, and their proof of concept has not yet been developed. As a result, traditional approaches for determining the startup business value/EV, such as the income approach, market approach, or net assets approach, are ineffective because startups and most early-stage companies lack the financial performance indicators required for those approaches.

Three factors must be taken into account: paying attention to future predictions rather than historical data, applying probability to analyze potential outcomes, and comprehending and paying attention to the startup's unique business strategy rather than market statistics on similar firms.

The valuation of a startup presents a number of challenges that require potential investors to approach the process differently. Because historical data is unavailable/limited and forecasts are uncertain, qualitative factors play an important role. Hidayat et al. (2022) suggested that because of the recent increase in the number of unicorns and their role in fostering entrepreneurship and social impact, venture capitalists, entrepreneurs, and regulators are concerned about the valuation of startup firms.

1.1 Characteristics of Startup Ventures

Although young companies vary in characteristics such as their regional development context, intellectual property rights, industry affiliation, and funding sources, which can all influence their outcomes and performance (Gao et al., 2020; Kim & Rhee, 2021), they have some common attributes too. We shall discuss these common attributes in this section with an eye toward the concerns and/or problems they pose for value.

Illiquid Investments Since it is difficult to exit an investment in a startup unless and until it has a very promising business strategy and a track record, which is typically not the case for startups as described above, investment in startups typically lacks liquidity. In this situation, the valuer must modify the discounting factor by including the liquidity premium, which is an additional return to the investor for investing in such illiquid companies. On the other side, the liquidity premium should not be included in the discounting factor in the case of established enterprises, as investors can exit the investment swiftly without sacrificing value in such cases.

No Background Most of the startups do not have sufficient financial background to make prediction for future cash flows and valuation. Making logical assumptions about important value drivers like growth, efficiency, cost structure, etc. is more difficult without a financial history. However, evaluating an established business is significantly simpler when taking into account the data that is readily available and its track record.

Uncertainty in Business Model One of the benefits for any business is having a different idea in the form of a product or service. The studies conducted by Gompers and Lerner (2001), Shane (2008), and Hsu and Eisenhardt (2018) highlight the inherent risks and uncertainties associated with starting a new venture, which can lead to a roughly equal chance of success or failure in the marketplace. While certain factors can increase or decrease these odds, such as the experience of the founding team or the viability of the product or service being offered, ultimately the outcome can be difficult to predict with certainty. Such a business model's estimates cannot be compared to those of successful businesses. Additionally, the valuer is unable to apply the relative technique in the absence of similar company/transaction multiples, and finding the necessary sensitivity factor (BETA) for the DCF method is equally challenging. Examples of such business models are OYO Rooms, Uber, OLA, etc., which are original and have never been used by another company.

High Probability of Failure Most new businesses fail. Failure must therefore be accounted for in the valuation. The majority of newly formed businesses fail when put to the test of commercial success. Although their failure rates vary, numerous research have been done to support this claim (Damodaran, 2009).

Small or No Revenue The majority of startups place a greater emphasis on building a clientele, finding a product or service that fits the market, etc. They therefore have very little or no revenue compared to the costs of starting a business, which leads to negative EBITDA. Business plans become extremely individualized and are susceptible to founder overconfidence biases and overoptimistic viewpoints. In these situations, the valuer should alter the discounting factor for the risk premium as well as the perpetual growth rate (in the case of the Gordon growth model used to derive terminal value) to handle the possibility of not attaining such an optimistic estimate.

Operating Loss The lack of operational detail in emerging enterprises makes the scant history that is available for them much less helpful. For idea companies, revenues are typically negligible or nonexistent, and costs are frequently related to establishing the business rather than earning income. They result in significant operating losses when combined.

Dependent on Private Equity Young enterprises rely more on equity from private sources than on public markets, though there are a few exceptions. Early on, the founder is largely responsible for funding the equity (and friends and family). In exchange for a stake in the company, venture capitalists provide equity financing as the likelihood of future success rises, driving up the need for more money.

This need for additional capital is known as the "funding gap," and it can be particularly acute for startups in the early stages of their development. In order to bridge this gap, many startups turn to venture capitalists and other sources of equity financing to raise the funds they need to continue operating and growing.

Studies have shown that VC investments can have a significant impact on the success of startups. For example, a study by Harvard Business School found that startups that received VC funding were more likely to experience rapid growth and achieve successful exits through acquisitions or initial public offerings (IPOs) than those that did not receive VC funding (Gompers & Lerner, 2001).

These difficulties make it more difficult to put together a business or financial strategy, calculate the cost of capital, employ relative valuation, and apply discounted cash flow techniques. In other words, they make it more difficult to value a start up.

1.2 Startup and VC Expectations

When a startup approaches a venture capitalist for financing, it typically has certain expectations and goals in mind. These expectations and goals can vary depending on the specific circumstances of the startup and the venture capitalist, but some common expectations include:

Funding The primary expectation of a startup when approaching a venture capitalist for financing is to secure funding for its operations and growth. The startup may require funding to finance research and development, expand its product line, increase marketing efforts, or hire additional employees.

Expertise Venture capitalists often bring a wealth of experience and knowledge to the table, and the startup may expect to benefit from this expertise. This can include guidance on business strategy, product development, marketing, and fundraising.

Network Venture capitalists often have extensive networks in the business community, and the startup may expect to benefit from these connections. This can include access to customers, suppliers, and industry experts.

Valuation The startup may also have an expectation of the valuation of its business. The venture capitalist will typically have its own valuation in mind, based on factors such as the startup's growth potential, financial projections, and market competition.

Similarly, when a venture capitalist considers financing a startup, they have several expectations and goals. Some common expectations are:

Generating Returns The main objective of a venture capitalist is to generate returns on their investment. They expect to receive a return that is higher than the return they could receive from more traditional investments, such as bonds or stocks.

Assessing Risk Venture capitalists also assess the risk associated with the investment. They expect to invest in a startup that has a strong business plan, a well-defined target market, and a clear path to profitability.

Supporting Growth Venture capitalists also expect to support the growth of the startup. They may provide advice, expertise, and connections to help the startup achieve its goals and reach its full potential.

Building Relationships Finally, venture capitalists expect to build relationships with the startup. This can help the venture capitalist understand the market, identify new opportunities, and support the startup in the future.

Achieving Exits Venture capitalists also expect to achieve exits, either through an initial public offering (IPO) or through an acquisition by a larger company. Exits provide an opportunity for the venture capitalist to realize the return on their investment and reinvest in new opportunities.

These expectations are based on the idea that the startup and the venture capitalist will work together to achieve common goals. By securing funding, building relationships, and generating returns, the startup can become more successful and achieve its goals.

Before signing a financing deal with a venture capitalist, a startup should be aware of all the terms and circumstances of the investment, including equity ownership, decision-making authority, and exit strategy. In a similar vein, the investor looks to find the best valuation while making investment choices. The extensive discussion of methodology in this chapter is followed by an in-depth analysis of the literature to explore various valuation methods in order to provide a wide understanding of these methods. Examples of a few ways are supplied along with them in order to compare various valuation techniques.

2 Literature Review

Startups have become a prominent feature of the modern economy, with their potential to create new markets, disrupt existing industries, and drive innovation. However, the valuation of startups is a complex and challenging task due to their high level of uncertainty and risk. This literature review aims to critically examine the existing research on the valuation of startups, exploring the different approaches and factors that influence startup valuation, and highlighting the gaps and opportunities for future research in this area.

Investors and analysts often rely on various methods and metrics to determine the value of startups, but the accuracy and reliability of these approaches are subject to debate. Davila et al. (2003) examined the link between the availability of venture capital (VC) and the expansion of startups' workforce. It also explored whether growth signals a need for VC or, alternatively, VC signals growth. The association between changes in staff numbers and increases in startup valuation over time is also shown by them. However, the study of Dittmann et al. (2004) examined a sample of 53 German venture capitalists in which investment performance is impacted by the usage of diverse valuation approaches. They discovered that while many investment managers utilize discounted cash flow (DCF) approaches, very few actually seem to apply a discount rate that is in line with the cost of capital.

Kaiser et al. (2007) examined the theoretical and empirical work on venture capital financing. The study explored best practices for the interactions between entrepreneurs and venture capital companies. The study emphasized on the fact that entrepreneurs should carefully evaluate the venture capitalist financing. Perhaps, the investors might chase their own objectives that might be contradictory to the objectives of the entrepreneurs. However, Khan et al. (2021) stressed that the venture capital financing can impact innovative entrepreneurial activities. The paper studied 41 countries for a period of 10 years on how venture capital fundraising supported such innovative entrepreneurial initiatives. The authors made a venture capital index using principal component analysis methodology to analyze the composite effect of venture capital on patent generation. The study showed a significant relationship between venture capital financing and patent registration. Therefore, the study concluded that the venture capital financing is critical for the innovative developments and growth. Hence, constructive policies are required to boost the innovative entrepreneurial initiatives through venture capital financing.

Timing for financing is critical for startups. The startup goes through different phases starting from pre-seed to going public. With every phase a startup faces certain unique issues and problems that can affect its valuation (Terpstra & Olson, 1993). The problems that were highlighted through open-ended questionnaire were classified into stages such as startup stage and later growth stage. The findings showed mixed sustenance for prior research concerning types of central problems to different phases of organizational development. The valuation of startup is strongly associated with the state of capital market. Under the given conditions of the market and economy the venture capitalist may have different hurdle rates.

Additionally, Bates and Bradford (2007) analyzed the performance of investments made by venture-capital funds that specialize in financing minority business enterprises and found that have less access to financing—equity as well as debt. The study concluded that the minority venture capital funds are earning yields on their realized investments that are at least equivalent to those of the broader VC industry. Highlighting a similar issue, Sass Rubin (2010) emphasized that the equity capital is critical for the growth of businesses, especially for young companies, which lack the cash flows necessary to repay loans. Not all companies, however, have been equally able to access such investments. Firms owned by women and people of color and those located in rural and distressed urban regions of the United States have been underserved by the venture capital industry.

Damodaran, A. (2009) mentioned that startups are more difficult to value due to their short history, reliance on private equity, and high failure risk. These factors are all exacerbated by the fact that they are also more prone to failure. The study of Cumming & Dai (2011) supports the idea that there is a diseconomy of scale in the venture capital business, which is partly caused by limitations on the type and amount of human capital available as fund sizes increase. However, Miloud et al. (2012) finds that attractiveness of the industry, the quality of the founder and top management team, as well as external relationships of a new venture significantly and positively affect its valuation by venture capitalists when it seeks venture capital financing in its early stages of development.

Gavious and Schwartz (2011) studied the relevance of financial information for the valuation of startup. They tried to explore valuation of ventures changed during the period of a technology bubble and the fluctuations that occurred in the capital market after the bubble burst. The study found that since the bubble burst, there has been a learning curve and a period of market adjustment. Specifically, during the time of the bubble the market did not rely on accounting information with respect to the valuation of startups. However, Köhn, A. (2018) found that understanding the various underlying factors that influence the valuation of startups is particularly crucial. Nevertheless, Dhochak & Doliya (2020) mentioned that the valuation of a new enterprise is frequently seen as a contentious area of discussion between entrepreneurs and venture capitalists. To close this gap, this chapter seeks to understand how existing strategic management theories relate to startup value.

Additionally, the findings of Montani et al. (2020) indicate that there isn't yet a "perfect" way to evaluate a startup's value. Although there are many opportunities for development, each of the models discussed has severe limitations. We are seeing a progressive move away from more arbitrary valuation models, and awareness of the premise that to more accurately determine a startup's value. According to Suwarni et al. (2020), Venture capitalists are willing to take a risk by investing in such organizations because they can profit greatly if these organizations succeed. Because of the vulnerability that comes with new and ambiguous companies, venture capitalists have a high rate of bankruptcy.

Hidayat (2022) Financial and nonfinancial information (social media), as well as sectoral and technological differences, all influence startup equity valuation. Big data, clean tech, mobile, and augmented reality technologies command significant equity valuation premiums, regardless of the subsectors from which the startups emerge. Que & Zhang (2021) discovered, based on a sample of 5621 financing rounds from 2006 to 2017, that firms in industries with an increase in investor attention exhibit higher valuations. This outcome is demonstrated to be attention-induced rather than the product of an information-based fundamental premium.

Several studies compared the accuracy of various startup valuation methods, including the discounted cash flow (DCF) method, the multiples method, and the real options method (Kretzer, 2017; Petrov, 2019; Vohra & Kaur, 2020; Mu & Ma, 2020; Li et al., 2021). The studies suggested that the DCF method is the most accurate and reliable method for valuing startups, but that the multiples method is also a useful tool for providing a rough estimate of value (Mu and Ma, 2020). However, Shill and Kaur (2020) found that the DCF method and the multiples method provide different results for startup valuation, and they provide recommendations for choosing the appropriate method based on the characteristics of the startup.

While doing a systematic of startups in China, Li et al. (2021) found that the DCF method is the most widely used method, but that the multiples method is also commonly used. The studies also discussed the advantages and disadvantages of each method and provide recommendations for choosing the most appropriate method for a given startup (Vohra and Kaur, 2020; Petrov, 2019). Hernandez and Sánchez (2021) examined the role of big data analytics in startup valuation. The authors find that big data analytics can provide valuable information for startup valuation, but they also discuss the challenges associated with using big data analytics and provide recommendations for improving its use in startup valuations.

Min and Lee (2017) found that growth prospects have a significant effect on startup valuation and that investors place a higher value on startups with high growth prospects compared to those with lower growth prospects. Kretzer (2017) discussed the challenges associated with valuing startups and provides recommendations for practitioners to improve the accuracy of startup valuations. Moradi and Fadaei (2021) did a meta-analytic review to investigate the impact of intangible assets on startup valuation. The authors found that intangible assets have a positive impact on startup valuation, and they provide recommendations for startups to enhance the value of their intangible assets. Kaitner and Dhanaraj (2020) examined the impact of startup stage and ownership structure on startup valuation. The authors found that startup stage and ownership structure have a significant impact on startup valuation, and they provide recommendations for startups to enhance their valuation by considering these factors.

In conclusion, startup valuation is a critical aspect of the venture capital industry, as it provides a way for investors to assess the potential value and risks associated with a startup. In this literature review, we have examined various methods used to value startups. Investors should carefully consider which method is best suited for their needs. Additionally, we have explored the role of venture capitalists in startup valuation, highlighting their unique expertise in identifying and assessing promising startups. Through their evaluation processes, venture capitalists can bring significant value to startups, helping them to grow and succeed in the highly competitive business landscape.

3 Research Methodology

The study aims at exploring the factors underpinning determining the hurdle rate to calculate exit value and ownership in an enterprise by a venture capitalist. The study will do an in-depth review of literature for such factors in the Indian context.

The study will further attempt to compare the valuation of the firm as determined by the venture capital with the current valuation of the firm. Some of the popular methods of valuation are Venture Capital Method, Scorecard method, and Comparable Company method. A comparative analysis of all the methods will be presented in the form of a case of a startup.

4 Methods of Startup Valuation

There are various methods to find the value of a startup such as the following:

1. **Venture capital (VC) method:** This method estimates the value of a startup based on the percentage of ownership that is being sold, the stage of the company, and the perceived risk of the investment. The VC method calculates the post-money valuation by dividing the Exit Value by the expected Return on Investment (RoI). The Exit Value (EV), or Terminal Value, is the value the company is expected to be sold for. In the Venture Capital method, this is usually calculated as a multiple of the company's revenues in the year of sale. The Rate of Investment, or Rate of Return, is often expressed as a multiple of the initial investment. The RoI is a function of risk perceived by investors. This method is useful when the startup is in its early stages and there is a high degree of uncertainty about its future success.
2. **Scorecard method:** This method uses a weighted average of scores assigned to various key factors to estimate the value of a startup. The key factors considered in the Scorecard Method include the product, market, team, financials, and legal & operational factors. The scores are assigned based on the relative strength of each factor compared to other startups in the same industry. This method is useful when the information available on the startup is limited, and the goal is to get a rough estimate of its value.
3. **Comparable company analysis:** This method involves comparing the startup to similar companies in the same industry to determine its value. This method is based on the assumption that similar companies should have similar valuations. The value of the startup is estimated by taking the average of the values of comparable companies, adjusting for differences in size, revenue, growth rate, and other factors. This method is useful when there is a sufficient number of publicly traded or privately held companies with similar business models.

5 Illustration of the Selected Startup Valuation Methods

In this section of the chapter, various methods of startup valuation that were discussed above will be illustrated using fictional data set.

1. Venture Capital (VC) Method

Steps Involved in the Venture Capital (VC) Method

The venture capital (VC) method for valuing a startup involves the following steps:

- Determine the pre-money valuation:

  This is the estimated value of the company before any new investment is made. It takes into account the company's financials, growth potential, industry, competition, and other relevant factors.
- Determine the ownership percentage being sold:

- This is the percentage of the company that the founders are willing to sell in exchange for investment.
- Calculate the post-money valuation:
- This is the value of the company after the new investment has been made. It is calculated by adding the pre-money valuation and the investment amount, then dividing by (1—ownership percentage being sold).
- Determine the implied value per share:
  This is the value assigned to each share of the company based on the post-money valuation and the number of outstanding shares.
  It's important to note that the VC method is subjective and heavily reliant on assumptions and perceived risk. The method may not always provide an accurate valuation of a startup, especially for early-stage companies with limited financial data.

Example

Here's an example of how to calculate the valuation of a startup using the venture capital (VC) method:

- Determine the pre-money valuation:
  Let's assume that the pre-money valuation of the startup is \$5 million.
- Determine the ownership percentage being sold:
- Let's assume that the founders are selling 20% of the company in exchange for investment.
- Calculate the post-money valuation:
  The investment amount is \$2 million, and the ownership percentage being sold is 20%, so the post-money valuation is calculated as follows:

$$\begin{aligned}&\$5\text{ million} + \$2\text{ million}/(1-0.20)\\&= \$5\text{ million} + \$2\text{ million}/0.80\\&= \$5\text{ million} + \$2.5\text{ million}\\&= \$7.5\text{ million}\end{aligned}$$

- Determine the implied value per share: Let's assume that the startup has one million outstanding shares. The implied value per share is calculated as follows:

$$\begin{aligned}&\$7.5\text{ million}/1\text{ million}\\&= \$7.50\text{ per share}\end{aligned}$$

So, based on this example, the valuation of the startup using the VC method is \$7.5 million, or \$7.50 per share.

2. Scorecard Method

Steps Involved in the Scorecard Method

The Scorecard Method of startup valuation involves assigning numerical scores to various qualitative and quantitative factors to estimate the value of a company. The steps are:

- Define relevant factors:
- Identify and define relevant factors such as the company's industry, market size, competition, management team, product/service, etc.
- Assign scores:
- Assign numerical scores to each factor, such as a 1–5 scale or a 0–100 scale, based on their relative importance and the company's performance in that area.
- Weight scores:
- Assign weights to each factor based on its relative importance to the overall value of the company.
- Calculate composite score:
- Calculate the composite score by multiplying each factor's score by its weight and summing the results.
- Determine valuation range:
- Based on the composite score, determine a valuation range using industry benchmarks or comparable companies.
- Make final determination:

Use judgment to make a final determination of the company's value based on the composite score and other relevant factors.

The Scorecard Method is not a precise method of valuation and should only be used as a starting point. It is important to consider additional factors, such as financial projections, when determining a company's value.

Example

Here's an example of how to calculate the valuation of a startup using the Scorecard Method:

- Determine the key factors:
- The Scorecard Method considers several key factors that impact the value of a startup, including the product, market, team, financials, and legal & operational factors.
- Assign a score to each factor:
- For each factor, assign a score based on its relative strength compared to other startups in the same industry. The score can range from 1 to 10, with 10 being the strongest.
- Calculate the weighted average:

Multiply each score by a weight to reflect its relative importance and then sum up the weighted scores to get the weighted average score.

For example, if the product score is 9, the market score is 8, the team score is 7, the financials score is 6, and the legal & operational score is 5, the weighted average score can be calculated as follows:

$$(9^{*}\ 0.3) + (8^{*}\ 0.25) + (7^{*}\ 0.2) + (6^{*}\ 0.15) + (5^{*}\ 0.1)$$
$$= 2.7 + 2 + 1.4 + 0.9 + 0.5$$
$$= 7.5$$

- Determine the valuation range:

  The final step is to use the weighted average score to determine the valuation range.

  For example, if the weighted average score is 7.5, the valuation range can be estimated as follows: $5 million to $10 million

  So, based on this example, the valuation of the startup using the Scorecard Method is estimated to be between $5 million and $10 million. It's important to note that the Scorecard Method is subjective and relies heavily on the assumptions and perspectives of the person conducting the analysis.

3. Comparable Company Analysis Method

Steps Involved in the Comparable Company Analysis Method

The comparable company analysis method of startup valuation involves the following steps:

- Identify comparable companies: Find publicly traded or privately held companies in the same industry with similar business models, target markets, revenue, and growth rates as the startup being valued.
- Gather financial information: Collect financial data on comparable companies, including revenue, earnings, market capitalization, and valuation metrics such as P/E ratio, price-to-sales ratio, and enterprise value-to-revenue ratio.
- Adjust for differences: Take into account differences between the comparable companies and the startup being valued, such as size, growth rate, profitability, and market position. Adjust the valuation metrics of the comparable companies to reflect these differences.
- Calculate average value: Calculate the average value of the comparable companies, using the adjusted valuation metrics.
- Apply average value to the startup: Apply the average value to the startup being valued, taking into account any further adjustments or differences. This will give an estimate of the value of the startup.
- Consider the range of values: The comparable company analysis method can produce a wide range of values, depending on the choice of comparable companies and the assumptions made. Consider the range of values obtained and the strengths and weaknesses of the comparable companies to arrive at a final valuation for the startup.

This method is only as accurate as the quality of the comparable companies and the adjustments made for differences between them and the startup being valued.

Example

Let's say we have a startup named "X" that operates in the online food delivery space and has $2 million in annual revenue. We want to estimate its value using the comparable company analysis method.

- Identify comparable companies
  We find three publicly traded companies in the same industry with similar revenue and growth rates as the startup: "Y" with $5 million in revenue, "Z" with $3 million in revenue, and "W" with $2.5 million in revenue.
- Gather financial information
  We collect financial data on these companies, including their revenue, earnings, market capitalization, and valuation metrics such as P/E ratio, price-to-sales ratio, and enterprise value-to-revenue ratio.
- Adjust for differences
  We adjust the valuation metrics of the comparable companies to reflect differences between them and the startup, such as size, growth rate, profitability, and market position.
- Calculate average value
  The average value of the comparable companies is estimated to be $100 million, using the adjusted valuation metrics.
- Apply average value to the startup
  We apply the average value of $100 million to the startup being valued and adjust for differences, such as revenue, growth rate, and profitability.
- Consider the range of values
  Based on the comparable companies used and the adjustments made, we estimate the value of the startup "X" to be between $50 million and $80 million. This range takes into account the strengths and weaknesses of the comparable companies and the assumptions made in the analysis.
  It's important to note that this is just an example and the actual valuation of the startup will depend on many other factors, such as the quality of the comparable companies, the accuracy of the financial information, and the strength of the startup's business model.

6 Practical Implication of the Study

The venture capital market in India is learning and maturing, which could bring performance-based work ethics to promote equitable distribution of finance to budding startups. To ensure that the factors affecting the venture capital decision to invest and entrepreneurs' decision to offer a stake in the newly established firm are critical. The study offers a comprehensive view of such factors that could offer a win-win valuation and stake in the firm that would lead to lesser disappointments.

7 Conclusion

It is undeniable that startups present the most challenging valuation estimation issues. Short and uninformative histories, operating losses, and the potential of a high risk of failure all contribute to valuation approaches that use a combination of forward multiples and arbitrarily large discount rates to try to avoid dealing with the uncertainty.

As previously mentioned, valuation is not a precise science. Since startups are new companies with little to no prior financial data, traditional methodologies like the income approach, market approach, or net assets approach are not always applicable for valuing them. For startups, alternative techniques like the VC or scorecard valuation methodologies might be more suitable. Such techniques, though, necessitate thorough knowledge of the market, the organization doing the appraisal, and the valuation procedure itself.

Young, startup enterprises must estimate inputs that are challenging to determine for both their intrinsic and relative worth. They make it necessary for the analyst to deal with potential sources of uncertainty, learn more about them, and, as usual, apply professional judgment to come up with the most accurate predictions.

References

Barney, J. B. (1991). Firm resources and sustained competitive advantage. *Journal of Management, 17*(1), 99–120. https://doi.org/10.1177/014920639101700108

Bates, T., & Bradford, W. (2007). Traits and performance of the minority venture-capital industry. *The Annals of the American Academy of Political and Social Science, 613*(1), 95–107.

Block, J. H., De Vries, G., Schumann, J. H., & Sandner, P. (2014). Trademarks and venture capital valuation. *Journal of Business Venturing, 29*(4), 525–542.

Burt, R. S. (1992). *Structural holes: The social structure of competition*. Harvard University Press.

Cumming, D., & Dai, N. (2011). Fund size, limited attention and valuation of venture capital backed firms. *Journal of Empirical Finance, 18*(1), 2–15.

Damodaran, A. (2009). *Valuing young, start-up and growth companies: Estimation issues and valuation challenges*. Available at SSRN 1418687.

Davila, A., Foster, G., & Gupta, M. (2003). Venture capital financing and the growth of startup firms. *Journal of Business Venturing, 18*(6), 689–708.

Dhochak, M., & Doliya, P. (2020). Valuation of a startup: Moving towards strategic approaches. *Journal of Multi-Criteria Decision Analysis, 27*(1–2), 39–49.

Dittmann, I., Maug, E., & Kemper, J. (2004). How fundamental are fundamental values? Valuation methods and their impact on the performance of German venture capitalists. *European Financial Management, 10*(4), 609–638.

Gao, Y., Huang, L., & Zhu, H. (2020). How do industry characteristics affect the relationship between entrepreneurial orientation and performance in Chinese SMEs? *Small Business Economics, 54*(4), 1165–1183. https://doi.org/10.1007/s11187-018-0097-9

Gavious, I., & Schwartz, D. (2011). Market valuations of start-up ventures around the technology bubble. *International Small Business Journal, 29*(4), 399–415.

Gompers, P., & Lerner, J. (2001). The venture capital revolution. *Journal of Economic Perspectives, 15*(2), 145–168. https://doi.org/10.1257/jep.15.2.145

Hernandez, J. C., & Sánchez, A. (2021). Start-up valuation and the role of big data analytics. *Journal of Business Research, 126*, 883–892. https://doi.org/10.1016/j.jbusres.2020.12.026

Hidayat, S. E., Bamahriz, O., Hidayati, N., Sari, C. A., & Dewandaru, G. (2022). Value drivers of startup valuation from venture capital equity-based investing: A global analysis with a focus on technological factors. *Borsa Istanbul Review, 22*(4), 653–667.

Hsu, D. H., & Eisenhardt, K. M. (2018). Extending the dynamic managerial capabilities perspective: A complex adaptive systems approach. *Strategic Management Journal, 39*(12), 3069–3092. https://doi.org/10.1002/smj.2957

Jensen, M. C., & Meckling, W. H. (1976). Theory of the firm: Managerial behavior, agency costs and ownership structure. *Journal of Financial Economics, 3*(4), 305–360. https://doi.org/10.1016/0304-405X(76)90026-X

Kaiser, D. G., Lauterbach, R., & Verweyen, J. K. (2007). Venture capital financing from an entrepreneur's perspective. *The International Journal of Entrepreneurship and Innovation, 8*(3), 199–207.

Kaitner, R., & Dhanaraj, C. (2020). The impact of stage and ownership structure on start-up valuation. *Journal of Business Research, 118*, 345–353. https://doi.org/10.1016/j.jbusres.2019.09.025

Khan, N., Qu, H., Qu, J., Wei, C., & Wang, S. (2021). Does venture capital investment spur innovation? A cross-countries analysis. *SAGE Open, 11*(1). https://doi.org/10.1177/21582440211003087

Kim, Y., & Rhee, J. (2021). Funding patterns and firm performance in Korean start-ups. *Asia Pacific Journal of Management, 38*(2), 369–398. https://doi.org/10.1007/s10490-020-09649-7

Köhn, A. (2018). The determinants of startup valuation in the venture capital context: A systematic review and avenues for future research. *Management Review Quarterly, 68*(1), 3–36.

Kretzer, M. (2017). A review of start-up valuation methods in practice. *Journal of Entrepreneurship, Innovation and Small Business, 2*(2), 149–163. https://doi.org/10.1186/s42513-017-0012-1

Li, J., & Zahra, S. A. (2012). Venture capitalists' evaluation of start-up teams: Trade-offs between human capital, social capital, and risk. *Journal of Business Venturing, 27*(6), 622–637. https://doi.org/10.1016/j.jbusvent.2011.09.001

Li, L., Li, X., & Guo, Q. (2021). A systematic review of start-up valuation methods: Evidence from China. *Journal of Small Business Management, 59*(2), 228–246. https://doi.org/10.1111/jsbm.12341

Miloud, T., Aspelund, A., & Cabrol, M. (2012). Startup valuation by venture capitalists: An empirical study. *Venture Capital, 14*(2–3), 151–174.

Min, J., & Lee, Y. (2017). The effect of growth prospects on start-up valuation. *Journal of Business Venturing, 32*(6), 567–583. https://doi.org/10.1016/j.jbusvent.2017.07.001

Montani, D., Gervasio, D., & Pulcini, A. (2020). Startup company valuation: The state of art and future trends. *International Business Research, 13*(9), 31–45.

Moradi, N., & Fadaei, M. (2021). The impact of intangible assets on start-up valuation: A meta-analytic review. *Journal of Business Research, 126*, 400–410. https://doi.org/10.1016/j.jbusres.2020.10.073

Moro-Visconti, R., & Moro-Visconti, R. (2021). *Startup valuation* (pp. 213–241). Springer International Publishing.

Mu, X., & Ma, L. (2020). A comparative study of start-up valuation methods: An empirical analysis. *Journal of Business Research, 117*, 361–373. https://doi.org/10.1016/j.jbusres.2019.06.074

Petrov, P. (2019). A review of start-up valuation methods. *Journal of Entrepreneurship, Innovation and Small Business, 3*(2), 149–167. https://doi.org/10.1186/s42513-019-0005-x

Que, J., & Zhang, X. (2021). Money chasing hot industries? Investor attention and valuation of venture capital backed firms. *Journal of Corporate Finance, 68*, 101949.

Ramelli, S., & Wagner, A. F. (2018). The value of investor attention in predicting stock returns. *Journal of Financial Economics, 129*(2), 367–382. https://doi.org/10.1016/j.jfineco.2018.04.011

Sass Rubin, J. (2010). Venture capital and underserved communities. *Urban Affairs Review, 45*(6), 821–835.

Shane, S. (2008). *The illusions of entrepreneurship: The costly myths that entrepreneurs, investors, and policy makers live by*. Yale University Press.

Shill, L. E., & Kaur, S. (2020). Start-up valuation: An empirical study. *International Journal of Entrepreneurial Behavior and Research, 26*(7), 1747–1758. https://doi.org/10.1108/IJEBR-02-2019-0140

Suwarni, R. N., Fahlevi, M., & Abdi, M. N. (2020). Startup valuation by venture capitalists: An empirical study Indonesia firms. *International Journal of Control and Automation, 13*(2), 785–796.

Terpstra, D. E., & Olson, P. D. (1993). Entrepreneurial start-up and growth: A classification of problems. *Entrepreneurship Theory and Practice, 17*(3), 5–20.

Vohra, R., & Kaur, S. (2020). Start-up valuation methods: A review. *International Journal of Innovation and Economic Development, 6*(4), 1–10. https://doi.org/10.11648/j.ijied.20200604.11

Venture Capital Method

Amar Rapaka

1 Introduction to VC Method

VC Method is a commonly used valuation method in the venture capital industry for valuing startups. Investors seek a return equal to some multiple of their initial investment.

Venture capital firms are pure financial investors. The purpose of venture capital firms is not to keep themselves invested in a startup indefinitely but to exit the investment at some point in the future. Typically, venture capitalists look for an exit within 3–7 years.

Unlike strategic investors that have other strategic reasons, such as technology and market access, venture capital firms invest for pure financial reasons. For this reason alone, the exit value of the startup assumes high importance in making an investment decision.

Another reason typical of venture capital investments is that venture capital firms invest in startups on behalf of other investors, hence fund management fee and carried interest assumes importance in their valuations.

Unlike other valuation methods, such as methods based on free cash flows or comparable companies, venture capital method incorporates the exit value, management fee, and carried interest in the valuation. Hence, the venture capital method is a widely adopted method in the venture capital industry.

A. Rapaka (✉)
London Business School, Andhra University, Hyderabad, India
e-mail: arapaka.sln2011@london.edu

S. Derindere Köseoğlu (ed.), *A Practical Guide for Startup Valuation*, Contributions to Finance and Accounting, https://doi.org/10.1007/978-3-031-35291-1_7

2 Seven Steps to Value a Startup Using the Venture Capital Method

There are seven steps to value a company using the venture capital method. Deciding on the quantity of investment is the first step. The second step is to find the investment exit value. Finding the present value of the exit value is the third step. Finding the value of the company is the fourth step. The fifth step is to estimate the value of the company owned by the VC. Estimating the management cost and carried interest, and incorporating them into the valuation is the sixth step. The last step is to decide on the investment.

Now let us look at each of the steps mentioned above in detail.

2.1 *Step 1: Determine the Investment Required*

Studying the business plan prepared by the entrepreneur is the first step to determine the investment required. The business plan summarizes all crucial information about the company; it includes the strategic plan, the competitors, and the financial projection. The financial projections focus on the use of funds and sources of funds. This gives an idea of the funds required by the startup. The business plan also will outline in detail how much the entrepreneur plans to raise in this round.

The financial projections from the business plan should be taken as a starting point, but not to be relied upon. Most startups have little to no sales, and the entrepreneur may have only the faintest idea about how the startup is going to perform in the future. With mature companies, forecasting sales, profits, and cash flow are relatively straightforward. However, for startups, VCs must put much more effort into getting inside the business and the opportunity. Deciding the investment required is both a science and art. Information such as on the size of the market, capability and experience of the management team, competitive edge of the product with respect to the competition, patents, and assessment of various risks can help decide on the quantum of investment.

2.2 *Step 2: Finding the Exit Value*

The focus of this step is to value the company at the time of exit. A successful exit is likely an IPO or a competitive sale. There are many techniques to estimate the exit value. The three main approaches are (1) relative valuation, (2) absolute valuation, and (3) successful exit method in the same industry.

2.2.1 Relative Valuation

In the relative valuation, we find a set of companies that can be compared to our startup. Among VC, among all the exit methods, relative valuation is by far the most popular method to value a company.

There are many multiples that can be used to estimate the target value. Some of the popular multiples are EV/EBIT, EV/EBITDA, P/E, EV/Revenue.

Out of all the ratios, P/E is probably the most widely used valuation multiple. Price refers to the market cap and earning refers to net income.

Let us see how we can use P/E valuation multiple to arrive at the exit valuation. Let us say our company, Startup Co, projected revenue, EBITDA, and net income are as follows:

	Year 1	Year 2	Year 3	Year 4	Year 5
Revenue	\$5 M	\$10 M	\$20 M	\$50 M	\$100 M
EBITDA	\$0 M	\$2 M	\$10 M	\$20 M	\$40 M
Net income	\$0 M	\$1 M	\$3 M	\$5 M	\$10 M

Let us say comparable public companies are trading at the 20X their earnings, then the exit value of Startup Co using P/E multiple is \$10 M*20 = \$200 M.

2.2.2 Absolute Valuation

In absolute valuation, we use the discounted cash-flow (DCF) model. There are two key inputs to DCF models. The first is the discount rate, and the second is the cash flow models.

Free cash flow (FCF) is the cash a company generates after considering all cash outflows, such as CAPEX, working capital, etc.

Free cash flows are estimated for a period until the company is stable. The perpetual value of the company at the point when the company is stable is estimated. Both the forecasted cash flows and the perpetual value of the company are discounted back to the time of the exit and are added to get the value of the company at the time of exit. Discount rate is the opportunity cost of the investment. It measures the required return from the investment given the riskiness of the future cashflows. This discount rate can be high given the high-risk nature of the startups.

2.2.3 Successful Exit Method in the Same Industry

This method is more prevalent than the above two methods in the venture capital industry. In this method, the venture capitalist will use the average valuation of successful exits in the same industry to arrive at the exit value.

For example, suppose the average valuation of successful IPOs in the same industry is \$500 M. Then the venture capitalist can assume the exit value to be \$500 M.

2.3 Step 3: Finding the Present Value of the Exit Value

To convert the exit value to today's date, we need an appropriate discount rate. VC usually uses high target return, reflecting the high failure rates of startups. Estimating the rate of return is a challenge, given that startups have little historical data to calculate betas. This discount rate represents not the target return, but the cost to the venture capital company. The cost to a venture capital company is calculated with a probability that indicates a successful exit. Let p represent the probability of a successful exit.

The expected value at exit is the exit value got from the previous step multiplied by p.

As explained in the previous step, the exit can be calculated using DCF, relative method, or exit method.

Let us assume that the expected exit will be after T years.

Then, the present discounted value at exit is an exit value multiplied by

$$\frac{p}{(1 + VC\_discount\_rate)^T}$$

where $VC\_discount\_rate$ is the cost of capital for the venture capital company, and $\frac{p}{(1+VC\_discount\_rate)}$ is the discount factor.

The inverse of the discount factor is the called target multiple of money. The target multiple of the money is later used in valuing the company.

Let us say $VC\_discount\_rate$ is 25%, and the probability of successful exit probability is 40%. Also, let us assume that a successful exit time is 7 years.

Then the target multiple of the money $= \frac{(1+VC\_discount\_rate)^T}{p} =$ 1.25^7/40% = 11.9.

The target multiple of money is one of the key parameters in the overall valuation and depends on assumptions regarding the value of T and p. So, conducting a sensitivity analysis on various values of T and p gives the venture capitalist a range of company's valuation.

2.4 Step 4: Estimating the Value of the Company

The value of the company is discounted value of exit value adjusted for retention rate. The reason for using the retention rate is to take into account later rounds of fundings.

Most startups need further rounds of funding as they don't turn cash flow positive for a considerable time. This results in dilution of ownership percentage for the previous investors. In reality, it is hard to predict the dilution of ownership that can arise from future funding rounds, hence most VCs use educated guesses and experience to arrive at the dilution.

To calculate the dilution, we take all the diluted share count of the startup after the current round of investment. The diluted share count is arrived when we add shares that have not been yet vested to the basic share count. The reason is that at the time of a successful exit, all the shares that have been vested will be realized.

The next step is to estimate the number of shares at the time of exit. This can be through an educated guess or experience.

The retention percentage = percentage of ownership after the current round of investment for the VC/percentage of ownership at the time of investment exit.

Let us say a VC buys 1 M share out of 4 M share of a startup. This means 25% (1 M/4 M) of the ownership of the startup is held by the VC. Now at the time of exit, the startup raised another 1 M. The share count now is 5 M shares, the ownership now fell to 20% (1 M/5 M).

The retention percentage is the percentage of ownership after the current round of investment/percentage of ownership at the time of investment exit = 0.20/0.25 = 80%.

Total valuation = exit valuation * retention%/target multiple of money.

Let us say the target multiple of money is 11.9, the retention is 80% and the exit value is $500 M.

Then the total valuation at present is $500 M * 80%/11.9 = $33.6 M.

2.5 Step 5: Estimating the Value of the Company Owned by the VC

Total valuation gives the valuation of the entire company, but the VC doesn't own the entire company, but part of the company. There are two major ways to value the part owned by the company.

The first one is through the option valuation. The second one is to make a simple approximation of the total company value multiplied by the proposed ownership of the company by the VC. In general, most VCs use the second one. We too will use the second one here.

Let us say the proposed ownership percentage by the VC today is 20%, and the total valuation is $33.6 M.

Then the partial valuation is 20% * $33.6 M = $6.7 M.

2.6 Step 6: Including Fund Management Fee and Carried Interest into the Valuation

The expenses of VCs, such as salaries, rents, administrative costs, legal costs, etc., should be included while deciding on the cost-benefit analysis of the investment. This cost is called the fund management fee.

Carried interest is the portion of future profits from an investment paid to general partners (GP) by the limited partners (LP) of the fund. Simply put, carried interest is a performance fee.

Limited partners (LP) are those who invest their capital in the venture capital fund. General partners (GP) are investment professionals who are responsible for making investment decisions and running the fund.

Committed capital is the money that LPs invest for venture capital fund. Investment capital is committed capital minus the fund management fee. Investment capital is the money available for investing for the GPs.

The fund management fee is calculated based on committed capital. Let us say the committed capital is $500 M. The life of the fund is 10 years, and management fees for years 1, 2, 3, 4, 5, 6, 7, 8, 9, and 10 are 2%, 2.5%, 2.5%, 2%, 2%, 1.5%, 1.5%, 1%, 1%, and 1.5% respectively. In general, management fees are high at the beginning of the fund's life and taper out at the end time of the fund's life.

Then the 10-year management fee = committed capital * (2% + 2.5% + 2.5% + 2% + 2% + 1.5% + 1.5% + 1% + 1% + 1.5%), which is $500 M * 13% = $87.5 M.

Investment capital = committed capital – management fee = $500 M – $65 M = $412.5 M. $412.5 M is the money available for investments in companies and not $500 M. Typically, 2% of the committed capital goes into fund management fee.

Let us say the VC is considering investing $10 M in a startup from the total available $412.5 M investment capital.

Then LPs cost for the $10 M investment = ($500 M/$412.5 M) * $10 M = $12.1 M.

Now let us investigate carried interest. The typical carried interest rate charged to LPs is 20%, although some GPs can receive even higher compensation. A carried interest rate of 20% means that after LPs have been paid their original investment back, the GPs will get 20% of the total profits from the investment fund, and the remaining 80% of fund's profits are paid to the LPs.

The general idea behind carried interest is that if the overall VC fund is profitable, some profits will belong to the GPs of the VC fund, and the rest will go to the LPs. This act has an incentive on the part of GPs to perform well.

Let us say the fund earned twice the invested capital at the end of 10 years, given the 20% carried interest of the GP, the GP profits are

(2*$412.5 M – $500 M) * 20% = $65 M
The GP% in the total profits = $65 M/ (2*$412.5 M) = 8%.
LPs valuation = (1 – GP% in the total profits) * partial valuation = 92% of $6.7 M = $6.1 M. (Here, as calculated in the previous step $6.7 M is the partial investment.)

2.7 *Step 7: Making the Investment Decision*

Investment recommendations are based on comparing costs to benefits. The costs are the money invested by the VC. The benefits are the present value of the exit valuation of the company. Investment recommendations are based on analyzing costs to benefits.

A good investments analysis takes a range of possible input values to test the sensitivity cost benefits analysis for various assumptions.

For some VC such an angel investor the management fee and carried interest doesn't make much sense as they invest their own money. For this section of VCs, we need not take the management fee and carried interest into consideration. Whatever fund management fee that is needed can be assumed to be included in the target multiple of money.

In this case, the investment decision is made based on comparing partial valuation to the investment amount.

For professional VC that run funds raised from LPs, the above may not be the ideal case. First, it mixes costs into valuation. Second, professional VCs need fund management fees to run the funds as it can take anywhere from 3 to 7 years to realize the investments. Last, the carried interest ties the VCs' interests to that of LPs' interests.

In this case, the investment decision is made based on comparing LPs' valuation to LPs' costs.

3 A Case to Illustrate the VC Method

Let us consider a VC is considering investing $10 M in a startup.

The committed capital is $150 M, and a 3% management fee over the fund life of the 10 years.

The founders of the Startup currently hold 10 M shares of common stock.

The VC proposes to add 5 M shares. Thus, following the investment, the Startup will have 15 M common shares outstanding.

The cost of venture capital fund (discount rate) is 20%.

The VC estimates a 40% probability for a successful exit, with an expected exit time in 5 years case.

The carried interest is 20%.

Now let us find out whether to invest.

3.1 Step 1

Suppose that, after due diligence, the VC estimates the startup needs an investment of $10 M.

The VC came to the $10 M required investment based on founders' business plans, industry trends, and the VC's own experience investing in this sector and previous transactions in the same industry.

3.2 Step 2

Exit value can be estimated based on relative valuation multiples, discounted cash flow valuation or exit valuation, as described in the above sections.

Let us say in this case, the VC has used an IPO exit of a similar transaction in the same industry to come with the exit value.

The average IPO exit in this industry is $500 M. We can use $500 M as our estimate for the exit value.

3.3 Step 3

As given in the case the cost of venture capital of 20%, 40% is the success rate for an IPO exit, and a successful exit time of 5 years.

As described in the above section, the required multiple of money.

$= \frac{(1+VC\_discount\_rate)^T}{p} = 1.2\hat{}5\ 40\% = 6.2$, where say $VC\ \_\ discount\ \_\ rate =$ 20%, $T = 5$ years and $p = 40\%$.

3.4 Step 4

To estimate the total value of the startup, we need exit valuation, target multiple of money, and retention rate. We already have the exit valuation, target multiple of money from the previous steps.

To find expected retention, we use stocks holding of the startup at different timelines.

The founder's stock before the investment = 10 M (from the case).

The proposed additional stock by the VC = 5 M (from the case).

After the investment, the VC holds 5 M/15 M = 33% of the company.

The startup is estimated to add another 20 M of shares in future funding rounds (from the case).

After the future rounds of funding, the VC will hold 5 M/35 M = 14%.

The expected retention rate = 14%/33% = 43%.

Now the total valuation = exit valuation * retention/M = $500 M*43%/ 6.2 = $34.45 M.

3.5 Step 5

The partial valuation is the proposed ownership * total valuation.

The proposed ownership percentage today is 5 M/15 M = 33.3%.

The partial valuation is 33.3%* $34.45 M = $11.48.

3.6 Step 6

To calculate the management fee, we need to calculate the investment capital.

The committed capital is $150 M. It is given in the case that the management fee is 3% over the fund life of the 10 years equaling $45 M.

The invested capital is committed capital – management fee = $105 M.

Then LPs cost = (Committed Capital/investment capital) * proposed investment.

= ($150 M/$105 M) * $10 M = $14.29 M.

Now it is given in the case that the fund earned 2.5 times the invested capital at the end of 10 years, given the 20% carried interest of the GP, the GP profits are (2.5* $105 M – $150) * 20% = $12 M.

The GP% in the total profits = $12 M/ (2.5*$105 M) = 8.6%.

Now the LPs Valuation = (1 – GP% in the total profits) * partial valuation.

= (1 – 8.6%) *$11.48 = $10.50 M.

3.7 Step 7

In this step, we need to decide on the investment.

Case 1: When a VC has negligible management fee and carried interest, to arrive at the investment decision, we need to compare the investment to the partial valuation.

As calculated, the partial valuation is $11.48 M, which is greater than the $10 M of investment. The VC should go ahead with the investment.

Case 2: In case the VC incurs fund management fees and carried interest, to arrive at the investment decision, we need to compare the LP's cost to the LP's valuation.

As calculated, the LP's cost = $14.29 M and LP's valuation = $10.50 M.

As the LP's cost is greater than the LP's valuation, the VC should not go with this investment.

3.8 Sensitivity Analysis for the Above Case

As described in this chapter, the target multiple of money is so important in the overall valuation that there is a need for doing a sensitivity analysis on various values of T and p that goes into calculating the target multiple of the money.

The following table is a sensitive table to calculate Target Multiple of Money by varying T and p for the above case.

	Probability of exit (p)			
		30%	40%	50%
Time of exit (T)	5	8.3	6.2	5
	6	10	7.5	6
	7	11.9	9	7.2

Given the various Target Multiple of Money, various valuation figures.

Target multiple of money	Valuation (in million)
5	$43.06
6	$35.88
6.2	$34.45
7.2	$29.90
7.5	$28.71
8.3	$25.83
9	$23.92
10	$21.53
11.9	$17.94

So, the range of valuations is from $17.94 M to $43.06 M. The venture capitalist should conduct a sensitivity analysis to understand the sensitivity of valuations before arriving at an investment decision.

4 Disadvantages of VC Method

There are two major disadvantages of the VC Method:

First, the VC Method demands the projection of company revenues and growth into the future, and this can be extremely difficult. Second, the VC Method needs the valuation multiples to arrive at a terminal valuation, which can be subjective and can change from investor to investor, which can give rise to less certain valuations.

Second, the discount rate required to decide on the valuation is subjective and is based on the risk perceived by the investor. Hence is not a universally accepted another for assessing risk, hence can change from one investor to another. Therefore, the VC Method can produce different valuations for the same startup from one investor to another and is based on the assumptions and risk perception among investors.

5 Conclusion

The VC Method is a favorite method for valuing companies in most venture capital companies across the world because its advantages outweigh its disadvantages.

Unlike strategic investors, venture capital firms exit the startup at some point in the future to realize their investments. For this reason, the exit value of the startup assumes high importance in making an investment decision.

Another reason for the popularity of the VC Method is that venture capital firms invest in startups on behalf of other investors, hence fund management fee and carried interest assume importance in their valuations.

Last, no venture capital company owns all the startups. There are founders, and future rounds of funding making sure there are other stockholders, hence partial valuation assumes importance.

VC Method accommodates all the above reasons, and hence, is widely adopted by the VC industry.

Terminology

General partners (GP)	General partners (GP) are investment professionals who make investment decisions and running the fund.
Limited partners (LP)	Limited partners (LP) are those who invest their capital in the venture capital fund.
Required investment	Capital needed by the startup to fund its operations.
Exit value	Value of a company/startup when venture capital firm plans to realize its investment. Typically, a value at an IPO or a strategic sale.

Exit time	Time when a venture capital firm plans to exit the investment. Typically, venture capitalists look for an exit within 3–7 years.
Discounted cash flow (DCF)	Discounted cash flow (DCF) is a valuation method that estimates the value of a company/ investment using its expected future cash flows.
Relative valuation	Relative valuation is a valuation method that estimates the value of a company/investment by comparing it to other similar company/ investment based on metrics such as EV/EBITDA, EV/Revenue, and P/E ratios, etc.
Successful exit valuation method	The average valuation of successful exits, such as an IPO or a strategic sale in the same industry.
Target multiple of money	The multiple of money that a venture capital firm expects when an investment goes to a successful exit, such as an IPO or strategic sale.
Retention rate	Retention rate is the ratio of current ownership to final ownership of the venture capital firm in the startup.
Fund management fee	Fund management fee is a charge levied by general partners (GP) for managing a venture capital fund.
Carried interest	Carried interest is a share of profits earned by general partners (GP) of the venture capital fund. It is the fee for performing the general partners (GP).
Total valuation	Total valuation is the present discounted value of the exit value, adjusted for the retention rate.
Partial valuation	Part of the value of the company/startup that the venture capitalist owns.
LP valuation	The profits earned by limited partners (LP) from an investment in a venture capital fund
GP valuation	The profits earned by general partners (GP) from making the investment.
LP costs	Cost incurred by limited partners (LP) to invest in a venture capital fund. This includes investment committed, fund management fee, and carried interest.

The First Chicago Valuation Method

Saeid Mashhadi

1 Introduction

In the 1960s, while serving as President of First Chicago Corporation (which no longer exists under that name), Stanley C. Golder developed the First Chicago valuation method. Many other financial institutions have since adopted this method, which revolutionized the way companies are valued. By using the First Chicago method, companies can be valued more accurately and more reliably than with alternative methods like the discounted cash flow methodology (DCF). Using this method, the firm's valuation is determined by estimating its earnings, cash flows, and capital structure. First Chicago valuation has gained widespread acceptance among investment banks and other financial institutions over the past few years, and it is now regarded as a reliable method of valuing companies.

The First Chicago valuation method is a tool for determining the value of a company based on the analysis of its expected future cash flows in multiple scenarios. According to this model, the value of a company is equal to its present value of future cash flows. This method takes into account multiple factors, such as industry trends, economic conditions, and the company's internal data, to make an accurate estimation of value. Additionally, the First Chicago method examines the company's operating risk and capital costs.

As an extension of the standard DCF, the First Chicago method runs three or more separate DCFs under varying assumptions, and then weights the values based on the probability of each outcome occurring. By doing so, it allows for more uncertainty to be considered as it weights the different scenarios. This makes it likely to provide more accurate values than the DCF for companies with high uncertainty levels. The First Chicago method involves analyzing multiple scenarios to determine what outcome is likely to occur for the organization. Therefore,

S. Mashhadi (✉)
Sharif University of Technology, Tehran, Iran

S. Derindere Köseoğlu (ed.), *A Practical Guide for Startup Valuation*, Contributions to Finance and Accounting, https://doi.org/10.1007/978-3-031-35291-1_8

probability values are assigned to a variety of scenarios, which also points out one of the method's shortcomings: it is highly subjective and judgmental.

While the DCF is most suitable for stable companies that have low risk and strong accounting records, the First Chicago method, with its assigned logical probabilities, may be more accurate in reflecting uncertainty. A startup's needs seem to be well met by this approach as well. This is due to the fact that these companies usually have a higher potential upside than their current market value, which could be accounted for by providing a scenario in which the company succeeds. Additionally, a higher default risk will be taken into consideration. As a consequence, the First Chicago method might be argued to be the most accurate valuation method for startups.

The First Chicago method is extremely versatile as it is characterized by a number of aspects. The primary advantage of this valuation method is that quantitative evidence about risk can be provided when compared to other valuation methods. This is because it considers both the qualitative and quantitative aspects of a business. Using this method, a more comprehensive picture of the company's value is provided by taking into account the company's financial performance, industry conditions, and competitive environment. Furthermore, the First Chicago method allows businesses to calculate their risk-adjusted return on investment, which is an important factor when deciding on an investment.

2 Literature Review

There have been several research studies conducted to evaluate the effectiveness of the First Chicago Valuation Method (FCVM). A study published by Babiarz (2016) examines the methods used by venture capital funds to value investments financed by public funds. In the study, the discounted cash flow and multiples methods were found to be the most frequently used methods. The article presents a comprehensive overview of the various valuation methods and recommends that the method chosen should depend on the specific characteristics of the investment project and the investor's preferences. Another study by Majercakova and Mittelman (2018) examines the valuation methods employed by a venture capital fund in the evaluation of technology start-ups. Based on the study, a combination of valuation methods was used, including the discounted cash flow and multiples methods. The article presents a comprehensive overview of these methods, highlighting the necessity of taking non-financial factors into account.

According to Achleitner and Lutz (2005), venture capital investors face difficulties when valuing innovative start-ups, and they usually use context-specific valuation methods. One such method, the FCVM, is based on the DCF method in large part and models three scenarios to account for payouts to investors during the holding period. The article explains the method in detail and illustrates how it can be applied to the valuation of startups. The authors conclude that while the FCVM has conceptual advantages over the Venture Capital Method, it is also more complex. Rothman (2020) discusses the FCVM and the use of real options in his book "Valuations of Early-Stage Companies and Disruptive Technologies." The book discusses both methods in detail, emphasizing the importance of observing the competitive landscape and market conditions when valuing early-stage startups.

In their study, Montani et al. (2020) noted that early-stage companies have unique characteristics that make determining their actual value difficult. Based on the authors' conclusions, there are no reliable methods for estimating the value of startups using the traditional methods. However, the FCVM is an alternative method to traditional methods of valuing startups. Every model analyzed in the article has significant limitations, and there are a lot of improvements that can be made. As outlined in this article, when selecting a valuation method, three factors must be considered: focusing on future forecasts rather than past data, utilizing probability to evaluate different scenarios, and understanding and paying attention to a startup's business model rather than historical data on comparable companies.

These studies indicate that the First Chicago valuation method can be an effective method of valuing startups, particularly when used in conjunction with qualitative analysis and adjustments to take into account the unique characteristics of early-stage companies. This method, however, may not be as accurate as it appears due to factors such as the quality of data available and the degree of uncertainty associated with the startup's future cash flow.

3 Applications

The First Chicago method can be used on a variety of assets and any type of business, regardless of its industry, making it a widely used valuation technique. In general, it is best suited to privately held companies with stable cash flow and an expected growth trajectory. Financial institutions utilize the FCVM when assessing the value of companies for the purposes of mergers and acquisitions, financing decisions, and other corporate transactions. The method is commonly utilized by financial professionals, such as investment bankers, venture capitalists, and private equity firms. Executives, such as CEOs and CFOs, also use it when making decisions regarding mergers and acquisitions. Moreover, this method can be used by individuals who are interested in investing in a company or an asset. The FCVM can be applied in the following ways:

Publicly Traded Companies
It is possible to estimate the value of publicly traded companies using the FCVM, especially if their cash flows are unpredictable or they do not pay dividends.

Private Companies
In addition to valuing public companies, the FCVM is suitable for evaluating private companies, especially those that are in their infancy and have little or no history of cash flows or earnings.

Real Estate
Real estate assets, primarily those that generate income through rent or other revenue streams, can be valued using the FCVM.

Project Finance
Especially for long-term cash flow-related projects in industries like infrastructure, energy, and natural resources, the FCVM can be used for project valuation.

Startups
As a result of its flexibility, the FCVM can be an excellent tool to use when valuing startups, since it allows for adjustments to be made in order to account for certain unique characteristics of these companies, such as their stage of development and degree of risk.

3.1 Application of the FCVM in Startups vs. Ongoing Businesses

Whether determining the value of an existing business or a startup, the First Chicago method is applicable to both, but there are certain key differences that should be considered.

Historical Performance
An ongoing business typically has a historical record of financial performance, including revenues, expenses, and earnings, which can be used in the calculation of the FCVM. In contrast, startups may not have a significant financial history, making it difficult to estimate future cash flows or calculate appropriate discount rates.

Growth Prospects
Historically, existing businesses have had more stable and predictable growth prospects than startups, which can be reflected in the FCVM calculation. A startup may, however, have more growth potential than an established company, which can be considered in the valuation process.

Risk
Generally, startups are considered to be more risky than existing companies, due to the lack of financial history, non-tested business models, and uncertain market conditions. Thus, to account for the higher level of risk, the discount rate used in the FCVM may be significantly higher for startups than for ongoing businesses.

Stage of Development
A startup is usually in the early stages of development, while an ongoing business is well established and has proven performance. Therefore, it may be necessary to adjust the FCVM according to the stage of development of the company.

In light of these differences between startups and ongoing businesses, the following describes the specific applications of the FCVM in startups:

Angel Investments
The FCVM can be used to value startups in the context of angel investments, as it allows for adjustments to be made to account for the stage of development and the level of risk associated with the company.

Pre-revenue Startups
The FCVM can be used to value startups in the pre-revenue stage, since it estimates the company's future cash flows and discounts them back to present value before the company is incorporated.

Early-Stage Startups
It is also possible to use the FCVM to value startups that are in the early stages of development. This is because the model allows adjustments to be made to account for the higher amount of risk and uncertainty associated with startups.

Venture Capital Investments
The FCVM is commonly used in the venture capital industry to value startup investments since it enables estimating the value of early-stage businesses which do not have a history of earnings or cash flows.

In summary, the FCVM can be used to provide an effective framework for valuing startups, particularly those in the pre-revenue or early-revenue stage without sufficient financial data to apply traditional valuation methods. While the FCVM can be applied to both existing businesses and new ventures, the valuation process may need to be tailored to account for the differences between their types. Depending on the specific characteristics of the company being valued, the FCVM calculation should be adjusted accordingly. Using the FCVM, investors and analysts are able to determine a startup's value more accurately, which can assist them in making informed investments and developing a strategic plan.

4 Pros and Cons

There are both advantages and disadvantages to using the First Chicago valuation method, which should be considered when evaluating the value of a company. Among its pros are its flexibility and wide application, while its disadvantages include its reliance on assumptions and complexity. The following sections examine in detail the pros and cons of using the First Chicago valuation method.

4.1 Pros

Focus on Future Cash Flows
The FCVM can provide a more accurate estimate of a startup's value than historical financial data. With this method, we can measure and quantify the risks associated with a company's operations or future performance.

Flexibility
Since the First Chicago method is an extension of the DCF method, it is an intuitive and straightforward approach to valuing a company. Based on a startup's stage of development and degree of risk, the FCVM can be customized to reflect its specific characteristics.

Widely Used
As a popular and widely used valuation method, the FCVM allows investors and analysts to compare startups' valuations more easily. Because it is relatively easy to use and understand, it is suitable for use by individuals who are not financial professionals. Moreover, it can be used to compare companies in different industries, as it is based on industry-specific factors such as the competition landscape and market trends.

Useful for Early-Stage Startups
The FCVM is useful for estimating the value of startup companies in the early stages of development, which often lack a solid financial history or an established track record. Because the method makes use of objective assumptions, it is more reliable than other relative or subjective methods which rely solely on the historical performance of the company.

4.2 Cons

Requires Assumptions
Similar to the DCF method, the FCVM requires a large number of assumptions about future cash flows and is highly sensitive to any changes in assumptions. It is especially pertinent in the case of startups which are prone to high levels of uncertainty. Furthermore, there is no basis for assigning probabilities to the various scenarios used in the valuation.

Discount Rate
As part of the FCVM, a discount rate must be used to calculate the risk of the investment, which is challenging for startups that are in the early stages of development.

Not Suitable for All Startups
The First Chicago method, like any other cash flow-based method, does not consider intangible assets such as brand recognition and customer loyalty, which can make a

significant impact on a company's value. In addition, the FCVM may not be suitable for all startups, such as those that have a non-standard business model.

May Not Reflect Market Conditions
The FCVM does not take into account external factors such as competitors' relative valuations, changes in economic conditions or technological advancements that may disrupt an industry or create new opportunities for competitors.

In summary, the FCVM can be an effective tool for valuing startups, but its limitations and potential drawbacks need to be considered when applying it to a particular situation. It is important to note that any valuation method should be used in conjunction with other analyses and judgments in order to arrive at a reasonable estimate of the value of a startup.

5 Methodology

The First Chicago valuation method is an effective and powerful tool for assessing the value of a company. This approach relies on the capability of a company to generate future cash flows as a measure of its value. As part of the analysis, the firm is evaluated in terms of its competitive position, growth prospects, and risk profile. In addition, other economic factors may influence the value of the company, such as the cost of capital.

In the FCVM, cash inflows and outflows are estimated for a forecast period (usually 5 years), a terminal cash flow value is calculated that captures value beyond the implied period of time, and these cash flows are discounted at a rate unique to the business known as the weighted average cost of capital. As part of the First Chicago method, essential data pertaining to a startup must be collected, such as revenue, earnings, cash flows, exit horizons, financial forecasts, etc. In order to accurately estimate the scenarios, you will also need to analyze industry and market trends.

Three types of scenarios are considered according to the First Chicago method: the least optimal outcome, the intermediate outcome, as well as the best-case outcome. Each scenario is then assigned a probability. A company's estimated valuation is calculated by multiplying each probability by the present value of its future cash flows in the corresponding scenario, then taking the average of those values. Figure 1 provides an overview of the FCVM. As shown in this figure, "EV" represents the Enterprise Value for the company under each scenario, while "p" denotes the probability of each scenario occurring.

Listed below is a step-by-step guide on how to use the First Chicago valuation method:

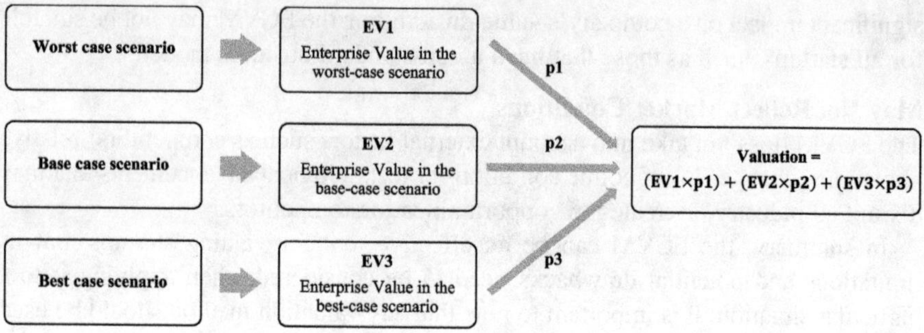

Fig. 1 Overview of the First Chicago valuation methodology. Source: Author's own creation

5.1 *Defining the Scenarios*

In the First Chicago valuation method, three different scenarios are considered: the best-case scenario, the base-case scenario, and the worst-case scenario. In the best-case scenario, the company's performance exceeds the expectations that were set out in the base-case scenario. It is a way to measure the potential upside of investments, as the best-case scenario is usually the most optimistic one. Under the base scenario, the company's performance meets expectations and falls within the range of expected performance. The outcomes of the base scenario are generally in accordance with the business plan. In the worst-case scenario, performance falls short of expectations, which results in a slower rate of growth and delays in completing the project, ultimately resulting in higher expenses. Based on the three scenarios offered, we are able to gain a better understanding of how our investments are likely to perform in the future.

5.2 *Estimating Future Cash Flows*

Upon defining the scenarios, you should begin by estimating the future cash flows of the company over the forecast period. To accomplish this, historical financial statements need to be analyzed in order to make assumptions regarding future growth and profitability. It may be challenging for startups or any company in its early stages to determine cash inflows and outflows over a 5-year forecast period. The forecasting process becomes more difficult when we are attempting to create a financial forecast for a technology startup. Specifically, this is due to the fact that the forecast must also include expected cash inflows and outflows from a digital product (e.g., an online platform or software), which has not been tested on the market or is in the early stages of its experimentation.

5.3 Determining the Discount Rate

In the First Chicago method of valuation, the discount rate used can have a significant impact on the calculated value of a startup, and it is critical to choose a discount rate that is appropriate for the stage and risk of the business. A discount rate can be calculated in the FCVM in a number of ways, depending on the stage of the startup.

Startups in the seed and early stages are typically subject to a higher discount rate than those in the later stages. For these startups, the Build-Up Method can be used to calculate the discount rate by adding a number of risk premiums together. A risk premium may include factors such as market risk, industry risk, size premium, and company-specific risks.

Startups that are at an advanced stage of development, where failure is less likely, may have a lower discount rate. It is possible to determine the discount rate for these startups according to the Weighted Average Cost of Capital (WACC) formula. In this case, the cost of equity is calculated using the Capital Asset Pricing Model (CAPM), which takes into account the risk-free rate, the expected market return, as well as the beta of the company. This discount rate can also be calculated using the Modified CAPM, which adjusts the beta according to the startup's specific risks.

As a startup progresses through different stages of development, the methods of calculating the discount rate in the FCVM are designed to reflect the changing risk profile of the startup. The FCVM provides a more accurate estimate of the startup's potential future cash flows by using appropriate discount rates according to the startup's stage of development. For startups at different stages of their business, the following general considerations should be taken into account when calculating the discount rate in the FCVM:

Seed Stage

At the seed stage, startups are typically facing an elevated degree of risk and uncertainty, as well as lack an established track record or a well-developed business plan. Depending on the level of risk involved in this type of startup, a discount rate of 50–100% might be appropriate.

Early Stage

A startup at the early stage has generally made some progress in developing its product or service, but may not yet have significant revenue or profitability. This type of startup may have a discount rate of 40–70%, depending on the level of risk and the development stage.

Growth Stage

During the growth stage, startups may have demonstrated traction and may be generating substantial revenue. However, they may still have a high degree of uncertainty regarding their future growth prospects. It is recommended that a discount rate of 30–50% be applied to these types of startups, based on the risk level and the stage of development.

Later Stage
It is typical for startups at the later stage to be more established and to have demonstrated a track record of revenues and profitability. Depending on the degree of risk and the stage of development, a discount rate of 20–40% may be appropriate for these types of startups.

These recommendations are intended as general guidelines. The discount rate used for a particular startup may vary due to a variety of factors, including country, global and local market conditions, competition, management team, and industry trends. In this regard, it is critical to evaluate each startup's unique characteristics carefully when determining an appropriate discount rate for the FCVM.

5.4 *Calculating the Terminal Value*

The terminal value of a company represents its value at some point in the future beyond the forecast period. A variety of methods can be used to calculate it, such as a multiple of earnings, or by applying a perpetual growth rate to the estimated free cash flow.

A terminal value within 5 years is generally used in the First Chicago valuation method to approximate the future cash flows that the business would generate if it were considered an ongoing business. By using this approach, it is assumed that the startup will continue to operate beyond the 5-year period, generating cash flows in perpetuity.

For established companies with a track record of success, this assumption may be reasonable, but it can be more problematic for startups, whose very nature is characterized by uncertainty and risk. In practice, however, the 5-year projection period is often used for startup valuations, in recognition of the fact that many startups have relatively short histories and uncertain prospects in the longer term.

The FCVM relies on a number of assumptions and factors for its determination of the terminal value within 5 years for a startup valuation. These assumptions and factors include:

Growth prospects: It is expected that the startup will grow rapidly over the next 5 years, as reflected in the cash flow projections.

Competitive landscape: In the 5-year period, the startup will be able to maintain or increase its market share due to its competitive advantage.

Management team: The startup is led by a strong and experienced management team that is capable of executing the business plan and driving the company's growth.

Industry trends: The startup is operating in an industry with favorable long-term trends, which is conducive to the success of its business model.

Despite these assumptions, it is important to realize that they may not always be accurate, and that using a terminal value within 5 years for startup valuations as if they were an ongoing business should be carefully reviewed and justified based on the particular circumstances of each startup.

5.5 *Calculating the Present Value of Future Cash Flows*

Once the expected future cash flows have been estimated and a discount rate has been determined, the present value of future cash flows can be calculated using a DCF model.

5.6 *Calculating the Total Enterprise Value*

In order to calculate the total enterprise value under each scenario, add up all of your estimated future cash flows over the forecast period and the present value of the terminal value. This estimate represents the cost of acquiring 100% ownership of the company under today's conditions, including both debt and equity.

5.7 *Assigning Probabilities to Each Scenario*

As a final step, assign a probability to each scenario and calculate the weighted average valuation by multiplying the probabilities by the valuation for each scenario.

6 Challenges Associated with the First Chicago Method

One of the primary challenges associated with this model is the ability to accurately predict future cash flows. This involves making assumptions about the company's growth rate, operating expenses, and other factors that are difficult to predict. In addition, it is also difficult to estimate the appropriate discount rate to use when calculating the present value of future cash flows. Moreover, the value of a company does not take into account non-cash items, such as goodwill or intangibles. Below, we will discuss these challenges in detail and explore how they can be addressed.

Difficulty in Determining the Appropriate Discount Rate
As part of the First Chicago valuation method, the present value of future cash flows is calculated using a discount rate. Identifying this rate can be difficult due to the lack of knowledge about a company's risk profile as well as its ability to generate future cash flows. A solution to this is to use the weighted average cost of capital (WACC), which takes into account the company's cost of debt and cost of equity, to determine the discount rate.

Difficulty in Estimating Future Cash Flows
Estimating future cash flows is a difficult task, as it requires an understanding of the company's operations, competitive environment, and industry trends. Creating a

DCF model is one solution to this problem, in which assumptions can be made about all aspects of the organization. A DCF model allows the user to create reliable assumptions that are based on the company's current and projected performance, while also taking into account external factors such as the industry's dynamics and competitive environment.

Subjectivity
The First Chicago valuation method is largely based on subjective inputs such as management's expectations and assumptions regarding the company's future performance. In this case, inaccurate assumptions may result in inaccurate valuations. To address these issues, the First Chicago method should be supplemented with more objective data points, such as past performance and industry trends, to ensure the accuracy of valuations.

Lack of Flexibility
The First Chicago valuation method employs a static approach that does not take into account changing market conditions or other factors that could affect the value of a company over time. Using a dynamic approach to define scenarios can enable a more accurate estimate of the value of a company. This involves incorporating market conditions in various circumstances into the valuation process.

7 Case Study for the First Chicago Method: Best Shop

7.1 Case Introduction

In this section, the First Chicago valuation model is applied to a case study that illustrates the practical application of the model based on the experience of "Best Shop, [1]" one of the leading e-commerce startups in the Middle East with approximately 20% share of the local online retail market. The company presents an ideal candidate for a detailed valuation using the First Chicago valuation method, since it has a solid market position and a resilient, continuously growing market. Additionally, Best Shop has a reliable historical financial record that can be used to estimate its future cash flows.

For late-stage startups such as Best Shop, the First Chicago valuation method offers a suitable solution since it emphasizes cash flows, considers risk factors, is flexible, and takes into account potential upsides. The FCVM provides a more accurate value of a startup's future earnings because it focuses on cash flows, which is particularly critical for startups that are approaching or have achieved profitability. The FCVM is a flexible valuation method that is adaptable to the specific requirements and circumstances of late-stage startups. Using this method,

[1] The actual name of the company has been changed for confidentiality reasons.

Table 1 Best Shop 2022 Income Statement (all values are in local currency)

Item	2021	2022
Sales	168,577	322,743
Cost of goods sold	(114,446)	(228,949)
Gross profit	**54,131**	**93,794**
Operating expenses	(25,850)	(49,350)
Operating profit	**28,281**	**44,445**
Other income/expenses	0	(3616)
Earnings before taxes	**28,281**	**40,829**
Income taxes	(7070)	(10,207)
Net income	**21,210**	**30,621**

different discount rates can be applied according to the startup's development stage and the exit options available to it.

The FCVM provides a more realistic and nuanced assessment of a startup's value by incorporating factors specific to startups, such as market risk, technology risk, and management risk. In general, the FCVM is more accurate and comprehensive than other valuation methods for assessing the value of a startup in its late stages, particularly in the case of businesses approaching potential liquidity events such as an initial public offering.

Table 1 illustrates Best Shop's 2021 and 2022 financial results. According to these figures, the company achieved a gross margin of 32.1% and 29.1%, respectively, in 2021 and 2022. A decrease in the EBIT margin was also observed from 16.8% in 2021 to 13.8% in 2022. Additionally, it is important to note that the company is subject to a 25% annual tax rate.

7.2 *Estimating Future Cash Flows*

The first step in building our model is to estimate the company's future cash flows. We begin by gathering the necessary financial information, including income statements, balance sheets, and cash flow statements. In addition, we will need to gather any relevant industry information and macroeconomic information that may influence the company's performance. The income statement for the next 5 years is estimated based on Best Shop's 2022 results.

To estimate Best Shop's future cash flow, it is necessary to forecast the company's revenue, expenses, and capital expenditures over a specified period of time. Forecasts are based on a combination of objective and subjective assumptions for a period of 5 years. In order for the assumptions to be reasonable and accurate, they must reflect both the history of the company and its potential for growth in the future. Based on these assumptions, which are always derived from an in-depth analysis of the company, it is possible to forecast the income statement. It is, however, also necessary to make assumptions regarding changes in working capital, depreciation, and capital expenditures in order to forecast cash flows.

Ideally, each item on the income statement should be divided into smaller components. For instance, in order to estimate the company's sales or revenue, we should take into account any information regarding Best Shop's revenue channels and analyze the methods by which the company generates income. This approach can be applied to the company's expenses or to any other item on the income statement. As a result, we will be able to make objective assumptions about each component based on the Best Shop's historical performance and its future potential.

7.2.1 Assumptions

Due to the fact that our model will be constructed under three different scenarios, we will have to create three sets of different macroeconomic and operational assumptions. There are a number of factors that influence the assumptions underlying these scenarios, and they differ from company to company. The first is, what would constitute success for this particular company in terms of exceeding expectations? Secondly, what is the expected performance of the firm? Finally, what does a company's failure look like?

With Best Shop, the company's sales are derived from its online platform through the sale of products. Accordingly, Best Shop's sales are determined by the number of users on its website and the amount of money they spend on its products. Following is a simple representation of how Best Shop generates income (Fig. 2):

We can begin by estimating the number of total users of Best Shop and proceed from there in order to determine the sales of the business. An example of how assumptions should be made in order to estimate the number of total users on our website is shown in Table 2. Using the same approach, assumption tables can be constructed in three different scenarios for estimating the remaining components of sales (conversion rates, active users, customers, and average revenue per customer).

Having estimated the company's sales, we can move on to the next items on the income statement, such as cost of goods sold, operating expenses, etc. As another

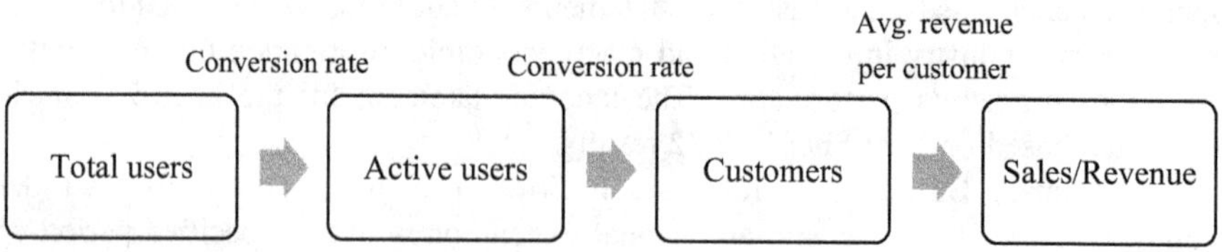

Fig. 2 Best Shop income generation process. Source: Author's own creation

Table 2 Sales assumptions: number of total users

Scenario	Current (2022)	Target (2027)
Worst-case	22,482,410	30,000,000
Base-case	22,482,410	35,000,000
Best-case	22,482,410	40,000,000

Table 3 Operating expenses assumptions: number of employees

Scenario	Current (2022)	Target (2027)
Worst-case	358	758
Base-case	358	843
Best-case	358	912

Table 4 Income statement forecast: worst-case scenario

Item	2023 (f)	2024 (f)	2025 (f)	2026 (f)	2027 (f)
Sales	506,548	737,399	1,033,944	1,322,111	1,685,501
Cost of goods sold	(322,500)	(480,233)	(682,675)	(872,732)	(1,112,839)
Gross profit	**184,048**	**257,166**	**351,270**	**449,379**	**572,661**
Operating expenses	(80,256)	(116,729)	(167,238)	(229,281)	(314,262)
Operating profit	**103,792**	**140,437**	**184,031**	**220,098**	**258,399**
Earnings before taxes	**103,792**	**140,437**	**184,031**	**220,098**	**258,399**
Income taxes	(25,948)	(35,109)	(46,008)	(55,024)	(64,600)
Net income	**77,844**	**105,328**	**138,023**	**165,073**	**193,799**

Table 5 Income Statement forecast: base-case scenario

Item	2023 (f)	2024 (f)	2025 (f)	2026 (f)	2027 (f)
Sales	538,860	832,432	1,235,798	1,674,004	2,257,807
Cost of goods sold	(338,393)	(527,950)	(786,313)	(1,053,323)	(1,407,345)
Gross profit	**200,467**	**304,482**	**449,485**	**620,681**	**850,462**
Operating expenses	(80,373)	(121,154)	(178,591)	(248,830)	(352,044)
Operating profit	**120,094**	**183,328**	**270,894**	**371,851**	**498,418**
Earnings before taxes	120,094	183,328	270,894	371,851	498,418
Income taxes	(30,024)	(45,832)	(67,724)	(92,963)	(124,605)
Net income	90,071	137,496	203,171	278,888	373,814

example, Table 3 shows the assumption table used for estimating human resource expenses, which is a component of operating expenses.

7.2.2 Income Statement Forecast

We have now constructed projections for each scenario using the actual numbers for 2022 and forecasted on the basis of those numbers for the next 5 years until 2027. After calculating gross profit and deducting SG&A expenses, depreciation, and interest payments, earnings before tax will be obtained. We will calculate tax expenses using the expected tax rate, which will result in the net income figure. Having forecasted all components, we are able to create a 5-year profit and loss projection. As shown in Tables 4, 5 and 6, the forecasted income statement for Best Shop in the worst-, base-, and best-case scenarios is presented.

Table 6 Income Statement forecast: best-case scenario

Item	2023 (f)	2024 (f)	2025 (f)	2026 (f)	2027 (f)
Sales	571,185	934,965	1,468,384	2,105,728	3,002,782
Cost of goods sold	(354,287)	(577,815)	(899,618)	(1,259,895)	(1,759,840)
Gross profit	216,898	357,150	568,766	845,833	1,242,942
Operating expenses	(80,380)	(123,287)	(186,032)	(262,686)	(387,605)
Operating profit	136,518	233,863	382,734	583,147	855,337
Earnings before taxes	136,518	233,863	382,734	583,147	855,337
Income taxes	(34,129)	(58,466)	(95,683)	(145,787)	(213,834)
Net income	102,388	175,397	287,050	437,360	641,503

Table 7 Capex forecast: all scenarios

Scenario	2023 (f)	2024 (f)	2025 (f)	2026 (f)	2027 (f)
Worst-case	2160	1163	2820	5311	10,554
Base-case	2160	1496	3146	6004	12,234
Best-case	2160	1850	3600	6417	13,569

Table 8 Depreciation forecast: all scenarios

Scenario	2023 (f)	2024 (f)	2025 (f)	2026 (f)	2027 (f)
Worst-case	(10,844)	(9107)	(7518)	(6579)	(6325)
Base-case	(10,844)	(9107)	(7585)	(6697)	(6558)
Best-case	(10,844)	(9107)	(7656)	(6845)	(6759)

7.2.3 Capex and Depreciation Forecast

As the business model does not depend on assets and does not require significant investments to expand, capex is assumed to only include the cost of purchasing equipment and computers for additional employees. Based on the old and newly incurred capital expenditures, depreciation is calculated using the straight-line method. In Tables 7 and 8, the forecasted capital expenditures and depreciation are presented for Best Shop.

7.2.4 Working Capital Forecast

In order to estimate the changes in working capital, we assume a reasonable working capital-to-sales ratio and multiply it by the total amount of sales for each period. Therefore, it is possible to calculate the changes in working capital, or more specifically, the additional investment in working capital per year. In order to make accurate assumptions about future capex and working capital quotas, it is always wise to consult with management and use historical data. Table 9 illustrates the forecasted working capital.

Table 9 Working capital forecast: all scenarios

Scenario	2023 (f)	2024 (f)	2025 (f)	2026 (f)	2027 (f)
Worst-case	29,492	48,440	78,439	129,296	219,977
Base-case	31,894	57,271	103,518	182,806	329,992
Best-case	34,296	70,136	136,924	254,183	480,876

Table 10 FCFF Calculation: worst-case scenario

Item	2023 (f)	2024 (f)	2025 (f)	2026 (f)	2027 (f)
EBIT	103,792	140,437	184,031	220,098	258,399
Minus: income tax	(25,948)	(35,109)	(46,008)	(55,024)	(64,600)
Plus: depreciation	10,844	9107	7518	6579	6325
Minus: capex	(2160)	(1163)	(2820)	(5311)	(10,554)
Minus: changes in working capital	(15,961)	(18,948)	(29,998)	(50,857)	(90,681)
FCFF	**70,567**	**94,323**	**112,723**	**115,484**	**98,890**

Table 11 FCFF Calculation: base-case scenario

Item	2023 (f)	2024 (f)	2025 (f)	2026 (f)	2027 (f)
EBIT	120,094	183,328	270,894	371,851	498,418
Minus: income tax	(30,024)	(45,832)	(67,724)	(92,963)	(124,605)
Plus: depreciation	10,844	9107	7585	6697	6558
Minus: capex	(2160)	(1496)	(3146)	(6004)	(12,234)
Minus: changes in working capital	(18,363)	(25,377)	(46,248)	(79,288)	(147,186)
FCFF	**80,391**	**119,730**	**161,362**	**200,294**	**220,953**

7.2.5 Free Cash Flow Calculation

Free cash flow to the firm (FCFF) is derived by adding depreciation to the after-tax operating profit (EBIT), subtracting capex, and taking into account the changes in working capital. The following equation can be used to calculate the firm's free cash flow:

$$\begin{aligned} \text{FCFF} = & \ \text{EBIT} - \text{Income Tax} + \text{Depreciation} - \text{CAPEX} \\ & - \text{Changes in Working Capital} \end{aligned}$$

In Tables 10, 11, and 12, the FCFF calculation for Best Shop is shown in the worst-case, base-case, and best-case scenarios, respectively.

7.3 Discount Rate

Once future cash flows have been estimated, we will need to calculate a discount rate that reflects the inherent risk associated with investing in this business. This

Table 12 FCFF Calculation: best-case scenario

Item	2023 (f)	2024 (f)	2025 (f)	2026 (f)	2027 (f)
EBIT	136,518	233,863	382,734	583,147	855,337
Minus: income tax	(34,129)	(58,466)	(95,683)	(145,787)	(213,834)
Plus: depreciation	10,844	9107	7656	6845	6759
Minus: capex	(2160)	(1850)	(3600)	(6417)	(13,569)
Minus: changes in working capital	(20,765)	(35,840)	(66,788)	(117,259)	(226,693)
FCFF	**90,308**	**146,814**	**224,318**	**320,529**	**408,000**

Table 13 WACC assumptions: all scenarios

Item	Value
Risk free rate	13.1%
Beta (levered)	0.81
Equity market risk premium	17.9%
After tax cost of debt	15.8%
W_e	0.88
W_d	0.12
WACC	**26.1%**

calculation can be carried out either utilizing a weighted average cost of capital (WACC) calculation or assuming a risk-free rate plus a premium based on the individual risk profile of the company. As mentioned earlier, Best Shop is currently in the later stages of its development. Therefore, we can calculate the discount rate of the company using a more comprehensive method, such as WACC. Other methods, however, might be more appropriate for estimating the discount rate of early-stage startups, depending on their development stage and the overall risks involved.

The assumptions used for calculating the WACC for Best Shop are shown in Table 13. While we assume that the WACC is the same for all scenarios, different discount rates can be applied based on the varying expected risks associated with the company in each scenario. The table shows that Best Shop should have a discount rate of 26.1%. Since Best Shop has largely been financed via private investors rather than debt, there is a greater weighting given to the cost of equity (0.88) compared to the cost of debt (0.12). A WACC may include additional risk premiums, such as illiquidity or early-stage risk premiums, reflecting the other risks associated with the company. We have not taken into account additional risk premiums when calculating the discount rate for Best Shop since it is a late-stage startup.

7.4 Terminal Value

The next step is to determine the terminal value of the company. A company's terminal value is what it will be worth at some future date after all its projected cash flows have been realized. Depending on the particular circumstances, you may choose to calculate the terminal value using either a perpetual growth rate or a multiple of earnings or revenue. As the name implies, the perpetual growth rate refers to the expected long-term growth rate of the startup's cash flows beyond the projection period. One method of calculating perpetual growth is to utilize the Gordon Growth Model, which assumes that the startup's cash flows will grow at a constant rate indefinitely. The startup's perpetual growth rate should be reasonable and reflect its long-term prospects. It is possible to overestimate a startup's value by considering a perpetuity growth rate too high. In addition, it is possible to underestimate its value by assuming a perpetuity growth rate too low. As a result, it is imperative that you use sound judgment and analysis when estimating the perpetual growth rate.

In the FCVM, it is generally not recommended to use perpetual growth rates when valuing early-stage startups. This type of growth rate is typically used to estimate the long-term growth rate of a mature business, assuming that cash flows will continue to flow at a stable rate indefinitely. Early-stage startups, however, are often subject to too much uncertainty and risk to make reliable long-term projections.

Since Best Shop is a late-stage startup, it is reasonable to assume that cash flows will grow at a stable rate for the foreseeable future. As the company should be able to adjust its prices in line with local inflation, we assume the long-term growth rate is 13.5%, 14.2%, and 14.8% for the worst-, base-, and best-case scenarios. The following equation can be used to calculate the terminal value:

$$TV_i = \frac{CF_N * (1 + g_i)}{(r - g_i)}$$

TV: terminal value
i: scenario index
N: forecast period
CF: cash flow
g: terminal growth rate
r: discount rate

Table 14 presents the calculations for terminal values in each scenario

Table 14 Terminal value calculation: all scenarios

Scenario	Growth rate	Terminal value
Worst-case	13.5%	890,104
Base-case	14.2%	2,118,663
Best-case	14.8%	4,141,414

7.5 *Present Value of Future Cash Flows*

The company's value in each scenario is derived from two parts, similar to the DCF method. The first is the company's present value during the forecast period (years 1 to 5), while the second is the company's present value of its terminal value (from year 5 into the future). The following formula shows how the present value of future cash flows is calculated in each scenario.

$$\text{Valuation}_i = \sum_{k=1}^{N} \frac{\text{CF}_k}{(1+r)^k} + \frac{\text{TV}_i}{(1+r)^N}$$

i: scenario index
N: forecast period
CF: cash flow in each period
r: discount rate
TV: terminal value

7.5.1 Present Value of Cash Flows in the Forecast Period

Using the estimated WACC, we may obtain the present value of the free cash flow in the forecast period (Table 15):

7.5.2 Present Value of the Terminal Value

Due to the fact that the terminal value represents the projected future cash flows of the company at the end of the forecast period (from year 5 to infinity), we must discount the terminal value at the required rate of return in order to determine its present value. By using the 26.1% discount rate, we can obtain the following present values for the terminal value for each scenario (Table 16):

Table 15 Present value of the FCFF: all scenarios

Scenario	2023 (f)	2024 (f)	2025 (f)	2026 (f)	2027 (f)
Worst-case	55,957	59,309	56,204	45,659	31,003
Base-case	63,747	75,284	80,456	79,190	69,272
Best-case	71,610	92,314	111,845	126,728	127,914

Table 16 Present value of the terminal value: all scenarios

Scenario	Terminal Value	PV of Terminal Value
Worst-case	890,104	279,060
Base-case	2,118,663	664,230
Best-case	4,141,414	1,298,390

7.6 Valuation in Each Scenario

We can now calculate the valuation of Best Shop in each scenario by adding up the present values of our future cash flows. As shown in Table 17, our valuation model results for Best Shop are the sum total of these discounted values.

7.7 Assigning Probabilities

The final step in the First Chicago method is assigning probabilities to each scenario. As with any probabilistic assessment, it is not possible to be precise in every case. The ultimate objective of this process is to generate significant changes in the valuation process. It is imperative to acknowledge that there is no one-size-fits-all solution for all types of companies. However, we assign predetermined probability estimates for startups, high-growth firms, and mature companies, which can be adjusted based on the specific characteristics and scale of the company being analyzed. In their analysis of various valuation methods for companies at different stages of their life cycle, Pettersen and Nylén (2017) present a predetermined probability for each scenario. Startups have a higher likelihood of either failing completely or achieving extraordinary success. A high-growth company has a close relationship between its expected and actual growth scenarios, while mature companies are less likely to experience higher or lower growth than expected. Table 18 presents sample predetermined probabilities, which are explained in the following paragraphs.

In each scenario, there is a different degree of uncertainty, which results in different probabilities. In the case of startups, failure is equivalent to default, which means the company is worth zero if it fails. As a result, we can give more weight to the likelihood of the worst-case scenario in startups. Successful development can also result in a soaring enterprise value, giving startups a higher chance of achieving the best-case scenario in comparison to high-growth and mature companies. High valuations will be derived primarily from scenarios of success in these cases.

Table 17 Valuation results: all scenarios

Scenario	Valuation
Worst-case	527,192
Base-case	1,032,179
Best-case	1,828,802

Table 18 Sample predetermined probabilities

Scenario	Startups (%)	High-growth (%)	Mature (%)
Worst-case	30	15	5
Base-case	50	70	85
Best-case	20	15	10

Table 19 The first Chicago valuation result

Scenario	Valuation	Probability (%)	Final valuation
Worst-case	527,192	30	1,040,008
Base-case	1,032,179	50	
Best-case	1,828,802	20	

As it is difficult to define what constitutes success for high-growth companies, assigning probabilities can be challenging. If a company has already achieved huge growth, success is measured by long-term growth above the normal level, even if the level is significantly lower than the current level. This means that in terms of long-term growth and valuation, the best-case and base-case scenarios are much closer compared to startups. Moreover, failure in this case does not represent default, but rather a level of growth below, or close to, the average, while the base scenario may still represent relatively high growth.

Due to the maturity of steady-state companies compared to startups and high-growth companies, there is a minimum amount of uncertainty. Therefore, there is a lesser degree of difference between the three scenarios as compared to other stages of a company. As an example, failure due to default is not considered since there is a very small probability that this will occur. However, there is the possibility of growth exceeding or falling below expectations.

In light of the above explanation, the final step is to sum the weighted valuations under all possible scenarios in order to obtain the final overall valuation. Table 19 summarizes the total enterprise value of Best Shop using the First Chicago method.

8 Summary

While the First Chicago method is similar to the DCF in many ways, it also offers more differentiation between companies at different stages and enables a better understanding of uncertainty. A distinguishing feature of this method is its consideration of various possible payoff scenarios for the target company. The method typically involves developing three scenarios: a best-case scenario, a base-case scenario, and a worst-case scenario.

Best-case scenarios for a company are usually what its management team anticipates, and are in line with the company's internal business plans and projections. Our assumption is that most things will follow management's plan for the most part. Additionally, the outcome should not be overly optimistic, but should be the result that management expects to achieve if all business and product development objectives are achieved.

A number of factors are taken into account in the base-case, including efficiency issues, reasonable delays in product development, and slow adoption of the product. In spite of these setbacks, the model assumes a relatively flat growth trajectory for the organization.

Under the worst-case scenario, the business model of the company fails to function effectively, causing minimal product adoption in the market, and revenue is restricted to existing products that are well established in the market.

All three scenarios are assigned a probability. The final valuation is the probability-weighted sum of all three scenarios. Venture capitalists and private equity investors can use this method to obtain an accurate valuation of a private company that incorporates both upside potential and downside risks.

References

Achleitner, A. K., & Lutz, E. (2005). First Chicago method: Alternative approach to valuing innovative start-ups in the context of venture capital financing rounds. *Betriebswirtschaftliche Forschung und Praxis (BFuP), 57*(4), 333–347.

Babiarz, A. (2016). Methods of valuing investment projects used by Venture Capital funds, financed from public funds. *Prace Naukowe Uniwersytetu Ekonomicznego we Wrocławiu, 428*, 11–28.

Majercakova, D., & Mittelman, A. (2018). *The analysis of the chosen methods of the evaluation of start-ups on the specific case* (pp. 484–490). Economic and Social Development: Book of Proceedings.

Montani, G., Gervasio, D., & Pulcini, G. (2020). Startup company valuation: The state of art and future trends. *International Business Research, 13*(10), 1–17.

Pettersen, R. Nylén, M. (2017). *Which valuation method yields the most accurate value in the valuation of companies in different stages of their life cycle?* Dissertation, BI Norwegian Business School.

Rothman, T. (2020). Valuation methods: The first Chicago venture method and the use of real options. In *Valuations of early-stage companies and disruptive technologies*. Palgrave Macmillan.

Scorecard Method of Valuation "The Subjective Analysis of Valuation"

Nataraja Nanjundaiah

1 Introduction

Storytelling and Valuation. The good valuation is always not just about numbers it is a combination of the story and the numbers, which is very well explained in the book by Aswath Damodaran, Narratives and Numbers, The value of Stories in Business. Valuation as a bridge between numbers and stories is very represented in the Fig. 1 below.

1.1 Valuation as a Bridge Between Numbers and Stories

And in the same book Damodaran has very well-articulated the process of coming with valuation from the story. Figure 2 describes the story-to-numbers process

It becomes more important for us to understand the story which the founders are trying to narrate while implementing the Scorecard method of valuation. Scorecard method deals with the translation of this story into numbers.

So our objective of this paper is to understand this process of converting the story into numbers using Scorecard method. I have dealt with this topic in two stages.

Bachelor of Commerce (B.Com), Fellow Member of Institute of Cost Accountants of India (FCMA), holds certification "International Valuation recognised by International Association of Certified Valuation Specialists (IACVS)", Registered Valuer—Securities or Financial Assets recognised by IBBI (Insolvency and Bankruptcy Board of India), Insolvency Professional recognised by IBBI (Insolvency and Bankruptcy Board of India), Completed one year Senior Management Program certified by Indian Institute of Management Calcutta (IIMC)

N. Nanjundaiah (✉)
Nataraja Nanjundaiah & Co, Bengaluru, Karnataka, India

S. Derindere Köseoğlu (ed.), *A Practical Guide for Startup Valuation*, Contributions to Finance and Accounting, https://doi.org/10.1007/978-3-031-35291-1_9

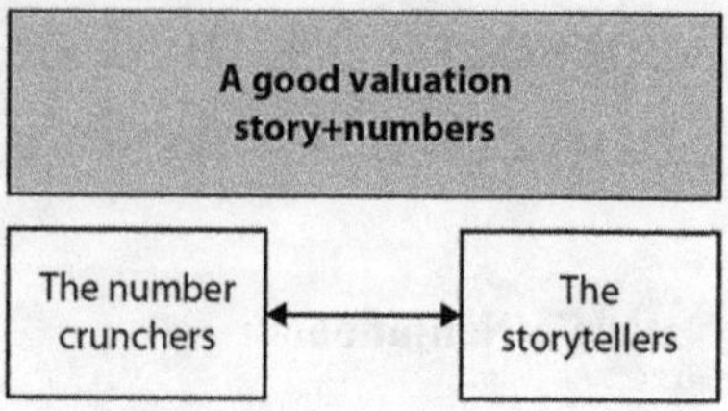

Fig. 1 Valuation as a bridge between numbers and stories. Source: Aswath Damodaran, Narratives and Numbers

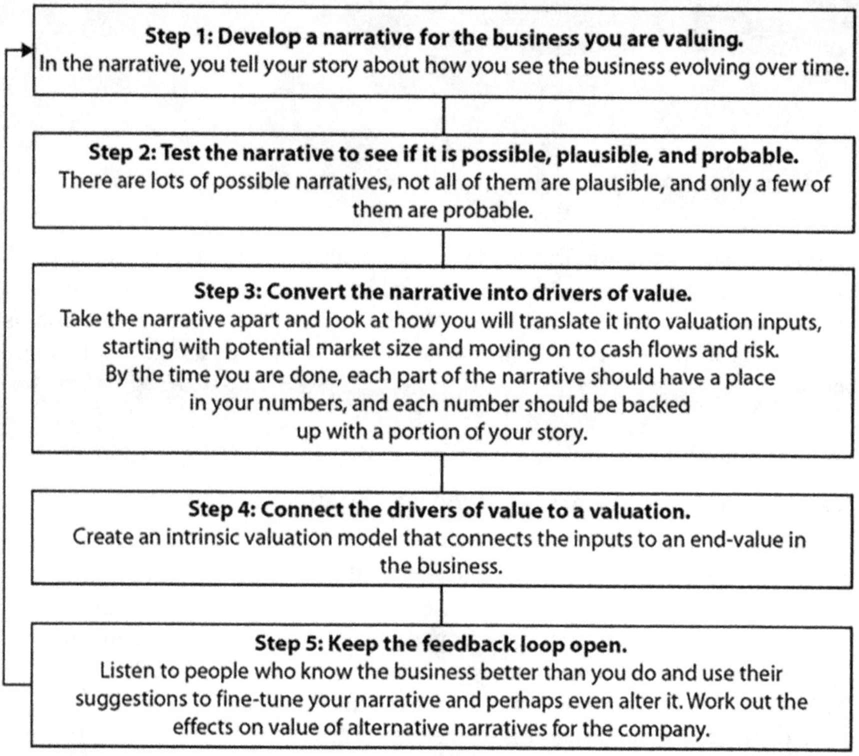

Fig. 2 The story-to-numbers process. Source: Aswath Damodaran, Narratives and Numbers

Firstly, we will understand the historic background and origination of this method, which is introduced by an Angel Investor community in the US and also understand the Scorecard Methodology developed by this Angel Investor community.

Secondly, I have used my experience and research to improve upon the Scorecard Method by modifying few of the criteria. The modification is a result of my research in this space, since the current scorecard method doesn't consider few more important qualitative factors which are vital, I have introduced the same in the modified scorecard model.

I have applied my experience of working for 24 years in various large corporates. I have had experience working in start-up where I led the finance function, I was instrumental in getting the funding at initial stages and worked closely with the Founders to grow and implement the Operations.

I was involved in handling various global business operations, handled various global projects and worked with global stakeholders when working with ADP & Amazon. I had the opportunity to learn from the business strategy, organization culture. I have applied the experience and learnings, which shaped me to think as a matured and holistic business professional. And have approached the topic from the entrepreneurial thought process to develop an appropriate learning methodology for valuation.

To summarize this paper is a result of the study of the scorecard method of valuation created by the US Angel Investors and also the modified scorecard method is a result of my practical experience working with various multinationals and the result of my curiosity in learning about entrepreneurship from a strategic perspective.

2 Background

Scorecard methodology was originally written in May 2001 and revised in January 2011. The method is detailed in the book written by William H. Payne published by Bill Payne in 2006 "The Definitive Guide to Raising Money from Angels". The Ohio Tech Angels adapted this valuation methodology in 2008 and named it Bill Payne method. This was further expanded in 2010 during a half-day workshop of the Angel Capital Education foundation, further renamed it the Scorecard Method. Some refer this as the Benchmark Method.

The angel investors in the US put personal investment at risk by investing in start-up companies. Generally, these investors invest between $25,000 and $1,00,000 in a round summing to $250,000 to $1,000,000. (These numbers are based on the article written in 2011, so we need to consider the inflation and other aspects which will change these numbers to the higher investments as of today.) In 2011, the valuation of pre-revenue start-ups was around $1 to $ 2 million and this used to be established as a result of negotiation between entrepreneurs and angel investors. For this amount of investment angels use to expect 20–40% stage and expected return on investment of 20–30 X within a period of 5 to 8 years.

Angels used to invest in 10 or more diversified companies, spreading their investment over few years. It is learnt through experience that 50% of these companies tend to fail (with returns less than the capital invested), and 3 to 4 companies may result in an average return on investment of 1X to 5X, and 1 or two of these 10 companies would result in 10X to 30X of initial investment over a period of 5 to 8 years of time. Summed up with the overall portfolio of the investor yields approximately 25% per annum. These outcomes have been validated by "Returns to Angel in Groups" by Professor Rob Wiltbank in November 2007. Angels usually invest in only those companies in which they are familiar. Diversification is not the focus of the angels unlike public markets.

In order to achieve a reasonable return on investment, an angel must ensure to invest in 1 or 2 companies with the ROI of 20–30X. While it is not easy to predict this early on.

3 Scorecard Method Explained

In the context of valuing Start-ups, the scorecard method can be a useful tool as traditional discounted cash flow analysis may not be applicable due to a lack of historical financial data and uncertain future cash flows. The scorecard method can provide a more qualitative and forward-looking assessment of a Start-up's value.

In a Start-up valuation scorecard, metrics such as the size of the target market, the strength of the business model, the quality of the management team, the level of competition, and the stage of the product development cycle can all be used to score the company. These metrics can be weighed and scored based on their importance to the success of the Start-up.

The overall score from the scorecard can then be used to estimate the value of the Start-up by comparing it to similar companies or by using multiples such as price-to-sales or price-to-earnings ratios. It is important to note that the scorecard method of valuation is subjective and may not provide a precise estimate of value. However, it can provide useful insights and a starting point for more in-depth valuation analysis.

The scorecard method of Start-up valuation is a method used to evaluate the potential of a Start-up by assigning a score to various elements of its business. The elements that are scored can include:

1. **Strength of the Team**
   Strength of the team can be ascertained by reviewing the experience and track record of the founders. While the current trend is that many youngsters are getting into entrepreneurship this point we may have to approach it differently. The team should consist of the required knowledge, passion, experience as necessary, commitment, clarity of thought and ownership. Ideally, the founders team should have the mix of all kinds of skillsets such as strategy, operational, marketing and technology.
2. **Size of the Opportunity**
   Size of the opportunity refers to the market potential, target addressable market (TAM) and the market potential. If the idea is unique and there is huge untapped market in this segment then the start-up holds better chance to capture the market. Also on the other hand if the start-up is entering into the well-organized market where the required awareness of the product and technology has been already created by the other players in the industry, even then that becomes easier to tap

the market since the predecessor innovators have done the work required, making it easier for the start-up to enter the marker.

3. **Competitive Environment**
   Competitive environment refers to the level of competition and barriers to entry due to competition. And how strong is the start-ups strategy to address the competitive environment.
4. **Product/Technology**
   Protection of the product/service refers to the Intellectual Property rights the company has acquired, which makes the company much stronger chances to get the higher valuation.
5. **Marketing/Sales Channels/Partnerships**
   Market penetration strategy and any signed contracts with the customers will help the company get higher chance of the valuation, due to guaranteed revenue possibilities.
6. **Need for Additional Investment**
   Funding required can be justified by the current level of capital structure with details of the founders capital infusion, with requirement of the funding justified with the reason for fund raise and the application fund.

4 Scorecard Method: Illustration

Using the scorecard valuation method, we can compare the target company with the angel funded Start-up ventures average valuation which is recently funded, and arrive at pre-money valuation of the target company. We must choose the comparable companies which are at the similar stage of lifecycle (which is pre-revenue Start-up).

As a first step, identify the pre-money valuation of the companies in that region which is at pre-revenue stage and which is in the similar business sector of the target company. Mostly the pre-money valuation is on similar scale with less variation. Following is a result of an informal survey of angel groups taken by Bill Payne in 2010, pre-revenue companies of different regions of North America. Table 1 below depicts the output of of the survey.

From Table 1 we can see that average pre-money valuation of the pre-revenue deals is \$1.67 million, mode is \$1.5 million. The range is with low of \$1.25 million, to high of \$2.7 million.

Taking the above results as our base we will use the mode value of \$1.5mn for our calculation.

Taking this study forwarded we will now ascertain the valuation using the Scorecard Method by using the following factors.

Determining the average pre-money valuation of similar companies, based on geography (Tables 2 and 3).

Considering \$ 1.5 million as the industry average. Considering the above example, the pre-revenue valuation of a setup is 1.5 into 0.83 which amounts to 1.245

Table 1 2010 Angel Valuation Survey

2010 Angel Valuation Survey	
(Pre-money Valuation of Pre-revenue Companies)	
Pre-money	
Angel Group Valuation (In Million Dollars)	
Tech Coast Angels	1.25
Phenomenelle Angels	1.3
New York Angels	1.3
Frontier Angel Fund	1.4
DC Dinner Clubs	1.5
Vancouver Angel Network	1.5
Midwest Groups (Okabe)	1.5
RAIN Funds	1.65
Ohio TechAngels	1.75
Band of Angels	1.75
Life Science Angels	2
Alliance of Angels	2.1
Common Angels	2.7
Mean	1.67
Median	1.50
Mode	1.50

Source: The article Scorecard Valuation Methodology Establishing the Valuation of Pre-revenue, Start-up Companies by Bill Payne (https://seedspot.org/wp-content/uploads/2021/02/Scorecard-Valuation-Methodology.pdf)

Table 2 Weights of the criteria

Criteria	Weights[a]
Strength of the team	0–30%
Size of the opportunity	0–25%
Product/Technology	0–15%
Competitive environment	0–10%
Marketing/Sales channels/Partnerships	0–10%
Need for additional investment	0–5%
Others	0–5%

Source: The article Scorecard Valuation Methodology Establishing the Valuation of Pre-revenue, Start-up Companies by Bill Payne (https://seedspot.org/wp-content/uploads/2021/02/Scorecard-Valuation-Methodology.pdf)
[a]Weights can be modified based on the user requirements

million. The above valuation is derived using the 2010 angel valuation survey (taken from the academic reference—Bill Payne Score Card Method Original Article, for the latest valuation you will need to compute these averages using the latest investment statistics in the applicable markets) and used this average valuation for the target company which is into Healthcare technology cum Fintech industry in

Table 3 Adjusted weightage

Criteria	Weights[a] (%)	Target company (%)	Adjusted weightage
Strength of the Team	30	81	0.24
Size of the Opportunity	25	85	0.21
Product/Technology	15	93	0.14
Competitive Environment	10	100	0.10
Marketing/Sales Channels/ Partnerships	10	88	0.09
Need for Additional Investment	5	50	0.02
Others	5	50	0.03
			0.83

Source: The article Scorecard Valuation Methodology Establishing the Valuation of Pre-revenue, Start-up Companies by Bill Payne (https://seedspot.org/wp-content/uploads/2021/02/Scorecard-Valuation-Methodology.pdf), relevant modifications done by the author to the scoring
[a]Weights can be modified based on the user requirements

India (which is considered for the reference learning point of view). The detailed analysis of the target company valuation is detailed further in this paper.

5 Modified Scorecard Method (Researched and Created by the Author)

While the above is the scorecard method which is currently used in the market, I wanted to improvise on the same by introducing another few of the qualitative parameters which are having major impact. Few of the factors which we may have observed in many situations why a start-up fails is mostly due to inappropriate business model, not aligning the competitive advantage to the current market conditions, lack of focus on financial modelling and unit economics, and poor execution and bad governance. We have seen many such examples of start-up failures. So, it is pertinent to bring in these factors into the scorecard method. Below is the modified scorecard method by including all these parameters. This method is researched and created by the author of this article. Find below the criteria of modified scorecard method (Table 4).

1. **Power of an Idea (Uniqueness, Technology Enabled)**
   In the current scenario of Start-up revolution, the uniqueness of the idea and utilization of technology is most important aspect. It can be a new idea or no issues in getting into the market where already there is huge competition, so you don't have to reinvent the wheel of creating the market and awareness. Usage of Artificial Intelligence (AI), Machine Learning (ML), Application programming

Table 4 Criteria

Criteria
Power of an Idea (Uniqueness, Technology enabled)
Strength of the founding team
Size of the Opportunity (Total Addressable Market)
Competitive advantage—Business Model defined
Strategy Execution and Governance mechanisms
Organisation culture
Financial Modelling and Unit Economics

Source: Author's own creation

interface (API), Mobile Application (App), and Block Chain are few relevant technologies which are used as per the requirement of that specific industry.

To understand and get the flavour of the power of a tech-enabled idea, let us look at few examples, following are some of the top business ideas that changed the world:

Apple Inc.—revolutionized the personal computer and mobile phone industries.
Amazon—transformed the retail industry with its online shopping platform.
Google—created the world's largest search engine and expanded into various technology markets.
Facebook—revolutionized social networking and changed the way people communicate and share information.
Uber—disrupted the taxi industry by creating a ridesharing platform and popularizing the concept of the sharing economy.
Tesla Motors—electric vehicles that are leading the shift towards sustainable transportation.
Airbnb—disrupted the hotel industry by creating a platform for short-term home rentals.
Alibaba—one of the largest online and mobile commerce companies in the world, particularly in e-commerce and retail.
Netflix—changed the way people consume media and entertainment by offering a subscription-based streaming service.
Microsoft—created the world's first widely used computer operating system and dominated the personal computing market.

Uniqueness of the Idea

In the current disruptive business world, the kind of ideas which are being thought about by the entrepreneurs are quite unique and unthinkable. Here are few Start-ups with unique ideas emerged in 2022.

Linktree is a freemium social media reference landing page developed by Alex Zaccaria, Anthony Zaccaria, and Nick Humphreys, headquartered in Melbourne and Sydney, Australia. Founded in 2016, it serves as a landing page for a person or company's entire associated links in social media, which rarely allows linking to multiple sites. The site was inspired by the developers' annoyance with social media that can't allow multiple hyperlinks.

Funnel Marketers rely on data to deliver insights to engage customers. As data grows, so does the pool of potential knowledge. Does more of it mean greater understanding? No! Data without context is meaningless—or even misleading. Funnel takes all your data and puts it where you need it. With Funnel know what's driving value, make quick, confident decisions and improve your business. Powered by Funnel, get your data at all times, business-ready!

So Syncd Based on the 16 personality types theory, So Syncd is the first dating app to connect compatible personality types. By pairing couples who have just enough similarities to understand each other and just enough differences to create a spark, we help you find that exciting, meaningful relationship that you've been looking for.

Manychat Engages Customers Instantly. Automate interactive conversations in Instagram Direct Messages, Facebook Messenger, and SMS to grow your brand.

Group Greeting At Group Greeting, allows you to create a digital card and have multiple people sign it. You'll never have to worry about running out of space to sign or losing the card. The days of passing around a manila folder are over.

2. **Strength of the Founding Team**

   Strength of the team can be ascertained by reviewing the experience and track record of the founders. While the current trend is that many youngsters are getting into entrepreneurship this point we may have to approach it differently. The Team should consist of the required knowledge, passion, experience as necessary, commitment, clarity of thought and ownership. Ideally, the founders team should have the mix of all kinds of skillsets such as strategy, operational, marketing and technology.
3. **Competitive Advantage: Business Model Defined**

   Competitive Advantage

   Start-up should be very clear on the way in which competitive advantage will be achieved. If we refer to the Michael Porter's competitive advantage, Porter describes three ways of gaining the competitive advantage: Differentiation, Cost and Focus.

   Differentiation is the matter of product or service differentiation and uniqueness of the product and service offering.

   Cost advantage is all about pricing the product competitively, here even if your product or service offering is not unique you compete by charging less/offering discounts, etc.

   Focus is where you bring in the combination of differentiated product or service and also cost advantage. Or you focus on a specific section of the market. Focus defined uniqueness of the specific companies' business model which makes it unique and helps positioning in the market and acquire the market.

Business Model

One of the important reasons any Start-up fails is having wrong business model or changes in business model without valid reason in the journey. Having the right business model and getting it right is so important.

Most successful business model in the recent years is marketplace business model. This model enables you to scale faster, since you are utilizing technology by being on the internet, utilizing the ecommerce platform, and next is not doing everything yourself and by only connecting the buyer with the seller, you are acting as an intermediary. Probably we can say Amazon revolutionized this model by inventing and making it successful and everyone now is following the footsteps of Amazon and then improvising on the same.

In recent years, some of the emerging popular business models are:

Subscription-based model: Companies offer access to products or services for a recurring fee, often on a monthly or annual basis.

Freemium model: Companies offer a basic version of their product for free, with paid upgrades for premium features.

Marketplace model: Companies create an online platform that connects buyers and sellers, often taking a commission on transactions.

Sharing economy model: Companies enable individuals to share underutilized assets, such as cars, homes, or tools, through a peer-to-peer platform.

Direct-to-consumer (D2C) model: Companies bypass traditional retail channels and sell products directly to customers online.

Artificial intelligence-powered model: Companies use AI and machine learning to automate various business processes, improve customer experience and drive efficiency.

On-demand model: Companies offer products or services that can be ordered and delivered on-demand, usually through a mobile app.

These are just some of the examples and new business models are constantly emerging as technology and consumer behaviour evolve.

Amazon Business Model Example

Here is an example of Amazon Business Model. One of the key strengths of Amazon is its business model which was drafted by Jeff Bezos when he was travelling in the flight on a napkin in early 2000s which is still valid, that is the strength and clarity the business model should carry which can stand the test of times. Here is the business model of the Amazon. Though Amazon entered into new businesses such as AWS and other verticals, the core business model of their Ecommerce business fuelled the growth of the business and the reason behind the market capitalization the company has achieved as of today (Fig. 3).

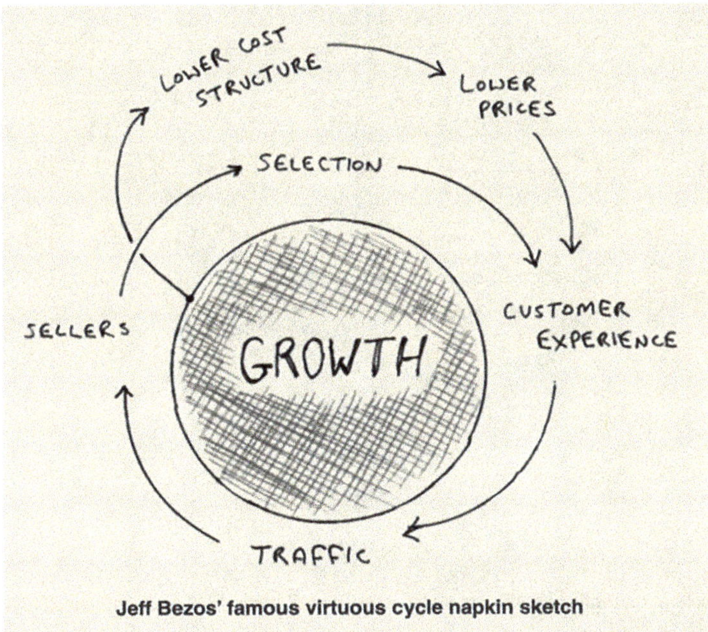

Fig. 3 Jeff Bezos' famous virtuous cycle napkin sketch. Source: Amazon business model

4. **Strategy Execution and Governance Mechanisms**

   Strategy Execution—Most of the cases where the failure of the start-up is not due to idea strength, it is due to the inappropriate business model and loose execution of the strategy. The interest of the founders and management die down during tough times and also due to poor planning the execution fails leading to the failure of the start-up, so it becomes more important to ensure and measure the executability strength. To measure this, we could look at the overall strategy in terms of what kind of business model is being adopted, strength of the business model. Best practices and industry frameworks implemented, to name a few Agile, Lean, Six Sigma, and Capability Models. Also, the latest technologies adopted such as Artificial Intelligence, Machine Learning, Analytics, Robotic Process Automation, etc.

   Governance Mechanisms—Jeff Bezos says in his famous speech to the employees, the good intention doesn't work and mechanism works. This is very much followed to the core ingrained in the Amazon work culture.

   What it means is that if someone has great intentions that is good, however there needs to be mechanism/process to implement and track the results and continuously improve. This is where the governance frameworks need to be implemented in all areas of the organization such as Business, Marketing, Operations, Financial aspects of the company.
5. **Organisation culture**—Organization culture becomes very important aspects in the success of the enterprise. Most of the organizations fail financially not

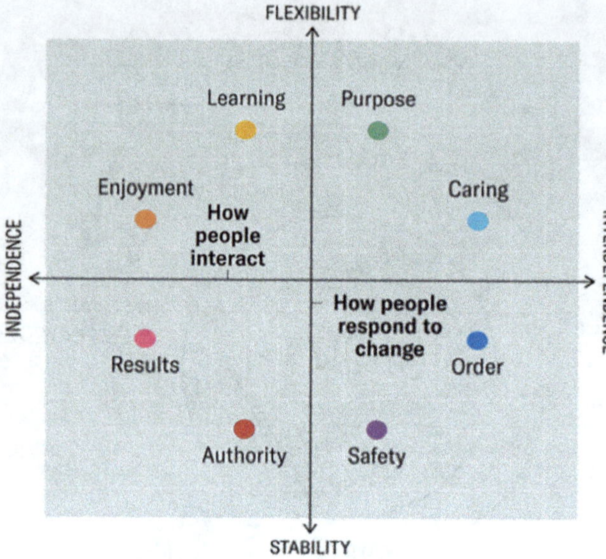

Fig. 4 Factors that influence the organization culture. Source: Picture courtesy—HBR (Harward Business Review article)

because of the issue with their business model, idea or technology, it is due to poor organization culture. Whatever needs to be achieved is through the people/employees/team so it becomes pertinent to keep the culture at its best to achieve the results to all stakeholders of the company. Organization culture brings in great employee engagement which is a key to the success of an organization.

Top few factors that influence the organization culture are as below (Fig. 4).

Here is the snapshot of the organization cultures of Amazon and ADP, Amazon is a renowned name worldwide. ADP is an HCM company and world leader in its space, and is well known in the corporate world. These are two organizations which I have picked up to demonstrate how important the Mission, Vision, Values, organization principles and its execution to the core, governance model, which brings sustainable success to the organizations. This is something every start-up should focus on in addition to the business idea, technology and passion to achieve exponential growth.

One of the key aspects of the Amazon culture is its focus on the leadership principles. Unlike most of the other organizations where the values are in the books and not ingrained in the culture, Amazon has integrated all its leadership principles into the organization culture, which helps them to walk the talk and achieve the results year on year and has created the history. In Amazon it is said "Work hard, have fun, create history". Here we go through below the snapshot of Amazon Leadership Principles. As I have worked in both these organizations I am sharing my experience as a testimonial of success factors associated with these company cultures.

Amazon Leadership Principles

Customer Obsession, Ownership, Are Right, A Lot, Learn and Be Curious, Hire and Develop the Best, Insist on the Highest Standards, Think Big, Bias for Action, Frugality, Earn Trust, Dive Deep, Have Backbone; Disagree and Commit, Deliver Results, Strive to be Earth's Best Employer, Success and Scale Bring Broad Responsibility.

To share few of my experiences with few of leadership principles:

Invent and Simplify—There is great importance placed at Amazon for continuous improvement, Amazon has integrated Six Sigma methodology and each employee is required to strive to continuously improve the processes they are involved in and accountable for the project they are driving. This helps the organization to always question the status quo and continuously strive to get better.

Hire and Develop the Best—Amazon is a place where there is a rigorous structured process of interview and selection of candidates. So it is very well known that it is not an easy thing to get hired at Amazon, so much is the importance given for hiring the best candidate. This makes the competition more fierce within the organization as you are working with the best team members.

Customer Obsession—Each of employee at Amazon strives to ensure customer delight, and they can go to any extent to ensure customer satisfaction. Customer is placed at the heart of the processes.

ADP Mission, Vision, Values

Automatic Data Processing, Inc. (ADP) is an American provider of human resources management software and services, headquartered in Roseland, New Jersey.

ADP's One-of-a-Kind Culture and Values

Insightful expertise, Service excellence, Inspiring innovation, Each person counts, Results-driven, Social responsibility.

6. **Financial Modelling and Unit Economics**

   Many a times start-up fail due to less or no focus on the financial planning. The successful companies have their numbers in place from the beginning, hence the focus on financial modelling and unit economics is very important.

   6.1 **Financial Modelling**

   Financial modelling is the process of creating a numerical representation of a financial situation, using mathematical and statistical tools, to forecast future financial performance. The models use inputs such as historical financial data, economic indicators, and industry trends to simulate financial scenarios and make predictions. Financial modelling is commonly used in corporate finance, investment banking, and financial planning and analysis. It helps companies make informed decisions by providing a visual representation of how changes in key assumptions will affect a company's financial performance. Some common applications of financial modelling include budgeting, valuation, risk analysis, capital planning, and mergers and acquisitions.

6.2 Unit Economics

Unit economics refers to the financial performance of a single unit or product, usually expressed in terms of revenue and cost. The aim of unit economics is to measure the financial viability of each unit of a product or service, and to understand the underlying drivers of profitability on a per-unit basis. This analysis helps a business determine the cost structure of producing and selling a unit of its product or service, and identify areas for improvement that can increase its margins. Ultimately, unit economics is a key factor in determining the overall financial health and sustainability of a business.

Unit economics is a tool to evaluate the business's profitability per unit. Unit can be customer, employee, transaction, output, etc., If you take example of a taxi company, the unit can be number of rides, driver, kilometre.

For a start-up unit economics is important. Following are the metrics you can analyse

(a) How much money you spend to acquire a client
(b) How many units you need to sell to make a business profitable
(c) How successful your marketing campaigns, and which marketing campaign you have to choose
(d) What is the growth potential of a business

Unit economics helps investors to make key decisions of whether to invest or not in a business.

For example, if we need to measure a Life Time Value of a Customer following is the formulae

LTV = (ARPU—CAC—COGS) * B
LTV = Lifetime value of a Customer
ARPU = Average Revenue per unit
CAC = Customer Acquisition Cost
COGS = Cost of Goods Sold
B = # of Units bought by the customer

Three Reasons Unit Economics Is Important

The outcome of unit economics analysis will be useful for the company in the short term and in the long run from the financial planning perspective.

1. Unit Economics helps in financial planning, forecasting and budgeting.
2. Unit Economics helps in the pricing decisions to ensure optimal utilisation of resources and helps in production planning and achieving maximise profits.
3. Unit Economics helps in assessing the future potential of the product and ensure business process reengineering of the product, technology and also focus on right business development to ensure sustainability of the business.

6 Modified Scorecard Method: Implementation Example (Table 5)

By implementing the modified scorecard for the example, we can see the results as below (Table 6)

Considering $ 1.5 million as the industry average Start-up valuation based on the trends (considered the same average as the scorecard method to be able to compare the scores using scorecard method and modified scorecard method). Considering the above example the valuation of a setup is $1.5 million into 0.75 which amounts to $ 1.125 million, for details of computation please refer to Appendix 2.

Table 5 Modified scorecard criteria

Criteria	Weights[a] (%)
Power of an Idea (Uniqueness, Technology enabled)	20
Strength of the founding team	15
Size of the Opportunity (Total Addressable Market)	15
Competitive advantage—Business Model defined	20
Strategy Execution and Governance mechanisms	10
Organisation culture	10
Financial Modelling and Unit Economics	10

Source: Author's Own Creation
[a]Weights can be modified based on the user requirements

Table 6 Adjusted criteria for modified scorecard

Criteria	Weights[a] (%)	Comparison (%)	Adjusted weighting
Power of an Idea (Uniqueness, technology enabled)	20	115	0.23
Strength of the founding team	15	84	0.13
Size of the opportunity (Total addressable market)	15	61	0.21
Competitive advantage—Business model defined	20	85	0.18
Strategy execution and governance mechanisms	10	53	0.05
Organisation culture	10	30	0.01
Financial modelling and unit economics	10	56	0.06
Total			0.75

Source: Author's own creation
[a]Weights can be modified based on the user requirements

7 Conclusion

The crux of this article on Scorecard Method of Business Valuation is for the professional valuer or appraiser to look at the valuation as not just a calculation activity, approach it holistically and look at the overall business model, idea, technology, organization culture, governance, unit economics, financial modelling, etc.

And most importantly as this method is used only in the absence of the quantitative data required for other methods such as DCF, Comparable transaction method and other methods, it is always better to calibrate the overall assessment again using DCF method and Comparable transaction method, and other Income and Market methods.

Also the reference to be made to the comparable companies on all parameters prescribed in the modified scorecard valuation method. Most of the times businesses fail due to poor governance, poor execution, lack of focus on financial planning and analysis and employee engagement and also due to lack of focus on the adopting to latest technologies.

One important caveat is that there are few criteria considered such as governance mechanisms and organisation culture, which one may argue is not applicable for a start-up since it is new and these things are work in progress. However, we need to understand that many organizations have failed due to these few issues as per the research which is outlined earlier in this article. So it may not be very easy to track these scores since the company is in the process of developing the people and process strategic aspects, however if we can examine and ask right questions to the founders we will be able to understand their plans with respect to people, process and compliance and the amount of importance the founders are laying getting these aspects in place. The founders who are concerned about building the sustainable business, will surely envisage the issues and build necessary control mechanisms in place. Great leaders who have made their company big and sustain for longer term have had their vision very clear and continuously developed it to adopt to the changing times.

Appendix 1: Scorecard Methodology Implemented with a Scoring Example for a Target Company—Healthcare Technology cum Fintech Company

The scoring model is shared below which will explain the various criteria considered for arriving at the above scores under each category.

The below scoring model is only an indicative example however the investor and the appraiser need to use their discretion to make necessary changes as per the requirement.

Explaining the Scoring Model

In the below scoring model which is depicted in Appendix 1, you can see that there is + and – sign used for scoring methodology. + (plus sign) sign means it is an adding to the strength of the valuation and – (minus sign) sign means it is working negatively for the target company and it will bring down the weightage of the scoring and bring down the valuation. This is the method used to provide points for every qualitative factor of the organization which adds into the company as an advantage or disadvantage in turn contributing to the valuation.

In the below scoring model depicted in Appendix 1, the author has used the target company example, the background of the target company explained below.

Brief Background of the Target Company The target company is into health tech/fintech business from India. It is a unique combination of this company which is both into lending in healthcare space and it is mainly technology enabled. In order to protect the confidentiality of the company and its uniqueness of the idea, I am refraining to disclose more details about the idea and the product. And important aspect is the idea is completely unique and there is no directly comparable company, however I have taken combination of few companies to arrive at comparable company scoring.

Target Company Information Below is the target company information and performance on each parameters of scorecard, which is aid you to relate on how the scoring is assigned.

Strength of the Product and Intellectual Property The company's product is totally unique as I have mentioned earlier and it has acquired IP rights for this product and it is a technology-enabled product which is using API/App based/ Machine Learning. This product is already live and has completed one year in the market so it has acquired the users and already making revenue.

Competitive Environment As I have detailed earlier this product is totally unique and there is no competitive product in this space however there are competitors in this space who are fintech players but their focus is not only healthcare industry, they are a generic fintech companies. So this company is into fintech space in the healthcare sector which is the uniqueness of the idea.

Marketing/Sales/Partners The target company has begun its operations and already acquired customers. However, only drawback is that when compared to other competitors who have captured market to a larger extent and have their customer acquisition strategy very clear, this target company is not too clear on the customer acquisition strategy.

Need for Additional Rounds of Funding The target company has completed 1 year of operations and has bootstrapped its operations and to take the operations to next stage and to achieve the set out target of growth, is looking for the additional funding, which is actually normal and will facilitate its growth.

Appendix 1 : Scoring Sheet

Scoring methodology - Working example (Target company in health/Fintech industry)					
		Scoring			
Scoring model		Target company scoring	Comparison company scoring	Target company scoring %	Comparison company scoring %
Strength of the Founding Team overall score				**81**	**100**
Impact	**Experience**				
+	Many years of business experience	+	+	100	100
++	Experience in this business sector	++	++	100	100
+++	Experience as a CEO	+++	+++	100	100
++	Experience as a COO, CFO, CTO	++	++	100	100
+	Experience as a product manager	+	+	100	100
+	Experience in sales or technology	–	+	0	100
–	No business experience				
Impact	**Willing to step aside, if necessary, for an experienced CEO**				
–	Unwilling				
0	Neutral				
+++	Willing	++	+++	75	100
Impact	**Is the founder coachable?**				
+++	Yes	++	+++	75	100
–	No				
Impact	**How complete is the management team?**				
–	Entrepreneur only				
0	One competent player in place				
+	Team identified and on the side-lines	+		75	
+++	Competent team in place		+++		100
0–25% Size of the opportunity				**85**	**100**
Impact	**Size of the target market (total sales)**				
–	< $50 million				
+	$100 million	$90 million		75	
++	> $100 million		$120 million		100

(continued)

Scoring methodology - Working example (Target company in health/Fintech industry)					
		Scoring			
Scoring model		Target company scoring	Comparison company scoring	Target company scoring %	Comparison company scoring %
Impact	**Potential for revenues of target company in 5 years**				
–	<$20 million				
++	$20 to $50 million	$45 million		60	
+++	>$100 million (will require significant additional funding)		$75 million		100

Source: The article Scorecard Valuation Methodology Establishing the Valuation of Pre-revenue, Start-up Companies by Bill Payne (https://seedspot.org/wp-content/uploads/2021/02/Scorecard-Valuation-Methodology.pdf), relevant modifications done by the author to the scoring

Scoring Methodology - Working example (Target Company in Health/Fintech industry)					
		Scoring			
Scoring Model		Target Company scoring	Comparison Company scoring	Target Company scoring %	Comparison Company scoring %
0–15% Strength of the Product and Intellectual Property				**93**	**100**
Impact	**Is the product defined and developed?**				
–	Not well define, still looking a prototypes				
0	Well defined, prototype looks interesting				
++	Good feedback from potential customers	++		90	
+++	Orders or early sales from customers		+++		100
Impact	**Is the product compelling to customers?**				
–	This product is a vitamin pill				
++	This product is a pain killer				
+++	This product is a pain killer with no side effects	+++	+++	100	100

(continued)

Scoring Methodology - Working example (Target Company in Health/Fintech industry)					
		Scoring			
Scoring Model		Target Company scoring	Comparison Company scoring	Target Company scoring %	Comparison Company scoring %
Impact	**Can this product be duplicated by the others?**				
–	Easily copied, no intellectual property				
0	Duplication difficult				
++	Product unique and protected by trade secrets	++		90	
+++	Solid patent protections		+++	100	
0–10% Competitive Environment				**100**	**100**
Impact	**Strength of competitors in this marketplace**				
–	Dominated by a single large player				
–	Dominated by several players				
++	Fractured, many small players	++	++	100	100
Impact	**Strength of competitive products**				
–	Competitive products are excellent				
+++	Competitive products are weak	+++	+++	100	100
0–10% Marketing/Sales/Partners				**88**	**100**
Impact	**Sales channels, sales and marketing partners**				
–	Haven't even discussed sales channels				
++	Key beta testers identified and contacted	++		75	
+++	Channels secure, customers placed trial orders		+++		100
–	No partners identified				
++	Key partners in place	++	++	100	100

(continued)

Scoring Methodology - Working example (Target Company in Health/Fintech industry)					
		Scoring			
Scoring Model		Target Company scoring	Comparison Company scoring	Target Company scoring %	Comparison Company scoring %
0–5% Need for additional rounds of funding				**50**	**100**
+++	None		+++		100
+	Another angel round	+		50	
–	Need venture capital				
0–5% Other				**50**	**100**
++	Positive other factors	+	++	50	100

Source: The article Scorecard Valuation Methodology Establishing the Valuation of Pre-revenue, Start-up Companies by Bill Payne (https://seedspot.org/wp-content/uploads/2021/02/Scorecard-Valuation-Methodology.pdf), relevant modifications done by the author to the scoring

Disadvantages of the Scorecard Method

One of the main disadvantages of the Scorecard Method is that it is more of a subjective method, and less of quantitative method. Due to unavailability of the historic track record of the company and also start-up being its early stages of life cycle (pre-seed, seed stage) mostly it is a nonrevenue generating company or minimum revenue generating company. The valuation arrived from the scorecard method might fail if the founders do not execute their plans successfully. Hence this method of valuation has to be applied cautiously, should be calibrated with other valuation methods like DCF method and Market method as much as possible. To arrest these disadvantages of the bad execution and few of the important factors which are not addressed in this scorecard method has been covered well in the Modified Scorecard Method (developed by author) which is being discussed in detail in the upcoming sections. However it is required to be noted that even the Modified Scorecard Method is not completely fool proof, calibrating the methods with other valuations methods and frequently carrying out the valuation at periodic intervals to assess the company's progress is important.

Why Start-Ups Fail

Before we go into the Modified Scorecard Method, I have done some research on why Start-ups fail, let us first review the same.

From the research done by CB Insights, of 111 start-ups failure stories from 2018 to 2022, it is learned that there is not one reason for start-up failure. It is broken down into 12 major reasons, which are depicted below.

The effort is made to address many of these issues in the Modified Scorecard Method developed by the author (Fig. 5).

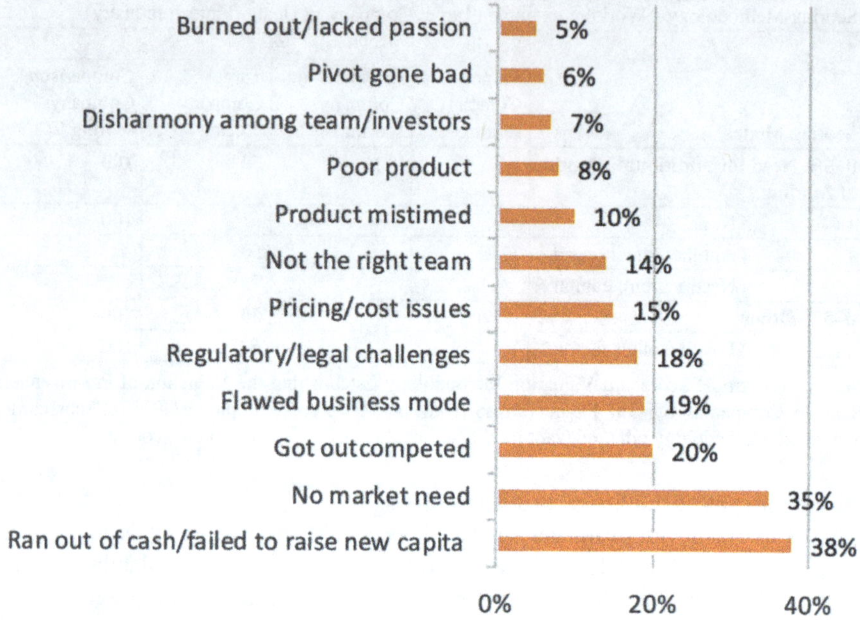

Fig. 5 Top reasons why start-ups fail. Source: CB Insights research

Appendix 2: Modified Scorecard—Illustrative Example

The scoring model is shared below which will explain the various criteria considered for arriving at the above scores under each category. The below scoring model is only an indicative example however the investor and the appraiser need to use their discretion to make necessary changes as per the requirement. The same target company which is into healthcare technology/fintech industry from India has been considered for computing the valuation using the modified scorecard method. For detailed characteristics of the target company do refer to the previous section where the valuation is performed using the scorecard method.

Below is the rationale explained for providing the scores as per the scoring sheet.

Power of an Idea (Uniqueness, Technology Enabled) The target company idea is totally unique and it is technology enabled and also utilising the API technology and Mobile App-based solution. It is already operational for more than an year and started generating the revenues. It is unique idea because there are only couple of competitors worldwide with the similar in the field of healthcare sector. In order to protect the confidentiality of the company and its uniqueness of the idea, I am refraining to disclose more details about the idea and the product.

Strength of the Founding Team The founding team has technology expert, operations expert and a strategic expert with industry influence. However there is high dependency on the founding team and the succession planning is not in place since the company is fairly new. Hence the scoring is accordingly impacted.

Size of the Opportunity (Total Addressable Market) The current focus of this product is within India, however this product can be scaled to implement in other countries as well which is not yet planned. There is scope for improvement in the customer acquisition strategy, as of now there is lack of clarity in this area hence the scoring is accordingly impacted.

Competitive Advantage: Business Model Defined The target company business model pretty clear and there is no diversion in the business model. The business focused in the healthcare sector and it is gaining the competitive advantage by identifying its customer very clearly and also the target market is identified very clearly. Overall scoring on this front is fairly good.

Strategy Execution and Governance Mechanisms Intellectual Property is registered. No clear strategy related to execution of strategy defined. No plans on implementing any operations or technology framework. Mission, Vision and Values are defined however not being reflected in the daily operations since the policy framework related to the various functions (Operations, HR, Finance, Compliance) is work in progress.

Organisation Culture The organization policies are under development and the organization culture is not yet established.

Financial Modelling and Unit Economics Financial Model is defined, as the company has already in operations for one year and has started generating revenues, and do have the prospective financial information, however the supporting required for the financial model can be improved, for example the investment in technology, marketing and capital expenditure is not fully in line with the revenue growth. The clarity in terms of forthcoming technology enhancements, version releases and associated costs are not estimated.

Unit economics is defined, the costs related to customer acquisition, and customer retention is available. The clarity with respect to fixed cost, variable cost is also available. However further refinement has to be done on the overall Management Accounting and Unit Economics so that the decision support system and Management information systems can be made further accurate and sophisticated. The opportunity to implement ERP systems and should be planned.

Appendix 2 : Coring sheet (Target company in health/Fintech industry)

Modified scorecard—Scoring methodology		Scoring		
Scoring	Category	Target company scoring	Comparison company scoring	% scoring
Power of an Idea (Uniqueness, Technology enabled)		15	13	**115**
0–5	Completely new product/solution	5	4	
0–5	Latest Technology enabled (Example—AI, ML, API, AWS, Block Chain, etc.)	5	4	
0–5	Unique solution/product	5	5	
0–3	Copied product/solution			
Strength of the founding team (marks added to each founder for each quality)		**26**	**31**	**84**
0–5	Technology	4	5	
0–5	Operations Excellence	4	4	
0–5	Proven track record/Experience	4	4	
0–5	Powerful network/Public figure	3	4	
0–5	Full time	5	5	
0–3	Part time	0	0	
0–3	Team identified and on the side-lines	0	0	
0–5	Team ready	4	5	
0–5	Succession planning in place	2	4	
Size of the Opportunity (Total Addressable Market)		**11**	**18**	**61**
0–5	Target Addressable Model clearly identified with appropriate research	4	5	
0–5	Market penetration strategy clearly defined	3	5	
0–5	Next five-year revenue opportunity relative to the competitor	2	4	
0–5	Already market penetration/revenue achievement on track	2	4	
Competitive advantage—Business Model defined		**11**	**13**	**85**
0–5	Cost Model	4	4	
0–5	Differentiation model	4	5	
0–5	Focus model	3	4	
Strategy Execution and Governance mechanisms		**9**	**17**	**53**
0–5	Intellectual Property registered	5	5	
0–5	Capability framework CMM, ISO, Agile, Six Sigma, Lean	0	3	
0–5	Execution capability Strategy clearly defined	2	3	
0–5	Mission, Vision and Values defined	1	3	
0–5	Policies of all functions defined (HR, Finance, Operations, Marketing, etc.)	1	3	
Organisation culture		**7**	**23**	**30**
0–5	Organisation culture aspects (Purpose, Caring, Order, Safety, Authority, Results, Enjoyment, Learning)	2	4	

(continued)

Modified scorecard—Scoring methodology		Scoring		
Scoring	Category	Target company scoring	Comparison company scoring	% scoring
0–5	Compensation and Rewards strategy defined	1	4	
0–5	Learning and Development framework	1	4	
0–5	Employee Engagement strategy	1	4	
0–5	Leadership principles	1	3	
0–5	Performance Management	1	4	
Financial Modelling and Unit Economics		**9**	**16**	**56**
0–5	Financial Modelling defined	3	4	
0–5	Unit Economics defined and implemented	3	4	
0–5	Financial Planning and Analysis and reporting	1	4	
0–5	Statutory Compliance framework/Status tracking mechanisms	2	4	

Source: Author's own creation

References

The Evolution of the Private Equity Market and the Decline in IPOs Michael Ewens and Joan Farre-Mensa∗ November 14, 2017 (http://gsf.aalto.fi/seminar_papers/ewens%20and%20farre%20mensa.pdf).

Book - Narratives and Numbers, The value of Stories in Business by Aswath Damodaran

Article Scorecard Valuation Methodology Establishing the Valuation of Pre-revenue, Start-up Companies by Bill Payne (https://seedspot.org/wp-content/uploads/2021/02/Scorecard-Valuation-Methodology.pdf)

https://www.forbes.com/sites/mariannehudson/2016/01/27/scorecard-helps-angels-value-early-stage-companies/?sh=26adf4276874

https://assets.aboutamazon.com/d4/9b/6d5662ec4a75961ae78c473e7d03/amazon-leadership-principles-070621-us.pdf

https://www.adp.com/about-adp/success-factors.aspx

https://lectera.com/info/articles/unit-economics

https://hbr.org/2018/01/the-leaders-guide-to-corporate-culture

Article from CB Insights on why the Start-ups fail - https://techcrunch.com/2022/12/20/remembering-the-startups-we-lost-in-2022/

Dave Berkus Method

Anjan Babu, Abraham Mathews, and A. M. Chinmaya

1 Introduction

The method adds "US$500,000" in each of the following risk reduction elements, allowing for a pre-revenue valuation of up to US$2 Million.

(a) Sound Idea (Basic Value)
The Method does not elaborate on any framework to assess and evaluate. However, one can access factors like Investment thesis, Problem being Solved and its Size, Scalability, and growth.

(b) Prototype (Reducing Technology Risk)
It is a replica of the actual concept of the product to test its viability. A working prototype with feedback from a few users would enhance the valuation.

(c) Quality Management Team (Reducing Execution Risk)
The attributes such as leadership, Integrity, commitments, etc., are generally considered in assessing the management capabilities to run the startup successfully.

(d) Strategic Relationships (Reducing Market Risk)
Product Integration, Partnerships targeting customers alongside scaling the product, etc.

(e) Product Rollout or Sales (Reducing production risk)
Giving attention to market demand, competition, and pricing strategies to access the chances of success.

However, the value need not be restricted to US$0.5 Million for each element and can be adjusted with market conditions and pre-money valuations claimed by similar companies in the space.

A. Babu (✉) · A. Mathews · A. M. Chinmaya
Agraga, Bangalore, Karnataka, India
e-mail: anjan.babu@agraga.co.in; abraham.mathews@agraga.co.in; chinmaya@agraga.co.in

S. Derindere Köseoğlu (ed.), *A Practical Guide for Startup Valuation*, Contributions to Finance and Accounting, https://doi.org/10.1007/978-3-031-35291-1_10

1.1 Background on Dave Berkus Method

The Dave Berkus Method is a venture capital investment evaluation framework developed by the American venture capitalist, Dave Berkus. Berkus has been involved in the venture capital industry for over four decades and has invested in numerous successful startups (By Dave Berkus, Berkus.com). The method is based on his experience as an angel investor and venture capitalist, and it provides a structured approach for evaluating early-stage startups.

Originally created in the mid-1990s to help with the imprecise problem of how to value early-stage companies, especially those in technology, Dave Berkus developed what soon became known as "The Berkus Method" when published in the popular book, *"Winning Angels"* by Harvard's Amis and Stevenson.

1.2 Purpose of Dave Berkus Method

The purpose of the Dave Berkus Method is to help investors and entrepreneurs quickly and efficiently assess the potential of an early-stage startup. It provides a set of guidelines and criteria that can be used to evaluate the chances of success of a startup, including factors such as Sound Idea, Viability of product tested through a prototype, assessment of management capabilities, strategic relationships that the startup has built and effective product roll out and achievement of sales.

Fewer than one in thousand startups meet or exceed their projected revenues in the planned periods. Relying on financial projections as valuation metrics would therefore yield unreliable valuations. Rather than ascribing value to projected financial success, the Berkus method values risk-reduction elements which capture the progress of the startup. The Dave Berkus Method is not meant to be a definitive valuation method, but rather a tool to help provide a rough estimate of a startup's value based on available information and industry data.

The Berkus technique provides aspiring business owners and early-stage investors with a simple framework that enables them to concentrate on risk factors rather than financial projections.

1.3 Popularity and Relevance of the Dave Berkus Method

The Dave Berkus Method has become a widely used and well-respected framework for evaluating early-stage startups. It has been adopted by venture capitalists, angel investors, and entrepreneurs around the world, and is considered one of the most comprehensive and effective approaches for evaluating startups in the early stages of development. Despite being developed over two decades ago, the Dave Berkus Method remains relevant and popular today, and is considered one of the key frameworks for evaluating startups and making investment decisions in the fast-paced and rapidly-changing world of venture capital.

The Dave Berkus Method is an important tool for startup valuations for several reasons:

- Practicality: The method is simple, straightforward, and easy to understand, making it accessible for both entrepreneurs and investors. It provides a basic framework for valuing startups that lack a significant track record or established revenue streams.
- Early-stage focus: The Dave Berkus Method is specifically designed for early-stage startups, which often have limited financial data and a lack of established market penetration. The method takes into account the unique challenges of early-stage startups and provides a way to estimate their value based on potential future growth.
- Relevance: The key components of the method, such as market size, market penetration, intellectual property, management team, and financial projections, are important factors that investors consider when evaluating a startup. By incorporating these components, the Dave Berkus Method provides a comprehensive view of a startup's potential for success.
- Flexibility: The Dave Berkus Method is not a one-size-fits-all solution, and its various components can be adjusted to reflect the specific circumstances of each startup. This makes it a useful tool for a wide range of startups, regardless of their size, industry, or stage of development.
- Widely used: The Dave Berkus Method is a widely recognized and respected valuation framework in the startup community. Many investors and entrepreneurs are familiar with the method and find it a useful tool for evaluating potential investment opportunities.

Overall, the Dave Berkus Method provides a practical, relevant, and widely used framework for valuing early-stage startups, making it an important tool for entrepreneurs, investors, and analysts.

Literature Review:

- **The Berkus Method: Valuing an Early Stage Investment** (**Berkus**, 2012)

  Let us first discuss the article on the Berkus Method written by Dave Berkus himself. In the article, he discusses the challenges of projecting the value of early-stage startups. In particular the technology industry. He argues that relying on revenue and profit projections from the entrepreneur to determine a company's worth is flawed. Very few startups meet or exceed their projected revenues in the planned period. To address this, the author proposes the "Berkus Method". It assesses critical elements of a startup's value without analyzing financial projections, except for the potential to reach over $20 million in revenues by the fifth year of business.

  The "Berkus Method" assigns a maximum value of up to $2 million (or up to $2.5 million post-rollout) to five critical elements of enterprise value, including sound idea, prototype, quality management team, strategic relationships, and product rollout or sales. But, the author notes that investors can assign much lower values to each element, resulting in valuations well below the maximum amount.

The article emphasizes the importance of keeping startup valuations low enough to account for the high risk involved in investing in early-stage companies and provide room for the investment to achieve a significant increase in value over its life. However, the "Berkus Method" is only applicable to pre-revenue startups, as revenue projections become more reliable once a company has been generating revenue for some time.

The article was then later updated in 2016 to provide for more flexibilities and leeways to the users in adopting the method. Berkus felt the original matrix was too restrictive and should be suggestive rather than rigid. As per Berkus "The Method should be flexible enough for its users to negotiate or create a maximum valuation they are willing to accept in a perfect situation, and to assign risk elements that might be more important to them than those listed above".

Berkus concludes by saying that early-stage startup valuations must reflect for any extreme risks taken by the investor while also enabling opportunity for the investment to achieve a tenfold increase in value over time. He also further states that once the company starts realizing actual revenues; this method no longer becomes applicable as most would start to project value over time.

- **Analysis of Key Factors Contributing Toward Valuation of Pre-Revenue Startups by Means of the Berkus Method (Mahajan et al.,** 2021)

This paper first establishes that the underlying problem of Berkus Method is that it is relatively simple and vague. It lacks proper reference as to how a founder while valuing his pre-revenue startup could assign an appropriate/apt value to the parameters specified in the method. With these problem statements the paper defines its objective to provide key sub-parameters or a guide for allocating values for each parameter under Berkus Method.

Upon conducting basic quantitative research, the method establishes following sub-categories for each of the parameters to evaluate an early-stage startup

Parameter as per Berkus Method	Sub-parameter established by the paper
Sound Idea	Proprietary nature of the idea
	Well-defined future plan
	Scalability of the idea
	Socio-political relevance
	Validation of idea
Prototype	Completion status of prototype
	Proof of concept and user feedback
	Possibility to license the product
	User interface and salability
	Presence of well-experienced personnel
Quality Management Team	Technical or commercial competency of founding team
	Management awareness of their limitations

(continued)

Parameter as per Berkus Method	Sub-parameter established by the paper
	Share or equity stake among the founding members
	Founder flexibility
	Diversity among founders
Strategic Relationships	Existing rivalry
	Effect of strategic relationship on efficiency of the startup
	Strategic relationship may bring new business/add to existing customer satisfaction
	Capability of strategic relationship to prevent threat from competition
	Whether strategic relationship covers most of the threat the startup is prone to
Product Rollout or Sales	Whether the product has been tested/run through QA
	Evidence that the target customer is willing to pay the target price.
	Customer support team has been properly trained
	Preparation to handle orders
	Clear Go-To Market Plan

1.4 Overview on "How the Dave Berkus Method Is Applied?"

The Berkus method assigns a financial value to each of the four major risks faced by early-stage startups—after crediting the entrepreneur some basic value for the quality and potential of the idea itself. The method adds "US$500,000" in each of the following risk reduction elements (Table 1):

It is to be noted that the above are the maximum limits that can be earned to form the Valuation, allowing for a pre-revenue valuation of up to US$2 million but also allowing the investor to put much lower values into each test.

The reason for this is that Berkus sets a 'soft-cap' of US$20 Mil valuation in the fifth year of the business, giving the investor a ten times return potential over the investment's life span in a pre-revenue stage company.

Table 1 Applying Dave Berkus Method

If exists	Add to company value
Sound Idea (Basic Value)	US$ 500,000
Prototype (Reducing Technology Risk)	US$ 500,000
Quality Management Team (Reducing Execution Risk)	US$ 500,000
Strategic Relationships (Reducing Market Risk)	US$ 500,000
Product Rollout or Sales (Reducing Production Risk)	US$ 500,000

1.4.1 Sound Idea

A sound startup idea is basically a hypothesis about why a company could grow rapidly. The Dave Berkus Method, as we understood assigns a value to the business and its key success factors or risk factors. Sound idea represents the basic value a startup can claim, with the highest value being at US$500,000.

Filters and Framework to Assess a Sound Idea
The Dave Berkus Method does not elaborate on any framework to assess and evaluate a "Sound Idea" but evaluation of an Idea by startup investors across the world can be summarized in the following framework:

- Investment thesis filter.
- Problem being solved and size of the problem.
- Scalability of solution.
- Advantages that would enable rapid growth.

1. **Investment Thesis Filter**

   The investment thesis outlines the specific criteria that the investor is using to make investment decisions and the expected outcome or return. It takes into consideration the investor's risk tolerance, investment goals, and market conditions. The investment thesis is based on extensive research and analysis of various factors such as market trends, company financials, and industry dynamics (Alexander Jarvis, 2021)

   A business idea, however good, would not be considered further for an investment round if it does not fit the Investment Thesis framework.
2. **Problem Being Solved and Size of the Problem**

   The problem statement is basically definition of the setting and environment for the subject company that allows it to grow rapidly. Problems not being solved rapidly or at scale may still be good businesses but are generally not considered good investments by VCs. Following are some of the attributes of "Good Problems" (Hale, 2019) to have "Sound Ideas" for:

   - **Popularity and Size:** Good problems are popular problems to solve. A large number of people experience the problem. Problems with smaller number of people are not quite promising to be solved.
   - **Growing Rate:** Problems that have a growing rate are considered good to be solved. More and more people facing the same problem as years go by is considered good as the startup has a growing addressable market.
   - **Urgency:** Problems that require an immediate solution are good problems to address with a solution. Problems that are not urgent to be solved struggle to get traction in the market.
   - **Expensive Problem:** Problems that are expensive if not resolved are good to be solved. It increases the size of the Total Addressable Market (TAM) and creates the opportunity to charge a lot of money from people to solve the problem.

- **Mandatory Problems:** Problems that cannot be done away with and are mandatory to be solved are great problems to solve.
- **Frequent and Recurring:** Problems that require usage of solution continuously and regularly are great problems to solve. The business has the potential to create recurring and predictable sources of revenue while gradually building a model to recover customer acquisition costs and increase profit margins.

3. **Solution that is Scalable**

   The solution statement is the actual "Sound Idea" under evaluation. Solutions are basically the experiments that the startup is running within the given conditions to grow rapidly (Hale, 2019).

   It is important that the solution is developed after a thorough understanding of the problem. Generally, the Solution should not be in search of the problem. The startup founder should not be so much in deep of the solution that they try to shoe horn a problem into the solution.

   Solutions that are also tech enabled with 'one to many' models are considered scalable with the ability to rapidly grow (Steve Blank, 2010).
4. **Insights and Unfair Advantages that Enable Rapid Growth**

   This is all about the reasons why the solution is going to work. What is the unfair advantage that the business holds that sets it up for rapid growth (Hale, 2019). Following are some of the attributes/analysis frameworks basis which the solution could be evaluated:

   - Why is this business in a position to win vs. everyone else?
   - Why would this business going to be the fastest one to grow?
   - Do they have an customer acquisition strategy that is at a scale, free or relatively cheap? Do they have to pay enormous amounts to acquire customers all the time?
   - Do they have unfair advantages that would make them a monopoly in the space that they operate?
   - Can they grow on network effects and 'one to many' method?

1.4.2 Prototype

A Prototype is a replica of the actual concept of the product to test its viability. The main objective with which a prototype is built to face the challenges and holes in the solutions in its practical implementation before making large investments in technology, time, energy, and priorities. ("What Is Technology Risk?", Retrieved from https://reciprocitylabs.com/resources/what-istechnology-risk/)

A working prototype, to a large extent, reduces the technological risks and allows for a confirmation of the technical viability of the product.

A working prototype need not, at its very core, have a beautiful UI/UX, fast processing speeds or use complicated tech stacks. It could be built on primitive technology or can even be human driven. However, it must be in a position to demonstrate functionality, reliability, and scalability of the solution (Ramirez, 2018).

A well-built excel sheet that takes a certain input to provide an output can also be a working prototype.

A lack of prototype would significantly reduce the valuation of the subject company while a working prototype with feedback from a few users in the target market would enhance the valuation and can potentially rank closer to US$500,000 mark in the Dave Berkus Method.

1.4.3 Quality Management Team

The quality of the management team, including the founders, is a crucial factor in venture capital investment decisions. VC firms assess the team's experience, skills, and ability to execute their plans, as well as their track record and unique advantages. The management team's leadership structure and ability to drive success and growth are also important factors. The quality of the team is seen as key to the success of the company and the potential for returns on investment, making it a critical consideration in VC investment decisions.

The Dave Berkus Method considers the Quality of Management as one of the attributes for valuation. A high-quality management team reduces the risk of execution and increases the likelihood of success of a startup.

Following attributes are generally considered (MOI, HBR, 2019) **by investment managers in assessing the management capabilities to run the startup successfully:**

- **Founder's Domain and Track Record**—The background and accomplishments of the founder in their respective field can greatly influence the potential of the startup. Previously successful founders are most likely to succeed in the venture than those founders who are starting up for the first time.
- **Founder Advantage**—If the founder is a product engineer at Google or Microsoft, it does not really establish a founder advantage. This is because there are hundred other product engineers at Google or Microsoft. However if the founder has developed, say a niche patent in battery manufacturing process or had earlier built a successful startup that scaled very well, the same would be considered a founder advantage. Founder advantage is rare to have and such startups deserve higher valuations.
- **Clarity of Thought**—Intellectual prowess is nowhere near as valuable as clarity of thought—the ability to take in disparate ideas, process them and process challenging questions. It takes extra effort and time to be crisp and concise in communicating the business model, strategy, and goals. Such founders effectively manage their teams, co-founders, and investors all alike.
- **Intellectual Integrity**—Founders who are introspective, understand their strengths and weaknesses very clearly. Founders who are self-aware tend to avoid mistakes, which are costly, in early-stage startups and instead seek for help in areas where they lack either from their co-founders or from the investor's team.

- **Solo Founder vs. Co-Founders**—Startup success rates have been closely linked with whether the company is run by a solo founder or a team of founders. Investors prefer co-founded startups for many reasons including better productivity because of leaders handling different priorities and moral support for one another. Founders who have worked together earlier or have known each other from a long time also stick together for longer periods of time.
- **No Other Commitments**—Founders who prioritize the success of their startup above other commitments are more likely to succeed than founders who run their startup on a part-time basis while running other startups or being in employment.
- **Clarity on Leadership**—Founders who have clarity on who the CEO or face of the company is, would work well together as there is minimal room for disputes as each of the co-founders are happy with their roles.

1.4.4 Strategic Relationships

Strategic Relationships can play a significant role in reducing market risk in early-stage startups. A company may enter into strategic alliances to expand into new markets, improve its product line or develop edge over a competitor. The arrangement allows two businesses to work towards a common goal that will benefit both (Kamau, 2019; Blakely, 2023, Picincu, 2018; Wakeam, 2003).

Following are a few examples of early-stage startups that have successfully leveraged strategic relationships:

- Stripe and Shopify: Stripe, a payments processing company, and Shopify, an e-commerce platform, have a strategic partnership that enables Shopify merchants to easily accept payments through Stripe. This strategic relationship has helped both companies grow by providing Shopify with a reliable payment processing option and giving Stripe access to Shopify's large merchant base.
- Airbnb and American Express: Airbnb, a platform for booking short-term rentals, has a strategic partnership with American Express that allows Amex cardholders to use their points to book Airbnb stays. This partnership has helped Airbnb expand its customer base and provide additional value to its hosts, while also increasing the value proposition of Amex's loyalty program.
- Lemonade and Google: Lemonade, a digital insurance startup, has a strategic partnership with Google that allows Google Home users to ask for insurance quotes and receive policy information. This partnership has helped Lemonade reach a wider audience and improve its brand awareness, while also providing Google Home users with a new functionality. Additionally, Lemonade has access to Google's technology and resources, which can help the startup innovate and improve its products.
- Impossible Foods and Burger King: Impossible Foods, a plant-based meat substitute company, has a strategic partnership with Burger King that has resulted in the popular "Impossible Whopper" menu item. This partnership has helped Impossible Foods gain visibility and market share, while also enabling Burger

King to appeal to a growing demographic of consumers interested in plant-based options.

Zerodha's multiple strategic tie-ups: Zerodha, an online discount stock brokerage firm in India has formed multiple strategic tie ups to enhance customer experience in investment and trading. Some of its strategic tie ups include

- Smallcase—Zerodha has partnered with Smallcase, an investment platform that allows users to invest in a basket of stocks that reflect a particular theme or strategy. Zerodha customers can use Smallcase to invest in a range of curated portfolios, including those based on themes such as "Smart Beta," "Value Investing," and "ESG Investing."
- Streak—Zerodha has also partnered with Streak, an algo-trading platform that allows users to create and backtest trading strategies. Zerodha customers can use Streak to create their own trading strategies or use pre-built ones, and automate their trades based on specific conditions.
- Sensibull—Zerodha has partnered with Sensibull, an options trading platform that provides users with real-time data and analytics. Zerodha customers can use Sensibull to analyze options strategies and make informed trading decisions.
- GoldenPi—Zerodha has partnered with GoldenPi, an online platform that allows users to invest in corporate bonds. Zerodha customers can use GoldenPi to invest in high-yield bonds issued by top-rated companies.
- Ditto Insurance—Zerodha's strategic partnership with Ditto an insurance advisory startup has further strengthened its ambition of expanding horizontally in the retail investment space.

In assessment of strategic relationships, following are some of the broad points to note:

- The partnership should increase target customer benefit and reduce friction or problems of the target customer.
- The partnership should compliment the business model in scaling the product offering of the startup.
- Both partners must understand each other's cultural environments. Since there is lot of uncertainty surrounding the offerings of early-stage startups, the partners must rely on intangibles such as executive leadership's vision, morals and values. Some of the matters to check alignment on include importance given to end users experience, customer relationship and its responsiveness, focus on building processes and integrity in business operations.
- Terms of the partnership—The terms of the partnership should be commercially beneficial and not lead to onerous arrangements where achievement of positive economics is a pipe dream.
- Integrations—Where product-level integrations are part of the partnership, such integrations should be relatively easy without requiring resource-intensive or distracting solutions. Partnerships that do not satisfy strategic objectives generally require detailed and customized solutions for integrations.

1.4.5 Product Rollout or Sales

A product rollout is a critical milestone for startups as it marks transition from development to market launch.

It involves careful planning and execution to ensure that the product meets the needs and preferences of the target audience (Kirsch, 2019). Early-stage startups must pay close attention to market demand, competition, and pricing strategies to optimize their chances of success. Additionally, startups need to adopt an agile approach to rollout, where they can adapt and refine the product based on feedback from early customers. Overall, a well-executed product rollout can have a significant impact on the long-term success and growth of a startup.

Following are the two key reasons why a product rollout is important in early-stage startups:

- Demonstrating proof of concept—A successful product rollout provides concrete evidence that the startup's product has value and is in demand in the market. This helps to demonstrate proof of concept for the startup, which is a key factor in valuing early-stage startups.
- Testing and refining the product—A product rollout provides an opportunity for the startup to test and refine its product based on customer feedback. This can help to improve the product's functionality, usability, and overall value proposition which is important for long-term success.

It is to be noted that Berkus method is best applicable primarily to pre-revenue early-stage startups. That means, the usual expectation is to assign a value of 'zero' to the Product Rollout or Sales criteria. Once the company starts generating revenue, projection of such revenue anyway becomes possible and a Discounted Cashflow approach to valuation may be better suited while the Berkus method would not be the best framework to value the startup (William Bruce, 2014).

Why a US$2 Million—2.5 Pre-money Valuation?

As we have discussed earlier, the Berkus model places as a maximum valuation of pre-revenue early-stage startup at US$ 2 Million and a startup with some revenues can be assigned valuation of up to a US$ 2.5 Million.

However, the matrix is not restrictive and the value that can be assigned to each of the element need not be restricted to US$0.5 Million. It is important that the investor or appraiser considers market conditions and has some knowledge of pre-money valuations claimed by similar companies in the space.

If, for example, the average pre-seed, pre-revenue companies' pre-money valuations in the Silicon Valley, USA is about US$10 Million then the value that can be assigned to each of the elements could be US$ 2.5 Million with a maximum pre-money of US$12.5 Million if the company is earning revenues. Similar adjustments could be made considering pre-money valuations in different sectors and geographies. (Berkus, D. After 20 years: Updating the Berkus method of valuation. Retrieved from https://www.angelcapitalassociation.org/blog/after-20-years-updating-the-berkus-method-of-valuation/#:~:text=The%20Berkus%20Method%20assigns%20a,potential%20of%20the%20idea%20itself)

2 Case Study

Let us go through the following case study to understand the practical application of Dave Berkus Method.

Startup: Silver Arrow HealthTech (Fictitious)

Business Model: Silver Arrow HealthTech is a software platform that uses machine learning algorithms to analyze health data and provide personalized health recommendations to users.

Milestones: The startup has developed a working prototype of their platform and has secured a partnership with a local hospital to pilot their product.

Management Team: The team consists of four experienced software engineers with expertise in machine learning and health data analysis.

Competition: There are several other companies in the healthtech space, but Silver Arrow HealthTech has a unique approach to personalized health recommendations that sets them apart from their competitors.

The company is yet to start earning revenues.

Solution

Allocation of value across various attributes can be made as follows, considering Maximum Pre-Money Valuation for Pre-Revenue Startups at US$2 Mil and US $500,000 for each attribute (Table 2).

The above valuation should be substantiated by a brief search of average pre-money valuations for pre-revenue startups in that geography.

Table 2 Solution of the Case Study

Attribute	Add to Value	Reasoning
Sound Idea	US$200,000	This is investor's subjective consideration for allocation of value. Typically, the full value is attributed if the investor is bullish on the idea.
Prototype	US$150,000	Since a fully functional working prototype is ready, a majority value can be attribute. However, the prototype is yet to be tested in real life scenario and the maximum value may not be attributed because of this reason.
Quality Management Team	US$100,000	Even though a competent panel of software engineers are heading the company, there is lack of skills diversity across other important aspects of running a startup like Sales, Marketing, Finance and experience of building startups
Strategic Relationships	US$50,000	The company has now built a relationship with a local hospital to test their prototype. However, strategic relationships in relation to confirmed usage by hospitals, channel partners who can strategical place SilverArrow in existing eco-systems are not present. Hence a lower valuation is attributed
Product Rollout or Sales	NIL	Since this a pre-revenue startup, no valuation for turnover or product rollout can be attributed.
Total valuation	US$600,000	

3 Conclusion

The Dave Berkus Method is particularly useful for early-stage startups that may not yet have significant revenue or assets to base a traditional valuation on. By taking into account attributes that were discussed above, the method provides a more holistic view of the company's potential value and risk reduction for an investor. It is also important to note that the method does not replace traditional valuation techniques but rather complements the. (Bruce, 2014; Teten & Allen, 2017).

The utility of the method also lies in its simplicity, in that it does not require detailed analysis but rather an opinion on various attributes that reduces risk and makes the startup worthy of success. The Berkus Method is not a precise formula but it simplifies valuation.

References

"What is technology Risk?", Retrieved from https://reciprocitylabs.com/resources/what-istechnology-risk/

de Mol E. (2019). What makes a successful startup team. Retrieved from https://hbr.org/2019/03/what-makes-asuccessful-startup-team

Berkus, D. *About Dave - Berkus.com.* Retrieved from https://www.berkus.com/?page_id=54

Berkus, D. *After 20 years: Updating the Berkus method of valuation.* Retrieved from https://www.angelcapitalassociation.org/blog/after-20-years-updating-the-berkus-method-of-valuation/#:~:text=The%20Berkus%20Method%20assigns%20a,potential%20of%20the%20idea%20itself

Berkus, D. *The Berkus method – Valuing the early stage investment.* Retrieved from https://berkonomics.com/?p=131

Berkus. (2012). https://berkonomics.com/?p=1214

Blakely. (2023). https://www.business.com/articles/connor-blakley-strategic-partnerships/

Bruce, W. The Berkus method: Valuing startups with realistic valuations. *Forbes*, January 22, 2014.

Business.com editorial staff, "5 Benefits of Strategic Partnerships," Retrieved from https://www.business.com/articles/connor-blakleystrategic-partnerships/

Berkus, D. *After 20 years: Updating the Berkus method of valuation.* Retrieved from https://www.angelcapitalassociation.org/blog/after-20-years-updating-the-berkus-method-ofvaluation/#:~:text=The%20Berkus%20Method%20assigns%20a,potential%20of%20the%20idea%20itself

Hale, K. (2019). https://www.ycombinator.com/library/6e-how-to-evaluate-startup-ideas

Jarvis, A. (2021). *Venture capital investment thesis.* "The Fundraising Canvas" website (https://thefundraisingcanvas.com/investor-types/venture-capital-investment-thesis/).

Kamau (2019). *Successful strategic alliances: 5 examples of companies doing it right.* Retrieved from https://www.allbound.com/resourcecenter/successful-strategic-alliances-5-examples-ofcompanies-doing-it-right/

Kirsch. (2019). Product launch checklists — They're more important than you think. Retrieved from https://www.productplan.com/product-launchchecklist/

Mahajan, A., Nallari, S., & Vyas, H. (2021). *Analysis of key factors contributing towards valuation of pre-revenue start-ups by means of the Berkus Method.*

Picincu. (2018). What is the meaning of a strategic partner? Retrieved from https://bizfluent.com/about6511465-meaning-strategic-partner-.html

Ramírez, V. (2018, September 5). *What is a prototype?* Retrieved from https://medium.com/nycdesign/what-is-a-prototype-924ff9400cfd

Steve blank. (2010). *Make No Little Plans – Defining the scalable startup*. Retrieved from https://steveblank.com/2010/01/04/make-no-littleplans-%E2%80%93-defining-the-scalable-startup/ 2010, January 25.

Teten, D., & Allen, S. *How to estimate value in early-stage ventures*. Columbia Business School Research Paper No. 17-46, August 2017.

Wakeam. (2003). The five factors of a strategic alliance. Retrieved from https://iveybusinessjournal.com/publication/the-fivefactorsof-a-strategic-alliance/

Risk Factor Summation Method

Anjan Babu, Chinmaya Arikutaram, and Abraham Mathews

1 Introduction

Early-stage valuations are challenging. How do we assess the Startup's future performance? Are the projections realistic? Is the valuation on par with market comparables? Have we assessed all risk factors? These are key concerns at the outset of any investment journey.

The **Risk Factor Summation** method addresses these concerns. It considers various factors that may impact a Startup's success. Its end goal is to provide the **possible pre-money valuation** for early-stage startups.

The **RFS or Risk Factor Summation** method was created by Ohio TechAngels (Bill Payne, 2011) and is utilized by angel investors and venture capitalists to assess the value of pre-revenue companies. This method is usually applied during the pre-seed or pre-Series A stages of funding. It expands on the principles of other techniques like the Venture Capital Valuation method and the Dave Berkus Valuation Method by taking into account a wider array of risk factors that can impact startups as they progress towards becoming established enterprises.

As reportedly described by Ohio Tech Angels *"Reflecting the premise that the higher the number of risk factors, then the higher the overall risk, this method forces investors to think about the various types of risks which a particular venture must manage in order to achieve a lucrative exit. Of course, the largest is always 'Management Risk' which demands the most consideration and investors feel is the most overarching risk in any venture. While this method certainly considers the level of management risk it also prompts the user to assess other risk types"*.

The risk factor summation method cannot be applied in a mechanical manner. It demands the **user's exercise of judgement**. It enables the user to think by providing

A. Babu (✉) · C. Arikutaram · A. Mathews
Agraga Valuers, Bangalore, Karnataka, India
e-mail: anjan.babu@agraga.co.in; chinmaya@agraga.co.in; Abraham.mathews@agraga.co.in

S. Derindere Köseoğlu (ed.), *A Practical Guide for Startup Valuation*, Contributions to Finance and Accounting, https://doi.org/10.1007/978-3-031-35291-1_11

various parameters. The user would be able to judge across these various parameters. The valuation would then be driven by what is beneficial and what is detrimental to the startup's ability to create a reasonable exit within a scheduled time frame (Reinfeld, 2018).

The risk factor summation method uses the value of comparable startups. Such value is the base value. It is then modified to account for 12 common risk factors. This comparison provides a framework. It assesses whether a startup carries a higher or lower level of risk in relation to other startups.

Following are the steps involved in applying the Risk Factor Summation Method:

1. Find the average Industry Pre-Money Valuation. The average serves as the base pre-money valuation.
2. Consider 12 Risk Factors that are correlated with the startup's industry.
3. Risk rating ranges between +2 Extremely positive with −2 being Extremely negative, which are as follows:

   (a) +2 = Very Positive/Very Low Risk
   (b) +1 = Positive/Low Risk
   (c) = Neutral/Medium Risk
   (d) −1 = Negative/High Risk
   (e) −2 = Very Negative/Very High Risk

4. Rate each of the 12 risk factors. Each rating carries a potential adjustment to the base pre-money value by $250 k for each point move either way (E.g.: +1 would add $250 k to the base valuation while −2 would reduce $500 k from the base valuation, 0 would not create any impact on the pre-money valuation adjustment).

   Find the total of the ratings castigated against adjustment to pre-money valuations.
5. Add the total of adjustments with the pre-money valuation arrived.

   Table 1 represents the result of application of steps to Risk Factor Summation Method of Pre-Money Valuation

2 Inputs of Risk Factor Summation Method

Now that a broad overview has been understood, we shall deliberate upon each ingredient that go into the valuation computation. Broadly, the following are the major inputs (Fig. 1)

Table 1 Risk factors

Base value (Average of comparables)		$25,00,000
Risk factors	Ratings	Addition/Subtraction ($)
Management risk	2	$5,00,000
Stage of the business	1	$2,50,000
Legislation/Political risk	1	$2,50,000
Manufacturing risk (or supply chain risk)	0	$0
Sales or marketing risk	2	$5,00,000
Funding/Capital raising risk	−1	−$2,50,000
Competition risk	−1	−$2,50,000
Technology risk	−1	−$2,50,000
Litigation risk	−1	−$2,50,000
International risk	0	$0
Reputation risk	0	$0
Exit value risk	−1	−$2,50,000
Net adjustment		$2,50,000
Total pre-money valuation		$27,50,000

Source: Author's creation

Fig. 1 Inputs of Risk Factor Summation Method

2.1 *Base Pre-Money Valuation*

The aim of this exercise is to determine the most common value of similar-stage companies.

The current valuation subtracted from the money raised provides us the pre-money valuation. We carry this exercise out for all companies in the industry. The average of pre-money valuations provides us with the base value.

It is important that we consider the valuation of similar-stage companies belonging to the same region. We must also be wary of outliers in our selected population.

Research reports on valuations may also be considered as a substitute.

Usage of research reports would allow us to adopt data from similar-stage companies. It will also ensure sanity of our computations while enabling removing of outliers.

Let us consider an example:

Say, we are assessing a seed round investment in a Fintech Company based out of the US. The median pre-money valuations of Seed Stage Companies for Fintech

Companies in the Americas is $12.6 Millions (Pulse of Fintech 2023) (KPMG, 2023). We can consider such valuation as the base for our exercise.

2.2 *Risk Factors*

The Risk Factor Summation Method directs the investor's focus towards the different types of risks associated with a particular Startup. By doing so, it compels the investor to consider all the potential risks to devise a viable exit strategy within a particular timeframe.

The risk factors that are listed down as by the Risk Factor Summation Method are listed in Table 2 (Payne, 2011).

Table 3 provides summary one liner questions to assess the risk factors.

Now we shall dwell into each of the Risk Factors with the intent of understanding its practical application.

2.2.1 Management Risk

As discussed earlier, Ohio Tech Angels consider Evaluation of the management/founder/promoter risk as a high priority among other risks which are part of the method.

Following are some of the ways Angel investors generally assess management risk:

- First-time founders are riskier in comparison to founders who have run Startups before.
- Solo Founders are riskier compared to team of founders/co-founders.
- Founders who have business interests outside the company are riskier than founders who have their 'skin in the game'.

Table 2 Risk factors

Risks
Management Risk
Stage of Business Risk
Legislation/Political Risk
Manufacturing or Service Delivery Risk
Sales and Marketing Risk or "Go to Market" Risk
Competition Risk
Technology Risk
Litigation Risk
Funding and Capital Raising Risk
Exit Risk
Reputation Risk
International Risk

Table 3 Assessing questions for risk factors

Sl. No.	Risk factor	Assessment question
1	Management Risk	Does the founding team pose a significant threat to the future of the business?
2	Stage of Business	Is the business in its initial stage of the maturity cycle, which entails a high risk of failure?
3	Legislation/Political Risk	Can regulations, legislation, and political conditions result in the collapse of the business?
4	Manufacturing or Service Delivery Risk	Can the business fail due to inability of suppliers and service providers?
5	Sales and Marketing Risk	Will the business be affected by sales and marketing problems?
6	Funding/Capital Raising Risk	Is it probable that the business will fail to raise funds in the future?
7	Competition Risk	Will the business fail due to the competitive environment?
8	Technology Risk	How much of a threat do you think the future emergence of new technologies poses to the survival of the business?
9	Litigation Risk	Do the circumstances indicate that the business may undergo litigation and fail?
10	International Risk	Will adverse international conditions lead to failure of business?
11	Reputation Risk	Will the business likely fail if it is exposed to brand reputation related crisis?
12	Potential Lucrative Exit	How probable is it for the future profitability of the business to be at risk such that the company may struggle to achieve a favourable profit margin for its products and services?

Source: Retiba, Online Valuation Tool

Apart from the above, the following are some practical insights on Founder assessment collated across few publications on Angel investing:

1. **Assess the founder's passion and commitment:** Founders who are passionate about their business idea are more likely to stay committed and work tirelessly to achieve their goals. Look for founders who are willing to make personal sacrifices to build their business, and who have a deep understanding of the problem they're trying to solve. The Gust Guide to Angel Investing (David.S.Rose) suggests that investors should ask themselves: ***"Does the founder have a vision that is inspiring and meaningful to them? Do they have the drive and tenacity to execute on that vision?"***
2. **Evaluate the founder's ability to handle uncertainty and adversity:** Starting a business is a challenging and unpredictable journey, and founders who can navigate through uncertainty and adversity are more likely to succeed. Look for founders who are resilient, adaptable, and have a history of overcoming challenges. The Angel Investor's Handbook (David S Rose) suggests that investors should ask themselves: ***"Has the founder demonstrated the ability to handle setbacks, learn from mistakes, and persevere in the face of adversity?"***

3. **Assess the founder's integrity and character:** Founders who have a strong sense of integrity and ethics are more likely to build a successful and sustainable business. Look for founders who are honest, transparent, and ethical in their dealings with others. The Due Diligence for the Entrepreneurial Investor (Howard Stevenson and Michael Roberts) book suggests that investors should ask themselves: ***"Do the founder's actions match their words? Are they transparent about the risks and challenges facing the business?"***
4. **Evaluate the founder's skills and experience:** Founders who have relevant skills and experience are more likely to build a successful business. Look for founders who have a deep understanding of the industry and market they're operating in, as well as relevant technical, operational, and leadership skills. The Angel Investment: Valuation and Diligence (Dr. Robert Wiltbank, Dave Berkus, and Andrew Romans) book suggests that investors should ask themselves: "***Does the founder have the skills and experience necessary to execute on their business plan? Are they able to assemble and manage a talented team?"***

2.2.2 Stage of Business Risk

For pre-seed and seed-stage startups, early traction reduces risks associated with Early stage Startups. Some of the examples of Early traction include:

1. Creation of a Beta or a Minimally Viable Product
2. Initial or Pilot Customers. Brand name customers are even better
3. Strategic Partnerships that enable any key area of business, be it Marketing, Sales, Procurement, Distribution
4. Customer Testimonials

Startups that are able to acquire early customers and generate revenue in their early stages are more likely to have found product-market fit. This means that their product or service meets a real need in the market and that there is demand for it. The Lean Startup by Eric Ries emphasizes the importance of finding product-market fit early in a startup's life cycle and using customer feedback to iterate and improve the product.

The founding team must have taken credible steps to achieve these low-fund but high-value milestones. Early-stage companies with evidence of customer traction, such as sales and/or users, and a plan to scale, can be more attractive to investors as it reduces stage of business risk to a large extent.

2.2.3 Legislation/Political Risk

Legislation and political risks can be a significant challenge for early-stage startups, particularly those operating in highly regulated industries or in countries with volatile political climates. Here are some insights and examples of legislation and political risks faced by early-stage startups:

1. **Regulations can create barriers to entry:** Startups operating in industries such as healthcare, finance, or transportation may face significant regulatory hurdles that can make it difficult to launch and scale their businesses. For example, startups in the healthcare industry may need to comply with strict regulations around data privacy and patient safety, while those in the transportation industry may need to navigate complex regulations around licensing and insurance. According to a report by CB Insights, "More than half of healthcare startups fail due to regulatory hurdles."
2. **Political instability can create uncertainty**: Startups operating in countries with unstable political climates may face uncertainty around issues such as taxation, trade policies, and labour laws. For example, a startup operating in a country that experiences frequent changes in government may find it difficult to plan for the long term or attract investment. A report by the World Economic Forum notes that "Political instability and regulatory risk are among the top three risks that companies face when investing in emerging markets."
3. **Legislation can change quickly:** Startups may also face the risk of sudden changes in legislation or policy that can impact their business models or revenue streams. For example, a startup that relies on a specific tax credit or subsidy may see its revenue decline if that policy is changed or eliminated. A report by Deloitte notes that "Startups need to be nimble enough to adapt to a rapidly changing regulatory landscape."

One example of legislation and political risks faced by early-stage startups is the sharing economy. Companies such as Airbnb and Uber faced significant regulatory hurdles and political opposition in their early days, as they disrupted traditional industries and challenged existing regulations. Airbnb, for example, faced legal challenges around issues such as zoning laws, hotel taxes, and safety regulations. Similarly, Uber faced regulatory challenges around issues such as licensing and insurance requirements for drivers. However, both companies were ultimately able to navigate these challenges and build successful businesses but the following startups failed mainly due to regulatory challenges:

1. Sidecar: Sidecar was a ride-hailing startup that launched in 2012, before Uber and Lyft became popular (CB Insights, 2019). However, the company faced significant regulatory hurdles, including fines from local transportation authorities and legal battles with taxi companies. In 2015, Sidecar announced that it would shut down its ride-hailing service and pivot to focus on a delivery platform.
2. Homejoy: Homejoy was an online platform that connected homeowners with cleaning services (WEF, 2018). However, the company faced legal challenges around whether its cleaners were employees or independent contractors, which impacted its ability to raise funding and operate in certain markets. In 2015, Homejoy announced that it would shut down its operations due to "unresolved challenges in the home services space."

3. Zenefits: Zenefits was a software company that provided cloud-based HR and benefits management software for small businesses (Deloitte, 2018). However, the company faced regulatory challenges around compliance with insurance laws and broker licensing requirements. In 2016, Zenefits announced that it would lay off 45% of its workforce and pay $seven million in fines to settle regulatory charges.

2.2.4 Manufacturing or Service Delivery Risk

According to a poll by CB Insights—a tech market intelligence platform, 42% of the startups believed that inability of a startup to deliver a great product according to the market needs is an important reason behind the failure of many startups.

While it may seem obvious that a poor product will not succeed, many entrepreneurs and investors believe that latent customer needs can be uncovered, and they will eventually buy the product. Investors often focus on other business parameters like market fit, valuation, and sales, overlooking the entrepreneur's ability to deliver the product.

However, not every market is as forgiving as the mobile phone market, where "average" products can succeed with some marketing and at the right price point. Product delivery is crucial for a startup's success, and underestimating its importance can have disastrous consequences.

Product delivery is the result of a great idea executed well for the right customer at the right time. This requires several elements to be done right, including building a winning team and having a strong and sustainable business model (Kunal Nandwani, 2022).

Investors sometimes commit startup investments without thoroughly evaluating the product delivery capabilities. But the difference between a successful startup and a failed one is the combination of several elements done right.

One example of poor product delivery is Juicero, which aimed to deliver perfect juice to customers with its $699 Wi-Fi-connected juicer that required proprietary juice packs. However, Bloomberg released a video that showed the juice packs could be squeezed by hand faster than the machine could squeeze them. The public was convinced that the product was useless, and investors realized that the machine was bulkier than the original plan. The company shut down sixteen months after launch.

One example of an early-stage startup that failed due to poor product delivery is Zano, a British drone startup. Zano aimed to produce a pocket-sized drone that could be controlled by a smartphone and could be used for aerial photography.

Zano raised over £2 million on Kickstarter and was able to attract additional investment. However, the company was unable to deliver on its promised product. The drone suffered from technical issues, had a short battery life, and lacked key features promised in the original campaign.

Despite efforts to rectify the issues, the company was unable to deliver a working product to its backers. Zano eventually went bankrupt, leaving its investors and backers empty-handed.

The failure of Zano is a clear example of the importance of good product delivery for startup success. No matter how innovative or promising an idea may seem, it ultimately depends on the ability of the startup to deliver a working product that meets the needs of the market.

2.2.5 Sales and Marketing Risk

Startups often face sales and marketing risks that can negatively impact their performance and ability to succeed. Sales and marketing is the process of bringing a product or service to market, including creating awareness, encouraging potential customers to buy, and managing customer relationships.

Two of the most common sales and marketing risks for startups are customer acquisition risk and customer retention risk. Customer acquisition risk relates to a startup's ability to convince potential customers to purchase their product or service, while customer retention risk relates to a startup's ability to keep customers engaged with their product or service (Foster Capital, 2022).

Aside from these two risks, there are several other sales and marketing risks that startups should also consider. Pricing risk is the risk of setting prices too low or too high, which can affect profits or deter potential customers. Distribution risk is the risk of not effectively reaching the target market, resulting in lost revenue. Branding risk is the risk of failing to create a strong connection with the target market, leading to a lack of interest in the product or service.

Examples of early-stage startups that failed due to poor sales and marketing include:

1. Pets.com: Pets.com was an online pet store that sold pet supplies and accessories. While the idea was great, the company failed to establish effective distribution channels, which made it difficult to get products to customers quickly and affordably. As a result, the company went bankrupt in 2000.
2. Quibi: A mobile video streaming platform that invested heavily in advertising but failed to generate enough interest from consumers, resulting in low subscriber numbers and ultimately, shutting down.

(Forbes, 2015)

Go-to-Market Strategies also play an important role in ensuring a success of Sales and Marketing. A well-crafted GTM strategy takes into account factors such as the target audience, distribution channels, pricing, and promotion methods. It helps a company to effectively launch its products or services, maximize customer reach, and ultimately achieve revenue and growth goals. (Williams, 2015)

Go-to-Market Strategies can fail for a variety of reasons, including inadequate market research, poor timing, ineffective messaging, and competition. Here are some examples:

1. Inadequate market research: Google Wave, a real-time collaboration tool, failed because it was too complex for most users and didn't meet their needs. Google

Wave was launched in 2009 with great fanfare but was discontinued a year later due to lack of adoption.

2. Poor timing: Apple's Newton, a personal digital assistant, was ahead of its time and failed to gain widespread adoption when it was released in 1993. However, when Apple released the iPhone in 2007, it was a huge success because the market was ready for a smartphone with advanced features.
3. Ineffective messaging: McDonald's launched a healthy menu option called the McWrap in 2013, but the messaging focused on its affordability rather than its health benefits. The McWrap failed to attract health-conscious customers and was eventually removed from the menu.

    (HBR—Schneider & Hall, 2011)

2.2.6 Funding/Capital Raising Risk

Funding risk is a common challenge faced by startups, which refers to the possibility of not being able to secure the necessary capital to grow and scale their business operations. This risk is particularly significant in the early stages of a startup's development, when access to capital can determine its survival.

There are several macroeconomic factors that can affect a startup's ability to secure funding. These include fluctuations in the global economy, changes in interest rates, and shifts in investor sentiment. Additionally, changes in government regulations and policies can also impact funding opportunities for startups.

One example of a startup that failed due to a lack of funding is the social networking site Friendster (TechCrunch, 2015). Despite being one of the first social media platforms to gain widespread popularity, Friendster was unable to secure additional funding after its initial round of investment, leading to its eventual decline and sale in 2009.

Another example is Admazely. Admazely offered retargeting tools for businesses (Failory, 2022a). They shut down in 2013 when they ran short on financing and didn't figure out how to secure more cash.

2.2.7 Competition Risk

Competition risk is a common challenge faced by startups, particularly in industries that are crowded with numerous players. This risk refers to the possibility of a startup losing market share or failing to establish a strong foothold in the market due to intense competition. The intense competition may result in price wars, lower profit margins, and difficulties in differentiating the product or service.

To assess whether a startup is facing intense competition, investors can examine various factors, including the number and size of competitors, market share, pricing strategy, customer loyalty, and product differentiation. An intense level of competition in the industry can negatively impact the startup's growth prospects and increase the likelihood of failure.

One example of a startup that failed due to intense competition is the mobile phone maker Essential (Verge, 2020). Despite being founded by Android co-creator Andy Rubin and raising $330 million in funding, the company struggled to compete against established players like Apple and Samsung, eventually shutting down in 2020.

Bitpass was a startup that offered a platform for making micropayments online (Failory, 2022b). However, the company eventually shut down due to intense competition, particularly from the free-to-use Google Checkout payment system. In an email to its users, Bitpass cited the emergence of Google Checkout as the main reason for its closure, stating that the new payment system made its business model redundant. The CEO of Bitpass had originally hoped to integrate its micropayment features into Google Checkout, but this never materialized. Despite raising around $12 million in funding and acquiring one of its competitors, Bitpass ultimately failed to sustain its operations and closed down in 2007.

2.2.8 Technology Risk

The emergence of new technologies in the future can pose a significant risk to the existence of businesses. This risk, known as technology risk, refers to the potential of a business becoming obsolete or losing its competitive edge due to new technologies that disrupt the market or render the company's products or services irrelevant.

Technology risk can manifest in various ways, such as the inability to adapt to new technologies, failure to innovate or keep up with the latest trends, or overreliance on outdated or obsolete technology. Companies that fail to keep up with technological changes risk losing market share, customer loyalty, and ultimately, their business.

One example of a Startup that failed was Jawbone (TechCrunch, 2017). Jawbone was a wearable technology company that produced fitness trackers and Bluetooth speakers. Despite raising over $900 million in funding and being valued at $3 billion, Jawbone failed to keep up with competitors like Fitbit and Apple. Jawbone faced several legal challenges and struggled to release new products, which ultimately led to its shutdown in 2017.

2.2.9 Litigation Risk

Assessing litigation risk is an important consideration for angel investors when evaluating startups. Some factors that may increase the likelihood of litigation risk include the nature of the industry, the presence of intellectual property issues, and the quality of the startup's legal counsel.

To assess litigation risk, investors should conduct due diligence on the startup's legal history, including any past lawsuits or legal disputes. They should also evaluate the startup's risk management strategies and assess whether the company has adequate insurance coverage in place. Additionally, investors should consider the potential impact of litigation on the company's reputation, financial stability, and future growth prospects.

One example of a Company that failed due to litigation is LimeWire (TechCrunch, 2017). LimeWire was a file-sharing startup that faced multiple lawsuits from record labels and music publishers over copyright infringement (NPR, 2011). The company was ultimately shut down and its founder was ordered to pay millions of dollars in damages.

2.2.10 International Risk

International risk can pose a significant threat to startups, particularly those that operate globally or rely on international markets for growth. Some factors that may contribute to international risk include political instability, trade barriers, cultural differences, and currency fluctuations.

One example of a company that limited its growth due to International Risk was TransferWise. TransferWise was a startup that offered international money transfer services at a lower cost than traditional banks (TechCrunch, 2016). The company faced challenges in some markets due to regulatory issues and restrictions on foreign exchange transactions. For example, TransferWise was unable to operate in India for several years due to restrictions on foreign investment in the country's payment industry. This limited the company's growth potential and forced it to focus on other markets.

37Coins, a BitCoin Technologies company failed due to International Risk. 37Coins, a California-based Bitcoin wallet provider, focused on developing new Bitcoin technologies for markets such as the Philippines and Singapore. The company developed SMS gateway systems, known as SMSGateways, which allowed users in specific regions to send and receive Bitcoins using their SMSWallets.

The company's effort to provide Bitcoin transfer technologies across different regions has proved to be nearly impossible for the company. 37Coins stated that delivering monetary funds across different carriers outside of the USA was "Unreliable."

2.2.11 Reputation Risk

Reputation risk is the potential loss that a company may face due to negative public perception of its products, services, or overall brand image. Reputation risk can have a significant impact on a startup's ability to attract customers, investors, and employees. In today's hyperconnected world, negative news or reviews can spread quickly, making it challenging for startups to recover from reputational damage.

An example of this is Teforia. Teforia was a startup that created a high-end tea brewing machine. The company marketed itself as a luxury brand, with machines costing up to $1000. However, the company faced significant reputational damage when a video by a customer went viral, showing that the machine was no better than a $20 tea kettle. Teforia eventually shut down in 2018.

2.2.12 Potential Lucrative Exit

An understanding of all the risk factors that were discussed above would equip an investor assessing investment in the Startup to come to an understanding whether a lucrative exit is possible.

Even if a startup has a great idea, if the team is not able to execute it properly or manage the company well, it can lead to failure and the investor losing their investment. According to a report by CB Insights, the top reason startups fail is due to "no market need," followed by "ran out of cash" and "not the right team."

Further, if a startup's business model is not scalable, it may not be able to generate significant revenue or attract a large enough customer base to be profitable. This can lead to a lack of interest from potential acquirers or investors, and ultimately, a low exit value for the angel investor.

2.3 Rating of Risk Factors

Each of the risk factors that were discussed above is rated, as part of the valuation exercise under Risk Factor Summation Method.

Each risk is assessed with regard to how it may impact the ability of the company to grow and execute a lucrative exit, and is assigned a score as follows:

- +2 = Very Positive/Very Low Risk
- +1 = Positive/Low Risk
- = Neutral/Medium Risk
- −1 = Negative/High Risk
- −2 = Very Negative/Very High Risk

The average industry valuation derived in step one is adjusted up or down depending on the score for each risk factor. The adjustment amount typically shifts around $250 k for each point move either way (e.g. +2 would add +$500 k to the valuation; −1 would subtract $250 k).

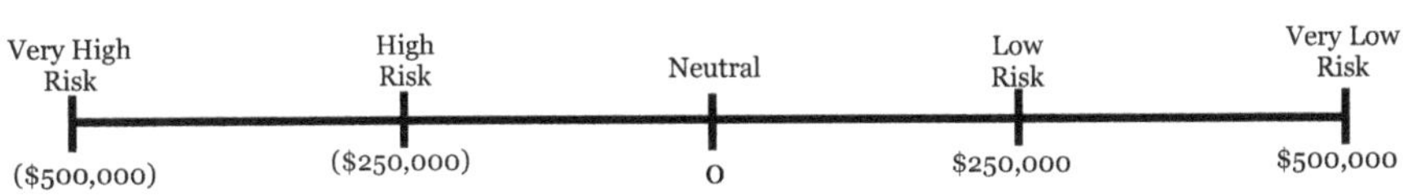

3 Case Study for Risk Facto Summation Method

3.1 Evaluation of Angel Investment in Pre-Revenue B2B SAAS Supply Chain Management Startup 'ProcuLink'

Problem Statement:

Small and medium-sized businesses often struggle with inventory management, demand forecasting, and order fulfilment due to the lack of efficient supply chain management systems. Manual processes are often time-consuming, error-prone, and lead to inefficient utilization of resources. Businesses need a solution that streamlines their supply chain management processes and provides insights for better decision-making.

Solution Provided by the Startup:

ProcuLink is a pre-revenue startup based out of Palo Alto, California that has developed a supply chain management software solution that streamlines inventory management, demand forecasting, and order fulfilment for small and medium-sized businesses. The software leverages artificial intelligence and machine learning algorithms to provide real-time insights and predictions for efficient utilization of resources. The solution is a B2B SAAS product that can be used on a subscription basis and is designed to be scalable and customizable to meet the specific needs of businesses.

Promoter Background:

The Startup was founded by Anuja, Rahul, and Priya, each bringing diverse backgrounds and skill sets to the table. Anuja has a background in data science and has previously founded and exited a healthcare technology startup. Rahul has experience in product management and has worked with leading B2B software companies, while Priya is a seasoned marketer with experience in B2B and B2C domains.

Strategic Business Relationships:

ProcuLink has established strategic partnerships with large corporations in the retail and logistics industries, providing access to a large customer base and helping the company validate its solution. The company's primary focus is on B2B relationships.

International Expansion:

ProcuLink's software solution intends to spend extensive time and investments in expanding their solutions and homogenizing software to shipping and logistics industries across the globe.

Dependence on Other Suppliers:

ProcuLink's software solution is not dependent on other suppliers. However, the company relies on cloud-based infrastructure and third-party APIs to provide some of its functionalities.

General Startup Funding Atmosphere:

The startup funding atmosphere for pre-revenue software development companies has been positive in recent years, and many venture capital firms and angel investors have shown interest in investing in startups with innovative solutions and strong growth potential.

Competition:

ProcuLink faces competition from several established large players like Oracle, IBM, Infosys, and Mindtree who have developed similar products and solutions along with their other activities. ProcuLink is the only company focusing on this particular solution.

Risk of Emergence of New and Competing Technology:

The risk of new and competing technology emerging in the supply chain management software industry is not that high. ProcuLink's focus on artificial intelligence and machine learning algorithms provides a strong defence against any risks of new technologies.

Potential Litigation Areas: There are no potential litigation areas for ProcuLink at the moment. However, the company will need to ensure that its software solution complies with data privacy and security regulations.

Likelihood of Scaling the Business: ProcuLink has a scalable business model that can be easily replicated in different industries and regions. The company's strategic partnerships with large corporations and logistics providers provide a strong foundation for scaling the business. Anuja's experience in running multiple startups, some of which were partly successful and one of them had a good exit, provides valuable experience in navigating the challenges of scaling a new venture. With the diverse skillset and backgrounds of all three promoters, ProcuLink is well positioned for growth and success in the highly competitive supply chain management software industry.

Go-to-Market: The company is yet to fully formulate its Go-to Market Strategy.

Solution

Step 1: Base Pre-money Valuations

Let us consider an average Angel Round Pre-Money Valuations for Startups at US$3.8 Millions (Venture Pulse Q2, 2022)

Step 2: Risk Rating

Sl. No.	Risk Factor	Rating	Reasoning
1	Management Risk	+2	Experienced and diverse founder group
2	Stage of Business	+1	Good Strategic Relationships, Prototype Solution in place. However no paying customers
3	Legislation/Political Risk	0	Appears that there is no Regulation related Risk
4	Manufacturing or Service Delivery Risk	0	Strategic matters not dependent on an any external provider. Not entirely self-dependent either.
5	Sales and Marketing Risk	−2	The company is yet to fully formulate its Go-to-Market strategy

(continued)

Sl. No.	Risk Factor	Rating	Reasoning
6	Funding/Capital Raising Risk	+1	Good market exists to raise funds in the future
7	Competition Risk	−1	Existence of large players, even though not specialized poses a threat to the company.
8	Technology Risk	+2	Given that it is an AI and ML-driven model, technology risk is minimum.
9	Litigation Risk	0	No litigation risk is foreseen as the IP is internally developed.
10	International Risk	−2	Given the focus segment is supply chain and shipping across the globe, unfavourable international conditions would have a large impact.
11	Reputation Risk	0	No reputation-related risks foreseen given the nature of industry
12	Potential Lucrative Exit	+1	Scalable model would enable a good exit. Since marketing strategy is not in place, competition is high and international expansion is required, the exit may be delayed.
	Total	+2	

Step 2: Adjustment to pre-money valuation

Net Total of Risk Rating	+2
Adjust per risk rating	$0.25 M
Total Adjustment	$0.5 M

Step-3 Pre-money Valuation

Base pre-money Valuation	US$3.8 M
Adjustment	US$0.5 M
Maximum Pre-Money Valuation	US$4.3 M

Case Study Source: Author's creation

4 Advantages and Disadvantages of the Method

The risk factor summation method offers several advantages, which include:

1. Simplified usability.
2. It is a good method to assess pre-revenue early-stage companies.
3. Easy assessment and control of risks without complex calculations.
4. Time and effort efficiency.
5. No requirement for specialized software or technical knowledge, making it suitable for inexperienced investors.
6. Minimal resource requirements.

However, there are also several to this method, which include:

1. Establishing the base pre-money valuation may be difficult.
2. Inability to function as a standalone valuation method. The analyst will require to corroborate this method with further assessments and other methods like multiples approach, Score Card or DCF.
3. The method may not be completely be scientific as the risks associated with a Startup may be much more diverse than the 12 common risks listed.
4. Risk rating and its impact on the valuation is purely judgemental as against being driven by an objective factor.
5. Positives could offset the Negatives and vice versa. Since the range of rating is limited to 0,1 and 2, a very large positive may be impacted offset by a small negative or conversely a very large negative may be offset by a small positive.
6. The base year is used as a benchmark for calculating the expected loss from each risk factor. This **could result in a bias** if the assumptions made about future changes in the base year are not valid.

5 Conclusion

The Risk Factor Summation Method (RFSM) is a technique for valuation of Startups by understanding the associated risks. It provides a very good framework to understand the risks associated with a Startup and getting a good exit.

The method is particularly useful for pre-revenue, early-stage startups where cash flows are unpredictable.

An analyst may corroborate the outcome of this method with other methods like the Venture Capital Method, Berkus Method and the Score Card Method.

References

Bill Payne, Gust. Valuations 101: The Risk Factor Summation Method, Bill Payne Angel Investor, Frontier Angel Fund (15 Nov 2011). https://gust.com/blog/valuations-101-the-risk-factor-summation-method/

Case Study Source: Author's creation.

CB Insights. *Why do startups fail? Top 20 reasons*. 2019.

CB Insights 2023. https://www.cbinsights.com/research/startup-failure-post-mortem/

Deloitte. (2018). *Navigating regulatory risk: The role of the board.*

Failory. (2022a). 63 Failed start ups with a lack of funds. https://www.failory.com/startups/lack-of-funds-failures

Failory. (2022b) What waa BitPass. https://www.failory.com/cemetery/bitpass

Faster Capital 2022.

Forbes - Why 90% of Startups Fail 2015.

Kunal Nandwani, Chandigarh Angels Network 2022. https://chandigarhangelsnetwork.com/product-delivery-capabilities-startup/

NPR. (2011). *LimeWire settles copyright lawsuits for $105 million*. https://www.npr.org/2011/05/13/136263292/limewire-settles-copyright-lawsuits-for-105-million

Pulse of Fintech H2'22 Global analysis of fintech Investment (February 2023). https://assets.kpmg.com/content/dam/kpmg/xx/pdf/2023/03/pulse-of-fintech-h2-2022-v14-web.pdf

Start-Up Valuation, Solving the valuation puzzle of new business ventures. Master Thesis HEC Paris Patrick Reinfeld (June 2018). https://www.vernimmen.net/ftp/Start_up_Valuation_Reinfeld_vF.pdf, Page 54, Semenchuck, 2017

Joan Schneider and Julie Hall Harvard Business Review - Why most product launches fail, April 2011.

Source: Retiba. Online Valuation Tools. https://retiba.com/risk-factors-summation/

TechCrunch. (2015). *The rise and fall of Friendster*. https://techcrunch.com/2015/08/30/the-rise-and-fall-of-friendster/

TechCrunch. (2016). *TransferWise hits profitability, plans expansion in Asia*. https://techcrunch.com/2016/05/19/transferwise-hits-profitability-plans-expansion-in-asia/

TechCrunch. (2017). *Jawbone is being liquidated as its CEO launches a related health startup*. https://techcrunch.com/2017/07/06/jawbone-is-being-liquidated-as-its-ceo-launches-a-related-health-startup/

The Verge. (2020). *Andy Rubin's essential is shutting down*. https://www.theverge.com/2020/2/12/21135405/andy-rubin-essential-products-shutting-down-new-mobile-os-email

Valuations 101: The Risk Factor Summation Method, Bill Payne Angel Investor, Frontier Angel Fund (15 Nov 2011). https://gust.com/blog/valuations-101-the-risk-factor-summation-method/

Venture Pulse Q2 2022. https://assets.kpmg.com/content/dam/kpmg/xx/pdf/2022/07/venture-pulse-q2-2022.pdf

David K. Williams. *According To Inc. Magazine*, October 28, 2015.

World Economic Forum. (2018). *Emerging market risk outlook 2018*.

Startup Valuation Based on the Real Options Approach

Jesus Cuauhtemoc Tellez and Aqila Rafiuddin

1 Introduction

The relationship between the investor's profile and the investment scope has led to alternative approaches of pricing opportunities such as Fintech startups which has been characterized as complicated due to dynamic attitudes of all stakeholders. As one venture capitalist Vinod Khosla put it: 'Our willingness to fail gives us the ability and opportunity to trade'.

After the global financial crisis, the role of digital transformation turned up as a pillar in the financial services industry where the financial intermediation function of fintechs widespread across developed and emerging countries with stellar growth investments by venture capitalists (Cumming et al., 2018). According to estimates of CB the flow of investments produced 206 unicorns (startups with valuations exceeding $1 billion) globally (Insights, 2021). The rise and expansion in the Fintech business models attracted researchers in the lending activities (Jagtiani & Lemieux, 2018). As large tech firms are expanding their products and services, an unprecedented speed is observed in the tech-focused startups (Vives, 2019; Allen et al., 2020; Boot et al., 2021). Fintech firms are technological startup firms (Cojoianu et al., 2020; Cumming et al., 2018; Gimpel et al., 2018; Haddad & Hornuf, 2019). The stages of startup development are explored based on entrepreneurial, organizational, and ecological factors (Van de Ven et al., 1984).

Valuation of Fintech startup is a kind of earlier studies and is also a dynamic process that is subject to change based on negotiation and mutually agreeable decisions of both entrepreneurs and investors (Yang et al., 2009; Heughebaert & Manigart, 2012). Business valuation for the startup is a crucial like a black box. An

J. C. Tellez (✉) · A. Rafiuddin
Tecnologico de Monterrey, Business School, San Luis Potosí, Mexico

Ajman University, Ajman, United Arab Emirates
e-mail: cuauhtemoc.tellez@tec.mx

S. Derindere Köseoğlu (ed.), *A Practical Guide for Startup Valuation*, Contributions to Finance and Accounting, https://doi.org/10.1007/978-3-031-35291-1_12

accurate measure on evaluation and monitoring of the performance of business identify the pursuit of the opportunities and costs to determine business worth, objective measures, and evaluate all aspects of the business; provide the owners with a snap on the facts and figures and the status of the company; considered to serve as a powerful tool to track the effectiveness of the company to all stakeholders that assess the value of all assets, reveal its company value for resale, provide broad access to the investors, and provide an insight into the mergers and acquisitions.

The startups are infant companies that are founded to develop a unique product or service and are at the initial stage of business cycle development. At this stage the goal is not the profit but to take the company ahead. On the other hand, the ongoing business is in the second or third stage of the life cycle of the business in which it is a permanent organization with an appropriate business that aims to create and maintain profit of the business.

An investment project evaluation refers to a cost-benefit analysis of a firm done before undertaking, rejecting, or delaying any project. Other factors like regulation, policies, external environment, production facilities, competition, consumers, and suppliers are determinants of investments. The Fintech market is dynamic based on demand and supply that are influenced due to change in government policies, targets, project size, business profits, etc. Uncertainties with the revision of regulations, laws, and policies are expected to affect the profits of business companies. The more crucial is the transition of ongoing projects from one policy framework to another causing a reasonable delay in investment until the amendment on policy.

Digitalization of the financial sector has given rise to "Fintech" term initial used in 1970, an umbrella concept that embedded multifold dimensions to serve finnovative products and services: Intense use of technological and digital services contributed as Blockchain, Internet-of-Things (IOT), data analytics, and artificial intelligence (Ma et al., 2020); Fintech from customer perspective, easy access, and less expensive financial services (Demirgüç-Kunt & Singer, 2017); Perspective of financial institutions, enhancement and effectiveness of operations, richness of the services (Currie & Lagoarde-Segot, 2017); A continuous development, emergence, and exploration of immense innovative opportunities (Gozman et al., 2018).

Fintech startups have come up in advanced and customized-related products and services such as Insurance, Wealth Management, Business Lending, Trading and Investments, Crowdfunding, Payments & Remittances, and Cryptos. As of November 2021, it was registered 26,346 Fintech startups compared to 12,131 in 2018, which represents an increase of 171% where the Americas region has led with a market share of 40% (Statista). If investments into fintech companies is considered, total value has increased more than 40% from 2018 to 2021. The investments in fintech globally reached US$210 billion in 2021 and with a projection of compound annual growth rate (CAGR) of 20% to US$305 billion by 2025.

With the burgeoning literature of Fintech and evidence of growth in Fintech allied industries fueled during the pandemic of Covid 19 attracted the investors and the service providers. One of the main objectives of Fintech is financial inclusion serving for No poverty the first sustainable development Goal (SDG1) of the United Nations. Growing demand attracted many investors to invest in the Fintech industry.

Thus, over the last few years with the increase in the startups and capital poured in by venture capitalists, valuation models have undergone set of complex methods and process as essential tools to assess the financial status of the company.

This chapter includes a general framework and practical guide to startups valuation through the Real Options approach which has gained an increasing importance in Corporate Finance since Myers (1977) introduced the term real option and who has been "Father of real options theory". Since then, abundant literature is available with different comparisons and perceptions about this valuation approach. Firstly, this work is an addition to the existing literature on startups valuation and secondly it considers a discussion of Fintech startups as a specific case of business valuation. This work is divided into different sections. Section 2 provides the review on the importance of RO approach as a specific case of valuation in Fintech. Section 3 describes the backgrounds and types of real options. Section 4 provides an application of the Discounted Cash Flow under different scenarios. Section 5 applies the real options approach to a startup business case under scenarios which highlights the Startup Financing Stages. Finally, conclusions and recommendations are given in Sect. 6.

2 A Review on the Real Options Approach

Application of real options by Meyers (1977) first proposed RO framework to invest, grow, and abandon that assists managers and other decision makers with more details on revised information. Investment analyzed with errors, which are unstructured, unplanned strategically could bring in loss to the project values and could lead to a bankruptcy of an enterprise. Therefore, for long-term success of a firm, a good financial management along with strategic capital investment is required (Bennouna et al., 2010). NPV and DCF methods are used worldwide to take the investment decisions (Graham & Harvey, 2001; Ryan & Ryan, 2002). However, in today's scenarios where businesses are dynamic, the risk and uncertainty associated with business could be unpredictable. NPV and DCF do not take the irreversibility and uncertain risks into account. Additionally, these two methods also do not have an explanation of deferring now and taking up the project later when market conditions are appropriate to it (Dixit et al., 1994).

Based on earlier works this section highlights few contributions. Business always seeks value by having an option to invest in later stage, or flexibility to expand (Fernandes et al., 2011), or simply not invest (Dixit et al., 1994). "Real Option", the term was first coined by Myers and Turnbull (1977). Charitou and Trigeorgis (2000) also supported Meyer by stating "An options approach to capital budgeting has the potential to conceptualize, and even quantify, the value of options for active management. This value is manifest as a collection of corporate real options embedded in capital investments opportunities". Unlike NPV, DCF and RO theories provide a support to managerial flexibility that addresses decisions under different scenarios with the account of high level of uncertainties. A modern approach to risk evaluation of a project was recommended by de Moraes Marreco and Carpio (2006).

There are a few definitions of "real options" available in the literature. According to Kogut and Kulatilaka (2001), real options are defined as "an investment decision that is characterized by uncertainty, the provision of future managerial discretion to exercise at the appropriate time, and irreversibility". Copeland and Antikarov (2003) define a real option "as a right, but not the obligation, to take an action (e.g., deferring, expanding, contracting, or abandoning) at a predetermined cost, called exercise price, for a predetermined period—the life of the option". Thus, investment opportunity is referred to as a call option. In other words, a firm that wants to invest money or exercise the right to buy has an option to invest now or later.

Broadly, there are two kinds of options. First, it gives a right to call (or buy) an asset at exercised price in a particular estimated time (or time of maturity). Second, it gives a right to put (or sell) an asset in specified time (time of maturity). Thus, Fernandes et al. (2011) mentions that when the choice to exercise price is less than the asset current price (a call option), or more than the current price of the asset (a put option), the option is said to be "in the money"; Otherwise, it is "out of the money". Options can be of two natures – either European or American. An option that can be exercised only on the maturity is designated to be a "European option"; whereas the "American option" can be exercised at any time before maturity.

Options may be addressed by different drivers. However, six major variables may affect option prices (Copeland & Antikarov, 2003). The first is related to the value of an asset: if there is an increase in the value of asset, the value of an option also increases. The second is associated with an exercised price: value of exercised price is inversely related with the value of an option. That means if exercised price increases, the value of an option decreases. The third is related with time: whether the value of an option increases with time. Whereas fourth is linked to the uncertainty: if the managerial decision has flexibility, the value of an option increases with increasing uncertainty. The fifth is associated with a risk-free rate of interest: if risk-free interest goes high, the value of an option enhances. The sixth and final variable is related to dividends: an increase in the amount of dividend paid would increase the value of an option.

In the standpoint of view of real options, Amram and Kulatalika (1999) suggested four-step solutions related to: (1) better frame the application of real options, (2) identify the inputs and the valuation models, (3) provide benchmarks for interpreting results, (4) implementation of the options valuation model and to review the results and the redesign if required. The first step reflects the framing and timing of possible decisions to be made. Chorn and Shokhor (2006) studied policies related to investment in the petroleum industry. They understood and framed the problems and used these problems as an option for development of policies. Further, they considered real options to address the uncertainty. Similarly, in different studies related to energy, real options are used to address the uncertainty (Yang & Blyth, 2007).

In the second step, for realizing the values of real options, it is important to express it mathematically. Black and Scholes (1973) proposed the mathematical

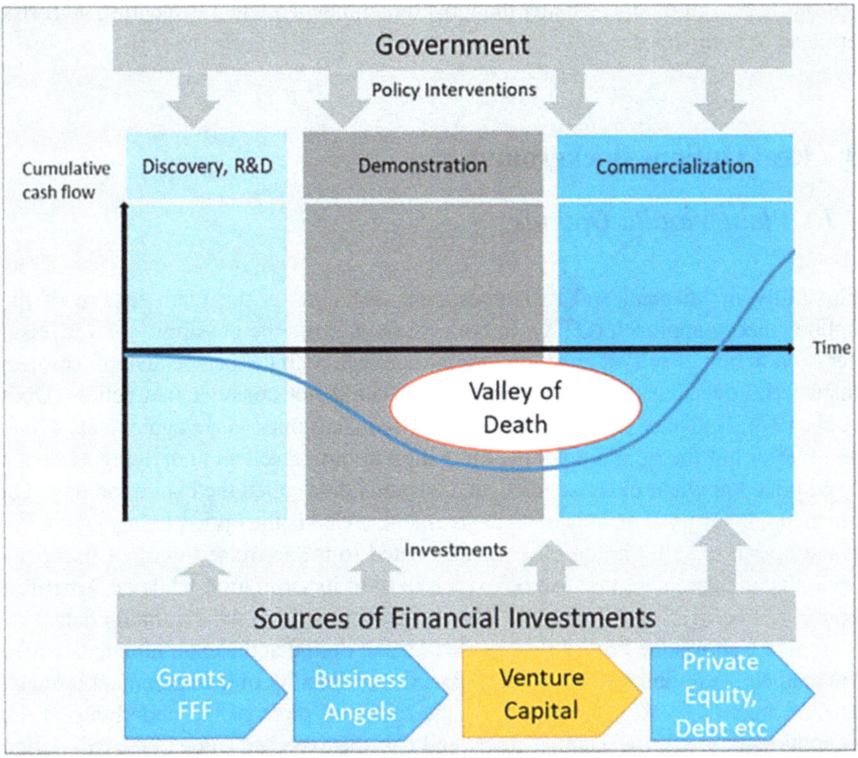

Fig. 1 Startups sources of financial investments. Source: Bürer and Wüstenhagen (2009)

formulation of such problems and later the formulation was applied by authors like Amram & Kulatalika (1999). Cortazar and Casassus (1998) proposed a model that mathematically explains the proper time of investment (in environmental technologies) by the firm. Description of how future payoffs are influenced by current decisions is also explained mathematically. The third step proposed by Amram and Kulatilaka (1999) is the review of the results, such as discounted cash flow. The fourth step proposes redesigning. D'souza (2002) mentions "redesigning the project enables managers to learn more about the market at an earlier stage, thereby creating an opportunity to modify the marketing plan and increase the chance of market success". Besides the Amram and Kulatilaka (1999) approach, other authors (e.g., Copeland & Antikarov, 2003; Dixit et al., 1994) also presented real options valuation processes.

According to Rencher (2012), valley of death is the period between the creation of the firm and the time at which it receives the positive cash flows as shown in Fig. 1. One of the main contributing factors is to cross this threshold. However, a better approach should incorporate all the uncertainties inherent to the business (Minardi, 2000). Similarly, Hartmann and Hassan (2006) have indicated the real options appraisal model as being the most recommended when evaluating high-risk projects or companies.

3 Real Options Background

3.1 Plain Vanilla Options

Flexibility in financial and real investment decisions is the main feature of the options theory approach (OTA). In both cases, it exists the possibility of a reversal decision to buy or sell, or abandon or continue, which in the perspective of a project managerial decision the Net Present Value would not consider that action (Dixit et al., 1994; Balliauw, 2021). In that sense, (financial) options are agreements where an investor has the right but not the obligation to buy or sell an underlying asset at a fixed price known as exercise price, at a terminal date called the expiration date. On one hand, in terms of exercising the agreement, a Call is the option to buy, and a Put is the option to sell. On the other hand, related to the exercise timing, a European option is an agreement that can be exercised until its expiration while an American option can be exercised during the life of the contract or at the expiration date.

Figure 2 shows the Profit/Loss profile of a call option at the expiration date where the mathematical function which describes the optionality of the agreement is stated as $C = \max(S_T - K, 0)$, where S_T is the expected price of the underlying at the expiration date, K is the exercise price, and C is the expected value of the call option at the expiration date T. If market conditions allow ($S_T > K$), then the call option is

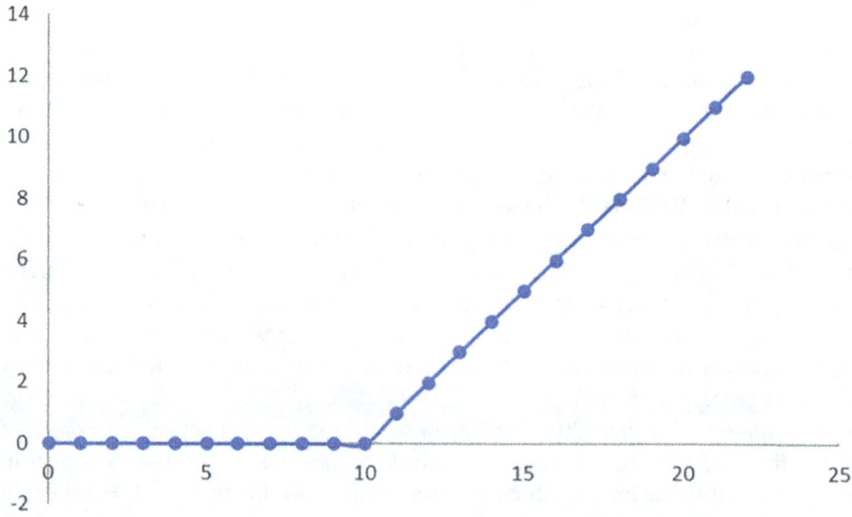

Fig. 2 Profit/Loss (*y*-axis) profile of a Call option in a long position when $K = 10$, given expected market prices (*x*-axis) at expiration date. Source: Author's Own Creation

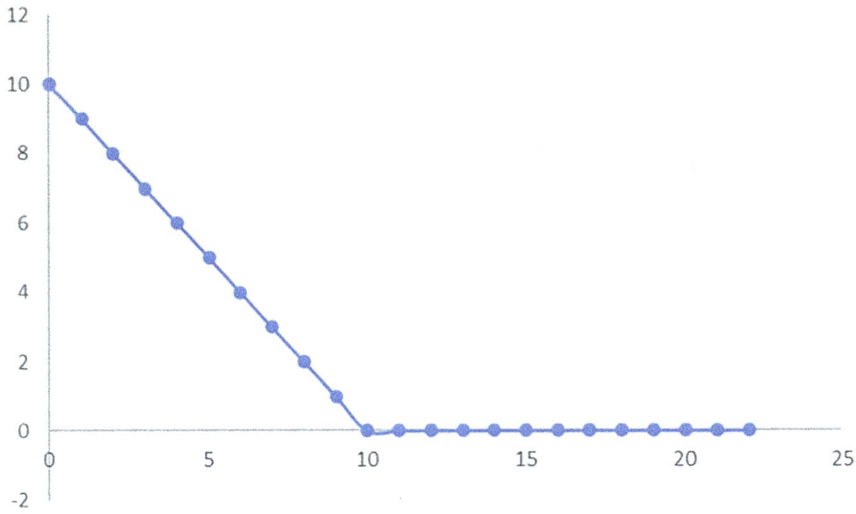

Fig. 3 Profit/Loss (y-axis) profile of a Put option in a long position when $K = 10$, given expected market prices (x-axis) at expiration date. Source: Author's Own Creation

exercised and the possible profit in the expiration date is ($S_T - K$). Otherwise, when ($S_T < K$) at the expiration date then the option is not exercised, and the terminal value of the contract is zero. As an example, when an investor enters into the agreement to buy an underlying asset at $K = \$10$, if the underlying asset price at the expiration date is $S_T = \$12$, then the investor can exercise the option and would make a profit of $2 per unit of the underlying asset bought. Otherwise, if the market price were $8 then the investor may not exercise the option to buy and would prefer to buy the asset outside the agreement at a lower price. In that sense, the terminal value of the call option will be $0.

Figure 3 shows the Profit/Loss profile when an investor faces a put option. Once at expiration T, if market conditions allow ($K - S_T$) then the investor may exercise the option to sell the underlying asset at the exercise price K. Otherwise, when the agreed price to sell at K is less than the market price S_T, then the investor may not exercise the option and the option value would be zero. As an example, an investor expects that prices will decrease so since now he/she agrees to sell the underlying asset at an exercise price $K = \$12$. Once the put option reaches the expiration date if the market price $S_T = \$10$ is less than the exercise price K, then the investor may exercise the option and would make a profit of $2. Otherwise, the investor may not exercise the option, sell the asset at the market price, and the put option will have a terminal value of $P = \$0$ (Fig. 3).

The option value type at the expiration date described above is known as the Intrinsic Value (V_T). However, differences could arise between the market price of the option and the intrinsic value, which is known as the Time Value. Although the Intrinsic value is zero, which may not allow to exercise the option, it is possible to make a profit, or the option market price be greater than zero. However, hedgers and investors would need to know in advance the option price they would need to pay at the inception of their hedging or investment strategy in this way to exercise the option or make a profit at the expiration date or before it. In that context, the Black and Scholes (1973) model has been considered as the reference approach to pricing options which originally was developed to pricing European options. The extended version is devoted to Merton who considered the pricing of American options.

Thus, following the previous background, the next section considers the main ideas of the Black-Scholes-Merton (BSM) model which is the leading support in the real options approach applied to a startup valuation.

3.2 Black-Scholes-Merton (BSM) Model

The BSM model is based on two main pillars, the Risk Neutral Valuation approach and the Normal Probability Distribution. The former basically consists of a time value discount process of the expected cash flow generated by the option at expiration date (V_{T}) discounted at the risk-free interest rate which also serves as the expected rate of return to estimate the future cash flow of the underlying (risky) asset. Even though uncertainty is the main driver addressing the risky feature of the underlying asset and the financial derivative, both are valued at the same expected rate of return where the derivative has shown itself to be riskier than the underlying asset.

The second pillar, Normal Probability Distribution, mainly considers that financial asset returns are distributed as a Normal Probability where extreme values may take a lower or even a zero-occurrence probability. In that context, expected sharp movements would have a lesser probability occurrence and the expected underlying asset values in a time frame will be distributed around an expected value which grows at the risk-free interest rate. The mathematical model that wraps the two pillars is called the Geometric Brownian Motion which consists of a drift and a random component which characterizes the uncertainty feature of the asset price evolution (Venegas-Martínez, 2008), as described in expression (1):

$$\frac{dS_t}{S_t} = \mu dt + \sigma dW_t, \tag{1}$$

where $\frac{dS_t}{S_t}$ is the asset rate of return, μ is the average annualized expected rate of return of the asset, σ is the annualized volatility of the asset returns, and dW_t is a random variable which models the asset movements which is Normally distributed $dW_t \sim N(0, dt)$.

Based on Black and Scholes (1973) hedging strategy which considers a long position in the stock and a short position in the option, and the mathematical model in expression (1), the option pricing formula of a European call option would be:

$$c_{BS}(S_t,t) = S_tN(d_1) - Xe^{-R(\tau)}N(d_2), \tag{2}$$

$$d_1 = \frac{\ln\left(\frac{S_t}{X}\right) + \left(R + \frac{1}{2}\sigma^2\right)\tau}{\sigma\sqrt{\tau}}, \tag{3}$$

$$d_2 = d_1 - \sigma\sqrt{\tau} \tag{4}$$

Expression (5) considers the Black-Scholes formula of a European put option:

$$p_{BS}(S_t,t) = Xe^{-R(\tau)}N(-d_2) - S_tN(-d_1), \tag{5}$$

where:

$c_{BS}(S_t, t)$ is the European call option value as a function of the current underlying asset price S_t at time t,
$p_{BS}(S_t, t)$ is the European put option value as a function of the current underlying asset price S_t at time t,
$d_1$and d_2 are standardized random variables,
$N(d_1)$ and $N(d_2)$ are the Normal Standard Distributions as a function of d_1 and d_2,
$N(-d_1)$ and $N(-d_2)$ are the Normal Standard Distributions as a function of $-d_1$ and $-d_2$,
R is the annual risk-free interest rate,
τ the option maturity proportional to a year basis,
σ^2 the annualized variance of the underlying asset returns, and σ the respective standard deviation (a measure of volatility).

As an example, consider a European call option which expires within 56 days. The agreement states an exercise price of \$45 to buy an asset for which the current market price is \$50 and pays no dividends. The annualized volatility of the asset returns is 15%, the annual reference (risk-free) interest rate is 10%, and the money market convention to be considered is 360 days a year. Then, based on the B-S model, the price of a call option would be:

$$d_1 = \frac{\ln\left(\frac{50}{45}\right) + \left(0.10 + \frac{1}{2}0.15^2\right)0.15}{0.15\sqrt{0.15}} = 2.0734,$$

$$d_2 = 2.0734 - 0.15\sqrt{0.15} = 2.0143,$$

where $\tau = \frac{56}{360} = 0.15$. Then,

$$c_{BS}(S_t,t) = 50N(2.0734) - 45e^{-0.10(0.15)}N(2.0143),$$

$$c_{BS}(S_t,t) = 50(0.9809) - 45e^{-0.10(0.15)}(0.9780),$$

$$c_{BS}(S_t, t) = 5.72.$$

So, a company facing the asset's market risk would agree to hedge its exposure by buying the call option at a price of $5.72. In this case the company agrees to buy the underlying asset at an exercise price of $45 that would be exercised within 56 days. If market conditions continue until the expiration date, then the company may exercise its right to buy the asset at $45. At the expiration date the intrinsic value of the option would be $C = \max(50 - 45, 0) = \$5$, which means that the expected underlying asset at expiration could be $50. Otherwise, the company could let the option expire and would rather buy the asset at the market price. Finally, the probability that the company may exercise the call option would be 0.9780, and the sensitiveness of the call option to the changes in the underlying asset price is 0.9809, which means that a change in the underlying asset price by 1 unit may outcome a change in the call option price by 0.9809 monetary units.

On the other hand, if the company or investor was the owner of the asset and expects that market prices can fall, then it could buy a Put option. In this case, the company may agree to sell the asset at the exercise price of 45. So, the cost of the hedging strategy using the B-S model would be:

$$p_{BS}(S_{BS}, t) = 45e^{-0.10(0.15)}N(-2.0143) - 50N(-2.0743)$$

$$p_{BS}(S_{BS}, t) = 45e^{-0.10(0.15)}(0.0220) - 45(0.0191)$$

$$p_{BS}(S_t, t) = 0.02.$$

Although the Put option intrinsic value is zero, which means that given market conditions the option would not be exercised at the expiration date, nevertheless the option currently holds a positive value related to Time Value. As the B-M model estimates, the probability of exercising the put option would be 0.0220 quite lesser than that of the call option. These outcomes arise since the current market price of the underlying asset is greater than the exercise price. In addition, since the days of expiration are not so far, then it can affect the probability of exercising both options. In that sense, the importance of the probability distribution assumption which the B-M model considers a Normal one, may not expect a large movement in the underlying asset that could significantly alter the option price given a 56 days of hedging horizon.

If days to expiration would be 90, ceteris paribus, then the value of both options could be

$$c(S, t) = 6.17,$$

$$p(S, t) = 0.06.$$

Results imply that as the expiration date lasts longer, the probability of exercising the call option increases due to the possibility that the expected underlying asset price would eventually be greater than the current asset price given market conditions. This situation would mean that the company or investor pays a greater premium for their hedging or investment strategy. However, a down movement of the expected asset price should also be possible as given by current market conditions, which may imply a greater probability of the Put option to be exercised at the expiration date. So, the company or investor would pay a greater premium to exercise their right to sell the underlying asset.

The previous analysis considered an extension of the expiration date. What about if the agreement to buy or sell considers a different exercise price? This scenario would mean that the company or investor are able to pay or accept a different investment amount at the expiration of the call or put option, respectively. Then, if the agreement states an exercise price of 42 given current market conditions and keeping the original 56 expiration days, the call and put options would be

$$c(S,t) = 8.65,$$

$$p(S,t) = 0.00.$$

The call option pricing implies a probability of 0.9993 to exercise the right to buy at the expiration date as compared to the original scenario where the probability was estimated at 0.9809. It is observed that as the intrinsic value increases, the probability of exercising raises, and the option price becomes higher. So, the opportunity cost to get a better chance of exercising the option is reflected in the option premium, given current market conditions. On the other hand, the put option pricing now implies an almost zero probability to exercise the right to sell which is reflected in an almost zero premium ($p = 0.0005$) to be paid by the company or investor. Both would have still considered the possibility that market conditions may change even if the expiration date is closer.

As shown by the scenarios when expiration lasts in 56 and 90 days, the call premiums are almost the same as the intrinsic value of the options. In the original scenario, the intrinsic value of the call option is \$5 while the call premium is slightly greater at \$5.72. About the put option case, its intrinsic value is zero while the estimated premium is slightly greater at \$0.06. So, even the put premium is slightly greater than the intrinsic value, this occurs because of the Time value implicit in the option, which means that even though the company or investor would have a near zero probability of exercising the right to sell in the expiration date there is a chance that conditions may change in the remaining days of the option life.

Related to the scenario where the exercise price is \$42 and expiration days do not change, the call option premium is gaining more value explained by the intrinsic value than what could be by the time value. In this case, the company or investor decides to buy the underlying asset at a lesser amount where under current market conditions they would have a greater probability of exercising the right to buy the asset. Such a case means that both economic agents would be willing to pay a higher premium for their hedging or investment strategies.

Table 1 Black-Scholes Option Greeks

Input	Situation	Call	Put	B-S Greek
Market price (S_t)	Current = 50	\$5.7156	\$0.0210	Delta (Δ)
	New = 52	\$7.6975	\$0.0029	
Expiration days	Current = 56	\$5.7156	\$0.0210	Theta (θ)
	New = 90	\$6.1695	\$0.0585	
Rate of change of Delta	delta =	0.9853	−0.0147	Gamma (Γ)
	Gamma =	1.4473	1.4473	
Volatility (σ)	Current = 15%	\$5.7156	\$0.0210	Vega (υ)
	New = 18%	\$5.7552	\$0.0606	
Reference rate (R)	Current = 10%	\$5.7156	\$0.0210	Rho (ρ)
	New = 14%	\$5.9851	\$0.0157	

Based on the above example, Table 1 shows the comparison of the option premiums whenever one of the B-S model inputs could change, ceteris paribus, where the effect on the option prices is called the Option Greeks.

It is observed that a direct relationship is held between the market price of the underlying asset and the call premium, while an indirect relationship with the put premium. Also, whenever the reference rate increases the call premium does it, meanwhile the put premium decreases. Accordingly, to the sensitive nature of the options to expiration days, it is found a direct relationship between both options and the number of expiration days. Something similar happens when volatility changes it would impact in a positive way to the call and put premiums.

The importance of the sensitiveness measurements based on the B-S Option Greeks is to identify the type and level of association which each input, ceteris paribus, holds with the call and put premium. Besides the main assumptions of the B-S model which may differ with current market behavior as those when the model was developed and published, however the option Greeks represent an approximation of the option changes to changes of any of the model inputs which support the flexibility feature of options to be applied on managerial decisions.

3.3 *Type of Options*

A summary of the types of real options is presented in this subsection which are related to deferring, time-to-build, alter operating scale, abandon, and switch and growth options. However, major real options are mentioned by Trigeorgis (2000).

3.3.1 Defer Option

This type of option refers to the ability of an investor to wait for pre-specified time and exercise an option when maximum profits are expected from the market changes. In other words, the investor has a choice to invest now or wait for further information related to uncertainty to invest later (Dixit et al., 1994). These options are commonly exercised on projects related to mining, farming, and real estate development.

The B-S formula which relates to the Defer Option is the same as expressions (2) to (4). However, interpretation of t should be as the "time expected to postpone the investment" (Venegas-Martínez, 2008). Therefore, if a financial option considers a 1-year expiration date, the real options approach would consider that the investment can be postponed in 1 year.

3.3.2 Time-to-Build Option

However, in another kind of industries such as pharmaceutical, energy, construction, etc., the long-term capital investment returns can be received only after a project is completed. This option refers to time-to-build (Trigeorgis, 2000). Kudankulam nuclear power plant (in India) could explain better the consequence of exercising such kind of an option in particular situations. The project started in 2002 and was formally commissioned in 2013 after 6 years from the scheduled date. Main reason quoted for this delay was the people's protest safety concerns (The Times of India, 2013). However, the return on investment in such kind of a project is also delayed, finally bringing in the loss to the business in the short run.

3.3.3 Scale of Operation Option

Whereas, in another kind of real option related to scale of operation, the investor is offered a flexibility to expand it if market conditions are expected to be favorable, and to reduce the level of production if market situation is bad (Trigeorgis, 2000). Examples of such industries are natural resource industries, manufacturing industries, construction industries, facility planning, and commercial real estate firms. In situations, when the market shift informs adverse conditions to the project, there is an option for an investor to sell the available assets. This might be important to avoid further losses in the investment on the project.

3.3.4 Abandon Option

Real options give a choice to the decision maker to abandon such projects if unfavorable information related to a project arrives (Majd & Pindyk, 1987). This option might sometimes be important in capital intensive industries like railroads, airlines, financial services, introduction of a new product, etc. (Myers & Majd, 1990). Further, when there is a sudden shift in the demand function of an industry, the firm can have the option to produce similar kinds of products from the same machinery (changing the output).

The B-S formula to pricing Abandon Option is the same as expressions (2) to (4). However, interpretation on its application should be careful. Whenever a company faces bad market conditions like a recession, it could take the option to abandon the project at a future date T. The company needs to check how much the expected cash flows could cover the salvage value (Venegas-Martínez, 2008). In that sense, the intrinsic value of the abandon option in T would be as in expression (6),

$$C(S,T) = \max(S_T, \mathrm{SV}_T), \tag{6}$$

where S_T are the expected cash flows and SV_T the Salvage Value in T.

So, if the SV_T is greater than S_T, then it is a signal that the company could sell the company or abandon the project. On the other hand, when the Salvage Value is constant and the possibility to abandon the project is only at T, then the intrinsic value would be as shown in expression (7),

$$C(S,T) = \max(S_T - K, 0) + K. \tag{7}$$

In that case, the B-S formula to pricing an abandon option would be

$$c_a(S,t) = c_{BS}(S,t) + K, \tag{8}$$

where c_a and c_{BS} denote the option to abandon and the call B-S pricing formula, respectively.

3.3.5 Option to Switch

On the other hand, using varying raw materials, a firm can produce the same product (changing inputs) or incur a technological change. These options are referred to as "Option to switch", as they offer a greater flexibility to an investor (Trigeorgis, 2000; Kulatilaka & Lenos, 1994).

If the company gets the possibility to switch from one technological process to another which may increase the expected cash flows, then the intrinsic value of the Option to Switch (Venegas-Martínez, 2008) would be

$$C(S,T) = \max\left(S_T^* - S_T^1 - K, 0\right), \tag{9}$$

where S_T^* and S_T^1 are the present value of the expected cash flows under the new production process and the expected cash flows of the current production process, respectively. Meanwhile, K is the cost from switching from the current to the new production process. Then, the option to switch could be exercised if $S_T^* > S_T^1 + K$.

3.3.6 Growth Option

Finally, another referred option is "growth". In strategic industries like R & D, high-tech, pharmaceuticals, etc., the option for acquiring necessary capabilities can be exercised by strategic acquisitions that can offer firm an advantage to grow in the future (Kulatilaka & Perotti, 1998).

4 The Discounted Cash Flow Approach

This subsection takes effect since the real options approach settles on the Discounted Cash Flow framework. Thus, different scenarios are considered which are based on a basic and pessimistic states of nature with different financing sources.

4.1 Scenario 1. The Basis Case When Financing with Internal and External Sources

Consider the stream of expected Net Cash Flows to be generated by an investment project as shown in Table 2, where the (net) initial installment is estimated at 10,000,000 USD. The investment horizon is 5 years, and an expected rate of return (WACC, Weighted Average Cost of Capital) of 15% which considers a capital structure of 50/50. Based on the NPV and IRR criteria, it is suggested that the project should be taken up.

Since the NPV is greater than zero, then the project should be accepted. Also, as the IRR is greater than the WACC, then it supports the criteria of the NPV as should be expected. It should be noted that as the capital structure is 50/50, then it is assumed that 50% of the whole initial investment will be financed by the company and the other 50% by external sources. In that sense, the project evaluation seeks to determine the capability of the Net Cash Flows to support the amount of capital invested by internal sources.

4.2 Scenario 2. The Pessimistic Case When Financing with Internal and External Sources

A second scenario can be run under negative expectations which could mean less expected cash flows, therefore the probability that the project would not be accepted. Table 3 shows the new project economic evaluation where the NPV is negative, and the IRR is lesser than the WACC.

Table 2 Net Cash Flows of an investment project and economic evaluation criteria, where: NCF, Net Cash Flow; PV, Present Value; PVCF, Present Value of Cash Flows; NPV, Net Present Value, and IRR, Internal Rate of Return

	0	1	2	3	4	5
NCF =	(10,000,000.00)	2,500,000.00	3,000,000.00	4,500,000.00	4,000,000.00	3,500,000.00
PV=	(10,000,000.00)	2,173,913.04	2,268,431.00	2,958,823.05	2,287,012.98	1,740,118.57
PVCF =	11,428,298.65					
NPV=	**1,428,299**					
IRR =	**20%**					

Table 3 Net Cash Flows of an investment project under negative expectations and economic evaluation criteria

	0	1	2	3	4	5
NCF =	(10,000,000.00)	1,800,000.00	2,500,000.00	4,000,000.00	3,500,000.00	3,500,000.00
PV=	(10,000,000.00)	1,565,217.39	1,890,359.17	2,630,064.93	2,001,136.36	1,740,118.57
PVCF =	9,826,896.42					
NPV=	**(173,104)**					
IRR =	**14%**					

4.3 Scenario 3. The Pessimistic Case When Financing with Internal Sources

A third scenario considers the simulation of the investment project when it is 100% financed with internal sources which means that the capital structure could be 100/0. In that context the expected rate of return based on WACC would be greater than 15% under the same market conditions as scenario 1. Table 4 shows the stream of Net Cash Flows and the economic project evaluation, where the expected rate of return is 18%. It is observed that the project should not be accepted since the present value of the expected cash flows is not able to cover the initial investment in this case held completely by the company. In addition, as the project is financed by internal sources then it would be expected to have a higher rate of return since no additional (external) sources are considered that could be benefited by the tax shield.

The previous scenarios show that under the Net Present Value approach it may be some kind of rigidity to take an investment decision, since at any time if NPV is greater than zero then the project should be accepted. Otherwise the project should be rejected. Nevertheless, how could a managerial decision be supported if the project wants to be taken when its NPV is negative?

5 The Real Options Approach Applied to Startup Valuation

The flexibility feature implied in Options has allowed us to apply the approach in managerial decisions, as shown in the Literature Review section. This section seeks to apply different types of real options to startup valuation where the main issue is the Startup Option Stages in which a decision should be taken to continue or quit from the investment made. Although the rate of return (WACC) is an important and crucial factor in business valuation, nevertheless the main contribution of this chapter is to support the application of the real options approach as a general and practical framework to startups valuation.

For this purpose, the main issue in this section concerns the startup business analysis when the timing in which target revenues are achieved at different financing stages. Figure 4 shows three different financing stages which cross with revenues levels and its timing. It is observed that the main financing source comes from Venture Capital, which could mean that the capital structure of the "option to invest in a new business" would be 100/0 (solely internal financing source). It makes sense since even at a Consolidation stage the startup could not have generated enough historical financial information or profits that would allow a credit rating to ask for a significant loan amount or make a debt issuance. However, as the financing cycle shows, after certain time and revenue levels the startup may engage in a stock issuance process.

For the real options approach purposes, the "Financing cycle for startups" is modified as shown in Fig. 5 which is named as the "Options Cycle for Startups". The

Table 4 Net Cash Flows of an investment project and economic evaluation criteria, when the project is financed with internal sources at an 18% expected rate of return

	0	1	2	3	4	5
NCF =	(20,000,000.00)	2,500,000.00	3,000,000.00	4,500,000.00	4,000,000.00	3,500,000.00
PV=	(20,000,000.00)	2,118,644.07	2,154,553.29	2,738,838.93	2,063,155.50	1,529,882.26
PVCF =	10,605,074.04					
NPV=	**(9,394,926)**					
IRR =	**−4%**					

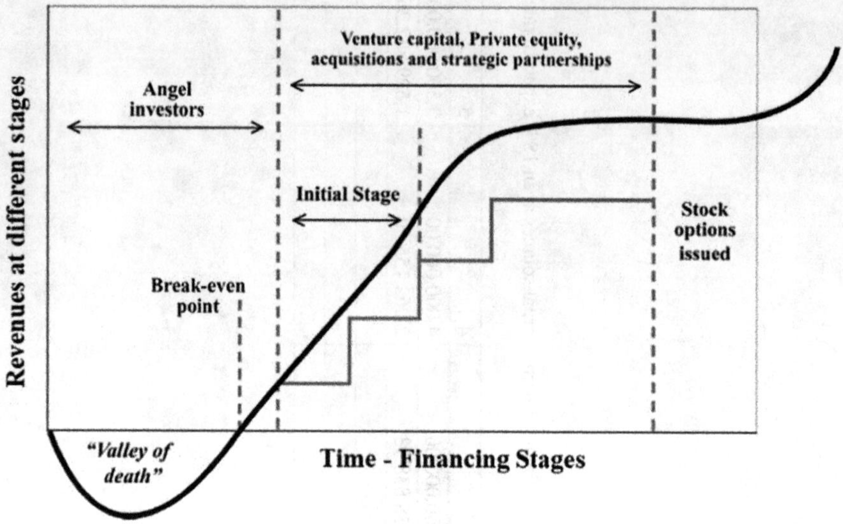

Fig. 4 Financing cycle for startups. Source: Félix et al. (2021)

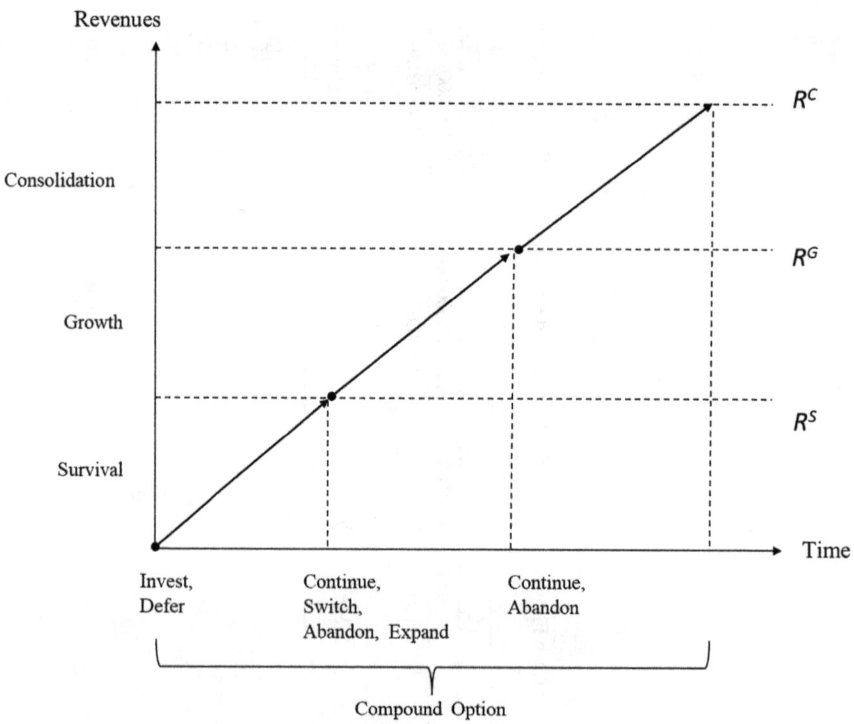

Fig. 5 The Options Cycle for Startups. Source: Author's Own Creation

main issue of this cycle is to show the importance of expected revenues to be achieved at different Startup Life stages, so the investor may determine the option to invest in the startup from the idea inception up to a mature stage. During a certain time, the investor may evaluate different options to be faced as the option to continue, abandon, switch, expand, or wrap the different stages in a single compound option.

Consider an investor facing the opportunity to finance a startup business. The investor can evaluate the investment project from the idea inception up to a certain time where the project has achieved target revenues that may allow to continue in the investment project. In the first startup cycle stage considered as the Survival stage, the company needs to achieve survival revenues R^S in such a way to continue to a second stage, the Growth stage. Then, since the beginning the investor could evaluate the option to invest or defer the investment where a crucial variable is the time that would take to reach the Survival Revenues given market conditions on which the evaluation is done and those expected in the terminal date T. The Survival Revenues are those revenues that at least may allow the investor to recover the initial investment.

Once the survival revenues have been achieved, the investor could have the option to abandon or continue, even to switch to another startup or expand the investment amount in the original. In this case, the startup has moved from the Survival to a Growth stage. However, the investor faces again the crucial question about the time required to reach a new target revenue known as Growth Revenues R^G which may allow to move to the third stage. The Growth Revenues are those revenues that may allow the investor to recover the initial investment and any additional installments that permitted an expansion of the original investment.

Finally, as the Fintech startup moves to a Consolidation stage, the investor can evaluate the option to continue or even abandon if the following revenues named as Consolidation Revenues may not allow the investor to recover the initial investment. Again, one of the investor's concerns is the time to achieve the Consolidation Revenues.

As described above, the investor would need a flexible analysis tool in such a way to determine the option to continue or abandon an investment done in a Fintech startup business. As was noted in the previous section, the real options approach would help and serve as a complement tool to take an investment decision even when market conditions are unfavorable. Also, as described above, not only the target revenues at different stages of Options Cycle for Startups have been based on the Financing Cycle for Startups, but supported by the lack of historical financial information and cost structures that startups face which would not make feasible to apply the traditional business valuation approach as a unique tool.

5.1 Scenario 1. The Survival Stage

The following is the application of the B-M approach to a Fintech startup business valuation. Consider a startup facing an investment of \$50,000,000 where investors' expected rate of return is 30% in the Survival stage which is estimated to expire in the next 3 years. Based on revenues of a similar startup, the volatility of revenues is 15% and the target revenues in the Survival stage has been considered at least as the lump sum of the initial investment. Table 5 shows the startup valuation based on the Discounted Cash Flow.

Although target revenues are equal to the initial investment, the startup investment should not be accepted because the NPV is negative. Certainly, this happens because of the time value of money. Results of the startup valuation based on the European call B-S formula are as follows:

- S_t: the present value of revenues,
- K: the initial investment,
- T: time to expiration of the Survival stage,
- R: expected rate of return (opportunity cost),
- σ: volatility of revenues.

$$d_1 = \frac{\ln\left(\frac{30{,}200{,}273}{50{,}000{,}000}\right) + \left(0.30 + \frac{1}{2}0.15^2\right)3}{0.15\sqrt{3}} = 1.6534$$

$$d_2 = 1.6534 - 0.15\sqrt{3} = 1.3936$$

$$c_{BS}(S_t, t) = 30{,}200{,}273N(1.6534) - 50{,}000{,}000e^{-0.30(3)}N(1.3936)$$

$$c_{BS}(S_t, t) = 30{,}200{,}273(0.9509) - 50{,}000{,}000e^{-0.30(3)}(0.9183)$$

$$c_{BS}(S_t, t) = 10{,}049{,}460$$

Analysis The intrinsic value of the option to invest in a startup that could be exercised at the expiration date of the Survival stage is $C = \max\,(30{,}200{,}273 - 50{,}000{,}000; 0) = \$0$. This means that at an expected level of revenues of \$30,200,273 that the startup could achieve at the expiration date, the investor would prefer to let the investment expire and do not continue to the following stage. This decision was initially suggested by the NPV approach which showed that investing in the Fintech startup could not have been a good decision. However, as the option value considers an intrinsic value and a time value, the real options approach suggests that the project should be taken because over time the Fintech startup may get value.

Table 5 Startup valuation in the survival stage

	0	1	2	3	4	5
NCF =	(50,000,000.00)	15,000,000.00	20,000,000.00	15,000,000.00	4,000,000.00	3,500,000.00
PV=	(50,000,000.00)	11,538,461.54	11,834,319.53	6,827,492.03	1,400,511.19	942,651.76
PVCF =	30,200,273.10					
NPV=	**(19,799,727)**					
IRR =	**0%**					

In that sense, once the investment has been made, the investor could get rid of the decision and transfer the business opportunity to a second investor. The latter could be willing to accept the startup project and pay a $ten million premium to have the right to exercise the investment installment at the revenues lump sum in the survival expiration date. The willingness to pay for a startup which initially would have been rejected is motivated by the fact that revenues during the survival stage could be greater than those expected in the initial evaluation.

If it happens that the first investor gets rid of the startup project since the initial Fintech startup stage and transfers it to a second investor, then this could be an example of an Abandon Option, and the estimated net effect for the first investor could be −$40 million. As the second investor is willing to pay a $ten million premium because market conditions may turn better, so the first investor is willing to abandon the startup project because market conditions may not be as favorable as the second investor has considered. This first scenario has shown the two sides of the same coin: an initial investor that after making an investment decision in a startup, which has shown to be rejected under the NPV, realizes the possibility to transfer it and wills to receive a $ten million premium with a net cash flow of −$40 million; and a second investor who is willing to pay $ten million because market conditions may change and get a payback greater than $60 million at the survival expiration stage.

5.2 *Scenario 2. The Growth Stage*

Assume the first investor survives to the initial stage because the revenues lump sum was at least equal to the initial installment. However, a decision should be taken to continue or abandon the project to a growth stage where revenues are expected to be higher than those in the previous stage. Despite the expected rate of return at that time could be less than the survival rate of return, the Fintech startup faces a stage which lasts longer than 3 years. The reason that expected rates of return in different stages could differ from each other is explained by the fact that each stage involves different investment risks where a survival stage would imply a high-risk investment in such a way to achieve the target revenues.

Table 6 considers the Growth stage evaluation under the NPV approach which considers a 5-year time stage and an expected rate of return of 20%. Also, it is assumed that revenues lump sum during the Growth stage should be at least equal to the initial investment.

Based on current and expected market conditions at the beginning of the Growth stage, the NPV approach signals that the decision to continue should be taken, which could mean an economic profit of $four million. So, the decision to stay in the startup project after surviving a critical stage was successful, even when the NPV of the survival stage showed to reject the project. In that respect, the real options approach was a complementary tool in the decision-making process because it showed that the Fintech startup business was keeping value that would make the possibility of

Table 6 Startup valuation in the growth stage

	0	1	2	3	4	5
NCF =	(50,000,000.00)	10,000,000.00	16,000,000.00	21,000,000.00	25,000,000.00	26,000,000.00
PV=	(50,000,000.00)	8,333,333.33	11,111,111.11	12,152,777.78	12,056,327.16	10,448,816.87
PVCF =	54,102,366.26					
NPV=	**4,102,366**					
IRR =	**23%**					

exercising the initial installment at the expiration of the survival stage. At this point before the investor could continue to a second stage, may decide to quit from the investment and just receive the initial investment.

The startup valuation under the B-S approach in the Growth Stage considers the same volatility of revenues as in the Survival stage.

$$d_1 = \frac{\ln\left(\frac{54{,}102{,}366}{50{,}000{,}000}\right) + (0.20 + \frac{1}{2}0.15^2)5}{0.15\sqrt{5}} = 3.3842$$

$$d_2 = 3.3842 - 0.15\sqrt{5} = 3.0488$$

$$c_{BS}(S_t, t) = 54{,}102{,}366N(3.3842) - 50{,}000{,}000e^{-0.20(5)}N(3.0488)$$

$$c_{BS}(S_t, t) = 54{,}102{,}366(0.9996) - 50{,}000{,}000e^{-0.20(5)}(0.9989)$$

$$c_{BS}(S_t, t) = 35{,}710{,}214$$

Analysis The intrinsic value of the startup project at the expiration of the Growth stage would be $C =$ max (54,102,366 – 50,000,000,0) = \$4,102,366. That means that if expected revenues during the Growth stage end at \$54,102,366, then the investor could exercise the right to buy the initial investment with a high probability and even continue to the next stage. The B-S approach shows that at the beginning of the Growth stage, the value of the startup business would be even greater than shown by the NPV. This happens because the expected Time Value of the option to continue in the Growth stage is still greater than the NPV of continuing it.

At this stage the investor may decide to abandon the Fintech startup and will accept a premium from a second investor of almost \$36 million. The net effect of the transaction would be –\$14 million, which is greater than the net cash flow of –\$40 million if the investor decides to abandon the startup project from the beginning of the Survival stage. On the other hand, the second investor willing to accept the startup business would expect that revenues at the expiration of the Growth stage be greater than \$86 million in such a way to exercise the right to buy the initial investment and recover the premium paid to the first investor.

5.3 *Scenario 3. The Consolidation Stage*

The consolidation stage can also be described as a Stability stage where revenues could be less volatile than in previous stages and the Fintech startup has entered a mature stage before making its IPO (Initial Public Offering). Also, as the Fintech startup has survived to the first critical years of life and has shown a strong growth in its revenues in such a way to make positive profits, then it could be expected a low

Table 7 Startup valuation in the consolidation stage

	0	1	2	3
NCF =	(50,000,000.00)	26,000,000.00	27,000,000.00	28,000,000.00
PV=	(50,000,000.00)	23,214,285.71	21,524,234.69	19,929,846.94
PVCF =	64,668,367.35			
NPV=	**14,668,367**			
IRR =	**28%**			

rate of return by investors. In that respect, uncertainty about the future of the startup may decrease and the investor could demand a less compensatory risk-return.

Assume that the same investor faces the option to continue to the Consolidation stage who has estimated a 3-year horizon before IPO occurs. Table 7 shows the stage evaluation where the investor expects a 12% rate of return. As in the previous stages, it is expected that target revenues during the consolidation process should be the revenues lump sum as equal as the initial investment.

Revenues during the consolidation stage could not be showing spectacular changes from year to year since the startup has entered a stability period where it has reached a specific market share in the industry and its cost structures may allow economies of scale. Results show that the investor could take the investment decision to continue into the Consolidation stage, since the NPV is positive.

The following results show the startup valuation based on the B-S model, where it is assumed a revenue volatility of 10%.

$$d_1 = \frac{\ln\left(\frac{64{,}668{,}367}{50{,}000{,}000}\right) + \left(0.12 + \frac{1}{2}0.10^2\right)3}{0.10\sqrt{3}} = 3.6503$$

$$d_2 = 3.6503 - 0.10\sqrt{3} = 3.4771$$

$$c_{BS}(S_t, t) = 64{,}668{,}367N(3.6503) - 50{,}000{,}000e^{-0.12(3)}N(3.4771)$$

$$c_{BS}(S_t, t) = 64{,}668{,}367(0.9999) - 50{,}000{,}000e^{-0.12(3)}(0.9997)$$

$$c_{BS}(S_t, t) = 29{,}784{,}922$$

Analysis Based on the intrinsic value of the right to buy the initial investment, $C = \max\,(64{,}668{,}367 - 50{,}000{,}000, 0) = 14{,}668{,}367$, where the NPV are the expected revenues at expiration of the consolidation stage; the investor would exercise the option with a high probability of 0.9999 given current and expected market conditions.

Besides the NPV indicates a startup value of $14 million, however the real options approach includes the Time Value of the investment decision and makes the startup increase its value. If the investor decides to quit the startup business, he will receive a payment of $29 million instead of $14 million. So, the investor would experience a net payment of −$21 million. On the other hand, a second investor is willing to pay \$29 million in such a way to exercise the right to buy \$50 million at the expiration of the consolidation stage. This happens since the second investor expects that revenues at expiration should be greater than those estimated by the first investor.

5.4 *Scenario 4. The Option to Switch in the Growth Stage*

The respective Fintech startup expects a technological change during its Growth stage which may contribute to an increase of 10% in the original expected revenues. However, the startup will face an additional investment cost of \$20 million. Table 8 shows the results of the option to switch where it is observed that the project should not be accepted since the NPV is not positive.

Besides the NPV states that the project should be rejected, the real options approach considers a chance to exercise the additional investment cost at the expiration of the growth stage. The B-S model estimates a probability of 0.67 of exercising the option to switch which estimated value is \$1.4 million.

$$d_1 = \frac{\ln\left(\frac{8{,}115{,}354}{20{,}000{,}000}\right) + \left(0.20 + \frac{1}{2}0.15^2\right)3}{0.15\sqrt{5}} = 0.4600$$

$$d_2 = 0.4600 - 0.15\sqrt{5} = 0.1246$$

$$c_{BS}(S_t, t) = 8{,}115{,}354N(0.4600) - 20{,}000{,}000e^{-0.20(5)}N(0.1246)$$

$$c_{BS}(S_t, t) = 8{,}115{,}354(0.6772) - 20{,}000{,}000e^{-0.20(5)}(0.5496)$$

$$c_{BS}(S_t, t) = 1{,}452{,}505$$

Even though the switch project may be rejected by the NPV approach, the investor still gets some value of its investment decision explained by the Time Value of the option to switch. If the investor would prefer to transfer the investment cost to a second investor, then a premium of \$1.4 million can be taken in this transaction and a net payment of −\$8.6 million. On the other hand, the second investor is willing to pay \$1.4 million to exercise the \$20 million investment cost at the expiration of the Consolidation stage. This happens since the second investor's expectations about future market conditions are better than the first investor. At the end, if the option to switch would not have generated enough new revenues, then the

Table 8 The Option switch in the Growth stage

	0	1	2	3	4	5
$NCF_1 =$		10,000,000.00	16,000,000.00	21,000,000.00	25,000,000.00	26,000,000.00
NCF*=		11,500,000.00	18,400,000.00	24,150,000.00	28,750,000.00	29,900,000.00
NCF* - $NCF_1 =$	(20,000,000.00)	1,500,000.00	2,400,000.00	3,150,000.00	3,750,000.00	3,900,000.00
PV=	(20,000,000.00)	1,250,000.00	1,666,666.67	1,822,916.67	1,808,449.07	1,567,322.53
PVCF =	8,115,354.94					
NPV=	**(11,884,645)**					
IRR =	**−8%**					

revenues differences will not allow the second investor to recover the additional investment cost. At that point, the investor could decide to quit from the startup business continuation.

As conclusion, the Real Options (RO) approach based on the B-S model has shown that even though an investment project could not be accepted by the NPV approach, there is a probability that the investment may get value over time. Also, it was observed that the NPV is an input of the RO approach. Therefore, both approaches should be complementary tools to managerial business decisions. A key feature in the RO analysis is the time to expiration of each startup stage. In this section the whole startup life cycle was 11 years which is a reasonable period before a startup enters an IPO. Also, it was not intended to discuss the rate of return to be applied in the startup valuation, instead it was intended to realize the importance of target revenues to be achieved in each of the startup stages. Consequently, the option to continue or abandon the startup investment was possible to be performed under the real options approach.

6 Conclusions

A managerial decision can be as straightforward as the use of a thumb rule or as roundabout as the use of advanced tools that could result in diminishing returns of the allocated sources in an investment project. Not only could have a negative impact on the investment performance, but a less than expected rate of return for investors and disagreement of all stakeholders. In that respect, a set of investment evaluation criteria and business valuation methodologies can be listed, which have been considered as traditional approaches. For example, an investment decision based on a thumb rule as the payback period up to a sophisticated framework as the discounted cash flow approach. However, all of them are useful in a decision-making process.

As a matter of fact, the Discounted Cash Flow methodology is the main framework of the Net Present Value approach for investment project purposes and to some extent the fundamental quantitative analysis reference in business valuation. In both cases, the expected rate of return plays a crucial role in determining the acceptance or rejection of the project or the value of a company. Consequently, criteria have been developed to help in the decision making: 1) the investment project evaluation is accepted when the NPV is positive, otherwise should be rejected; 2) in business valuation, once cash flows are discounted if the estimated value of the company is greater than its market price then the company is undervalued, otherwise it could be overvalued.

In that perspective, no more choices could the investor get when facing an investment decision: to accept or reject the project, or to buy or sell (even keep) the company's stocks. Therefore, some kind of "sticky choices" may face the investor when solely applying non-flexible tools that could not allow to build a wide portfolio of choices, besides current and expected market conditions have been incorporated into the analysis. Furthermore, how could the investor decide in advance when the economy may show swings or downturns?

This is shown as the application of the real options approach as a complementary tool for managerial decision-making, specifically it was focused on startups valuation. First, it was presented scenarios related to the NPV approach in such a way to realize the fact of "sticky-choices" an investor could face: no other alternative, yes or no. Also, the importance of the NPV relies on the fact that it is the main input in the real options approach. Despite the RO approach could consider different option pricing methodologies, in this chapter the Black-Scholes formula was applied. Second, the intention in this chapter was not to discuss or propose estimations of the startup expected rate of return. Third, in consequence, the main goal was to show the application of the RO approach in startup business valuation where the meaningful issue in the analysis was the Options Cycle for Startups which derives from the Financing Cycle for Startups.

Four startup business valuation scenarios were performed. The first scenario, Survival stage, where an investor may face a high-risk investment decision because of uncertainty that the startup may not achieve target revenues to cover the initial installment. Also, during this stage it was considered a high- expected rate of return that would resemble the high-risk life period of the startup. Results based on the NPV showed that the investment in the startup should not be accepted. However, the RO approach shows that the option to invest in the startup could be made with certain probability to exercise the invest installment at the expiration of the stage. A crucial factor plays an important role: the time to expiration of the Survival stage in which the target revenues should be achieved.

The second scenario, Growth stage, considers a lesser expected rate of return and an expiration date longer than the Survival stage. The NPV was positive and could signal to the investor the feasibility to invest in the second stage of the startup. Since the NPV is an input of the RO approach, then under the RO approach it shows that the investor may have a high probability to exercise the right to buy the initial investment at the expiration of the Growth stage. Even if current market conditions would not be favorable to the investor, the RO approach suggests that expected conditions could change. In that sense, the investor could have the option to abandon the startup investment and still gain a premium because of the probability that target revenues would be higher than expected.

The third scenario, Consolidation stage, a stage in which it is expected stability of revenues. Since this stage the startup may hold enough historical financial statements and consolidated cost structures that could address the startup to make an initial public offering. The NPV estimated in this stage was positive given: expected revenues, current market conditions, and a lesser expected rate of return than the previous stage. Accordingly, the RO approach suggests that the initial investment could be exercised with a high probability at the expiration date of the stage. Therefore, if the investor has survived to a critical period and experienced the startup growth, then it would be highly recommended the option to continue in the Consolidation stage.

Finally, a fourth scenario was performed which considers an additional investment to support a technological change that would contribute to increase the target revenues during the Growth stage. The NPV approach shows that the additional investment should not be made since in the expected time frame of the stage, the investor would not recover the investment. Nevertheless, the RO approach suggests that the investment can be made with a medium probability of recovering the investment at the expiration of the Growth stage.

Why is the RO approach pricing the startup business at different stages higher than the NPV approach? The answer relies on the fact that any option may hold an Intrinsic Value and a Time Value. Even though the Intrinsic value of the option would be zero at the expiration date, the option would still have value because the probability that market conditions could change may also be favorable to a change in the underlying asset (revenues). The probability of change over time makes the option to get Time Value. In addition, there is always someone willing to pay for the opportunity that in the future will get better benefits than what were originally expected. In spite that the RO approach would help to improve managerial decision-making, care should be taken when applied the B-S model. On one hand, the B-S model assumes that the option and the underlying asset grow at the same rate (the risk-free rate), and that the underlying asset returns are Normally distributed. On the other hand, the B-S model assumes that the underlying asset and the financial derivative are marketable securities, which are known as Complete Markets. However, investment projects and startup businesses are not marketable securities which means that the valuation process is facing a problem of Incomplete Markets.

This chapter applied the RO approach to evaluate startups in different life stages before an IPO. It was emphasized on a Fintech startup because of its importance in the financial services digitization, financial inclusion, and its contribution towards economic growth and development of the nation. The scenarios were limited to consider the options to continue, to abandon, and to switch. Therefore, the scope of this chapter was to propose a "general startup business valuation framework" based on the RO approach. The next work can be extended to apply the compound option and other types of options in the respective startup stages.

Finally, a question that may arise from starters, investors, or stakeholders: when is the real options approach useful to apply? Answer: At any time as if we're using the Net Present Value framework. However, attention should be paid to the case when the discounted cash flows are showing negative values or as a whole the NPV is negative. In this respect, the real options approach rescues the flexibility behind any investment decision that cannot be shown solely by the NPV as compared to the real options approach which is able to unmask the Intrinsic Value and Time Value of investment decisions.

References

Allen, F., Gu, X., and Jagtiani, J. A., (2020). "A Survey of Fintech Research and Policy Discussion", Review of Corporate Finance 1 (2021), pp. 259–339, *FRB of Philadelphia Working Paper* No. 20–21, Available at SSRN: https://ssrn.com/abstract=3622468 or doi: https://doi.org/10.21799/frbp.wp.2020.21

Amram, M., & Kulatilaka, N. (1999). *Real options: Managing strategic Investment in an Uncertain World*. Oxford University Press.

Balliauw, M. (2021). From theoretical real options models to pragmatic decision making: Required steps, opportunities and threats. *Research in Transportation Economics, 90*, 101063.

Bennouna, K., Meredith, G. G., & Marchant, T. (2010). *Improved capital budgeting decision making: Evidence from Canada*. Management Decision.

Black, F., & Scholes, M. (1973). The pricing of options and corporate liabilities. *Journal of Political Economy, 81*(3), 637–654.

Boot, A., Hoffmann, P., Laeven, L., & Ratnovski, L. (2021). Fintech: What's old, what's new? *Journal of Financial Stability, 53*, 100836.

Bürer, M. J., & Wüstenhagen, R. (2009). Which renewable energy policy is a venture capitalist's best friend? Empirical evidence from a survey of international cleantech investors. *Energy Policy, 37*(12), 4997–5006.

Charitou, A., & Trigeorgis, L. (2000). *Option-based bankruptcy prediction*. Available at SSRN 248709.

Chorn, L. G., & Shokhor, S. (2006). Real options for risk management in petroleum development investments. *Energy Economics, 28*(4), 489–505.

Cojoianu, T. F., Clark, G. L., Hoepner, A. G., Veneri, P., & Wójcik, D. (2020). Entrepreneurs for a low carbon world: How environmental knowledge and policy shape the creation and financing of green start-ups. *Research Policy, 49*(6), 103988.

Copeland, T., & Antikarov, V. (2003). *Real options: A practitioner's guide*, revised edition. Thomson/Texere.

Cortazar, G., & Casassus, J. (1998). Optimal timing of a mine expansion: Implementing a real options model. *The Quarterly Review of Economics and Finance, 38*(3), 755–769.

Cumming, D. J., Hervé, F., Manthé, E., & Schwienbacher, A. (2018). Hypothetical bias in equity crowdfunding. In *2nd emerging trends in entrepreneurial finance conference*.

Currie, W. L., & Lagoarde-Segot, T. (2017). Financialization and information technology: Themes, issues and critical debates–part I. *Journal of Information Technology, 32*(3), 211–217.

de Moraes Marreco, J., & Carpio, L. G. T. (2006). Flexibility valuation in the Brazilian power system: A real options approach. *Energy Policy, 34*(18), 3749–3756.

Demirgüç-Kunt, A., & Singer, D. (2017). *Financial inclusion and inclusive growth: A review of recent empirical evidence*. World Bank Policy Research Working Paper, (8040).

Dixit, R. K., Dixit, A. K., & Pindyck, R. S. (1994). *Investment under uncertainty*. Princeton University Press.

D'Souza, D. (2002). Toward an understanding of how organizations create manufacturing flexibility. *Journal of Managerial Issues, 14*(4), 470–485.

Félix, J. C., De Moares, J. G., & Yao, P. (2021). Are Fintechs worth investing? Case study for startup using real option theory. *International Journal of Development Research, 11*(4), 45999–46007.

Fernandes, B., Cunha, J., & Ferreira, P. (2011). The use of real options approach in energy sector investments. *Renewable and Sustainable Energy Reviews, 15*(9), 4491–4497.

Gimpel, H., Hosseini, S., Huber, R., Probst, L., Röglinger, M., & Faisst, U. (2018). Structuring digital transformation: a framework of action fields and its application at ZEISS. *Journal of Information Technology Theory and Application (JITTA), 19*(1), 3.

Gozman, D., Liebenau, J., & Mangan, J. (2018). The innovation mechanisms of fintech start-ups: insights from SWIFT's innotribe competition. *Journal of Management Information Systems, 35*(1), 145–179.

Graham, J. R., & Harvey, C. R. (2001). The theory and practice of corporate finance: Evidence from the field. *Journal of Financial Economics, 60*(1–2), 187–243.

Haddad, C., & Hornuf, L. (2019). The emergence of the global fintech market: Economic and technological determinants. *Small Business Economics, 53*(1), 81–105.

Hartmann, M., & Hassan, A. (2006). Application of real options analysis for pharmaceutical R & D Project valuation – Empirical results from a survey. *Research Policy, 35*(3), 343–354.

Heughebaert, A., & Manigart, S. (2012). Firm valuation in venture capital financing rounds: The role of investor bargaining power. *Journal of Business Finance and Accounting, 39*(3–4), 500–530.

Insights, C.B., *12. Tech trends to watch closely in 2021.*

Jagtiani, J., & Lemieux, C. (2018). Do fintech lenders penetrate areas that are underserved by traditional banks? *Journal of Economics and Business, 100*, 43–54.

Kogut, B., & Kulatilaka, N. (2001). Capabilities as real options. *Organization Science, 12*(6), 744–758.

Kulatilaka, N., & Lenos, T. (1994). The general flexibility to switch: Real options revisited. *International Journal of Finance, 6*(2), 778–798.

Kulatilaka, N., & Perotti, E. (1998). Strategic growth options. *Management Science, INFORMS, 44*(8), 1021–1031.

Ma, Y., Ping, K., Wu, C., Chen, L., Shi, H., & Chong, D. (2020). Artificial intelligence powered internet of things and smart public service. *Library Hi Tech, 38*(1), 165–179.

Majd, S., & Pindyck, R. (1987). Time to build, option value, and investment decisions. *Journal of Financial Economics, 18*(1), 7–27.

Minardi, A. M. A. F. (2000). Teoria de opções aplicada a projetos de investimento. *Revista de Administração de Empresas, 40*, 74–79.

Myers, S. C., & Majd, S. (1990). Abandonment value and project life. *Advances in Futures and Options Research, 4*, 1–21.

Myers, S. C., & Turnbull, S. M. (1977). Capital budgeting and the capital asset pricing model: Good news and bad news. *The Journal of Finance, 32*(2), 321–333.

Rencher, M. (2012). *Crossing the Valley of Death: A multi-sited, multi-level ethnographic study of growth startups and entrepreneurial communities in post-industrial Detroit*. Wayne State University.

Ryan, P. A., & Ryan, G. P. (2002). Capital budgeting practices of the fortune 1000: How have things changed? *Journal of Business and Management, 8*(4), 355–364.

The Times of India. July 14, 2013. "Kudankulam nuclear plant goes critical". Retrieved from: http://timesofindia.indiatimes.com/articleshow/21061780.cms?utm_source=contentofinterest&utm_medium=text&utm_campaign=cppst

Trigeorgis, L. (2000). *Innovation and strategy, Flexibility, Natural Resources and Foreign Investment: New Developments and Applications in Real Options.* Oxford University Press.

Van de Ven, A. H., Hudson, R., & Schroeder, D. M. (1984). Designing new business startups: Entrepreneurial, organizational, and ecological considerations. *Journal of Management, 10*(1), 87–108.

Venegas-Martínez, F. (2008). *Riesgos financieros y económicos* (2ª edición ed.). CENGAGE Learning.

Vives, X. (2019). Digital disruption in banking. *Annual Review of Financial Economics, 11*, 243–272.

Yang, M., & Blyth, W. (2007). Modeling investment risks and uncertainties with real options approach. *International Energy Agency, 23*.

Yang, B., Lee, C., Xiang, W., Xie, J., He, J. H., Kotlanka, R. K., et al. (2009). Electromagnetic energy harvesting from vibrations of multiple frequencies. *Journal of micromechanics and microengineering, 19*(3), 035001.

Startup Valuation with Data Envelopment Analysis

Yusuf Ozan Üzgün

1 Introduction

Widely used mature firm valuation approaches in the literature are "accounting-based", "market-based" and "cash flow-based" approaches. These are also called traditional approaches. Apart from these, there are also methods which are called non-traditional valuation methods such as real option valuation, Economic Value Added (EVA) and Cash Flow Return on Investment (CFROI).

When we look at startup valuation methods, it is seen that traditional methods used for mature companies are used with various modifications, but there are also developed methods specific to startup companies. Apart from these, there are also non-traditional valuation methods used for startup companies, just like mature companies, and these can be listed as follows: Venture Capital, Berkus, Scorecard, First Chicago, Risk Factor Summation, Cost-to-Duplicate (Roig & Vicen, 2020).

Moreover to these approaches and methods used for mature and startup companies, there is another method that seems to give very satisfactory results, although it has been seen to be studied in a limited area in the literature. This method is called valuation with Data Envelopment Analysis (DEA) method.

It should also be noted here that valuation with DEA tool can be evaluated within the scope of the market-based valuation approach, as it searches for companies that are comparable to the firm whose value is being estimated, and thus estimates the firm's value by comparison.

Valution with DEA is mostly used for mature companies. On the other hand, within the framework of various assumptions, it can be used in startup valuation by estimating the input and output values (which will be explained later) to be used in the process of finding the efficiencies of the startup to be valued with DEA. The

---

Y. O. Üzgün (✉)
Presidency of Republic of Türkiye – Defense Industry Agency, Ankara, Turkey

S. Derindere Köseoğlu (ed.), *A Practical Guide for Startup Valuation*, Contributions to Finance and Accounting, https://doi.org/10.1007/978-3-031-35291-1_13

purpose of this chapter is to create an applied framework on how DEA can be used in startup valuation.

In this context, first of all, in order to understand the theory of firm valuation with DEA, since DEA is a market-based valuation tool, information on the theory of market-based valuation will be presented and after that a brief theory of the DEA will be presented. Following the information about the theory, the methodology of firm valuation with DEA will be discussed and a startup firm valuation will be made using DEA over a sample application.

2 Market-Based Valuation Approach

Valuation is the process of estimating the value of an asset or liability according to the International Valuation Standards Council (IVSC, 2019, p. 5) and is a very important concept as they form the basis of decisions involving significant amounts of money or wealth transferred from one party to another (Rawley & Gup, 2010, p. xvii.).

Firm valuation can also be defined as the activities of determining the value of a firm based on the above definition, and it is done in order to determine the appropriate and reasonable market value of the firm subject to the valuation (Chambers, 2011, p. 6–7).

Although many valuation methods are used, starting from very simple methods to more complex methods, some of these methods are classified together because they have some common features. With the classification of these valuation methods, which have a common feature, the broader concept of "valuation approach" has emerged (Sipahi et al., 2016, p. 25).

In the market-based valuation approach, the value of an asset is valued based on how similar assets are priced in the market. For example, a prospective home buyer decides how much to pay for a home by looking at the prices paid for similar homes in the neighborhood. Likewise, a potential investor in a stock tries to estimate its value by looking at the market prices of "similar" stocks (Damodaran, 2006, p. 56–57).

Company valuation with DEA is mainly seen as an extension of a market-based valuation approach. Firm valuation with DEA follows a similar principle. Here too, first of all, the relative efficiency of Decision-Making Units (DMUs) that produce similar outputs by using similar inputs in the value creation process is measured with DEA. As a result of this measurement, the peer DMUs that the inefficient DMUs take as examples for themselves are determined. Here in valuation with DEA by using "taking as an example" feature, the most similar DMUs are determined.

Returning again to the market-based valuation approach, while it is an advantage that the methods under the market-based valuation approach are easily applicable, it is the disadvantage of this method that this valuation method does not give reliable results when there is no comparable firm (Sipahi et al., 2016, p. 123).

With market-based methods, when searching for whether a publicly traded and therefore market-priced firm is overvalued or undervalued, first of all, comparable firms are determined and then the average multipliers of these firms are found. Finding a multiplier is essentially a standardization (normalization) operation to make an absolute value comparable. The most commonly used multipliers are "price/earnings ratio", "market cap/book value ratio" and "company value/EBITDA ratio". These multipliers are compared with the multipliers of the firm whose value is searched for, and comments are made about the market value of the firm whose value is being researched as if it is undervalued, correctly valued or overvalued.

It should also be noted that the disadvantages of the market-based valuation approach become more evident in the valuation of startup companies. For example, it may not be possible to make a relative valuation using a parameter such as EBITDA, as startups often have negative EBITDA. Again, there are difficulties in the use of the book value of these companies, since the book values of the newly established companies are very low due to their very short-term history. Nevertheless, sales amounts in relative valuation are also a problematic parameter for newly established companies since they cannot make sales yet. Again, it is very difficult to find the multipliers to be taken as a basis in the relative valuation, since the shares of young companies are less likely to be traded on the stock exchanges. In this case, the valuation of a young firm will involve the use of multipliers of a mature firm. But here too, this approach will also contain errors, as the risk, cash flow and growth characteristics of young and mature firms are different. Again, it is not easy to include risk factors related to the survival of these highly risky companies in the valuation processes of startup companies (Damodaran, 2009, p. 12).

3 Data Envelopment Analysis

To put it simply, DEA finds a frontier and analyzes the efficiency of each unit in the comparison set relative to its distance from this frontier. This method can provide the integrity that traditional methods cannot provide for the evaluation of multiple inputs and multiple outputs with the logic of total factor productivity. In the DEA technique, the weights of inputs and outputs are used for DMUs to maximize their efficiency ratios. Weights are allocated for the inputs and outputs of each decision-making unit separately (Kutlar & Babacan, 2008, p. 150).

DEA is a non-parametric tool. Being non-parametric means not belonging to a class of functions that have a finite number of parameters and a functional form for the relevant production technology (for example, the Cobb-Douglas functional form) (Tarım, 2001. p. 45). In parametric efficiency measurement methods, it is assumed that the production function of the decision unit to be measured is known and usually a single output (dependent variable) is tried to be explained with one or more inputs (independent variable). While measuring performance with regression analysis, the regression line is used. If a decision unit is above the regression line, it is considered efficient, and if it is below it, it is considered inefficient. The regression line can be thought of as a boundary between efficient units and inefficient units (Yücel İşbilen, 2017, p. 16). Non-parametric methods have a parameterless structure that is based on linear programming as a solution technique. It does not require any production function to be defined for performance measurement and can correlate multiple inputs and multiple outputs at the same time. Data envelopment analysis is the first thing that comes to mind when non-parametric method is mentioned in efficiency analysis (Yücel İşbilen, 2017, p. 19–20). Since the majority of non-parametric efficiency measures are independent of the units of measurement of inputs and outputs, they allow different dimensions of firms to be measured simultaneously. These measures determine the appropriate cluster for each decision unit by optimizing the objective functions separately while calculating the relative efficiency for each decision unit (Kutlar & Babacan, 2008, p. 108).

DEA is essentially a method developed for measuring the comparative efficiency of homogeneous DMUs using the same type of inputs and obtaining the same type of output (Keskin Benli & Bozdan, 2019, p. 30–31). The first original idea of this method was to provide a methodology for measuring a non-profit DMU's efficiency compared to a set of comparable DMUs. But since then, DEA, with the help of its modified versions, has become a tool that provides a lot of additional information for exploring the production process and managing performance.

The DEA model can basically be formed with two types of linear programming models—Envelopment and Multiplier models—which are dual[1] of each other. These models are solved for each DMU. Although the efficiency scores represented by the objective function value in both models are obtained as the same value, different inferences can be reached over the values of the variables of the models. The envelopment model takes into account the production possibilities set approach and it produces the target values required for the DMUs to reach the efficient limit. Multiplier model, which takes into account the weighted output/weighted input ratio of the DMUs, is used to determine the inputs and outputs that are the source of the efficiency or inefficiency of the DMUs (Atıcı et al., 2016, p. 4).

It should be noted here that classic DEA models have two types of orientation, defined as input- and output-orientated models. While input-oriented models ask, "How much can inputs be proportionally reduced by keeping output constant?",

[1]Every linear programming problem has an associated twin problem. Any linear programming problem is called primal and original, while the other, that is, its twin, is called duality or dual. Duality is used both institutionally and practically in linear programming problems. We can list them as follows:

- In some cases, it is easier to solve the dual problem than the primal.
- Duality allows to use the simplex method when the initial solution is not possible. This technique is called dual simplex.
- It provides powerful theorems that explain duality linear programming problems.
- The dual solution of a primal problem brings important economic interpretations as well as its mathematical properties.
- Duality is used to investigate how changes in the formulation or coefficients of a linear programming problem will affect the solution (i.e. sensitivity analysis) (Patır, 2020, p. 175).

output-oriented models ask "by how much can output quantities be increased proportionally by keeping the input amount constant?" (Torun et al., 2020, p. 486).

Below is a mathematical representation of the output-oriented CCR (initials of Charnes, Cooper, and Rhodes) multiplier model which is the first DEA model introduced by Charnes, Cooper, and Rhodes in 1978 (Zhou et al., 2008, p. 3).

If there are M inputs and N outputs for each of the *K* DMUs in DEA;

$$
\begin{aligned}
&\max \sum_{(m=1)}^{M} u_m Y_{mo} \\
&s.t. \\
&\sum_{(m=1)}^{M} u_m Y_{mk} - \sum_{(n=1)}^{N} v_n X_{nk} \leq 0 \\
&k = 1, 2, \ldots, K. \\
&\sum_{(n=1)}^{N} v_n X_{xo} = 1 \\
&u_m, v_n \geq 0, \quad m = 1, 2, \ldots, M; \\
&n = 1, 2, \ldots, N
\end{aligned}
\tag{1}
$$

u_m : weight given to the mth output by the *K* decision – making units,
v_n : weight given to the nth input by the *K* decision – making units,
Y_{mk} : *m*th output produced by *K* decision – making units,
X_{nk} : *n*th input used by *K* decision – making units.

Accordingly, *K* models are generated for *K* DMUs in the above model, and *K* maximization models are solved so that the relative efficiency of each DMU can be measured.

v_n ve u_m are virtual weights in the model. It is called virtual because these weights are derived, not observed. For this reason, the inputs and outputs found by multiplying the virtual weights are called virtual inputs and outputs. Virtual weights are determined separately for each DMU (Yücel İşbilen, 2017, p. 22).

Below is the dual of the above multiplier form (input-oriented CCR envelopment model):

$$
\begin{aligned}
&\mathrm{Min}\theta_k \\
&\sum\nolimits_{(n=1)}^{N} \lambda_k X_{nk} \leq \theta_k X_{no}, \quad n = 1, 2, \ldots, N, \\
&\sum\nolimits_{(m=1)}^{M} \lambda_k X_{mk} \leq Y_{mo}, \quad m = 1, 2, \ldots, M, \\
&\lambda_k \geq 0, \quad k = 1, 2, \ldots, K.
\end{aligned}
\tag{2}
$$

The envelope form is preferred more because it contains fewer constraints than the multiplier model. Again, in envelope form, instead of weights related to inputs and outputs, the weights on the DMUs, that is, the density vector λ, are obtained. The density vector λ indicates how much an inefficient DMU should resemble the efficient DMUs (Yücel İşbilen, 2017, p. 27–28).

The efficient peer DMU of an inefficient DMU can be determined with optimal λ values. The peer DMU represents radially closest efficient DMU at the efficient boundary to the inefficient DMU. The inefficient DMU can determine how it can become efficient by taking the practices of the peer DMU as an example (Ulucan et al., 2018, p. 309).

The basic DEA model given above takes into account the assumption of constant returns to scale. This type of modeling is used when a proportional relationship between inputs and outputs can be assumed. For problems where there is no proportional relationship between inputs and outputs, DEA models with variable returns to scale were derived by Banker, Charnes, and Cooper in 1984. The BCC (initials of Banker, Charnes, and Cooper) model can be set by adding a convexity constraint to CCR model, which makes the sum of the λ variables equal to 1. The reflection of this in the dual model is a free variable added to the left side of the first constraint group (Atıcı et al., 2016, p. 5).

The convexity constraint is:

$$\sum_{k=1}^{K} \lambda_k = 1. \tag{3}$$

The fact that a set is convex means that all linear combinations of, for example, X and Y in this set are also included in this set. This simple but illuminating idea causes the efficient frontier to envelop the observed points more tightly (Yücel İşbilen, 2017, p. 28).

The steps required for the implementation of DEA can be listed as follows:

1. Selection of decision-making units
2. Input and output selection
3. Model selection (CCR, BCC, etc.)
4. Measurement of relative efficiency with DEA (mostly by a software)
5. Evaluation of results

Detailed explanations regarding the implementation of these steps are given in the DEA valuation application section of the study.

4 Firm Valuation with DEA

4.1 Literature on Firm Valuation with DEA

The purpose of the first study (Simak, 2000, p. 102–115), which deals with the firm valuation with DEA, is to find the group of publicly traded companies that are most similar to the firm to be valued. In this study, first of all, with the input-oriented BCC model, efficiency analysis was carried out by using the input and output data of the year 1997 of 51 publicly traded companies operating in the production sector. By this analysis, efficient and inefficient firms and inefficient firms peer groups were determined. The set of efficient firms, which were taken as a peer, together with the firms that took the same efficient firms as a peer, were taken as a group. Within the scope of the study, total assets and total liabilities were taken as inputs, and net profit, working capital and retained earnings were used as outputs. As a result of this initial study, it was concluded that encouraging results were obtained, this methodology can be used in multidimensional comparison of companies (Simak, 2000, p. 102–115).

In the second study on this subject, the first study conducted by Simak was expanded and it was revealed that DEA could be used not only for the firm value range, but also for maximum value calculations for firms found inefficient and minimum value for firms found efficient. All analysis are performed using the input-oriented BCC model, and using total assets and total liabilities as inputs, and equity, net sales, profit and cash flows as outputs (Anadol, 2000, p. 54–115).

In the third study on firm valuation with DEA, variable returns to scale (VRS) assumption was used, as in the first two studies. The reason for choosing VRS was VRS efficiency frontier's being formed by more DMUs than the CRS efficiency frontier and consequently containing more reference set for classifying DMUs in the analysis. Main difference in this study is that the slack-based model (SBM) is used instead of the BCC model. It has been stated that the SBM model is used because both inputs and outputs are important in deciding the efficiency state of a DMU and it is difficult to say which is more critical. While only inputs or outputs are controllable factors in the objective function of classical DEA models, all inputs and outputs are included in the objective function in SBM (Anadol et al., 2014, p. 16–27).

In another study on firm valuation with DEA Üzgün, 2022), the estimated values of firms traded in İstanbul Stock Exchange are compared with the market values of these firms. Separate valuation studies were conducted for different sectors and very satisfactory results were obtained.

4.2 Firm Valuation Methodology with DEA

The DEA valuation approach is essentially a market-based valuation method, and its key component is finding the cluster of companies most similar to the company to be valued. Similarity should exist in all relevant dimensions of the company's operating characteristics. DEA allows for such a multidimensional comparison between firms.

The simple two-dimensional example below illustrates the DEA process. First, the efficient frontier is determined, which consists of the best practice units (A, B, C, D). Second, for each DMU, efficiency measures reflecting its distance from the border is calculated. For every inefficient firm, there is a peer group, a set of efficient firms that are "closest" to the firm being evaluated (Table 1 and Fig. 1).

Table 1 Two-dimensional input-oriented DEA (variable return to scale) example

DMU	Input (*X*)	Output (*Y*)	Efficiency score	λA	λB	λC	λD
A	2	2	100%	1	0	0	0
B	4	4	100%	0	1	0	0
C	6	5	100%	0	0	1	0
D	8	6	100%	0	0	0	1
E	5	2.5	50%	0.75	0.25	0	0
F	7	3	43%	0.5	0.5	0	0
G	5.8	3.8	66%	0.1	0.9	0	0
H	6.5	4.2	68%	0	0.8	0.2	0
I	7.8	4.8	72%	0	0.2	0.8	0

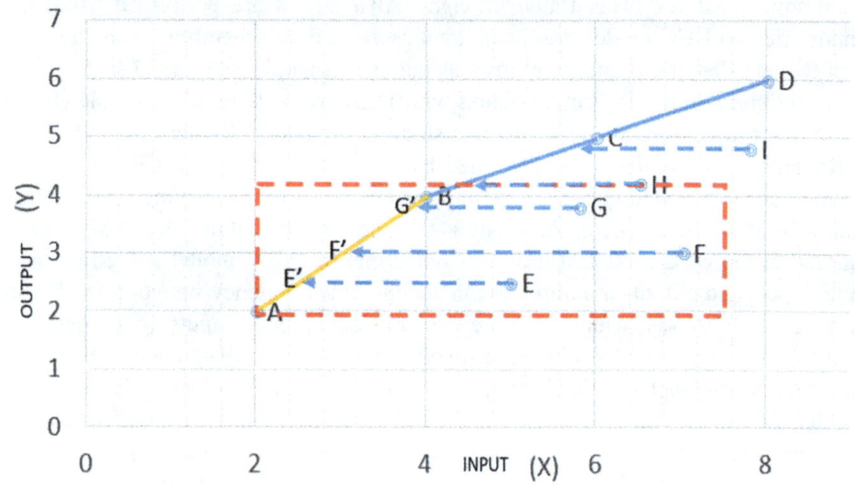

Fig. 1 Two-dimensional DEA. Source: Author's own creation

For example, the peers of firms E, F, G are companies A and B, and firms B and C are peer of H and I. When considering the input-oriented projection, companies belonging to the same peer group have similar levels of output. Using this feature of peer groups, DEA can be used to identify similar firms multidimensionally. Firms E, F and G have the same set of peers, and their lambda values show how close they are to each other. In this example, the three relevant lambda vectors for firms E, F and G are [0.75, 0.25, 0, 0], [0.5, 0.5, 0, 0] ve [0.1, 0.9, 0, 0] (the corresponding efficient firms are A, B, C and D). Lambda values also show that company E is closer to company F than company G (in terms of output). This represents a two-dimensional example, but the same theory applies in multiple dimensions. The difference indicator calculation has been developed to move this two-dimensional example to multiple dimensions. Variable δ_{ij} for each company *i*, difference indicator between companies *i* and *j* as follows (Anadol, 2000, p. 106–107):

$$\delta_{ij} = \sum \left(\lambda_{ik} - \lambda_{jk}\right)^2 \tag{4}$$

Here k is the coefficient of all efficient companies in the analysis. For companies belonging to the same peer group, the presence of a low difference indicator value is an indicator of the similarity in the output dimensions of the DEA model.

The λ value in the same formula shows the contribution level of efficient firms to the virtual DMU created by reflecting an inefficient DMU to the efficiency frontier. These units, which contribute to the creation of the imaginary unit, will have non-zero dual weights, namely lambda, and will form the reference set for the DMU (the DMU in question). The reference set for the DMU therefore consists only of efficient units and serves as a basis for calculating the DMU's efficiency score. The magnitude of the lambda indicates the extent to which the properties of the efficient DMUs are used to create the virtual DMU at the boundary to which the inefficient DMU is projected.

Another indicator to look for similarity is the efficiency score. The efficiency score is an input radial measure of efficiency and can be used to determine similarity across input dimensions. Since firm E has an efficiency score of 0.5 and firm F has an efficiency score of 0.43, it can be seen that they are quite similar in the input-oriented dimension as well.

In order to understand the valuation method with DEA, the example given by Simak will be used. In Simak's study, data from 51 publicly traded companies operating in the manufacturing sector for 1997 were used and 13 firms were found to be efficient and the rest were found to be inefficient. As a result of the DEA, for example, the peer companies of the company no. 2 were determined as firms no. 19, 22 and 45. Other firms that take the same firms as a peer are firms no. 14, 32, 33, 34, 42 and 43.

Firms no.19, 22 and 45, which are the peer companies of the firm no. 2, as well as firms no. 14, 32, 33, 34, 42 and 43, which take no 19, 22 and 45 firms as peer just like the firm no. 2 were examined altogether in terms of similarity for the firm no. 2.

The δ_{2j} values, which are the indicators of the difference between these companies and companies no. 2, were calculated. Difference indicators calculated together with lambda values are given in the table below (Table 2). For example, the difference indicator between firm no. 2 and firm no. 42 is found by solving the following formula:

$$\begin{aligned} \delta 2.42 &= \sum \left(\lambda_{2,k} - \lambda_{42,k}\right)^2 = (0.57 - 0.65)^2 + (0.19 - 0.09)^2 \\ &\quad + (0.24 - 0.26)^2 = 0.018. \end{aligned}$$

Firms with a low difference indicator and an efficiency score close to 0.49 will be similar to firm 2. The most similar firm in the data set is firm 42 with the lowest difference indicator and with its 0.45 efficiency score it is very close to firm 2. Firms

Table 2 Firm no. 2 example

Firm number	Lamda values of efficient firms λ_{i19}	λ_{i22}	λ_{i45}	Difference indicator δ_{2j}	Efficiency point θ	Market value Milion $
2	0.566	0.192	0.242	0	0.49	372
42	0.65	0.09	0.26	0.018	0.45	375
33	0.387	0.396	0.217	0.074	0.8	690
32	0.456	0.04	0.54	0.124	0.54	295
19	1	0	0	0.284	1	341
43	0.1	0.164	0.736	0.462	0.82	109
34	0.054	0.106	0.84	0.627	0.8	122
13	0.042	0.021	0.937	0.787	0.85	54
45	0	0	1	0.932	1	43
22	0	1	0	1032	1	380

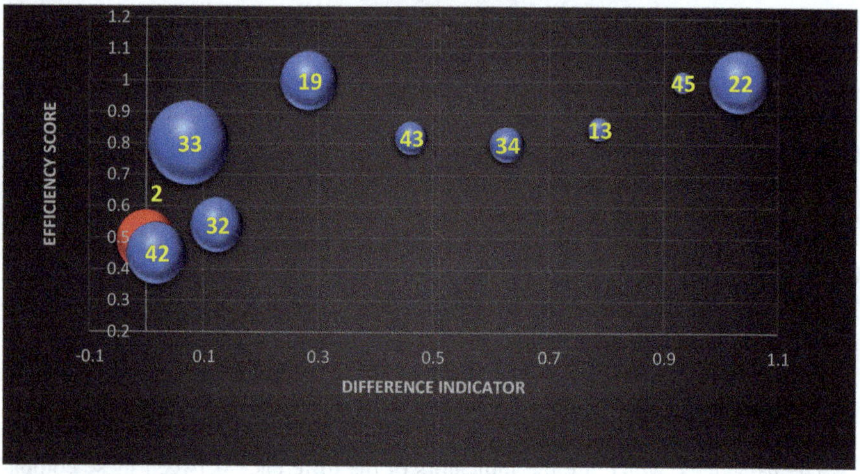

Fig. 2 Balloon chart for firm no. 2. Source: Author's own creation

32 and 33 have a relatively low difference indicator, but efficiency scores of 0.8 and 0.54 may be too far from 0.49 to establish a sufficiently high degree of similarity. The purpose of the analysis is to find a set of firms similar to firm 2 and use their market values to estimate the market value of firm 2. If we were to use the market value of firm 42 ($375M) to estimate the market value of firm 2, we would be very close to the real market value of $371M. The next two similar firms define the $295 million to $690 million range, but are less usable for market cap estimation as noted there is a larger difference in efficiency scores to that of company 2. Representation of this analysis for the firm no. 2 is given in below figure in which the size of the bubbles is proportional to the market values of these firms (Fig. 2).

Accordingly, the closest balloon to the balloon (shown in red) representing firm 2 (firm numbers are shown with yellow numbers) is the balloon belonging to firm

42 and they are almost exactly the same size. Firm 32 is the second closest firm, and the size of the bubble is slightly smaller than the bubble of firm 2. The bubble of firm 33 is farther away from firm 2 (compared to firm 32) and noticeably larger. When these results are evaluated together, it is concluded that the values of companies no. 42 and 32 can be used to determine the value range of firm no. 2.

With DEA, not only value range estimation can be made, but also maximum value estimation can be made for firms that are found to be inefficient as a result of DEA. For this, the lambda values of the efficient firms, of which the firms that are found to be inefficient as a result of DEA, are taken as a peer, are multiplied by market values of efficient firms and then summed together. Value found in the total is the maximum value for the inefficient firm analyzed.

If this analysis is to be done for firm 13 in the above example, the lambda values of firms no. 19, 22 and 45, which are the efficient firms that firm no. 13 takes as a peer are multiplied with the market values of these firms and after that those multiplications are summed together for finding the maximum value of firm 13. This operation will be as follows:

$$= (0.042^{*}341\text{ M}) + (0.021^{*}380\text{ M}) + (0.937^{*}43\text{ M}) = 62.5\text{ M}$$

The market value of firm 13 is $54 Million less than the maximum value found as a result of the analysis. Based on this example, analysis of maximum firm (no 13) value with DEA gives a reasonable result.

5 Startup Valuation Application

5.1 *Selection of DMUs*

In DEA, the efficiencies of units that convert to similar outputs using similar inputs are compared. This approach is generally equivalent to making comparisons of units operating in the same sector. In startup valuation, in addition to operating in a similar sector, being in a similar developmental stage should also be a criterion for DMU selection.

In the application to be made, Sendbox Inc., which is assumed to have just started its activities in the technology sector "Computer Software: Prepackaged Software" industry in the USA, will be valued with DEA. The input and output data of this firm to be used in DEA will be determined hypothetically, and in the light of these data, the value of the firm will be predicted.

The data of the companies that will be included in the analysis and will be the basis for comparison with the company to be valued were selected among the companies in the "Computer Software: Prepackaged Software" industry operating in the NASDAQ technology sector. The companies that are subject to comparison, just like the company to be valued, were selected from among the companies operating in the USA. The fact that the companies to be compared operate in a similar sector and geography is important in terms of ensuring the homogeneity condition in DEA.

On the other hand, since the company to be valued is relatively new, it is assumed that its income generation potential is low and its market value may be as low as this, it is assumed that the companies that will be used as a basis for comparison in DEA are companies with a market value of between \$ 0 and \$ 50 million. Accordingly, Nano Cap companies in the NASDAQ "Computer Software: Prepackaged Software" industry were chosen as the benchmark companies. Nano cap refers to small, publicly traded companies with a market capitalization below \$50 million and is as small as you can get in terms of market capitalization.

When determining the DMUs, it is also very important to determine the number of DMUs. In the literature, there is a view that the number of DMUs should be at least twice the sum of the number of inputs and the number of outputs, and there is also a view that the number of DMUs should be more than three times the sum of the number of inputs and the number of outputs. Nevertheless there is a view that the number of DMUs included in the analysis should be at least 20, and there is also a view that argue that if the number of inputs selected is m and the number of outputs is s, at least $m + s + 1$ DMUs is a necessary constraint for the reliability of the research (Okursoy & Tezsürücü, 2014, p. 7–8).

The number of companies included in the analysis is 22, including the company to be valued. As can be seen under the next heading, the analysis was carried out with three inputs and two outputs. Considering the number of firms included in the analysis is 22 and the sum of the number of inputs and outputs is five, the number of DMUs included in this analysis (22) satisfies all the above-mentioned constraints.

Within the scope of the study, the market values used in the valuation tests are the total market values of the companies calculated on the basis of the stock prices of NASDAQ at 11.11.2022. The input and output data obtained from the financial statements of the related companies are taken from the financial statements that are closest to 11.11.2022 (when the valuation is made) and are currently in publication. All data, obtained from NASDAQ's web site, *are real* except the data of the Sendbox Inc. which is a hypothetic firm whose value is being searched.

5.2 Selection of Inputs and Outputs Included in DEA

The second step in the application of DEA is the selection of the input and output variables to be used in the analysis. Since DEA is a data-based efficiency measurement technique, the accuracy of the measurement results depend on selecting significant inputs and outputs. In DEA application, different measurement units can be used for inputs and outputs (Okursoy & Tezsürücü, 2014, p. 8).

With DEA, service efficiency of companies and their ability to transform input into output can be analyzed. Considering this logic, inputs and outputs that reflect the firm's value creation process and measure its ability to transform assets into profits must be included in valuation with DEA. Net income, net sales, total assets, total liabilities, equity, cash flow, capital expenditures, retained interests, working capital and other quantitative and qualitative factors that make the firm more profitable, valuable and competitive can be included in the model (Anadol, 2000, p. 56–57).

The inputs and outputs within the scope of the study were selected from among the inputs and outputs that reflect the value creation process of companies in the "Computer Software: Prepackaged Software" industry operating in the NASDAQ technology sector. In this respect, cost of goods sold, R & D expenses and total assets were used as inputs, and total revenue and net profit were used as output.

Apart from this, although not used in this study, if it can be obtained or strongly estimated, other factors such as the number of patents owned or applied by startup companies, the amount of intangible assets owned, the experience of the firm's entrepreneurs, the age of the startup, its market share, brand value and existence of companies' management control systems (1 if any, 0 if not) can be taken as output in DEA. Moreover (with a scaling to be made), scores can be used as output by giving a higher score if the startup whose value is searched for operates in countries where the startup culture and markets are developed. All of these are factors increase the efficiency and therefore the value of the startup if maximized with given inputs level.

Different input-output mixes can be used for companies operating in different sectors. For example, fixed assets such as machinery and equipment are important input items in the valuation of an iron and steel factory. For a sugar factory, for example, while the amount of processed beet is an important input item, the amount of sugar produced can be taken as an output.

It should be noted that the data envelopment analysis allows the inputs and outputs to be in different units, for example, the number of personnel can be included in the model, and R & D expenditures can be included in the model as $ amount, similarly, outputs can be included in units with different units.

The following table contains the input and output data and market values of the companies to be used in the analysis. The last line contains the information of Sendbox Inc., whose value we will estimate. Its input-output data are given hypothetically (Table 3).

Estimation of the inputs and outputs to be included in the analysis emerges as a separate compelling issue since the Sendbox Inc., which we will value, is just newly started to operate. At this point, the realism of the estimates will contribute to the accuracy of the valuation.

For example, the estimation of the revenue item to be used as output can be based on the result of the market analysis to be made, and the estimated growth rate can be used for estimating revenue for the next 5 years. Then, those revenues are discounted with a discount rate that reflects the appropriate level of risk to find their net present values. These are then averaged to find the estimated revenue amount to be used as output in DEA.

Table 3 Firms input-outputs and market cap (thousand $)

Name	Input			Output		Market cap
	Cost of revenue	R & D expenses	Total assets	Total revenue	Net profit	
Amesite Inc.	0	3.060	8.884	697	−9.060	7.327
authID Inc.	184	538	21.920	607	−5.301	22.310
Auddia Inc.	44	151	6.470	0	−2.050	17.771
Cuentas Inc.	615	0	7.470	670	−3.186	5.453
CYREN Ltd. Ordinary Shares	2.845	3.280	41.760	4.209	−12.436	7.957
DatChat Inc.	0	0	17.678	38	−2.582	10.715
Duos Technologies Group Inc.	2.335	530	14.992	3.617	−1.343	23.561
Fast Radius Inc. Class A	7.015	1.897	69.329	7.275	−22.187	18.380
GSE Systems Inc.	9.573	182	37.193	12.745	−1.401	15.515
T Stamp Inc. Class A	348	529	7.618	708	−2.922	19.146
Inpixon Common Stock	1.396	4.912	117.846	4.725	−19.872	9.108
Marin Software	3.203	2.980	51.565	4.720	−5.374	19.338
NetSol Technologies Inc.	8.727	581	72.609	13.544	−2.167	34.544
NextPlat Corp	2.304	0	25.089	2.871	−1.656	16.544
NextPlay Technologies Inc.	565	242	101.469	456	−9.155	24.364
Oblong Inc.	926	398	14.570	1.333	−9.033	6.293
RealNetworks Inc.	2.705	5.332	53.439	11.856	−5.136	34.197
Sonic Foundry Inc.	1.907	1.924	21.236	6.465	−1.503	11.204
SilverSun Technologies Inc.	6.511	0	18.311	10.638	−88	16.070
Minerva Surgical Inc.	5.322	1.274	93.958	12.967	−5.613	8.219
Waitr Holdings Inc.	15.983	1.242	154.508	31.171	−11.671	23.771
Sendbox Inc.	4.000	3.000	100.000	3.000	−16.000	?

Again, the net profit amount to be used as an output is a data that can be estimated based on the proforma income statements that can be prepared as an estimate. It is expected that the net profit amount of the startup will take a negative value during the establishment periods, and it will turn positive with the adaptation of the company to the market over the years. Considering this situation, a 5-year forecast and the average of their net present values can be used as output in DEA.

5.3 Model Selection

One of the most important stages of DEA application is the determination of the model to be used. The model to be chosen is determined according to the purpose of the analysis and the relationship between inputs and outputs.

In the model selection in DEA, input-oriented models are selected if the relevant DMU has control over the inputs, and output-oriented models are selected if it has control over the outputs. While input-oriented models are used in the analysis of operations and management, output-oriented models are preferred in planning and strategy analysis (Acer, 2021,p. 2980).

In the application phase of this study, input-oriented DEA model was preferred, because it was evaluated that the control over the input set was more than the control over the output set.

Another issue in model selection is the scale relationship between inputs and outputs. If there is a fixed return on scale of DMUs, the CCR model should be preferred, and if there is a variable return to scale, the BCC model should be preferred (Yücel İşbilen, 2017, p. 35). Since the rate of changes in inputs and outputs are thought to be unequal in the model established within the scope of this study, variable return to scale approach was chosen.

Another important issue in the selection of the model is whether there are negative input and output data. In Simak's study (Simak, 2000, p. 36), this issue was addressed as "scale and transformation invariance in DEA". Scale invariance and translation invariance are features of some basic DEA models. Scale invariance means that the efficiency scores of DMUs will not be affected if one or more of the DMUs' inputs or outputs are scaled by a certain amount (for example, multiplied by a certain constant). Transformation invariance means that efficiency scores are not affected by transforming the inputs and outputs by a scalar (for example, adding a certain constant to all of the outputs). The BCC model is both scale and translation invariant due to its variable returns to scale, while the CCR model only has scale invariant feature. The input-oriented BCC model to be used in this study has both scale and transformation invariant properties for outputs. This means that the efficiency of a given DMU is unaffected if one or more outputs of all DMUs are converted by a scalar quantity or scaled by a certain amount.

5.4 DEA Analysis and Valuation Findings

In order to carry out DEA, Efficiency Masurement System (EMS), a software for solving DEA problems, is used. You can find this software at https://www.holger-scheel.de/ems/link. There are many programs, for example, WIN4DEAP, that can be downloaded for free apart from EMS.

After preparing and loading the MS Excel file as indicated in the EMS user manual, we choose the model in the "run model" tab of the EMS. The screenshot of

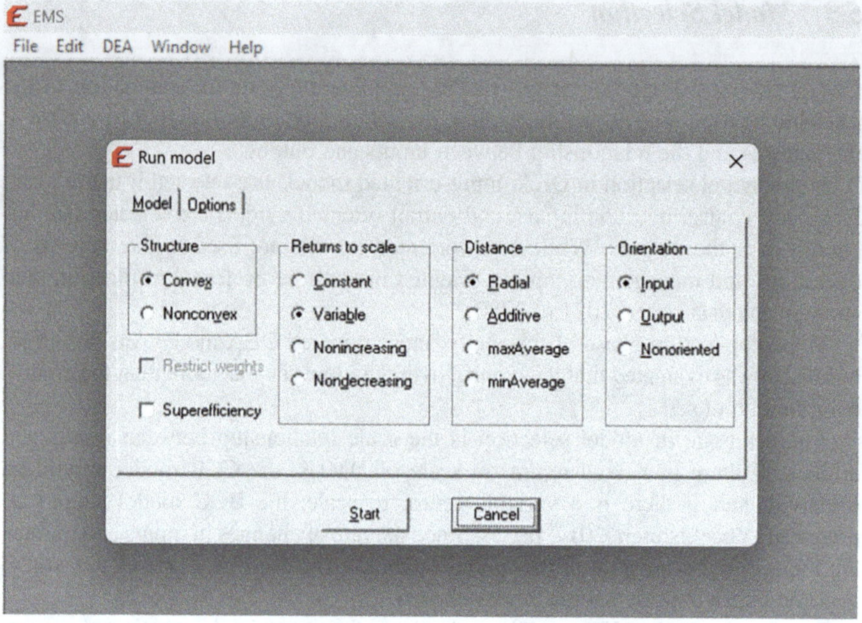

Fig. 3 DEA model selection screen in EMS. Source: Author's own creation

the model selection screen is below. As you can see in the figure, we choose the structure, returns to scale, distance and orientation of the model. In order to run the classical input-oriented VRS DEA model, the distance is selected as radial and structure is selected as convex. You can find extensive information on this subject (structure and distance of the model) in the literature, but as valuation practitioners, it is enough for us to know this much for now (Fig. 3).

As a result of the analysis carried out with the help of EMS, efficiency scores, peer firms, and lambda values for inefficient firms are found. Below you can see a screenshot of the output of the Efficiency measurement software program as a result of this analysis. In the screenshot, you can see the DEA scores and which inefficient firm takes which efficient firm as a peer (benchmark) (Fig. 4).

As a result of the analysis, 12 of the 22 companies were found to be efficient. In the valuation phase, firms that take the same efficient firms as a peer for themselves and the efficient firms that these companies take as a peer are considered together as a peer group.

The table regarding the efficiency scores found as a result of the DEA analysis and the lambda values (values in parentheses) with the companies that inefficient companies take as a peer are given below.

Accordingly, Sendbox Inc., for which we are looking for its values, is also among the inefficient firms, and the firms it takes as peer are DatChat Inc., Sonic Foundry Inc. and Minerva Surgical Inc.

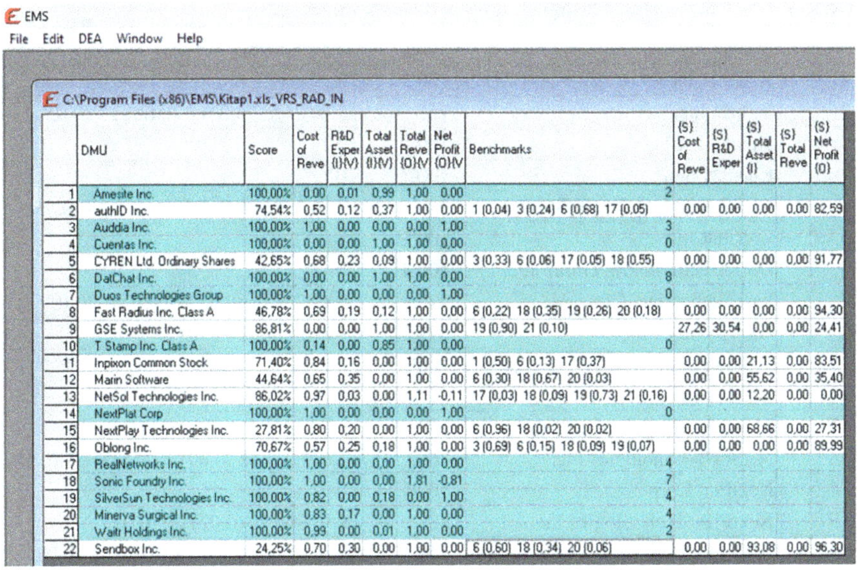

EMS
File Edit DEA Window Help
C:\Program Files (x86)\EMS\Kitap1.xls_VRS_RAD_IN

	DMU	Score	Cost of Reve	R&D Exper {I}{V}	Total Asset {I}{V}	Total Reve {O}{V	Net Profit {O}{V	Benchmarks	{S} Cost of Reve	{S} R&D Exper	{S} Total Asset {I}	{S} Total Reve	{S} Net Profit {O}
1	Amesite Inc.	100,00%	0,00	0,01	0,99	1,00	0,00	2					
2	authID Inc.	74,54%	0,52	0,12	0,37	1,00	0,00	1 (0,04) 3 (0,24) 6 (0,68) 17 (0,05)	0,00	0,00	0,00	0,00	82,59
3	Auddia Inc.	100,00%	1,00	0,00	0,00	0,00	1,00	3					
4	Cuentas Inc.	100,00%	0,00	0,00	1,00	1,00	0,00	0					
5	CYREN Ltd. Ordinary Shares	42,65%	0,68	0,23	0,09	1,00	0,00	3 (0,33) 6 (0,06) 17 (0,05) 18 (0,55)	0,00	0,00	0,00	0,00	91,77
6	DatChat Inc.	100,00%	0,00	0,00	1,00	1,00	0,00	8					
7	Duos Technologies Group	100,00%	1,00	0,00	0,00	0,00	1,00	0					
8	Fast Radius Inc. Class A	46,78%	0,69	0,19	0,12	1,00	0,00	6 (0,22) 18 (0,35) 19 (0,26) 20 (0,18)	0,00	0,00	0,00	0,00	94,30
9	GSE Systems Inc.	86,81%	0,00	0,00	1,00	1,00	0,00	19 (0,90) 21 (0,10)	27,26	30,54	0,00	0,00	24,41
10	T Stamp Inc. Class A	100,00%	0,14	0,00	0,85	1,00	0,00	0					
11	Inpixon Common Stock	71,40%	0,84	0,16	0,00	1,00	0,00	1 (0,50) 6 (0,13) 17 (0,37)	0,00	0,00	21,13	0,00	83,51
12	Marin Software	44,64%	0,65	0,35	0,00	1,00	0,00	6 (0,30) 18 (0,67) 20 (0,03)	0,00	0,00	55,62	0,00	35,40
13	NetSol Technologies Inc.	86,02%	0,97	0,03	0,00	1,11	-0,11	17 (0,03) 18 (0,09) 19 (0,73) 21 (0,16)	0,00	0,00	12,20	0,00	0,00
14	NextPlat Corp	100,00%	1,00	0,00	0,00	0,00	1,00	0					
15	NextPlay Technologies Inc.	27,81%	0,80	0,20	0,00	1,00	0,00	6 (0,96) 18 (0,02) 20 (0,02)	0,00	0,00	68,66	0,00	27,31
16	Oblong Inc.	70,67%	0,57	0,25	0,18	1,00	0,00	3 (0,69) 6 (0,15) 18 (0,09) 19 (0,07)	0,00	0,00	0,00	0,00	89,99
17	RealNetworks Inc.	100,00%	1,00	0,00	0,00	1,00	0,00	4					
18	Sonic Foundry Inc.	100,00%	1,00	0,00	0,00	1,81	-0,81	7					
19	SilverSun Technologies Inc.	100,00%	0,82	0,00	0,18	0,00	1,00	4					
20	Minerva Surgical Inc.	100,00%	0,83	0,17	0,00	1,00	0,00	4					
21	Waitr Holdings Inc.	100,00%	0,99	0,00	0,01	1,00	0,00	2					
22	Sendbox Inc.	24,25%	0,70	0,30	0,00	1,00	0,00	6 (0,60) 18 (0,34) 20 (0,06)	0,00	0,00	93,08	0,00	96,30

Fig. 4 DEA results. Source: Author's own creation

Similarly, NextPlay Technologies Inc. and Marin Software Incorporated took DatChat Inc., Sonic Foundry Inc. and Minerva Surgical Inc. as peer firms.

In this case,

1. Sendbox Inc.
2. NextPlay Technologies Inc.
3. Marin Software
4. DatChat Inc.
5. Sonic Foundry Inc.
6. Minerva Surgical Inc.

firms form a peer group (Table 4).

The table in which the lambda values of the companies displayed separately is given below (Table 5).

The table regarding the calculation of the difference indicator made for Sendbox Inc. using lambda values in the table above is given below (Table 6):

In the table below, the difference indicators, market values and efficiency scores of the firms in Sendbox Inc.'s peer group are given. Accordingly, the firms with the closest difference indicator to Sendbox Inc. is Marin Software Incorporated and its efficiency score is relatively close to Sendbox Inc. The other firm that is closest to Sendbox with its efficiency score and difference indicator is NextPlay Technologies Inc. (Efficiency score is 28%, difference indicator is 0.23). In this case, the value of Sendbox is expected to be between 19.338 thousand $, the market value of Marin

Table 4 Efficiency scores, benchmark firms and lamda values

No	DMU	Score	Benchmarks
1	Amesite Inc.	100%	2
2	authID Inc.	75%	1 (0.04) 3 (0.24) 6 (0.68) 17 (0.05)
3	Auddia Inc.	100%	3
4	Cuentas Inc.	100%	0
5	CYREN Ltd. Ordinary Shares	43%	3 (0.33) 6 (0.06) 17 (0.05) 18 (0.55)
6	DatChat Inc.	100%	8
7	Duos Technologies Group Inc.	100%	0
8	Fast Radius Inc. Class A	47%	6 (0.22) 18 (0.35) 19 (0.26) 20 (0.18)
9	GSE Systems Inc.	87%	19 (0.90) 21 (0.10)
10	T Stamp Inc. Class A	100%	0
11	Inpixon	71%	1 (0.50) 6 (0.13) 17 (0.37)
12	Marin Software Incorporated	45%	6 (0.30) 18 (0.67) 20 (0.03)
13	NetSol Technologies Inc.	86%	17 (0.03) 18 (0.09) 19 (0.73) 21 (0.16)
14	NextPlat Corp	100%	0
15	NextPlay Technologies Inc.	28%	6 (0.96) 18 (0.02) 20 (0.02)
16	Oblong Inc.	71%	3 (0.69) 6 (0.15) 18 (0.09) 19 (0.07)
17	RealNetworks Inc.	100%	4
18	Sonic Foundry Inc.	100%	7
19	SilverSun Technologies Inc.	100%	4
20	Minerva Surgical Inc.	100%	4
21	Waitr Holdings Inc.	100%	2
22	Sendbox Inc.	24%	6 (0.60) 18 (0.34) 20 (0.06)

Table 5 Lambdas of peer group companies for Sendbox Inc.

No	DMU	Lamda of DatChat Inc.	Lamda of Sonic Foundry Inc.	Lamda of Minerva Surgical Inc.
12	Marin Software Incorporated	0.30	0.67	0.03
15	NextPlay Technologies Inc.	0.96	0.02	0.02
22	Sendbox Inc.	0.60	0.34	0.06
6	DatChat Inc.	1.00	0.00	0.00
18	Sonic Foundry Inc.	0.00	1.00	0.00
20	Minerva Surgical Inc.	0.00	0.00	1.00

Software Incorporated, and 16.544 thousand $, which is the market value of NextPlay Technologies Inc. (Table 7).

Below is the figure in which the market values of the companies in the peer group of Sendbox Inc. and their efficiency scores, as well as the difference indicators of these firms with Sendbox Inc., are displayed. The size of the balloons is proportional to the market values of the firms concerned. In this figure Sendbox Inc's market

Table 6 Difference indicator calculation of peer group firms for Sendbox Inc.

DMU	DatChat Inc. $(\lambda_{\text{peer firm}} - \lambda_{\text{Sendbox Inc.}})^2$	Sonic Foundry Inc. $(\lambda_{\text{peer firm}} - \lambda_{\text{Sendbox Inc.}})^2$	Minerva Surgical Inc. $(\lambda_{\text{peer firm}} - \lambda_{\text{Sendbox Inc.}})^2$	Difference Indicator $\Delta_{\text{peer firm, Sendbox Inc.}}$ $\Sigma(\lambda_{\text{peer firm}} - \lambda_{\text{Sendbox Inc.}})^2$
Marin Software Incorporated	0.09	0.11	0.0009	0.20
NextPlay Technologies Inc.	0.13	0.10	0.0016	0.23
Sendbox Inc.	0.00	0.00	0.0000	0.00
DatChat Inc.	0.16	0.12	0.0036	0.28
Sonic Foundry Inc.	0.36	0.44	0.0036	0.80
Minerva Surgical Inc.	0.36	0.12	0.8836	1.36

Table 7 Difference indicator, market values and efficiency scores of peer group companies for Sendbox Inc.

No	DMU	Difference indicator $\delta_{\text{peer firm, Sendbox Inc.}}$	Market value (thousand $)	Efficiency score
12	Marin Software Incorporated	0.20	19.338	%45
15	NextPlay Technologies Inc.	0.23	16.544	%28
22	Sendbox Inc.	0.00	?	%24
6	DatChat Inc.	0.28	10.715	%100
18	Sonic Foundry Inc.	0.80	11.204	%100
20	Minerva Surgical Inc.	1.36	8.219	%100

capitalization is assumed ($17,941 thousand) to be the arithmetic average of market values of Marin Software Incorporated and NextPlay Technologies Inc. companies (Fig. 5).

The maximum value for Sendbox Inc. is 11.202 thousand $. The calculation for this is given in the table below. As can be seen from the table, the maximum value for Sendbox Inc. is found by multiplying the market values of the efficienct firms that Sendbox Inc. takes as a peer and the lambda values assigned to Sendbox for these firms as a result of DEA (Table 8).

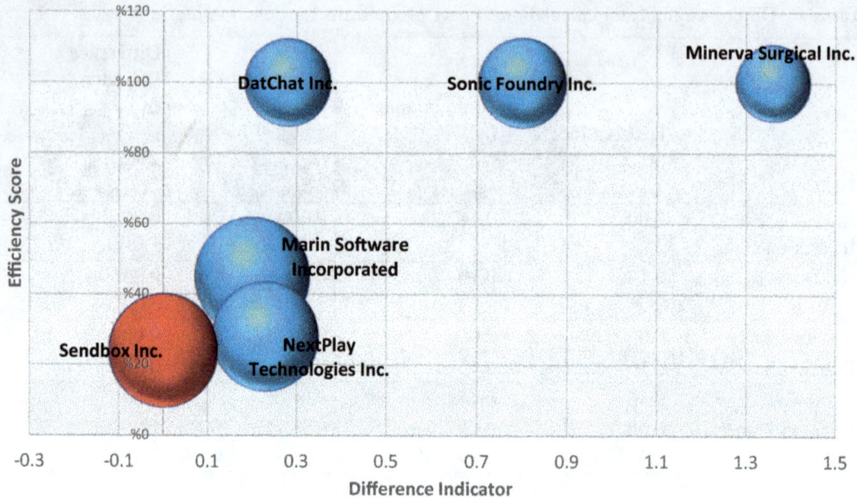

Fig. 5 Difference indicator, efficiency score and market value graph for Sendbox Inc. Source: Author's own creation

Table 8 Maximum value calculation for Sendbox Inc.

	DatChat Inc.	Sonic Foundry Inc.	Minerva Surgical Inc.	Total (maximum value) (thousand $)
Lambdas of Sendbox Inc. (a)	0.60	0.34	0.06	
Market value of efficient peers (thousand $) (b)	10.715	11.204	16.070	
Lamda x market value of efficient peers (a) x (b)	6.429	3.809	964	11.202

6 Conclusion

Firm valuation method with DEA is a tool that can be used to find out what the value of a firm should be. It has been observed that there are a limited number of studies in the literature regarding the use of this tool, whose main area of use is efficiency comparison, in firm valuation.

It is seen that this method gives very good results in valuation of mature firms. Similarly, although some assumptions are needed for the generation of the input and output data to be used in DEA to be included in the model as an estimation, this method can also be used in startup valuation.

An exemplary valuation application has been made above. Although the method is theoretically difficult to understand at first, it is a very easy method to implement. With this method using the lambda values obtained with package programs that perform DEA analysis, both the market value range and the maximum value of a firm can be estimated. Use of the input-output sets that best reflect the value creation process for different sectors' and opportunity of the model modification according to the scale relationship between those inputs and outputs make the valuation method with DEA a flexible method.

The method has advantages over market-based valuation methods using multiplier as well. While valuation with multiples is done by taking into account a single parameter that creates value in the valuation process, the inclusion of more than one input and output in the value creation process in the modeling of the valuation with DEA can be seen as an advantage of valuation with DEA compared to valuation with multipliers.

The biggest disadvantage of the firm valuation with DEA is that the estimated value ranges reach very wide margins if the DMUs with very different market values are included in the analysis. In order to eliminate this disadvantage and to estimate the value in a narrower margin, homogeneous units with closer market values should be included in the analysis.

The difficulty of finding comparable firms in the market-based valuation approach also applies to this method. It is one of the difficulties of firm valuation with DEA as well to find and include companies with a similar risk and growth potential in the same sector, geography and growth potential as the firm that will be tried to find its value range or maximum value.

The purpose of valuation, which is frequently mentioned in the valuation literature, is to "make estimations according to different methods and reveal a reasonable value, rather than to find the firm value with a single valuation method", which is also valid in startup valuation with DEA. The value obtained with DEA is not an absolute value. The aim here is to estimate the value closest to the company's required value, just like in other valuation approaches and methods.

References

Acer, A. (2021). Determining the efficiency of entrepots in logistics activities by data envelopment analysis. *Journal of Business Research-Turkey, 13*(4), 2976–2989.

Anadol, B. (2000). Valuing private companies: A DEA approach. Master Thesis, University of Toronto.

Anadol, B., Paradi, J., Simak, P., & Yang, X. (2014). Valuing private companies: A DEA approach. *International Journal of Business and Management, 9*(12), 16–27.

Atıcı, K. B., Şimşek, A. B., Ulucan, A., & Tosun, M. U. (2016). Performance measurement studies by data envelopment analysis in Turkey: Literature review and evaluations. *Journal of Productivity, 2016*(1), 7–47.

Chambers, N. (2011). *Firm Valuation*. Beta Releases.

Damodaran, A. (2006). *Valuation approaches and metrics: A survey of the theory and evidence*. Working paper (Stern School of Business). Available at: http://people.stern.nyu.edu/adamodar/pdfiles/papers/valuesurvey.pdf

Damodaran, A. (2009). *Valuing young, start-up and growth companies: Estimation issues and valuation challenges*. Working paper (Stern School for Business). Available at: https://pages.stern.nyu.edu/~adamodar/pdfiles/papers/younggrowth.pdf

International Valuation Standards Council. (2019). International Valuation Standards (IVS). Available at: https://www.rics.org/globalassets/rics-website/media/upholding-professional-standards/sector-standards/valuation/international-valuation-standards-rics2.pdf

Keskin Benli, Y. and, D.N. Bozdan, 2019, Measuring the efficiency of deposit banks in Turkey with data envelopment analysis İksad Publishing House.

Kutlar, A., & Bakırcı, F. (2018). *Data envelopment analysis-theory and practice- DEA-solver Win4DEAP MALMQUIST index*. Orion Bookstore.

Okursoy, A., & Tezsürücü, D. (2014). Comparison of the relative efficiencies by the data envelopment analysis: An application in Turkey for the provinces of cultural indicators. *Journal of Management & Economics, 21*(2), 1–18.

Patır, S. (2020). Doğrusal Programlamada Primal ve Dual İlişkisinin İrdelenmesi ve Bir Örnek Uygulaması. *Elektronik Sosyal Bilimler Dergisi, 6*(21), 172–191.

Rawley, T., & Gup, B. E. (2010). *The valuation handbook: Valuation techniques from today's top practitioners*. John Wiley & Sons, Inc.

Roig, A., & Vicen, C. (2020). Startup valuation. Master Thesis, HEC Paris.

Simak, P. C. (2000). Inverse and negative DEA and their application to credit risk evaluation. Doctorate Thesis, University of Toronto.

Sipahi, B., Yanık, S., & Aytürk, Y. (2016). *Company valuation approaches principles – Methods – Practices*. Seçkin Publishing.

Tarım, A. (2001). *Data envelopment analysis mathematical programming based relative efficiency measurement approach*. Turkish Court of Accounts. Available at: https://armagan.github.io/SAT/DeaBook.pdf

Torun, N., Atan, M., & Ayanoğlu, Y. (2020). An analysis of financial efficiency of public hospitals according to statistical region classification. *World of Accounting Science, 22*(3), 476–505.

Ulucan, A., Atıcı, K. B., & Özkan, A. (2018). Benchmarking in higher education using data envelopment analysis and the bologna process data. *Croatian Operational Research Review, 9*(2), 301–316.

Üzgün, Y. O. (2022). Firm valuation approach with data envelopment analysis -Borsa İstanbul example. Doctoral Thesis, Ankara Hacı Bayram Veli University, Institute of Graduate Studies.

Yücel İşbilen, L. (2017). *Data envelopment analysis, example of portfolio activity measurement with Frontier Analyts and WinDeap, and various applications*. DER Publications.

Zhou, P., Ang, B. W., & Poh, K. L. (2008). A survey of data envelopment analysis in energy and environmental studies. *European Journal of Operational Research, 189*(1), 1–18.

GPSR Compliance
The European Union's (EU) General Product Safety Regulation (GPSR) is a set of rules that requires consumer products to be safe and our obligations to ensure this.

If you have any concerns about our products, you can contact us on

ProductSafety@springernature.com

In case Publisher is established outside the EU, the EU authorized representative is:

Springer Nature Customer Service Center GmbH
Europaplatz 3
69115 Heidelberg, Germany

www.ingramcontent.com/pod-product-compliance
Lightning Source LLC
Chambersburg PA
CBHW070728190226
39777CB00028B/134
9783031352904